TRAILS, ROCK FEATURES AND HOMESTEADING IN THE GILA BEND AREA

Unititled mural by Emil Pedro for the exhibit He'kugam V:og,
Huhugam Heritage Center, Gila River Indian Community.

Gila River Indian Community
Anthropological Research Papers
Number 4

Arizona State University
Anthropological Field Studies
Number 43

TRAILS, ROCK FEATURES, AND HOMESTEADING IN THE GILA BEND AREA

A REPORT ON THE STATE ROUTE 85, GILA BEND TO BUCKEYE ARCHAEOLOGICAL PROJECT

Edited by John L. Czarzasty, Kathleen Peterson, Glen E. Rice, and J. Andrew Darling

Contributions by Karen Adams, Matthew Chamberlin, John L.Czarzasty, J. Andrew Darling, B. Sunday Eiselt, Kathleen Peterson, Glen E. Rice, Arleyn Simon, Susan Smith, Pat H. Stein, Erik Steinbach, Michael Waters

A draft of this volume of the Gila River Indian Community,
Anthropological Research Papers was previously distributed by

Glen E. Rice
Arizona State University, Department of Anthropology
Office of Cultural Resource Management

for the

Arizona Department of Transportation
Environmental Planning Group
205 South 17th Avenue, MD 616E
Phoenix, Arizona
ECS Contract #02-59
TRACS NO. 085 MA 120 H3225 02L

as

*Trails, Rock features, and Homesteading in the Gila Bend Area; A Report on State Route 85,
Gila Bend to Buckeye, Archaeological Project; Anthropological Field Studies no. 43*

September 15, 2003
(Revised April, 2008)

Gila River Indian
Cultural Resource Management Program
Sacaton, Arizona

Cover: Ryan Stone, archaeologist for the Cultural Resource Management Program, Gila River Indian Community, recording a trail in the Maricopa Mountains near State Route 85.

ISBN 0-9723347-3-4

TABLE OF CONTENTS

LIST OF FIGURES

FOREWORD

The archaeology of the Gila Bend region—the area encompassing the great S-curve in the Gila River Valley from the town of Gila Bend on the south to Buckeye on the north—is slowly coming into view. Lying at the transition between the prehistoric cultures identified as Hohokam and Patayan, the Gila Bend also generally marks the northeastern limit of the Western Papaguería where it overlaps with the traditional territories of the O'odham, Pee Posh, and their ancestors. Later immigrants to the region, Spanish, Mexican, Euro-American and African-American, perpetuated the role of the Gila Bend as a crossroads and a place to occasionally settle.

The fourth volume of the Anthropological Research Papers series represents a unique collaboration. First, in preparation for the widening of State Route 85, it is a report of archaeological investigations conducted in 2002 by the Office of Cultural Resource Management, Arizona State University for the Arizona Department of Transportation. Second, it is a report of the efforts of the Cultural Resource Management Program of the Gila River Indian Community. The Program at the time was engaged in developing an inventory of O'odham and Pee Posh traditional cultural properties both on and off the reservation under funding by the Pima-Maricopa Irrigation Project,[1] and a grant from the National Park Service. The collaborative efforts of Arizona State University and the Gila River Indian Community along State Route 85 provided unique insights, particularly for understanding trails and trail features, with far-reaching geographical implications. The original draft of this report, identified on the title page, was completed in 2003 and since that time it has been cited by several recent publications. These include Altschul and Rankin's 2008 compendium, entitled *Fragile Patterns*, on the archaeology of the Western Papaguería, and a chapter by Darling and Lewis (2007) in the volume, *The Hohokam Millennium*, edited by Fish and Fish (2007). The exhibit, *He'kugam V:og, Ancient Trails of the Arid Southwest,* opened in 2003 as one of the inaugural exhibits of the Huhugam Heritage Center, the Gila River Indian Community's museum and artifact repository, and was based in large part on the results of the State Route 85 work.

It is remarkable that the great S-curve of the Gila River Valley has received so little archaeological attention; yet, as a landscape, its shape practically invites research. Even after this study, it remains impressive to find so many trails and historic routes descending from the eastern bajada of the Maricopa Mountains into the floodplain. Ironically, the only main north-south road through the area is State Route 85, which receives the least attention, historically, but is the central reason for the studies reported herein. State Route 85 has its role to play, too. As a consequence of its location, this report tells a coherent story about the prehistoric and historic transportation infrastructure of the valley, which is only visible along the State Route 85 corridor. This includes the roads, the trails, the travelers, and the African-American family, who for a time made a living in the valley of the Gila Bend.[2]

J. Andrew Darling, Coordinator
Cultural Resource Management Program

---

[1] Except where otherwise noted, traditional cultural property research by the Gila River Indian Community, Cultural Resource Management Program, was conducted in conjunction with the Pima-Maricopa Irrigation Project with funds from the U.S. Department of the Interior, Bureau of Reclamation, under the Tribal Self-Governance Act of 1994 (P.L. 103-413), for the design and development of a water delivery system utilizing Central Arizona Project water.
[2] To further appreciate the history of the Warner Goode homestead and the exodus of blacks to the American West, see Greta LeSeur's wonderful book, *Not All Okies are White,* published in 2000.

A project of this magnitude depends on the collective commitment and efforts of many people. We take this opportunity to acknowledge those who contributed to the success of the State Route 85 Project and express our sincere gratitude for all they have done.

The State Route 85 Project was under the guidance of the Environmental and Enhancement Group of the Arizona Department of Transportation. We are grateful for and acknowledge the efforts of the Group staff: Owen Lindauer, Serelle Laine, Jon Schumaker, Saskia Grupp, David Zimmerman and Ruth Greenspan. Their requirements and guidance were clear, and it was a pleasure to work with the professionals of the Environment and Enhancement Group.

A special acknowledgement of, and thanks for, the efforts of the field crew are in order. Field conditions included a span of typical Arizona summer. We endured days that fortunately did not go above 117° F, but reached it. In spite of the environmental conditions and our labor's stern demands, high spirits and good humor never sagged, enthusiasm never dragged, and the lofty levels of professionalism never flagged. So thank you Frances Black, Barbara Brady, Matt Chamberlain, Travis Cureton, Emily Higgins, Jennifer Jones, Chris Loendorf, Bobbie Jo Miller, Tatsuya Murakami, Elizabeth Murphy, Ryan Peterson, Stanley Plum, Erik Steinbach, and Densie To for a job very well done. We are also grateful to the field crews of the Gila River Indian Community, Cultural Resource Management Program including Brett Couchyouma, B. Sunday Eiselt, Jennifer Johnson, Lavaria Jones, Wesley Miles, Brenda Randolph, and Ryan Stone who endured other seasons featuring their share of cold and rainy winter days.

We required assistance with specialized topics in several spheres in order to successfully complete the State Route 85 Project. Mike Waters examined the geomorphology of the project area. Kelly Schroeder documented the historic glass artifacts from a Depression Era farmstead along State Route 85. Desert Rose provided important help with the cartography. Matthew Chamberlain assisted with the analysis of prehistoric ceramics recovered during the project. Susan Smith analyzed and reported on the pollen recovered in environmental samples, while Karen R. Adams did likewise for the macrobotanical specimens recovered through flotation. Pat Stein documented the historic trails, Depression Era homestead, and historic canals (reported separately) in the project area. Sunday Eiselt collaborated on the report on the prehistoric trails in the project area after personally assisting with tracing one of the more prominent trails, thus contributing to this effort with her feet as well as her intellect. Lynn Simon, Brian Lewis, and Russell Talas of the Cultural Resource Management Program at Gila River ably assisted with instrument surveying and cartography. Tom Herrschaft, also of the Gila River Cultural Resource Management Program deserves special mention for being constantly on deck from beginning to end to assist in exhibit and report production. Finally, much appreciation is due to Mr. Calvin P. Goode, a prominent civic leader of Phoenix, who devoted his time to provide an oral history of the Depression Era homestead at which he had spent years of his childhood.

We would also like to acknowledge the authors of the survey report upon which we relied so heavily to locate sites and identify features within the project area. Elizabeth Hunt Harmon and Lisa J. Beyer, authors of *Cultural Resources Survey of Approximately 40 Miles of Proposed State Route 85 Right-of-Way (and Associated Alternative Routes) between Gila Bend and Buckeye, Southwestern Maricopa County, Arizona,* provided us with as clear a roadmap to, and description of, the objectives of our research efforts as could be desired. To both of them we are very grateful.

This report is accompanied by a permanent exhibit entitled *He'kugam V:og, Ancient Trails of the Arid Southwest* at the Huhugam Heritage Center of the Gila River Indian Community. Highpoints of the exhibit include a video tape of O'odham songs about trails, and a mural by the renowned Pee Posh (Maricopa) artist Mr. Amil Pedro featured on the frontispiece. Our thanks to John C. Ravesloot of the Cultural Resource Management Program of the Gila River Indian Community, Russell B. Varineau, Exhibit Designer, Monica King, Education Curator, and to the following individuals who also assisted: Diane Bedonie, Letricia Brown, Elvin Crewell, Diane Dittemore (Arizona State Museum), Angela Garcia-Lewis, Suzanne Griset (Arizona State Museum), Veronica Hernandez, Thomas Herrschaft, Shirley Jackson, Barnaby V. Lewis, Jarrod Lewis, Marjorie Lewis, Brenda Randolph, Verna Red Bear-Stone, Bonny Rockette, Josh Roffler, Chris Soke, Sr., Eloise Pedro, and M. Kyle Woodson. We honor the memory of two colleagues and dear friends who contributed to the exhibit and so much more and have passed since the completion of the exhibit, the late Hartman Lomawaima (Arizona State Museum) and Anne Powers. We miss them both very much.

An important outcome of this project was the collaboration between archaeologists and members of the Gila River Indian Community, and the full results of that collaboration occur in the context of the exhibit. The Community Members provided artwork, traditional songs and memories to accompany the archaeological enumeration of artifacts and features. The State Route 85 archaeological project was in large part about Native American trails, and the involvement of the Community Members provided the context needed to view these trails in their cultural landscape. The archaeological contribution was the demonstration that these trails had been used for at least a thousand years. In a very real way the trails link the modern Akimel O'odham and Pee Posh to their Hohokam and Patayan ancestors.

The Editors

CHAPTER 1

INTRODUCTION

John Czarzasty and Glen E. Rice

The Arizona Department of Transportation plans to widen State Route 85 to a four-lane freeway in the area between Buckeye and Gila Bend. This report presents the results of archaeological data recovery investigations conducted along State Route (SR) 85 (Figure 1.1) for the Arizona Department of Transportation (Contract No. 02-59) by a research team assembled by the Office of Cultural Resource Management, Department of Anthropology at Arizona State University. The Area of Potential Effect (APE) was located between mileposts 121 and 147 on State Route 85 between the towns of Gila Bend to the south and Buckeye to the north (Figures 1.2 through 1.4). The Gila River Indian Community (CRMP) provided technical assistance on Traditional Cultural Property (TCP) and treatment, particularly trails, funded in part by the Pima-Maricopa Irrigation Project (P-MIP) and a National Park Service grant to support TCP inventory. The project consisted of the investigation of six sites (Table 1.1, Figures 1.2 through 1.4), five of which were prehistoric and one that was historic. The project area is southwest of the Phoenix metropolitan area.

The historic site (T:14:96) was a Depression era African-American homestead occupied during the 1930s. For the five prehistoric sites, the results of the investigations were that three of the sites (T:14:113, T:14:94, T:14:92) contained rock cairns and rock circles associated with trails, one site (Z:2:46) was a roasting pit very likely associated with *ak chin* agricultural fields dating to the Pioneer Period, and the remaining prehistoric site (T:10:86) was an area of irrigated agricultural fields on the terrace of the Gila River. The trails in the project area were generally oriented east–west, and could have been used by occupants from settlements west of the project area along the Gila River for procurement trips to the bajada and the Maricopa Mountains for lithic and food resources. Some of the trails also provided direct routes to other settlements on the upper portions of the Gila River.

Table 1.1. List of Investigated Sites, from North to South

Site	Site Type	Land Ownership
AZ T:10:86 (ASM)	Hohokam artifact scatter	ADOT, Private
AZ T:14:113 (ASM)	Patayan rock cairn	ASLD
AZ T:14:96 (ASM)	Historic homestead	ADOT, ASLD, Private
AZ T:14:94 (ASM)	Hohokam/Patayan rock cairns, trails	ASLD, BLM
AZ T:14:92 (ASM)	Hohokam rock cairns, trails	ASLD
AZ Z:2:46 (ASM)	Pioneer Period roasting pit, trails	ADOT, BLM, Private

Key: ASM = Arizona State Museum; ADOT = Arizona Department of Transportation; ASLD = Arizona State Land Department; BLM = Bureau of Land Management

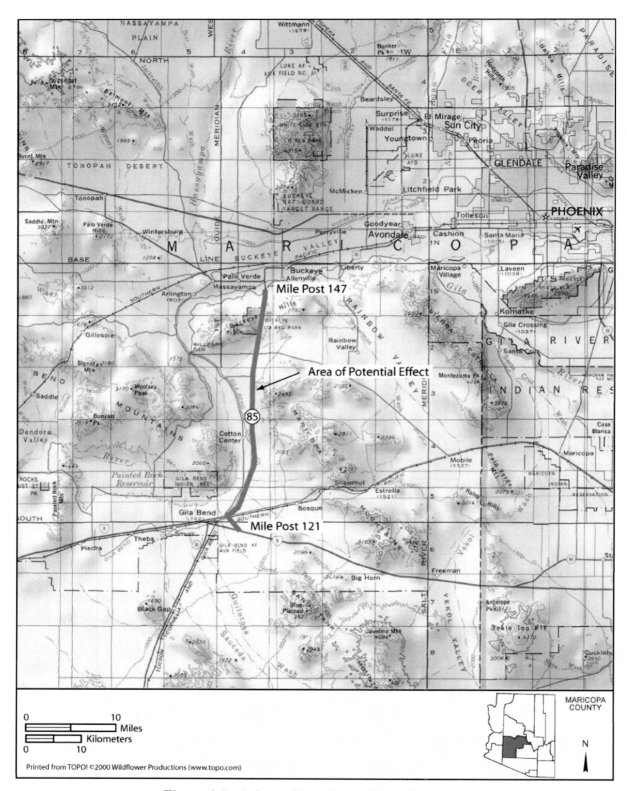

Figure 1.1. Arizona State Route 85 project area.

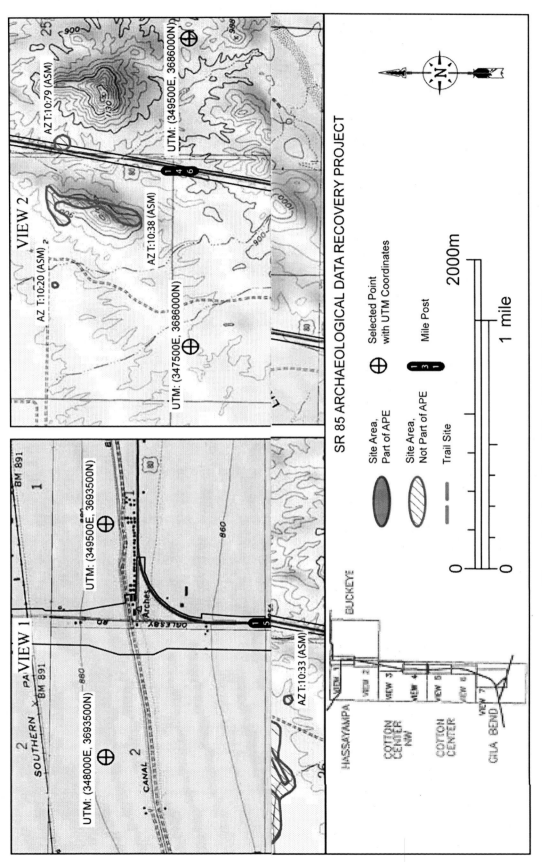

Figure 1.2. Location of the AZ T:10:86 (ASM)

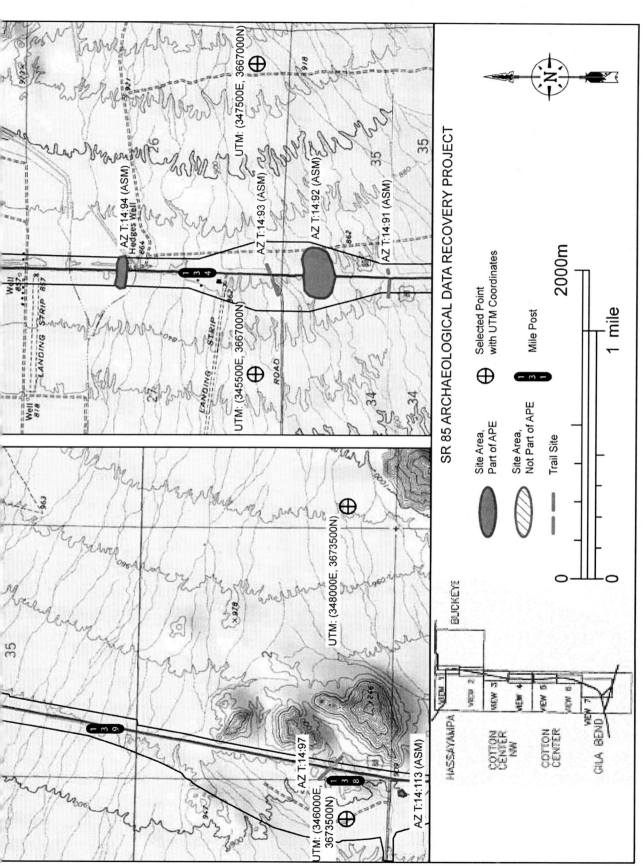

Figure 1.3. Locations of sites AZ T:14:113 (ASM), AZ T:14:96 (ASM), and AZ T:14:92 (ASM).

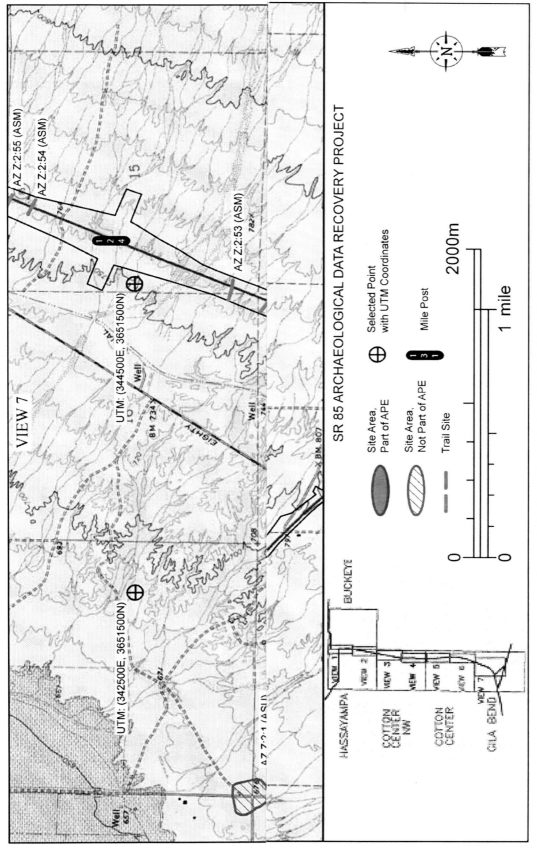

Figure 1.4. Location of site AZ Z:2:46 (ASM)

Among the five investigated prehistoric sites, exclusively Hohokam wares were found at one site (T:10:86 [ASM]), exclusively Patayan wares were found at one site (T:14:113 [ASM]), and a mixture of both wares was found at two sites (T:14:92 [ASM], T:14:94 [ASM]). No ceramics were recovered from Z:2:46 (ASM). Prehistoric occupation at the location of the historic site was not investigated. It appears that members of both Hohokam and Patayan cultural systems were present in the project area. An alternate explanation for the artifact distribution is movement of Patayan wares into the Hohokam area as a result of exchange.

ENVIRONMENTAL SETTING

The dominant environmental feature of the project area is the Gila River valley, with its active channel, floodplain and terraces. Along the Gila River, the terraces created by over bank flooding have soils suitable for agriculture (Johnson 1997). The Gila River channel is sufficiently high to allow for irrigation of the terrace, and the Hohokam used irrigation during prehistoric occupation of the Gila River valley (Wasley and Johnson 1965:80).

All of the investigated sites are located in the Gila Bend area of the Gila River Valley between the towns of Gila Bend and Buckeye, Arizona. One investigated site (T:10:86 [ASM]) was located on the river's terrace, while the remaining five investigated sites were located on the bajada. The bajada is the relatively undisturbed, gently sloping desert surface with primarily colluvial and some alluvial deposits delivered from the mountainous uplands. The lower reaches of the bajada are Holocene deposits. The elevations of Holocene deposits on the bajada are too high to have been irrigated by canals from the Gila River, but the soils are suitable for growing crops using *ak chin* agriculture (Waters 1982). The upper reaches of the bajada are Pleistocene deposits with incised drainages. Though similar terrain was used for dry-farm agave fields in the Tucson Basin (Fish et al. 1992), this use has not been observed in the study area. The mountainous uplands in the project area include the Maricopa Mountains, the Buckeye Hills, and the Gila Bend Mountains. The mountains and hills consist of bedrock formations containing small drainages and valleys.

The larger area encompassing the project sites is essentially bounded by uplands: on the north and west by the Gila River and Gila Bend Mountains, on the east by the Maricopa Mountains, and on the south by the Sand Tank Mountains and the southern foothills of the Maricopa Mountains. The project sites were limited to a narrow corridor within the larger area, which is characterized by basin-and-range topography and encompasses an area approximately 55 km N–S by 45 km E–W. The elevation of the floodplain of the Gila River drops from 860 feet to below 630 feet within the study area. Gross topographic relief varies from below 630 feet in the floodplain near the town of Gila Bend to over 3200 feet in the Maricopa Mountains. There are few springs in the area, and the only permanent water occurs along the Gila River channel. The only other major drainage in the area is Rainbow Wash, a seasonal ephemeral tributary of the Gila River, providing inflow to the Gila River only following storms. A field-based study of the geomorphology was conducted by Waters and is presented in Chapter Four of this report.

The project area is in the Sonoran Desert scrub biome, and is set within an area that includes portions of the Lower Colorado River valley and Arizona Upland subdivisions of the biome (Brown 1994). It is an arid environment subject to bimodal rainfall patterns. During the summer the area receives severe thunderstorms of short duration, and during the winter precipitation arrives in the form of longer, more frequent, gentle rains. The project area is in a creosote-bursage vegetation zone within a larger mixed paloverde-cactus zone (Turner and Brown 1982). The immediate areas of the sites are dominated by creosote bushes, paloverde and ironwood trees, with some saguaro cacti present. Other floral species are present within site areas, although they are more common in the larger environmental setting as a whole. These species include acacia, agave, barrel cactus, bursage, cholla, desert broom, desert grasses, hedgehog cactus, mesquite, ocotillo, rabbitbrush, snakeweed and wolfberry (see Brown 1994, Turner and Brown 1982, and Rea 1997). Specific locations for these species are delimited by elevation, aspect and differences in the availability of water.

The project area and its surrounding environment are home to numerous species of fauna, including black-tailed jackrabbit, cottontail rabbit, coyote, desert mule deer (rare), desert tortoise (very rare), gray fox, javelina, kangaroo rat, woodrat, and several species of birds (including Gambel quail, mourning dove, red-tailed hawk, roadrunner, and white-winged dove), lizards and snakes (Hoffmeister 1986). Pee Posh (Maricopa) groups hunted mountain sheep in the Gila Bend Mountains surrounding the project area (Spier 1933:70).

Agricultural villages were spaced along the Gila River to the west of the project sites, and the populations of these villages used the project area and the larger area surrounding the sites for resource exploitation. Leguminous trees are present in the washes. Saguaro cacti are scant but present in the project area, and at higher elevations where agave are also present the saguaro become denser. Spring and summer would have been the prime seasons for harvesting plant resources, with collection limited to wild seeds during the fall and winter. Faunal resources were likely to have been even more seasonal.

CULTURAL SETTING

The project area is located in the Gila Bend subarea, a periphery of the Phoenix Basin Hohokam core area. This overlaps with the Papaguería, a large arid area that covers southwestern Arizona and parts of northern Sonora, Mexico. The Papguería is considered to be a peripheral area of the Hohokam tradition by some (McGuire 1991) and a cultural area in its own right by others (Tucker 2000). In either case, the Gila Bend subarea was near the contact point of different major cultural groups; the most important to the sites in the project area were the Hohokam and the Patayan. Human use of the area, however, began during the Archaic, before the development of the archaeological traditions.

Paleo-Indian Period

The Paleo-Indian Period is the earliest evidence of human occupation in the American Southwest. The primary manifestation of the Paleo-Indian Period in Arizona began approximately 12,000 years ago and ended between 8,000 and 10,000 years ago (McGregor 1965; McGuire 1982). The record is scant and dominated by projectile points and stone tools. Clovis and Folsom points are conspicuous components of the archaeological record, and they are used to infer a tradition of hunting large mammals (McGuire and Schiffer 1982:166). Paleo-Indian remains in Arizona consist of camps in southeastern Arizona (Haury 1956; Haury et al. 1959; Hemmings and Haynes 1969), isolated Clovis points from central Arizona (Crownover 1994) and the northwest Papgueria (Ezell 1954), a point from Ventana Cave (Haury 1950), and closer to the project area, a Folsom point near Gila Bend (Effland et al. 1982).

A secondary manifestation of the Paleo-Indian tradition was the San Dieguito tradition. It was not as widespread in Arizona as Folsom and Clovis traditions, occurring mainly in southeastern California. The San Dieguito tradition has been attributed to only the northwest corner of Arizona and to Tucson area drainages (Hayden 1976; Rogers 1958). The tradition spans from 15,000 years ago (Hayden 1976) to 9,000–7,000 years ago (Irwin-Williams 1979). It differs from the Folsom and Clovis traditions in that it is characterized by stone scrapers and other stone tools rather than by projectile points, perhaps suggesting a much lower emphasis on big game hunting.

Archaic Period

The Archaic Period represented a shift from a reliance on large game (the Paleo-Indian Period) to a dependence on a broad spectrum of plant foods and small game, a shift in food preparation from roasting to boiling, and the adoption of grinding implements (Huckell 1996b). In the Sonoran Desert the Early Archaic (10,000 to 7,000 B.P.) is associated with Ventana/Amargosa I style (or Lake Mojave and Silver Lake style) projectile points, which were stemmed with convex bases. Although Pinto style stemmed points with concave bases occur in both the Early and Middle Archaic of the Great Basin, they seem to occur only in the Middle Archaic of the Sonoran Desert (Huckell 1984:190–193). Large parts of the Sonoran Desert and Colorado Plateau may have been abandoned during the Altithermal (6,700 to 5,500 B.P.), a period of drier climate associated with down cutting of fluvial terraces (Matson 1991; Huckell 1996a; Waters 1985).

During the Middle Archaic (5,500 to 3,500 B.P.) three different populations with different mobility, subsistence strategies and styles of projectile points lived simultaneously in the Sonoran Desert (Rice et al. 2003:48). Sedentary hunter-gatherer groups associated with *Chiricahua* style points lived year round within the Sonoran Desert, while highly mobile hunter-gatherer groups using *Pinto/San Jose* and *Gypsum* style projectile points wintered in the Sonoran Desert but ranged into the surrounding mountains and plateau during the rest of the year (Bayham et al. 1986). A third population in the Tucson Basin using *Cortaro* style points were also sedentary hunter-gatherers who may have experimented with maize cultivation, although the early dating of maize is limited to a single example that has yet to be replicated (Gregory 1999:118, 121).

The Early Agricultural Horizon (3,500 to 2,000 B.P.) is relatively new terminology for pre-ceramic populations with maize agriculture (Huckell 1996b:334–345); many components once called Late Archaic are now assigned to the Early Agricultural Horizon. Because maize agriculture may have spread first along the large valleys and only later into the more arid parts of the Sonoran Desert, there is the potential for the Early Agricultural Horizon and Late Archaic tradition to occur concurrently in different parts of the Sonoran Desert. The Early Agricultural Horizon and Late Archaic are associated with *San Pedro* and *Cienega* style projectile points (Loendorf and Rice 2004; Rice et al. 2003).

The Hohokam Tradition

The Phoenix Basin and the Middle Gila River valley, with the confluence of the Salt and Gila Rivers, are the core area of the Hohokam tradition. The Gila Bend area, in which the project is located, is considered by some investigators to be the southwest edge of the core area (Doyel 2000:101) and by others to be a periphery of the core area (McGuire 1991:348). The Gila Bend area sits astride major travel corridors (Doyel 2000:125), and the influence of the Patayan tradition from the southwest is visible in the archaeological evidence in the area. The travel corridors connected distant resource areas, such as the Gulf of California, to the Hohokam core area. The corridors also enhanced travel between Hohokam settlements in the Gila Bend area and settlements in the core area, as well as settlements to the east on the upper Gila River. The travel corridors remained important into historic times.

In addition to the Phoenix Basin and Gila Bend area, the Hohokam inhabited the area of present day Tucson and surrounding lowlands near rivers and large drainages region wide, with late expansion into peripheral drainage systems to the north of the core area. During the florescence of the Hohokam tradition from approximately A.D. 300 to approximately A.D. 1450, the Hohokam developed a complex social system and a material culture subsisting primarily on irrigated agriculture. Their society was remarkable for their agricultural adaptation to a desert environment. The temporal span of the Hohokam tradition is divided into periods, and the periods into phases, based primarily on differences in ceramic styles, architecture, and mortuary practices (Haury 1976; Dean 1991).

Hohokam occupation began with the Pioneer Period, which consisted of a proposed Red Mountain phase followed by the more firmly established Vahki, Estrella, Sweetwater, and Snaketown phases (Cable and Doyel 1987; Morris 1969; Haury 1976; Gladwin et al. 1938). Chronologies vary with regard to the start of the Vahki phase. Early investigators placed it as early as 300 B.C. (Gladwin et al. 1938; Wheat 1955; Haury 1976), while later investigators (Wilcox and Shank 1977; Plog 1980; Dean 1991) placed the start closer to A.D. 300. The end of the Pioneer Period was placed at A.D. 550–700. The Colonial Period followed the Pioneer Period and consisted of the Gila Butte and Santa Cruz phases. The Colonial Period ended approximately A.D. 900. The ensuing Sedentary Period consisted of only one phase, the Sacaton. The Sedentary Period was the last period of the pre-Classic Hohokam era, and it ended at approximately A.D. 1100 or later. The Classic Period of the Hohokam lasted until approximately A.D. 1450, and consisted of the Soho and Civano phases. An additional, post-Classic Polvoron phase has been proposed (Doyel 1991; Sires 1983), but like the Red Mountain phase it has yet to achieve the same status of the other widely accepted phases. Other phase names appear in the literature, but usually refer to Hohokam presence outside of the core area.

The Patayan Tradition

Patayan society appeared in southwest Arizona during the first millennium A.D. Although similar to the Hohokam in that both were desert-adapted cultures with riverine and upland variations, the Patayan of the Lower Colorado River basin and the Papaguería were not irrigation agriculturalists. In the Papguería, gathering was much more important for subsistence than in the Hohokam core area (McGuire 1991:350), and Patayan settlements were of a more seasonal nature than Hohokam settlements. The inferred riverine and upland adaptations of the Patayan and their material culture are sufficiently similar to the culture and adaptations of the Yumans that continuity from the Patayans to the Yumans is indicated (McGuire and Schiffer 1982).

Patayan presence in Arizona is believed to have originated in southern California. Patayan sites are present in the project area, and their type and distribution are covered in a subsequent chapter addressing settlement patterns. Beyond the project area, evidence for the main Patayan presence is roughly bounded by the southern California desert regions on the west, the Sierra Pinacate, Mexico on the south, the Buckeye Hills at the north of the Gila Bend periphery on the east, and Parker, Arizona on the north (Rogers 1945; Wallace 1989; Stone 1986; McGuire and Schiffer 1982), though Patayan presence is not strictly limited to this area. At the site of Las Colinas, a Hohokam village in the metropolitan Phoenix area, an isolated cluster of two residential structures produced high frequencies of Patayan wares (Teague 1988:131), which was interpreted as evidence of some interaction between the Hohokam and Patayan cultures.

The artifact record of the Patayan is dominated primarily by Lower Colorado buffware ceramics, which are sufficiently ubiquitous over time to be less than optimal as chronological indicators. Patayan ceramics, a distinct ceramic tradition, do not appear at Hohokam sites in the Gila River valley before the end of the Colonial Period, but Hohokam ceramics from the Colonial Period's Santa Cruz phase do appear at sites in the Patayan area (Waters 1982:287). In addition to Lower Colorado buffware, Patayan assemblages are characterized by Palomas and Tumco buffwares, redwares, stucco plainwares, shallow basin metates, and triangular projectile points (Rogers 1945).

Proto-historic/Historic Developments

After the end of the Hohokam tradition and before the arrival of the Spanish, the Gila Bend area was occupied by numerous small groups of Yavapai, Tohono O'odham, Akimel O'odham

(Pima) and Pee Posh peoples who subsisted on gathering, hunting, fishing, and some non-irrigation agriculture (McGuire and Schiffer 1982; Spier 1933; Bostwick 1988). The settlement pattern was fluid, and population movement and intergroup friction documented in historical accounts were already underway.

The historical period began at the approximate date of contact between the Spanish and local natives around A.D. 1540 and continued to the 1950s (with everything following 1950 being termed "modern"). Native populations in the project area continued to use the area as a transit corridor, and perhaps for special procurement and ceremonial purposes. One notable use of the area was as a migration route for the Pee Posh. The Pee Posh, who are present day neighbors of the Akimel O'odham on the Middle Gila River, lived on the lower Colorado River until approximately the end of the fifteenth century. Over the course of the next few centuries, the Pee Posh migrated to the Gila Bend area, then farther up the Gila River to escape attacks from their former neighbors (and traditional enemies), Yuman-speaking tribes on the lower Colorado River basin (Spier 1933). Another modern Native American group with stated ties to the project area is the Hopi.

Early non-Native Americans in the area were primarily Spanish explorers and missionaries, who were followed by settlers and miners from the eastern United States. Trapping expeditions worked the Gila River during the 1820s (Davis 1982). The project area, previously an important north-south travel corridor during prehistoric times, continued to be important for travelers from Mexico to Gila River settlements during Spanish and Mexican dominance. (Indeed the very reason that this report is being written is because of the continued use of the travel corridor into modern times.) The area was also part of an important east-west travel corridor between northern Mexico and California, the Camino del Diablo. Father Eusebio Kino used the route in 1698, 1699 and 1701 (Ahlstrom and Tucker 2000:65), as well as other routes in the area.

The earliest American contact with local residents occurred during the Mexican-American War as American troops moving along the Gila River toward California made contact with Akimel O'odham and Tohono O'odham. After the United States gained possession of the area in 1848 at the conclusion of the war, homesteading slowly increased. The Camino del Diablo remained in use and saw heavy duty as a route to the California gold fields in 1849 (Ahlstrom and Tucker 2000:67). The presence of the United States Army suppressed tribal warfare, such as that between the Yuman-speaking tribes and the Pee Posh cited above (Kroeber and Fontana 1986).

Modern water projects recreated and surpassed the conditions that permitted intense agricultural use of the land seen during the Hohokam florescence, though with uneven results throughout the project area. (See Chapter 10 on the historic site that includes a description of an attempt at farming within the project area during the Great Depression.) Agriculture remains a major life way in the area, though cash crops have replaced subsistence crops. Cattle ranching was introduced to the area in the 1920s, but was widely abandoned in the 1940s (Mitchell and Solometo 2002). Only trace amounts of the practice remain in the project area today. Mining, primarily for gold, silver and manganese, was present in the southern portion of the project area throughout the historic period, though it was not extensive or particularly successful (Ahlstrom and Tucker 2000:69).

CHAPTER 2

RESEARCH QUESTIONS

John Czarzasty and Glen E. Rice

THE NATURE OF THE SITES

This chapter presents questions that influenced research objectives and the field methods used to pursue these objectives. Objectives and methods followed as closely as possible those stated in the treatment plan (Office of Cultural Resource Management 2002) submitted for this project.

The project included three different categories of sites based on their settings in the landscape, their internal spatial structure, and the variety of activities conducted at the site. The first category included a single 20th century Depression-era historic homestead, AZ T:14:96 (ASM) (see Figure 1.3). The site contained the remains of structures, animal pens, and the considerable diversity of artifacts and features expected of residential settlements. The study of this site consisted of survey, archival research, and oral histories.

The second site category included a single prehistoric site on the Gila River terrace, AZ T:10:86 (ASM) (see Figure 1.2). It was difficult to tell from survey information if this site was a Hohokam village, a hamlet, or a series of field houses associated with agricultural fields on the river terrace. Because it was located in an alluvial setting the site was considered likely to have buried artifact deposits and features. The scale, internal spatial organization and function of this site could not be determined without subsurface testing as a minimum measure. Subsurface investigations eventually showed this to be the location of prehistoric agricultural fields.

The third category of sites consisted of activity areas located on the bajada away from the Gila River floodplain and included four sites: AZ T:14:113 (ASM), AZ T:14:94 (ASM), AZ T:14:92 (ASM), and AZ Z:2:46 (ASM) (see Figures 1.3 and 1.4). The sites were located on residual surfaces (Ruble 1998), frequently covered with desert pavement, and had almost no depositional depth. Most of the artifacts and features associated with the sites were visible on the surface, and survey observations provided considerable information about the internal spatial structure of the sites. Overall, the sites had sparse artifact assemblages mostly consisting of ceramics; the features included a variety of rock piles, rock scatters, rock rings, and trails.

Among the six sites in the project there was one historic residential settlement located on the bajada, four prehistoric activity areas located on the bajada, and one prehistoric site that was an activity area on the alluvium of the Gila River terrace. The large prehistoric villages in the area were located on or near the alluvial terraces of the Gila River, but they did not fall within the SR 85 construction area right-of-way.

WHAT SUBSISTENCE ACTIVITIES WERE ASSOCIATED WITH THE SITES?

In this landscape the best agricultural land with a reliable source of water is found on the alluvial soils of the Gila River terraces. Most of the large Hohokam villages were located on or near terraces along the edges of the floodplain (Teague 1981; Wasley and Johnson 1965) and fields were located on the alluvial terraces (Wright 1995). Surveys of the bajada, bedrock pediments and hills away from the floodplains have found numerous small sites including rock piles, rock rings, trails, light density artifact scatters, and petroglyphs (Rodgers 1976; Harmon and Beyer 1995). This settlement dichotomy will be illustrated clearly in the following chapter where it is shown that surveys have identified large sites along the river and small sites in the hills. The pediments and rougher terrain of the Buckeye Hills and Maricopa Mountains provided a range of resources such as cactus fruits, mesquite beans, small (and occasional large) game, various grass seeds, and greens that added diversity to the diet of farmers along the floodplain. The use of river terraces for agriculture and of pediments for collecting wild resources was common among the O'odham and other Native groups in early historic times and is evident in the prehistoric periods as well (Doelle 1976; Fish et al. 1992; Goodyear 1975; Rodgers 1976).

While site AZ T:10:86 (ASM) (see Figure 1.2) was likely to provide data on the Hohokam use of Gila alluvial terraces for irrigation farming, some of the sites on the bajada also had the potential to provide subsistence information. Other sites, or features within the sites, may pertain to the ceremonial use of the landscape. One of the bajada sites, AZ Z:2:46 (ASM) (see Figure 1.4), had a roasting pit or hearth containing potential macrobotanical evidence for the kinds of resources that were processed in the uplands. The balance of the project's Hohokam sites on the bajada and pediments consisted of rock piles, rock rings, and rock clearings, from which pollen samples may provide information on subsistence activities.

THE TRAILS

The numerous trails identified during the survey of SR 85 (Harmon and Beyer 1995) were apparently the routes that linked Hohokam villages along the Gila River to

    a) other settlements,
    b) resources found on the pediments and foothills of the Maricopa Mountains, or
    c) ceremonially important parts of the landscape marked by petroglyphs or shrines.

Three of the four prehistoric sites on the bajada (AZ T:14:92 [ASM], AZ T:14:94 [ASM], and AZ Z:2:46 [ASM], see Figures 1.3 and 1.4) were associated with trails. The sites, features and artifacts along the trails provide evidence of who used the trails, when they were used, and how they were used. Field research and an archival study of the trails are included in Chapter 12.

Trails were visible only when they occurred on old surfaces covered with desert pavement, and their spatial distribution coincides with the maximum extent of the desert pavement. For example, the northern distribution of trails does not extend beyond the northern extent of the Maricopa Mountains; the area to the north of the Maricopa Mountains is part of the Rainbow Wash drainage, and the Holocene soils are too recent to have desert pavement. Thus evidence for prehistoric trails no longer exists in that area.

A well known historic route used by Native American tribes, Spanish explorers, and eventually the Butterfield Stage Line (AZ T:14:61 [ASM]), led from the Gila Bend area eastward to the location of Maricopa Wells on the Middle Gila River (Stein 1994; Ahnert 1973). This shortcut saved a considerable amount of time for people traveling east or west. It eliminated the circuitous route following the Gila River northward around the Estrella Mountains and Buckeye Hills and then south again. The trip on the trail was conducted in two days, and natural tanks about midway sometimes held water and provided a convenient place for an overnight stay.

Additionally, we suggest that some of the trails in the southern part of the distribution were leading from Hohokam settlements in the Gila Bend area (e.g., the Gatlin site, AZ Z:2:1 [ASU], see Figure 3.1), heading east through Pima Pass in the southern tip of the Maricopa Mountains, continuing around the southern point of the Estrella Mountains to the vicinity of Maricopa Wells and Pima Butte on the Middle Gila River.

The "Wide Trail Site" (AZ T:14:28 [ASM], see Figure 3.1) is a particularly good candidate for trails that might fit this latter category. This trail varies from 0.5 to 1 meter in width, and was followed out by survey crews for a distance of more than one mile (1.6 km) to the west of the highway right-of-way (Harmon and Beyer 1995). The trail also continues to the east of the right-of-way in the general direction of Pima Pass at the southern tip of the Maricopa Mountains.

WHO USED THE LANDSCAPE AND DID THIS CHANGE OVER TIME?

The artifact assemblages found along trails can provide considerable information about the material culture that was transported over them (Stone 1991:83), and recent developments in the compositional analysis of Hohokam ceramics (Abbott 2000; Burton and Simon 1993; Simon 1998) and obsidian (Shackley 1995) have greatly improved the resolution with which these materials can be attributed to their source of origin. Three of the project's six sites provided features and artifact assemblages associated with trails, and thus can be used to characterize trails.

The answer to who used the sites in the pediments depends on having a method for distinguishing between the kinds of trails. Trails used for short, daily trips to collect resources ought to have been used mostly by local people, and therefore the artifacts dropped by the sides of the trail should be the kinds of materials found in the nearby villages. People from many different areas would have used the long distance trails. The artifacts dropped along those trails ought to contain higher percentages of non-local materials than are found in the local villages.

In order to distinguish between these two kinds of trail assemblages it is necessary to know what the artifact assemblages in the local Hohokam villages on the Gila River look like. Several Hohokam villages located on the Gila River in the vicinity of the trails have been excavated and their assemblages analyzed for the Painted Rocks Reservoir project reported by Wasley and Johnson (1965). Comparing the assemblages from sites and features excavated during this project against the data recorded for the sites excavated by in the Painted Rocks Reservoir project (Table 2.1), we were able to detect three different scenarios. First, Hohokam wares overwhelmingly dominated the ceramic assemblages of the majority of sites and features. Second, substantial amounts of both Hohokam and Patayan wares were associated with a closely spaced group of five rock features at one site. Finally, Patayan wares overwhelmingly dominated the ceramic assemblage of one site.

HOW WERE THE SITES USED FOR RESOURCE EXCHANGE?

What information do the sites associated with trails provide about long distance exchange and communication? Archaeological studies suggest that obsidian from the Sauceda source and marine shell from the Rocky Point area may have been traded through the Gila Bend area into the Middle Gila and Phoenix basin areas (McGuire and Howard 1987; Shackley 1988), and villages in the Gila Bend area received pottery in trade from the Hohokam on the Middle Gila River, the Patayan area along the Lower Colorado River, and possibly from populations in the northern periphery of the Phoenix Basin (Stone 1986:78–83; Teague 1981). Hohokam pottery, ground stone axes and shell jewelry were traded from the Gila River area to the Lower Colorado River area (Stone 1991:83), and

Table 2.1. Village Sites Excavated during the Painted Rocks Reservoir Project

Agency Number	Site Name	Time Period	Diagnostic Ceramics
AZ T:13:2 (ASM)	Citrus Site	Sedentary	Sacaton r/b, Gila plain, Lower Colorado Buff
AZ T:13:7 (ASM)		Colonial to Sedentary	L.C. Buff, Sacaton r/b, Gila plain
AZ T:13:8 (ASM)	Fortified Hill Site	Late Classic	PW, redware, Tanque Verde red-on-brown, Gila Plain (Gila), L.C. Buff
AZ T:13:9 (ASM)	Rock Ball Court Site	Colonial	Gila Butte r/b, Santa Cruz r/b, plainware, buffware
AZ T:14:11 (ASM)	Bartley Site	Classic period	Casa Grande r/b, Tanque Verde red-on-brown, Gila Red, buffware, Gila Plain (Gila)
AZ T:14:12 (ASM)		Classic period	Casa Grande r/b, Tanque Verde red-on-brown, Gila Red, buffware, Gila Plain (Gila)
AZ T:14:14 (ASM)		Sedentary period	Sacaton r/b, L.C. buff, Mimbres black-on-white
AZ T:14:15 (ASM)		Colonial to Sedentary	Gila Butte r/b, Santa Cruz r/b, Sacaton r/b
AZ T:14:16 (ASM)	Hi-Vu Ranch Site	Late Sedentary- Early Classic	Gila plain
AZ T:14:17 (ASM)	Enterprise South	Colonial-Early Classic	Gila plain, Gila Butte r/b, Casa Grande r/b, Sacaton red, Tanque Verde red-on-brown
AZ T:14:19 (ASM)	Enterprise Ranch Site	Sedentary-Early Classic	Sacaton r/b, Gila plain, Sacaton red, Classic red
AZ Z:1:11 (ASM)		Late Classic	Gila Plain (Gila), Gila red, Gila smudged, L.C. Buff,
AZ Z:2:1 (ASM)	Gatlin Site	Colonial to Classic	Santa Cruz r/b, Sacaton r/b, Sacaton red, Gila plain, Sacaton buffware, Lower Colorado Buff
AZ Z:2:2 (ASM)		Colonial-Sedentary	Santa Cruz r/b, Sacaton r/b, Gila plain (Gila)

conversely, pottery from the Lower Colorado River area was traded into the Hohokam core settlement in the Lower Salt and Gila River basin.

In early historic times Native groups in southern Arizona traveled long distances for trade, communication and war. The Pee Posh on the Middle Gila River traveled periods of 8 or 9 days, averaging about 30 miles (48 kilometers) a day, to visit related groups in southern California (Spier 1933:44). Both the Pee Posh and their Yuman adversaries traversed the distance from the Middle Gila to the Lower Colorado, passing through the Gila Bend area, when waging war against each other (Kroeber and Fontana 1986). Trails used for long distance travel, whether for purposes of war, trade, or visiting, will tend to have diverse assemblages of artifacts from different parts of the region.

WHAT KINDS OF FEATURES AND ARTIFACTS OCCUR WITH TRAIL SITES?

Trails, associated features and co-occurrences of artifacts when combined with settlement data provide important clues about inter-community relationships and communications. Long distance, linear routes suggest travel and communication between culturally affiliated and non-affiliated populations. Trails connected areas that had different resources and they identify routes between task-specific sites and base camps or villages. Mapping and analysis of trails and trail systems is necessary to evaluate processes related to mobility, exploitation and communication.

Native American trails are commonly associated with rock cairns, piles or clusters, cleared circles and ceramic sherd scatters (Breternitz 1975; Brown and Stone 1982; Harmon and Beyer 1995; Rodgers 1976; Stone 1986, 1991). Woodall (1995:13–14) notes that the most frequently observed feature within the vicinity of trails is the rock cluster. These features were composed of concentrations of locally available rock and range from 1 to 3 meters in diameter. Rock clusters and piles have been observed both along trails and independent of trails, and could represent roasting pits, hearths and/or trail markers (Brown and Stone 1982; Stone 1991; Woodall 1995). Rock piles may also represent trail shrines as noted by Treutlein (1949:228), cited in Ezell (1961:78–79):

> Near roads are seen small heaps of piled-up stones…Each traveler placed a stone at a certain place near the road, and the unconverted still have the habit… If the Indians themselves are asked why they heap up these stones, they answer, "We do it so that we shall not tire, but rather shall be able to run actively and swiftly over hill and dale, and so that no misfortune will overtake us on the journey."

Ezell (1961:79) noted the existence of this trait by commenting on a San Dieguito shrine identified in the saddle of the Buckeye Hills northeast of Gila Bend and a similar shrine found in the saddle of Gila Butte along the Gila River.

One feature on site AZ T:14:94 (ASM) and two features on site AZ T:14:92 (ASM) (see Figure 1.3) had quartz cobbles present. Rock piles and quartz flaked stone might have ideological significance. Areas containing quartz and white quartz along trails may be considered sacred by Native American communities. Ethnographic research relates that some Yuman-speaking groups shattered quartz in order to free supernatural powers embodied in it (Ezzo and Altschul 1993; Rogers 1976; Stone 1991). Rogers (1976) has identified possible quartz quarries along trails in the Buckeye Hills and the potential link between Buckeye Hills and mountain resources. Farther south, quartz cobbles and white quartz shatter have frequently been found as manuports in the vicinity of trails recorded in the SR 85 project area (Woodall 1995:13), possibly originating from quartz outcrops in the Estrella Mountains. Trail shrines may exhibit fist-size quartz stones potentially left as offerings. Large quartz outcroppings are identified readily in the Estrella Mountains and occur near trails. Certain of these outcrops served as quarries for raw material or, as in the case of Quartz Peak, are Traditional Cultural Properties for the Gila River Indian Community. As reported in the chapter on trails (this volume), a more practical explanation of quartz rock along trails has been suggested by Gila River Indian Community members who noted that accumulations of quartz fragments served to mark the trail, particularly on moonlit nights (E. Pedro, Personal Communication 2003). This may have facilitated travel during the hot summer months when night or early morning travel was preferred over walking during the day.

WHERE DO THE TRAILS GO?

One of the most intriguing questions about the trails concerns their points of origin and destination. These points do not fall within the SR 85 right-of-way, so this research question could not be addressed using data collected directly within the area of potential effect of SR 85 widening. The study team made use of archival research, analysis of aerial photographs, and a complete pedestrian survey and mapping of a few of the trails in the project area. Staff members of the Gila River Indian Community, Cultural Resource Management Program conducted the pedestrian survey and mapping using a GPS unit, and the results, included in Chapter 12, provide field corroboration of the archival research. Air photographs and the survey data concerning isolated artifacts were used to distinguish prehistoric cultural trails from historic livestock trails. For the prehistoric period the cultural trails are grouped with respect to their origin and destination. Prehistoric trails went from settlement to settlement, from a settlement to a general location, and from a settlement to a specific, non-settlement location on the landscape, such as a shrine, petroglyph panel, or ceremonial locality.

As the research progressed, special attention was given to the mapping of a trail that passed through AZ T:14:92 (ASM) and led from the Gila River valley eastward through a pass in the Maricopa Mountains, across Rainbow Valley, and through a second pass in the Estrella Mountains. Historic research showed that Father Kino used this trail.

AN AFRICAN-AMERICAN HOMESTEAD OF THE DEPRESSION ERA

Site AZ T:14:96 (ASM) (see Figure 1.3) was the location of a homestead patented by Warner Goode in 1936 (Harmon and Beyer 1995:54–56). The material remains at the site consisted of concrete foundations, wood and wire pens, woodpiles, ashy areas and an extensive historic artifact scatter dating mainly to the 1930s and 1940s.

Preliminary research by Pat Stein indicated that Warner Good was an African-American born in Chandler, Oklahoma, on March 23, 1902. He began to homestead in the Gila Bend area circa 1927. The homestead included 160 acres, described as the NW ¼ of the SW ¼ of the SW ¼, and the SW ¼ of the SW ¼ of the SW ¼ of Section 11, Township 3 South, Range 4 West, and the NE ¼ of the SE ¼ of the SE ¼, and the SE ¼ of the SE ¼ of the SE ¼ of Section 10, Township 3 South, Range 4 West. Goode received his homestead patent in 1936. The Goode family continued to reside on the homestead until 1948, when they moved to Phoenix, establishing a permanent residence at 1446 East Jefferson Street. For much of his productive life, Warner Goode worked in construction. During one period of his life, he ran a road grader for Maricopa County; during another, he owned a cement-and-rock masonry business. He was a member of the Sky Harbor Congregation of the Jehovah's Witnesses. When Warner Goode died in 1982 at age 80, his survivors included his wife, three sons, four daughters, three brothers, five sisters, 20 grandchildren, and 12 great-grandchildren (*Arizona Republic* 1982; Government Land Office 1936; Social Security Death Index n.d.). His son Calvin was a Phoenix City Councilman for many years, and is currently involved in the effort to develop a Black History Museum in historic Carver High School in Phoenix (James Garrison, personal communication).

To date, several Arizona homesteads have been archaeologically excavated (Ayres and Seymour 1993; Solometo 2001; Stein 1981, 1988); however, they have all been associated with Euro-American or Mexican-American settlers. SHPO sponsored a study of Mobile, AZ (about 20 miles east of the project area), focused on African-American homesteads (Swanson 1992); however, that study was a survey that did not examine any of the homesteads in detail. The State Route 85 investigation may mark the first detailed study of an African-American homestead in Arizona.

The archival research examined primary and secondary data sources, including homestead case files, serial records, contemporary newspapers, county records, and miscellaneous other records. Interviews were conducted with Mr. Calvin Goode about his family's use of the homestead.

SUMMARY

In order to address the research questions fully and completely, multiple methods were required and they were applied to those areas for which they were best suited. The methods of fieldwork, archival research, and oral histories all proved to be valuable components in the implementation of the research. Fieldwork was used to investigate the sites and the trail systems. Archival research was used to identify the settlement patterns in the larger identify containing the project area, and also contributed to the development of the trail overview. Finally, archival research and oral histories were used to document the historic site.

CHAPTER 3

THE GILA BEND SETTLEMENT PATTERN

John Czarzasty and Glen E. Rice

INTRODUCTION

The Gila Bend area of southwest Arizona was a periphery of the Hohokam core. It is located southwest of the Hohokam core area in the basin of the Gila and Salt Rivers near present-day Phoenix. Landforms of the Gila Bend can be divided into four main categories: floodplain, terrace, bajada and mountain. The floodplain is the low level terrain immediately adjacent to the river channel that is the first to flood when the river leaves its banks. Terraces are elevated above the floodplain along rivers, formed by aggradation during past overbank flooding. Terraces can also be formed when floodplains are left behind at a higher elevation as an incising river cuts the river channel deeper. The bajada is the piedmont area above the terraces, formed by the deposition of materials from surrounding mountains. The bajada is usually sloped, and does not consist of alluvium except from local washes. (Chapter 4 provides further discussion of these landforms.)

A map of known prehistoric sites in the Gila Bend area is presented in Figure 3.1. This is based on a records search of 16 USGS 7.5' map quadrangles (Table 3.1) using the site records at the Bureau of Land Management and AZSITE. Site types are discussed below. Figure 3.2 shows the prehistoric sites in the Gila Bend area that are attributed to the Hohokam culture, the Patayan culture, to both cultures, and the more ephemeral sites for which no cultural assignment could be made based on the contents of their artifact assemblages. Site distribution by cultural tradition supports Roger's findings (1976:71) that Patayan ceramics were more often found in upland sites.

The Hohokam periphery in the Gila Bend overlaps the Patayan cultural area centered in the Papaguería to the southwest. The Gila Bend area was a travel corridor through which both people and material passed from locations in the Papaguería and farther south into the Hohokam core. The traffic moved both ways as Hohokam people and material from the core area and the Gila Bend area traveled southwest into the Papaguería. However, the area was more than just a traffic thoroughfare. Separate and distinct elements of Patayan and Hohokam populations were present in the Gila Bend area's uplands, each with their own characteristic ceramic tradition.

There are two major indicators of contact between the Hohokam of the Gila Bend and the people located to the southwest. The first is the presence of Patayan ceramics, such as Lower Colorado, Palomas and Tumco buffwares in the Gila Bend area and Hohokam core. The buffwares are discussed in a subsequent chapter on artifacts. The other indicator is the presence of shell. Shell from the Gulf of California's Adair Bay was transported or traded northward through the Gila Bend area into the Phoenix basin (Tucker et al. 2000), and this apparent trade intensified during the Hohokam Sedentary period (McGuire 1982). Connections with people to the southwest resulted in an overlapping of material cultures. An examination of the settlement pattern in the area must consider cultural, spatial and functional components.

Table 3.1. Map Quadrangles (USGS 7.5') Covered in the Records Search

Arlington, AZ	Hussayampa, AZ	Buckeye, AZ	Avondale, AZ
Spring Mtn, AZ	Cotton Center NW, AZ	Margies Peak, AZ	Mobile NW, AZ
Citrus Valley East, AZ	Cotton Center, AZ	Cotton Center SE, AZ	Butterfield Pass, AZ
Smurr, AZ	Gila Bend, AZ	Bosque, AZ	Estrella, AZ

SETTLEMENT SYSTEM COMPONENTS

The records search covered the 16 map quadrangles listed in Table 3.1. The site search covered approximately 2,000 square kilometers and was bounded by the Buckeye Valley to the north, the Maricopa Mountains to the east, the Sand Tank Mountains to the south and the Gila Bend Mountains to the west. The search resulted in 202 prehistoric sites in the greater Gila Bend area (Appendix A). The prehistoric sites are broken down into the following categories: village, temporary habitation, campsite, activity area and trail. (See Downum [1993] for an alternate breakdown of site categories.)

Villages are the largest of the five categories, and they are characterized by an aggregation of population with a sedentary residential pattern. Villages are locations of multiple activities and usually have a variety of features and artifact classes spread over a large horizontal expanse. Features may include trash mounds, middens, platform mounds, pit houses or other residential structures. Activity areas may be found within the perimeter of a village.

Temporary habitations are residential structures, but their isolation, fewer artifact classes, and the absence of indicators of intense occupation, such as large trash mounds, distinguish them from villages. Temporary habitations may not have been occupied as continuously as villages, and they may have been used by special work groups rather than by a full social complement. A typical example of a temporary habitation site is an agricultural fieldhouse.

Activity areas are loci associated with the exploitation of a subsistence resource and are normally located in the immediate vicinity of the resource. Activity areas usually involve the procurement or processing of a single type of resource and are of a limited temporal duration. Activity areas are characterized by a limited horizontal expanse, a restricted number of artifact types and features, the utility of which are directly related to the resource being exploited.

Campsites are a subset of activity areas. The distinguishing characteristic of campsites is the concept of a sojourn, a brief stay for rest and possibly nourishment, rather than the performance of an activity or activities followed by a departure from the site, though such activities can occur at a campsite. Campsites are temporary residences occupied while one is traveling away from one's permanent residence. Campsites may be needed while traveling to a specific destination, or while away from the permanent residence on a round to gather resources.

Campsites frequently have campfires and rock rings large enough to enclose a sleeping area for one or more persons. Some activity areas may also have campfires for processing resources or for preparing a meal, so the difference between campsites and activity areas is often subtle.

Consideration of a site's propinquity to a village may help as a discriminator between activity areas and campsites, since an overnight or longer stay would not normally be necessary when one is

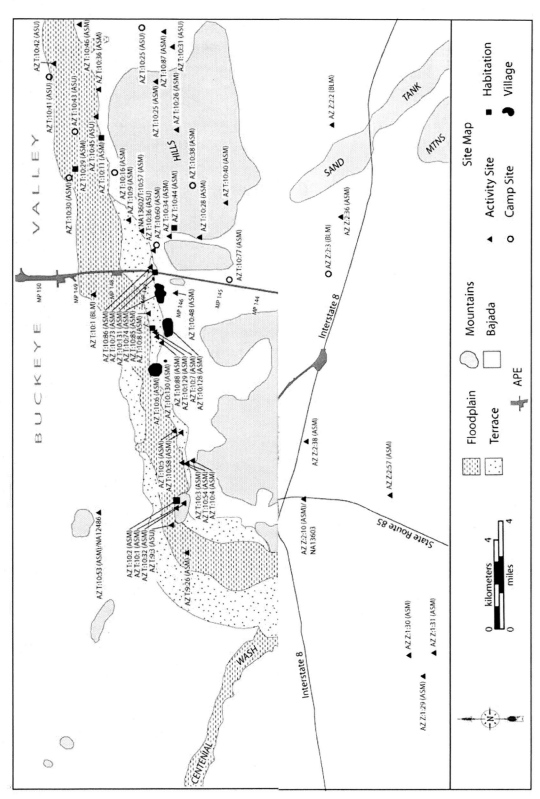

Figure 3.1. Prehistoric sites in the Gila Bend area, shown by site type.

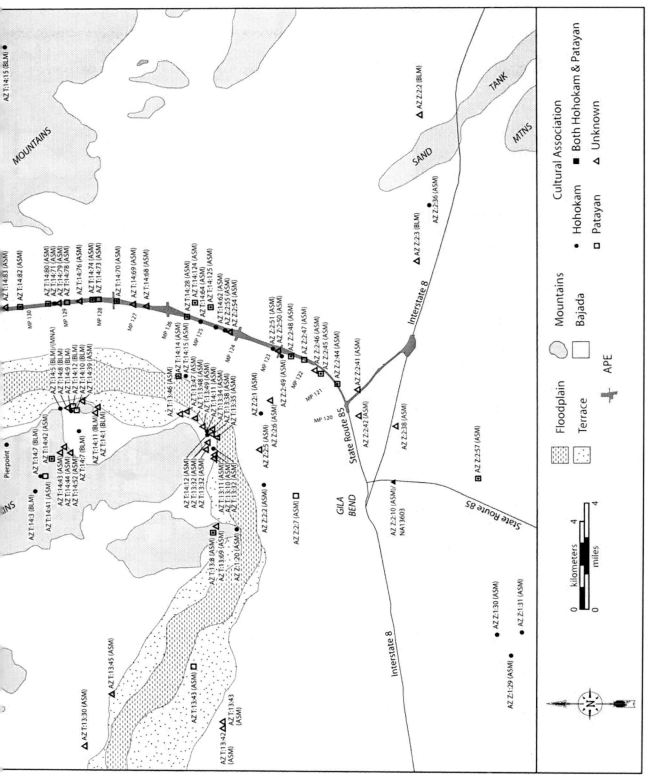

Figure 3.2. Prehistoric sites in the Gila Bend area, shown by cultural attribution.

in close proximity to a village, assuming that both campsite and village were occupied simultaneously and parties involved were not socially distant from one another. Once beyond a certain distance from a village, campsites would have been necessary for travelers, gatherers and procurers. In determining between campsites and activity areas during the site records search, site types recorded by the original site investigators were generally honored. If the original investigator did not make the determination, the presence of shelter-sized rock rings and thermal features in addition to artifact scatters left by various activities led us to classify sites as campsites.

Trails are associated with both campsites and activity areas, and they are generally oriented so as to link those sites with villages. On a larger scale, some trails linked the Gila Bend area to other settlement areas, notably settlements to the east on the Middle Gila River. Trails were the arteries of the settlement system, used for travel from settlement to settlement, for gathering resources, or for both purposes. Resource trails from a village to the bajada were not necessarily shorter than travel trails connecting settlement areas. The Yuman descendants of the Patayan covered distances of 50 miles or more on trails in order to reach areas with favorable distributions of wild resources (McGuire 1982:191).

PREVIOUS ARCHAEOLOGICAL RESEARCH IN THE GILA BEND AREA

During the last three-quarters of a century, more than 50 major archaeological surveys and many more minor surveys have been conducted in southwestern Arizona, with most of the surveys occurring since the Cultural Resources Management legislation of the 1970s (Schiffer and Wells 1982). A list of some of the major surveys and excavations within the Gila Bend area are provided in Table 3.2. The majority of the surveys took place within an area bounded by the Buckeye Valley to the north, the Maricopa Mountains to the east, the Papaguería to the south and the Gila Bend Mountains to the west. In addition, Rogers' (1928, etc) work covered all of Southern California and southwestern Arizona east to the Gila Bend area.

RESULTS OF PREVIOUS SURVEYS

United States Bureau of Land Management (BLM) files were utilized to obtain records of 134 surveys within the Gila Bend Hohokam periphery area. A list of these surveys, along with acreage covered, form of survey (linear or block), number of sites found, and dominant terrain, is attached as Appendix B. The records were used to create Table 3.3, a compilation of the number of acres surveyed and the number of sites found by landform. In the table, the acreage from 12 surveys that covered multiple landforms have been split by landform and added to the acreage totals of surveys conducted on a single landform type. Additionally, it is apparent that site records and descriptions do not exist for all sites recorded in surveys, since survey records show 355 prehistoric sites encountered, while BLM and Arizona State Museum records show only 202 unique sites in the same area. Survey boundaries did not indicate the likelihood of duplicate encounters of sites.

Table 3.3 indicates that surveys on the bajada recorded more than their expected share of sites, assuming here as in subsequent analysis that a random dispersion of sites would place a number of sites in each landform category in proportion to the percentage of the acreage associated with that category. The percentage of sites recorded on the bajada (86%) exceeds the percentage of bajada acreage within total surveyed acres (57%) by a factor of 1.5.

The analysis of the survey results indicates that the greatest number of sites was discovered on the bajada. The bajada was exploited at numerous small sites (as were the mountainous uplands).

Table 3.2. Major Surveys and Excavations in the Gila Bend Area

Surveys

Buckeye Hills East (Rodgers 1976)

Northeast Papaguería (Coe 1979)

Southern California and Southwestern Arizona (Rogers 1928, etc.)

Northwestern Papaguería (Ezell 1954, 1955)

Painted Rock Reservoir (Schroeder 1961; Ezell 1963)

Gillespie Dam to the Granite Reef Dam (Wasley 1965)

Liberty to Gila Bend 230KV Transmission System (Brook et al. 1977)

Probability Sample Survey of the Painted Rock Reservoir Area (Teague and Baldwin 1978)

State Route 85 Right-of-Way, Gila Bend to Buckeye, AZ (Harmon and Beyer 1995; Woodall 1995, 1997)

Butterfield Stage Overland Route, Gila Bend to Mobile, AZ (Hackbarth 1995)

An Archaeological Survey of a Portion of the Robbins Butte Wildlife Area (Rice and Smith 1999)

Excavations

Painted Rock Reservoir: Prehistoric Sites (Johnson and Wasley 1961; Wasley and Johnson 1965)

Fortified Hill Site, Gila Bend (Greenleaf 1974, 1975)

Test Excavations at Painted Rock Reservoir (Teague1981)

Table 3.3. Survey Data Compilation, Total by Landform of Surveyed Area

Landform	Surveys	Acres Surveyed	Sites per 100 Acres	Sites Recorded	Expected in Random Distribution
Bajada	80	20,203	1.51	306	201
Terrace/floodplain	21	14,128	0.25	36	141
Mountains	21	1,319	0.99	13	13
Multiple forms	12	N/A	N/A	N/A	N/A
Total	134	35,650	0.997	355	355

While the floodplain and terrace may have had more people performing more activities, the people and activities there tended to be clustered in fewer, larger sites. In addition to cultural factors, geological forces are at work. Floodplain and terrace sites are more likely to have been erased from the landscape due to erosion or covered by alluvium deposition during the intervening centuries following deposition of archaeological materials. Site detection is also hindered on the floodplain and terrace due to restricted visibility caused by proliferation of vegetation and agricultural fields. These factors are much less of an issue when searching for sites on the bajada. Figure 3.3 shows the percentages of site types (excluding isolated trails) by landform. Although all landforms are dominated by activity areas, a

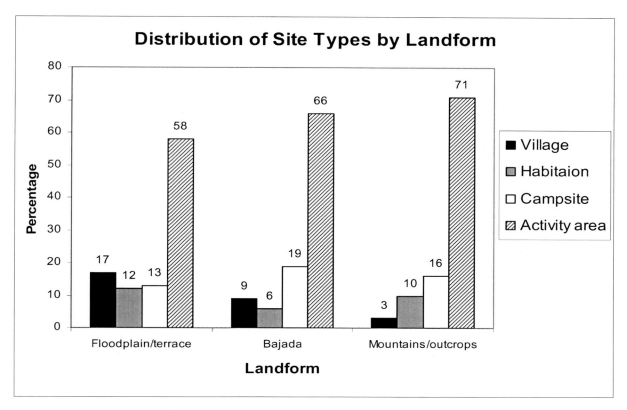

Figure 3.3. Distribution of site types by landforms.

land-use pattern is discernible in which the presence of long-term occupational sites, both large scale (villages) and small scale (habitations), is greatest in the floodplain/terrace, while the reverse holds for campsites and activity areas. This topic is addressed further later in this chapter.

One must temper any conclusions based on the surveys included in this analysis because the surveys were in no real sense a random sampling of the project area. Many of the surveys were conducted to ensure compliance with cultural and environmental laws and regulations. Specific areas were investigated in order to meet specific regulatory needs. Although the surveys used here allow us to make extrapolations regarding the larger area in which they were conducted, we must recognize that a rigorous random sample is not present.

RESULTS OF PREVIOUS EXCAVATION

A literature search uncovered reports of excavations at 11 sites in or near the project area. The sites were mostly village sites, with one habitation site and one ball court included, and they were part of the system of villages spaced along the Gila River that formed the backbone of the Hohokam settlement system.

Site AZ T:13:8 (ASM) - Fortified Hill Site

Site AZ T:13:8 (ASM) was a Hohokam village (Downum's [1993] type 3, Noncompound Settlement) on the top of a volcanic escarpment projecting from the bajada north of the Gila River approximately 7.1 km (4.4 mi) northwest of the town of Gila Bend (see Figure 3.1). The site, occupied during the Civano phase of the Classic period (based on the presence of Gila Polychrome ceramics), covered approximately 2 acres. Site AZ T:13:8 (ASM) consisted of artifact scatters, 57 rooms, bedrock mortars, middens, outside hearths, cremations and inhumations. Wasley excavated the site (Greenleaf 1975).

Site AZ T:13:9 (ASM) - Rock Ball Court Site

Site AZ T:13:9 (ASM), the Rock Ball Court site, was a Hohokam village (Downum's [1993] subtype 1b, Settlement with Ballcourt) occupied during the Colonial and Sedentary periods and excavated by Wasley and Johnson (1965). The site was approximately 200 m x 300 m in size, and located on the terrace north of the Gila River approximately 24 km (15 mi) northwest of the town of Gila Bend (beyond the area covered by the maps in this report). The Rock Ball Court Site consisted of pit houses, a storage unit, a ball court, cremations, a pit oven, and several small trash mounds, borrow pits, and an artifact scatter.

Site AZ T:14:11 (ASM) - Bartley Site

Site AZ T:14:11 (ASM) was a Hohokam village (Downum's [1993] type 3, Noncompound Settlement) founded during the Classic period. The site was located on the Gila River terrace north of the river, directly north of the modern town of Gila Bend (see Figure 3.1). The size of the site was at least 50 m x 50 m. The site consisted of a large, expansive trash mound, burials, artifact scatters, and a primary cremation (recorded separately as AZ T:14:10 [ASM]). Wasley and Johnson (1965) excavated the site.

Site AZ T:14:12 (ASM)

Site AZ T:14:12 (ASM) was a Hohokam temporary habitation, possibly a fieldhouse, (Downum's [1993] type 2, Compound Settlement) occupied during the Classic period. The site was located on the Gila River terrace approximately 8 km (5 mi) north of the modern town of Gila Bend (see Figure 3.1). The site was approximately 50 m x 60 m. Site AZ T:14:12 (ASM) consisted of an outer ring wall, a rectangular structure, a trash mound, a single burial, and artifact scatters. Wasley and Johnson (1965) excavated the site.

Site AZ T:14:14 (ASM)

Site AZ T:14:14 (ASM) was a Hohokam village (Downum's [1993] subtype 1b, Settlement with Ballcourt) occupied during the Sedentary period. The site was badly disturbed by modern agriculture and vandals. Though several trash mounds and a ball court were identified, only the north-south-oriented ball court was excavated (Wasley and Johnson 1965). The site was located on the bajada north of the modern town of Gila Bend (see Figure 3.1).

Site AZ T:14:15 (ASM)

Site AZ T:14:15 (ASM) was a Hohokam ball court. No other features were reported to be associated with it. The site was on the bajada one-half mile west of site AZ T:14:14 (ASM) (see Figure 3.1) and may be associated with that site. The east-west oriented ball court was excavated by

Wasley and Johnson (1965), and assigned to the Sedentary period. However, the east–west orientation of the ball court and the presence of both Gila Butte and Santa Cruz red-on-buff sherds suggest an earlier Colonial period construction, with use persisting into the Sedentary period. The dimensions of the ball court were 9.5 m x 23.7 m and its depth was 1.4 m.

Site AZ T:14:19 (ASM)

Site AZ T:14:19 (ASM) was a Hohokam village (Downum's [1993] type 1, Settlement with Public Architecture) founded during the Sedentary period with occupation into the early Classic period. The site was approximately 388 x 866 meters in size and located on the bajada west of the Gila River approximately 25 km (16 mi) north of the town of Gila Bend (see Figure 3.1). The site consisted of a large trash mound, several smaller trash mounds, 2 north–south oriented ball courts, and walled enclosures. Wasley and Johnson (1965) excavated only the large trash mound, and halted the excavation once they determined that it was not a platform mound.

Site AZ Z:1:11 (ASM)

Site AZ Z:1:11 (ASM) was a Hohokam village (Downum's [1993] type 3, Noncompound Settlement) located on the terrace south of the Gila River, approximately 8 km (5 mi) northwest of the town of Gila Bend. The site was occupied during the Classic period, and it spanned 50 m x 100 m. Despite its small size and the fact that only one structure was discovered at the site, it is still considered to be a village due to the presence of a substantial trash mound (15-m diameter, 0.5-m thickness) and three cremations. This indicates a continuous occupation of the site. Additionally, multiple artifact classes were recovered at the site: ceramics, flaked stone, ground stone and shell. This indicates that a wide range of activities took place at the site, more than would have occurred at a limited activity site. Wasley and Johnson (1965) excavated the site. They recovered intrusive Lower Colorado buffware sherds, indicating contact with the Patayan culture, and Gila Polychrome, indicating occupation during the Civano phase of the Classic period.

Site AZ Z:1:7 (ASM)

Site AZ Z:1:7 (ASM) was a Hohokam village (Downum's [1993] type 3, Noncompound Settlement) located on the terrace south of the Gila River, approximately 9.6 km (6 mi) northwest of the town of Gila Bend. The site was occupied during the late Colonial and Sedentary periods and it spanned 130 m x 350 m. Site AZ Z:1:7 (ASM) contained an artifact scatter, one structure, cremations, and trash pits. The site was excavated in order to mitigate for pending agricultural development (Teague 1981).

Site AZ Z:1:8 (ASM)

Site AZ Z:1:8 (ASM) was a Hohokam village (Downum's [1993] type 3, Noncompound Settlement) located on the terrace south of the Gila River in close proximity to site AZ Z:1:7 (ASM). The site was occupied during the Sedentary period, and it covered 300 m x 400 m. Site AZ Z:1:8 (ASM) contained an artifact scatter and a trash pit. The site was excavated in order to mitigate for pending agricultural development (Teague 1981). It is possible that this site and site AZ Z:1:7 (ASM) were components of one site.

Site AZ Z:2:1 (ASM) - Gatlin Site

Site AZ Z:2:1 (ASM), the Gatlin site (Doyel 2000; Wasley 1960), was a Hohokam village (Downum's [1993] subtype 1, Settlement with Public Architecture) founded late in the Colonial period and occupied through the Sedentary period. The site was approximately 385 m x 410 m in size, and was located on the bajada south of the Gila River near the town of Gila Bend where the direction of flow of the Gila River changes from south to west (see Figure 3.1). The Gatlin Site consisted of a Sedentary Period style platform mound, 22 trash mounds, 2 north-south-oriented ball courts, a crematorium, pit houses, a canal, and artifact scatters. Wasley and Johnson (1965; Wasley 1960) excavated the site.

OTHER SIGNIFICANT SITES

Additional significant settlement sites have been discovered along the Gila River but have not been excavated. In order to present a more complete picture of the village settlement pattern in the greater area encompassing the project sites, these sites are described below.

Site AZ T:10:74 (ASM)

Site AZ T:10:74 (ASM) was a Hohokam village (Downum's [1993] type 3, Noncompound Settlement) located on the bajada southwest of the SR 85 crossing of the Gila River (see Figure 3.1). The site, occupied from the late Sedentary period into the Classic period, covered approximately 540 m x 660 m. Evidence for the site consisted of artifact scatters and 14 trash mounds (Rice and Smith 1999).

Site AZ T:10:128 (ASM)

Site AZ T:10:128 (ASM) was a Hohokam village (Downum's [1993] type 3, Noncompound Settlement) located on the bajada south of the Gila River approximately 1.6 km (1 mi) east of Robbins Butte (see Figure 3.1). The site, occupied from the late Pioneer period into the Sedentary period, covered approximately 640 x 780 meters. Evidence for the site consisted of three expansive high intensity surface scatters containing multiple artifact categories (Rice and Smith 1999).

Site AZ T:10:130 (ASM)

Site AZ T:10:130 (ASM) was a small Hohokam village (Downum's [1993] type 3, Noncompound Settlement) located on the bajada south of the Gila River approximately 0.25 km (0.16 mi) southeast of Robbins Butte (see Figure 3.1). The site, occupied from the late Pioneer period into the Sedentary period, covered approximately 60 m x 80 m. Evidence for the site consisted of an expansive high intensity surface scatter containing multiple artifact categories (Rice and Smith 1999).

Site AZ T:10:131 (ASM)

Site AZ T:10:131 (ASM) was a small Hohokam village (Downum's [1993] type 3, Noncompound Settlement) located 200 meters east of site AZ T:10:74 (ASM) (see Figure 3.1). The site was possibly an outlying part of site AZ T:10:74 (ASM) during the early portion of the occupation of AZ T:10:74 (ASM). The site, occupied from the late Pioneer period into the Sedentary period, covered approximately 30 m x 50 m. Evidence for the site consisted of surface scatters and a trash mound (Rice and Smith 1999). Though small in size, the multiple artifact categories found at the site suggest that it was used for long-term occupation as a village.

DISTRIBUTION OF SITE TYPES: OVERVIEW

The lifeblood of the Hohokam desert farmers in the Gila Bend area was the Gila River, and as would be expected, the largest agglomerations of people, represented by village sites, were spaced along the Gila River (Doyel 2000; Wasley and Johnson 1965). Villages were located on the terrace and bajada, away from seasonal flooding yet close enough to the river for easy access to water and to make effective use of irrigation potential. Towards the end of the Classic period, villages relocated to easily defended bedrock pediments such as Robbins Butte, though of necessity their agricultural activity remained on the terrace and floodplain. Though villages were located on the bajada in the Gila Bend area, they do not occur there as frequently as in the Tucson Basin with its greater network of reliably flowing tributary washes on the bajada (Fish et al. 1992).

Temporary habitations had more flexibility regarding where they could be located. Temporary habitations found in the site search were located on the terrace, bajada, and on hilltops. When used in conjunction with agriculture as fieldhouses, they were usually located on the edge of the floodplain or terrace. Agricultural fieldhouses were occupied during the growing season when the threat of flooding was minimal and the need to be near the fields was immediate. Temporary habitations on the bajada and on hilltops may have also served a subsistence role, such as a semi-permanent collection point for upland resources. Some of the hilltop temporary habitations may actually be remnants of elevated villages from the Classic period, when pre-Classic villages were depopulated, settlement became more dispersed, and easily defended locations were favored (Tucker et al. 2000:67; Wilcox 1979; Greenleaf 1975; McGuire 1982).

Campsites were generally located away from the Gila River, often along trails. Campsites were used during travel and resource gathering expeditions. Though some campsites were located near the river, this is not common in the archaeological record. Opportunities for other accommodations (assuming contemporaneity and small social distances between the parties involved) would be available in the villages spaced along the river. Some of the campsites and nearby villages may not have been occupied at the same time. An alternate explanation for the low occurrence of campsites near the river is that site preservation may be poor in the face of erosion, alluvial deposition and modern agriculture. Campsites on the floodplain and terrace may have been covered or disturbed beyond recognition.

Generally, activity area locations were not restricted by landform. Activity areas were found across the entire Gila Bend area. Some were near villages, others were far from the villages, at resource-rich locations on the bajada or in the mountains. Certain ideological activities were sensitive to landform type. Ceremonial activity areas, identified as such due to the presence of petroglyphs and rock piles (thought to be shrines), occurred almost exclusively on the uplands where suitable raw materials were abundant. For the 26 sites within the study area with petroglyphs, all but one occurred on the bajada or mountains/outcrops.

The preservation of trail sites, due to their lack of depth and ephemeral nature, was highly dependent on the kind of landform that they traversed. The vast majority of trails were found on the bajada where they cross stable surfaces covered with desert pavement. The trails connected villages

Table 3.4. Archaic Sites

Sites/ Names	Quad	Land-form	Type	Size	Period/ Phase	Features	Assem-blage	Diagnostics
ASM								
T:13:35	Cotton Center	Gila River floodplain	habitation	6-m diameter	"Archaic"	depression (1)	FS	none
T:14:59	Cotton Center NW	Gila River floodplain	activity area	not recorded	"late Archaic"	artifact scatter (1)	FS, GS	none
Z:1:20	Smurr	rock outcrop	activity area (quarry)	200m x 250m	Archaic through Hohokam	lithic quarry (1), petroglyph panels (7)	FS, GS	Archaic and Gila style petroglyphs

Key: FS - flaked stone   GS - ground stone

with resource areas and other villages, and those portions of the trails closest to the villages on the floodplain and terrace were not as well preserved, if at all, as were trails on the bajada and in the mountains.   Bajada and mountain trail segments have not been subjected to the same types of weathering and sedimentation as trail segments on the floodplain and terrace. Preservation factors are not the only possible explanation for the preponderance of trails on the bajada.   A dendritic trail system, linking villages to various resource-gathering locations by branching out as the trails move away from their points of origin at or near a village, may account for the apparent greater presence of trails on the bajada.

In summary, the distribution of site types across the landscape is aligned with expectations. Hohokam villages were anchored on, or perhaps shackled to, the only reliable source of water in the area, the Gila River.   Temporary habitations conformed to expectations, particularly in light of the interpretation of many as agricultural fieldhouses. Activity areas and campsites were not bound to a particular area, and in fact, campsites exhibited an inclination to be removed from the vicinity of villages. In the following section, the spatial array of sites over time is examined.

TEMPORAL AND CULTURAL DISTRIBUTION OF SITES

Archaic Period

Only three sites in the Gila Bend area are assigned to the Archaic period (Figure 3.4, Table 3.4).   AZ T:13:35 (ASM) (Teague and Baldwin 1978), recorded as being "Archaic," was a depression with flaked stone present that was possibly the substructure of a habitation. Its location in the Gila River floodplain makes for a remarkable preservation history, if the site is in fact Archaic. AZ T:14:59 (ASM) (Douglas and Crary 1993) was an activity area. A scatter of flaked stone and groundstone mark the site, which was recorded as "late Archaic." Diagnostic artifacts were not reported for either of the two sites. The third site, Z:1:20 (ASM) (Wallace and Holmlund 1989), was a long-used quarry site with flaked stone and groundstone, and with petroglyphs recorded as being of "Archaic" and "Gila" styles. Firm dating to the Archaic Period seems weak, but assuming that the three sites are Archaic, the overall picture for the Gila Bend area during this period is one of sparse, non-nucleated population.

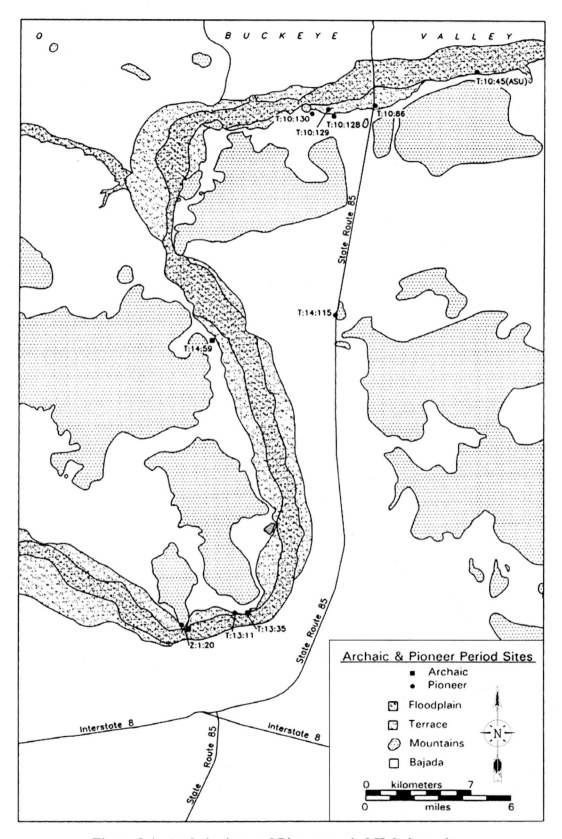

Figure 3.4. Archaic sites and Pioneer period Hohokam sites.

Pioneer Period

Early Hohokam occupation of the Gila River area was concentrated in the north (see Figure 3.4, Table 3.5). There were two villages south of the Gila River near Robbins Butte, AZ T:10:128 (ASM) and AZ T:10:130 (ASM), and both have been described earlier in this chapter. In addition to the villages, there are five activity areas dating to the Pioneer and one designated as "Preclassic" that might also be a Pioneer site within the Gila Bend area.

The activity areas were spread across the Gila Bend area. Two of the activity areas were in the immediate vicinity of the villages within a 3-km radius. The sites were located on the terrace, and they were most likely agricultural fields exploited by the village occupants.

Table 3.5. Pioneer Period Sites

Sites/ Names	Quad	Land-form	Type	Size	Period/ Phase	Features	Assemblage	Diagnostics
ASM								
T:10:86	Buckeye	terrace	activity area	230m x 246m	Pioneer-Classic periods	ash stains (11), artifact scatters	C, FS, GS	Salt red, Gila plain, Hohokam buff, Hohokam R/B
T:10:128	Hassayampa	bajada	village	780m x 640m	Pioneer-Sedentary periods	artifact scatters	C, FS, GS, FCR	Gila Butte R/B, Sweetwater red-on-grey
T:10:129	Hassayampa	terrace	activity area	30m x 70m	Pioneer-Sedentary periods	artifact scatters	C, FS, GS, S	Gila Butte R/B
T:10:130	Hassayampa	bajada	village	80m x 60m	Pioneer-Sedentary periods	artifact scatters	C, FS, GS, FCR	Hohokam R/B, PW
T:13:11	Cotton Center	bajada	activity area	not recorded	Preclassic period	artifact scatter (1)	C, L, FS, GS	not recorded
T:14:115	Cotton Center NW	bajada	activity area	40m x 91m	Preclassic to Classic periods	petroglyphs (6)	none	N/A
Z:1:20	Smurr	rock outcrop	activity area (quarry)	200m x 250m	Archaic through Hohokam	lithic quarry (1), petroglyph panels (7)	FS, GS	Archaic and Gila style petroglyphs
ASU								
T:10:45	Buckeye	Gila River flood-plain	activity area	120m x 170m	Snaketown and Gila Butte phases	artifact scatter (1), hearth (1)	C, FS	Gila plain, Gila Butte & Snaketown, R/B

Key:
C - ceramics   FCR - fire-cracked rock   FS - flaked stone
GS - ground stone   L - Lithics   S - shell
R/B - red-on-buff   PW - plainware

A third activity area site, AZ T:10:45 (ASU), was also in the north and located along the floodplain, but its distance from the villages indicates that it was not involved in daily agricultural exploitation by village residents. Judging from the limited artifact types present, the site was most likely used for resource gathering. The size of the site and the presence of a hearth suggest that the site was used frequently.

The remaining three activity areas were even greater distances from the villages. All were on the bajada or pediment. AZ Z:1:20 (ASM) was a lithic quarry that also contained petroglyphs. AZ T:14:115 (ASM) was exclusively a petroglyph site. Activities at site AZ T:13:11 (ASM) could not be precisely determined. The site was originally recorded as "Preclassic" and may actually date to the Colonial or Sedentary periods.

In summary, Hohokam sites in the Gila Bend area during the Pioneer period were scant, indicating a low population during the earliest stage of Hohokam occupation. Settled villages with associated activity areas could be found only in the north, and a very few additional activity areas were scattered throughout the area. Patayan artifacts are not recorded in the Gila Bend area during the Pioneer period.

Colonial Period

During the Colonial period, Hohokam occupation of the Gila Bend area expanded significantly both in extent and density (Figure 3.5, Table 3.6). Seven villages and at least 46 additional smaller sites were present, as agricultural exploitation of the river valley and use of the adjacent uplands intensified in order to support growing populations.

At AZ T:14:15 (ASM), near the present day town of Gila Bend, the area's earliest known ball court was excavated by Wasley and Johnson (1965:49–51). Although Wasley and Johnson dated the site to the Sedentary period, the presence of Colonial period ceramic sherds and the east-west orientation of the ball court suggest an earlier date for the construction of the ball court, though its use apparently persisted into the Sedentary period.

The archaeological record for the Colonial period presents evidence for the most extensive exploitation of the bajada and mountains during the Hohokam occupation of the area. This may be an artifact of the nonrandom surveys conducted in the area, or it may reflect a time in the Hohokam sequence before commitment to irrigation agriculture became total and complete.

The Colonial period also has the greatest number of Patayan sites in the archaeological record. Wasley and Johnson (1965:70–72) concluded that Patayan presence did not appear before the Sacaton phase. Subsequent surveys showed that this was not the case. Patayan artifacts are present at 27 sites, 10 of which contain exclusively Patayan artifacts. The desert-adapted Patayan were clearly exploiting many of the same upland desert resource sites as the Hohokam, yet maintained a distinct ceramic tradition. It seems unlikely that substantial numbers of Patayan artifacts were traded into the Hohokam area because of the infrequent presence of Patayan artifacts in Hohokam villages during the entire Hohokam occupation of the area. Alternatively, the later presence of Patayan artifacts at AZ T:14:14 (ASM), a Sedentary period site (Figure 3.5) and Patayan artifacts associated with specific rooms at the Hohokam village of Las Colinas in the Phoenix Basin (Teague 1988:131) suggests that Patayan trade goods in the Hohokam villages along the Gila River in the project area may have been overwhelmed by the Hohokam artifacts and not identified by the investigators who recorded the villages.

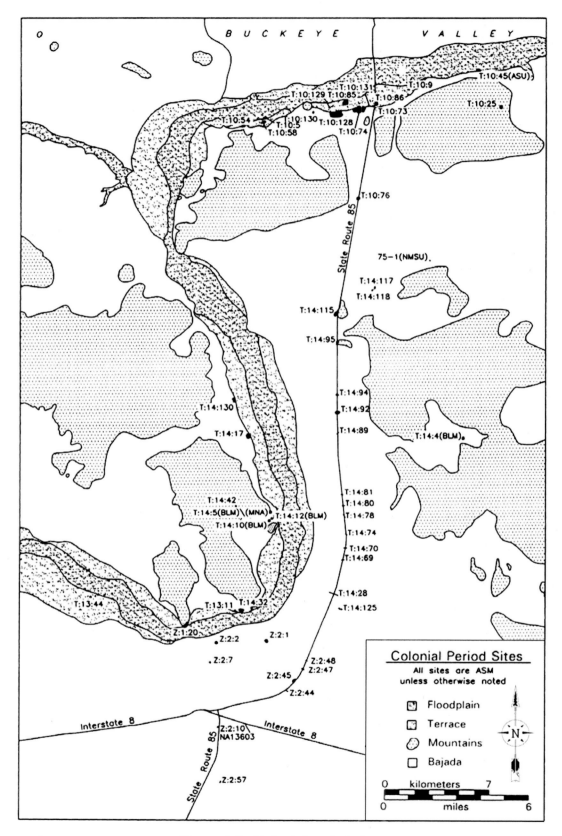

Figure 3.5. Colonial period sites.

Table 3.6. Colonial Period Sites

Sites/Names	Quad	Landform	Type	Size	Period/Phase	Features	Assem-blage	Diagnostics
ASM								
T:10:5	Hassa-yampa	Gila River floodplain	activity area	100m x 100m	Patayan I	artifact scatter (1)	C, FS	LC buff, PW
T:10:9	Buckeye	terrace	activity areas	300m x 500m	Colonial period	artifact scatter (1)	C, FS, S	Gila plain, Gila butte-Santa Cruz R/B, PW
T:10:25	Buckeye	Buckeye Hills	activity area	200m x 300m	Gila Butte phase	artifact scatter (1)	C, FS, GS, S, M, G	Gila Bend plain, Gila Butte R/B, Gila Bend red, Gila Bend beige
T:10:54	Hassa-yampa	terrace	activity area	not recorded	Gila Butte phase	artifact scatter (1)	C, L	Hohokam buff, Gila Butte R/B
T:10:58	Hassa-yampa	terrace	activity area	not recorded	Patayan I	artifact scatter (1)	C, L	LC BW
T:10:73	Buckeye	terrace	habitation	90m x 65m	Santa Cruz-Sacaton phases	artifact scatter (1), pithouse (1)	C, FS, FCR, GS	Santa Cruz R/B, Sacaton R/B, Gila plain
T:10:74	Hassa-yampa	bajada	village	660m x 540m	Santa Cruz-Sacaton phases	trash mounds (14), artifact scatters	C, FS, GS, S	Hohokam R/B, PW
T:10:76	Hassa-yampa	bajada	activity area	150m x 120m	Patayan I	rock features (2)	C, FS, G, GS, FCR	Colorado beige
T:10:85	Hassa-yampa	terrace	activity area	not recorded	Santa Cruz through Polvoron phases	canals (2), artifact scatter (2), roasting pit (1)	C, FS, S, GS, FA, FCR, MB	Santa Cruz R/B, Sacaton R/B
T:10:86	Buckeye	terrace	activity area	230m x 246m	Classic period	ash stains (11), artifact scatters	C, FS, GS	Salt red, Gila plain, Hohokam buff, Hohokam R/B
T:10:128	Hassa-yampa	bajada	village	780m x 640m	Pioneer-Sedentary periods	artifact scatters	C, FS, GS, FCR	Gila Butte R/B, Sweetwater red-on-grey
T:10:129	Hassa-yampa	terrace	activity area	30m x 70m	Pioneer-Sedentary periods	artifact scatters	C, FS, GS, S	Gila Butte R/B
T:10:130	Hassa-yampa	bajada	village	80m x 60m	Pioneer-Sedentary periods	artifact scatters	C, FS, GS, FCR	Hohokam R/B, PW
T:10:131	Hassa-yampa	terrace	village	30m x 50m	Santa Cruz-Sacaton phases	trash mound, artifact scatters	C, FS, GS, S, FCR	Hohokam R/B, PW
T:13:11	Cotton Center	bajada	activity area	not recorded	Preclassic period	artifact scatter (1)	C, FS, GS	not recorded
T:13:44	Citrus Valley East	floodplain	activity area	not recorded	Patayan I	artifact scatter (1)	C, FS	LC buff

Continued

Table 3.6. Colonial Period Sites *(Continued)*

Sites/ Names	Quad	Landform	Type	Size	Period/ Phase	Features	Assem- blage	Diagnostics
T:14:17 Enter- prise South	Cotton Center	terrace	village	273m x 369m	Colonial- Early Classic periods	trash mounds (10), depressions (5), rock features (2), artifact scatter (1)	C, FS, S, GS, FCR	Gila plain, Gila Butte R/B, Casa Grande R/B, Sacaton red, Tanque Verde red-on-brown
T:14:28 Wide Trail Site	Cotton Center	bajada	trail w/campsite	60m x 1200m	Patayan I, Santa Cruz phase	trails (2), artifact scatter (1)	C, FS	Hohokam buff, Santa Cruz R/B, LC buff, Gila plain
T:14:32 Gate Site	Cotton Center	bajada	activity area	85m x 210m	Gila Butte- Sacaton phases	rock clusters (2), artifact scatter (1)	C, FS, GS	Sacaton R/B, Gila Butte, PW, BW
T:14:42	Cotton Center	Red Rock Canyon, Gila Bend Mountains	habitation	15m x 20m	Patayan I	petroglyph panels (3), pictogram panels (1), artifact scatter (1), rock align-ment (1)	C, FS, GS	LC buff, stucco jar, Gila plain, redware, Patayan stuccoware
T:14:69	Cotton Center	bajada	trails w/campsite	305m x 490m	Patayan I and Classic period	trails (13), rock features (3), roast pit (1), lithic scatter (2)	C, FS, FCR	LC buff, Salt red, Hohokam buff
T:14:70	Cotton Center	bajada	trails w/campsite	275m x 400m	Patayan I	trails (6), rock features (6), clearings (5), ceramic scatter (1)	C, FS	LC buff
T:14:74	Cotton Center	bajada	trails w/activity area	180m x 365m	Patayan I	trails (6), artifact scatter (2)	open air, surface	LC buff, Gila plain
ASM								
T:14:78	Cotton Center	bajada	trails w/activity area	120m x 470m	Patayan I	trails (2), rock features (2), artifact scatter (3)	C, FS	LC buff
T:14:80	Cotton Center	bajada	trails w/activity area	240m x 305m	Patayan I	trails (7), artifact scatters (6), rock features (1)	C, FS	LC beige & buff, Gila plain
T:14:81	Cotton Center	bajada	trail	150m x 275m	Patayan I	trails (4)	C, L	Colorado beige, Gila plain (Salt)
T:14:89	Cotton Center	bajada	trail w/campsite	60m x 365m	Patayan I	trail (1), rock features (1)	C, FCR	Gila plain (Salt), Colorado beige
T:14:92	Cotton Center NW	bajada	trails w/ activity area	170m x 425m	Patayan I	rock features (9), trails (3)	C, FS	Hohokam buff, PW, LC Buff
T:14:94	Cotton Center NW	bajada	trails w/activity area	60m x 365m	Patayan I and Classic period	trails (3), rock features (8)	C, FS	Colorado red, Colorado beige, Gila plain (Salt), Salt red
T:14:95	Cotton Center NW	bedrock	activity area	not recorded	Patayan I	petroglyphs (6)	C, FFS	LC buff, Gila plain, Hohokam buff

Continued

Table 3.6. Colonial Period Sites *(Continued)*

Sites/ Names	Quad	Landform	Type	Size	Period/ Phase	Features	Assem- blage	Diagnostics
T:14:113	Cotton Center NW	bajada	activity area	6m x 8m	Patayan I	rock feature (1), artifact scatter (1)	C	LC buff
T:14:115	Cotton Center NW	bajada	activity area	40m x 91m	Preclassic to Classic periods	petroglyphs (6)	none	N/A
T:14:117	Margies Peak	bajada	activity area	80m x 240m	Patayan I	artifact scatter (1)	C, FS	Gila plain, Hohokam buff, Hohokam R/B, LC red
T:14:118	Margies Peak	bajada	activity area	60m x 82m	Patayan I and Classic period	artifact scatter (1)	C, FS	Gila plain (Salt), Gila plain (Gila), Salt red, LC buff, LC red, Wingfield plain, Wingfield red
ASM								
T:14:125	Cotton Center	bajada	activity area	57m x 173m	Patayan I, Gila Butte-Santa Cruz phases	artifact scatter (1)	C	Hohokam buff, Santa Cruz R/B, LC buff, Gila Butte R/B
T:14:130	Cotton Center NW	bajada	village	164m x 333m	Colonial to Classic periods	ball courts (2), rooms (2), trash mound (1), artifact scatter (1)	C, FS, S, GS, FCR	Gila plain (Gila & Salt), Sacaton R/B, Sacaton red, Gila Butte R/B
T:15:6	Mobile NW	bajada	habitation	90m x 160m	Colonial period	artifact scatter (1)	C, FS, S, GS	R/B
Z:2:1 Gatlin Site	Gila Bend	bajada	village	385m x 410m	Colonial-Sedentary periods	trash mounds (22), ball courts (2)	C, FS, GS, S, W, FR	Santa Cruz R/B, Sacaton R/B, Sacaton red, Gila plain, Sacaton buff
Z:2:2	Gila Bend	bajada	habitation	not recorded	Colonial-Sedentary periods	artifacts scatters, trash mound (1)	C, FS, GS, FCR, M	Gila plain (Gila)
Z:2:7	Gila Bend	bajada	habitation	30m x 30m	Patayan I	artifact scatter, midden (1)	C, FS, S	LC buff
Z:2:10	Gila Bend	bajada	activity area	10-m diameter	"Colonial period"	artifact scatter (1)	C	Hohokam sherds
Z:1:20	Smurr	rock outcrop	activity area (quarry)	200m x 250m	Archaic through Hohokam	lithic quarry (1), petroglyph panels (7)	FS, GS	Archaic and Gila style petroglyphs
Z:2:44	Gila Bend	bajada	trails w/activity area	165m x 430m	Patayan I	trails (3), rock ring (1), artifact scatters (3)	C, FS, G	LC buff, Hohokam buff, Gila plain (Salt and Gila)
Z:2:45	Gila Bend	bajada	trails w/campsite	150m x 275m	Patayan I	trails (2), roasting pits (6)	C, FFS, GS, W, FCR	LC buff, Hohokam R/B, Gila plain (Salt and Gila)

Continued

Table 3.6. Colonial Period Sites *(Continued)*

Sites/ Names	Quad	Landform	Type	Size	Period/ Phase	Features	Assem- blage	Diagnostics
Z:2:47	Gila Bend	bajada	trails w/activity area	305m x 400m	Patayan I	artifact scatters (2), trails (2), rock features (5)	C, FS, G	LC buff
ASM								
Z:2:48	Gila Bend	bajada	trails w/campsite	400m x 460m	Patayan I	artifact scatters (3), trails (15), rock features (5)	C, FS, FCR	LC buff, Gila plain (Salt)
Z:2:57	Gila Bend	bajada	activity area	40m x 128m	Patayan I	artifact scatter (1)	C	Hohokam R/B, LC buff, Gila plain (Salt and Gila)
T:10:24	Buckeye	terrace	activity area	not recorded	recorded as Colonial to Sedentary	rock rings (3)	C	not recorded
ASU								
T:10:45	Buckeye	Gila River floodplain	activity area	120m x 170m	Snaketown and Gila Butte phases	artifact scatter (1), hearth (1)	C, FS	Gila plain, Gila Butte & Snaketown, R/B
BLM								
T:14:4	Cotton Center SE	Maricopa Mountains	activity area	160m x 220m	recorded as Santa Cruz phase	artifact scatters (21 knapping stations)	C, FS, GS	not recorded
T:14:5	Cotton Center	bajada	activity area	4.5x5m	recorded as Santa Cruz phase	artifact scatter (1), rock feature (1)	C, FS, GS	Hohokam R/B
T:14:10	Cotton Center	bajada	trail w/ activity area	1.5x24m	Patayan I	trail (1), rock feature (1), artifact scatter (1)	C, FS	LC Buff
T:14:12	Cotton Center	bajada	trail w/ activity area	8m x 8m	Patayan I	trail (1), rock feature (1)	C, FFS, GS	LC Buff
Z:3:3	Estrella	Maricopa Mountains	activity area	50m x 150m	recorded as Santa Cruz phase	artifact scatter (1)	C, FFS, GS	not recorded
NMSU								
75-1	Margies Peak	bajada	activity area	not recorded	Patayan I	artifact scatter (1), petroglyph panel (1)	C	LC BW

Key: C - ceramics   FS - flaked stone   L - lithics   S - shell

       FA - faunal remains   G - glass   M - metal   W- wood

       FCR - fire-cracked rock   GS - ground stone   MB - macrobotanical remains   PW- plainware

       LC- Lower Colorado   R/B- red-on-buff   BW- buffware

Sedentary Period

The archaeological record of the Hohokam Sedentary period (Figure 3.6, Table 3.7) in the Gila Bend area is not as prolific or widespread as that of the previous Colonial period. There are fewer sites (28 vs. 53) and less of a presence outside of the floodplain and terrace areas during the Sedentary period. However, villages do proliferate during the Sedentary period in the Gila Bend area, increasing from 7 villages during the Colonial period to 11 villages during the Sedentary period. An intensification of agricultural exploitation of the fertile lowlands may have drawn efforts away from exploitation of the uplands. Such a shift may explain both the dearth of upland sites and the increase in the number of villages poised to exploit lowland agriculture. The record does not appear to have been unduly altered by geomorphologic events.

There are a total of 10 ballcourts in the area, and all are associated with village sites (Doyel 2000). The presence of ball courts indicates a higher level of community integration during the Sedentary period. Besides being sites for the ritual expression of community identity, or *communitas,* ball courts could also be used in the aggrandizing strategies of ambitious individuals (Hill and Clark 2001). The distribution of ball courts in the Gila Bend area is not continuous. All ballcourts in the Gila Bend area occur in the southern half of the area, where the Gila River flows from north to south. Although four villages are recorded for the northern end of the area, none of the four northern villages had a ball court (or at least none that survived modern agriculture in recognizable form). The ball court complex was to be eventually eclipsed by the platform mound as a locus of community ritual. Though platform mounds are more commonly associated with the Classic period, the only platform mound in the Gila Bend area, found at AZ Z:2:1 (ASM), the Gatlin site, dates to the Sedentary period (Doyel 2000; Wasley 1960).

Only 2 sites in the Gila Bend area during the Sedentary period were found to have Patayan artifacts present. AZ T:10:8 (ASM) was a habitation on the terrace at the northern end of the area. AZ T:14:14 (ASM) was a village on the bajada at the southern end of the area (see Figure 3.5). Both were Hohokam sites with intrusive Patayan ceramics. There were no sites recorded with exclusively Patayan artifacts, yet another departure from the preceding pattern of the Colonial period during which there were 10 sites with Patayan artifacts only. This may represent the exclusion of outsiders from an area that was experiencing greater community and regional identity, as indicated by the replication of the ball court complex in the area. However, even if the Patayan were being kept out of the area, Hohokam presence on the bajada and in the mountainous areas would still be expected, unless as suggested above, subsistence resource production had become concentrated on agriculture. Indifference by the Hohokam toward upland resources might have presented opportunity for more Patayan presence there, not less. The archaeological record of the uplands during the Sedentary period requires closer examination.

Classic Period

Settlement patterns during the Hohokam Classic period underwent radical change (Figure 3.7, Table 3.8). Though villages remained the centerpiece of the settlement system, their numbers decreased from Sedentary period levels (8 vs. 11), along with site size, reflecting both population decline and the consolidation of domiciles on fortified hilltop sites, such as Robbins Butte (AZ T:10:6 [ASM]), Power's Butte, the Fortified Hill Site (AZ T:13:8 [ASM]), and the Pierpont Site.

At least two of the village sites took a form new to the Classic period. Designated as *trincheras,* the new type of site was characterized by "dry-laid masonry walls located on isolated hills or bluffs" (McGuire 1982:195). Robbins Butte (AZ T:10:6 [ASM]) and the Fortified Hill Site (AZ T:13:8 [ASM]) fit this description. Patayan presence was recorded on the bajada at campsites and activity areas, though the presence of Patayan artifacts at Hohokam villages was not recorded.

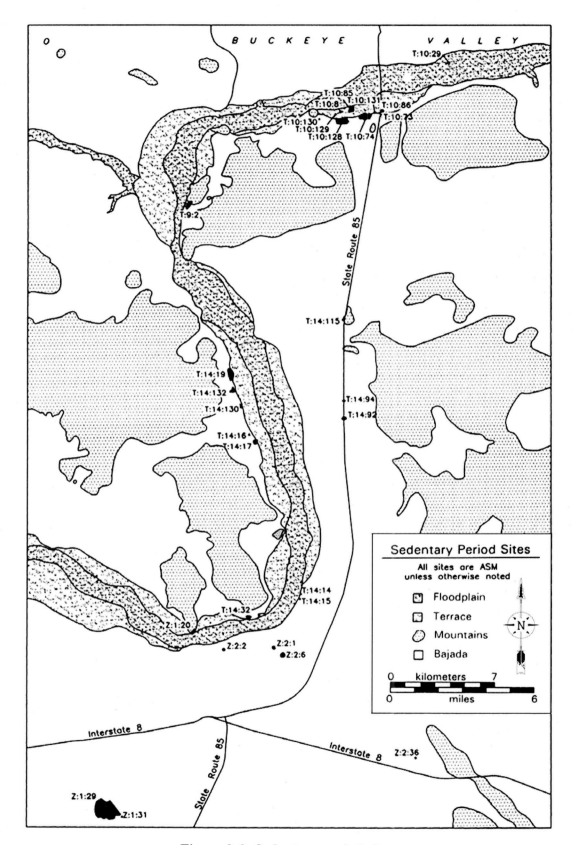

Figure 3.6. Sedentary period sites.

Table 3.7. Sedentary Period Sites

Sites/ Names	Quad	Landform	Type	Size	Period/ Phase	Features	Assem- blage	Diagnostics
ASM								
T:9:2	Arlington	bajada	habitation	100m x 100m	Sedentary-Classic periods	trash mounds (2), room block (1)	C, GS	Gila plain, Sacaton R/B, Gila & Salt red
T:10:8	Hassa-yampa	terrace	habitation	25m x 25m	Sacaton phase	small mound/ structure	C, FS, GS	Sacaton R/B, Gila plain, LC stucco
T:10:29	Buckeye	Gila River flood-plain	habitation	not recorded	Sacaton phase	artifact scatter, pithouses	C, L	Sacaton R/B, buffware
T:10:73	Buckeye	terrace	habitation	90m x 65m	Santa Cruz-Sacaton phases	artifact scatter (1), pithouse (1)	C, FS, FCR, GS	Santa Cruz R/B, Sacaton R/B, Gila plain
T:10:74	Hassa-yampa	bajada	village	660m x 540m	Santa Cruz-Sacaton phases	trash mounds (14), artifact scatters	C, FS, GS, S	Hohokam R/B, PW
T:10:85	Hassa-yampa	terrace	activity area	not recorded	Santa Cruz through Polvoron phases	canals (2), artifact scatter (2), roasting pit	C, FS, S, GS, FA, FCR, MB	Santa Cruz R/B, Sacaton R/B
T:10:86	Buckeye	terrace	activity area	230m x 246m	Classic period	ash stains (11), artifact scatters	C, FS, GS	Salt red, Gila plain, Hohokam buff and R/B
T:10:128	Hassa-yampa	bajada	village	780m x 640m	Pioneer-Sedentary periods	artifact scatters	C, FS, GS, FCR	Gila Butte R/B, Sweetwater red-on-grey
T:10:129	Hassa-yampa	terrace	activity area	30m x 70m	Pioneer-Sedentary periods	artifact scatters	C, FS, GS, S	Gila Butte R/B
T:10:130	Hassa-yampa	bajada	village	80m x 60m	Pioneer-Sedentary periods	artifact scatters	C, FS, GS, FCR	Hohokam R/B, PW
T:10:131	Hassa-yampa	terrace	village	30m x 50m	Santa Cruz-Sacaton phases	trash mound, artifact scatters	C, FS, GS, S, FCR	Hohokam R/B, PW
T:14:14	Cotton Center	bajada	village	not recorded	Sedentary period	artifact scatters, ball court, trash mounds	C	Sacaton R/B, L.C. buff, Mimbres black-on-white
T:14:15	Cotton Center	bajada	activity area	9.5m x 23.7m 1.4m depth	Sedentary period	ball court	C, S	Sacaton R/B, Gila Butte R/B, Santa Cruz R/B
T:14:16 Hi-Vu Ranch	Cotton Center	terrace	village	258m x 288m	Late Sedentary-Early Classic periods	ball courts (2), trash mounds (4), artifact scatters (5), rock feature (3)	C, FS, S, G, GS, FCR, M	Gila plain
T:14:17 Enterprise South	Cotton Center	terrace	village	273m x 369m	Colonial-Early Classic periods	trash mounds (10), depressions (5), rock features (2), artifact scatter (1)	C, FS, S, GS, FCR	Gila plain, Gila Butte R/B, Casa Grande R/B, Sacaton red, Tanque Verde red-on-brown

Continued

Table 3.7. Sedentary Period Sites *(Continued)*

Sites/ Names	Quad	Landform	Type	Size	Period/ Phase	Features	Assem- blage	Diagnostics
T:14:19 Enterprise Ranch	Cotton Center NW	bajada	village	388m x 866m	Sedentary- Early Classic periods	ball courts (2), trash mounds (16), architecture	C, FS, S, G, GS, FCR, M, W	Sacaton R/B, Gila plain, Sacaton red, Classic red
T:14:32 Gate Site	Cotton Center	bajada	activity area	85m x 210m	Gila Butte- Sacaton phases	rock clusters (2), artifact scatter (1)	C, FS, GS	Sacaton R/B, Gila Butte, PW, BW
T:14:115	Cotton Center NW	bajada	activity area	40m x 91m	Preclassic to Classic periods	petroglyphs (6)	none	N/A
T:14:130	Cotton Center NW	bajada	village	164m x 333m	Colonial to Classic periods	ball courts (2), rooms (2), trash mound (1), artifact scatter (1)	C, FS, S, GS, FCR	Gila plain (Gila & Salt), Sacaton R/B, Sacaton red, Gila Butte R/B
T:14:132	Cotton Center NW	bajada	habitation	457m x 610m	Sacaton phase	trash mound (1), possible rooms (2), surface scatter (1)	C, FS, G, GS, W, FCR	Gila plain (Salt & Gila), Sacaton red
Z:2:1 Gatlin Site	Gila Bend	bajada	village	385m x 410m	Colonial- Sedentary periods	platform mound (1), trash mounds (22), ball courts (2)	C, FS, GS, S, W, FA	Santa Cruz R/B, Sacaton R/B, Sacaton red, Gila plain, Sacaton buff
Z:2:2	Gila Bend	bajada	habitation	not recorded	Colonial- Sedentary periods	artifacts scatters, trash mound (1)	C, FS, GS, FCR, M	Gila plain (Gila)
Z:2:6 South Allentown Site	Gila Bend	bajada	village	not recorded	recorded as Sacaton phase (by Wasley)	houses, cremations (2)	C	not recorded
Z:1:20	Smurr	rock outcrop	activity area (quarry)	200m x 250m	Archaic through Hohokam	lithic quarry (1), petroglyph panels (7)	FS, GS	Archaic and Gila style petroglyphs
Z:1:29 Mobak/ Aux 6 Site	Smurr	bajada	agriculture activity area	1100m x 1300m	Sedentary- Classic periods	artifact scatters, rock piles, rock features	C, FS, GS, S, FCR, G, W, M	R/B, Gila plain
Z:1:31 Wash Away Site	Smurr	bajada	activity area	2m x 8m	Sedentary period	artifact scatter (1)	C	R/B, brown PW
Z:2:36	Bosque	bajada	activity area	110m x 250m	Sedentary period	artifact scatter (1)	C, FS (1)	Gila plain (Gila), Gila R/B, PW
ASU								
T:10:24	Buckeye	terrace	activity area	not recorded	recorded as Colonial to Sedentary	rock rings (3)	C	not recorded

Key:	C - ceramics	FS - flaked stone	L - lithics	S - shell
	FA - faunal remains	G – glass	M - metal	W - wood
	FCR - fire-cracked rock	GS - ground stone	MB - macrobotanical remains	PW- plainware
	LC- Lower Colorado	R/B- red-on-buff	BW- buffware	

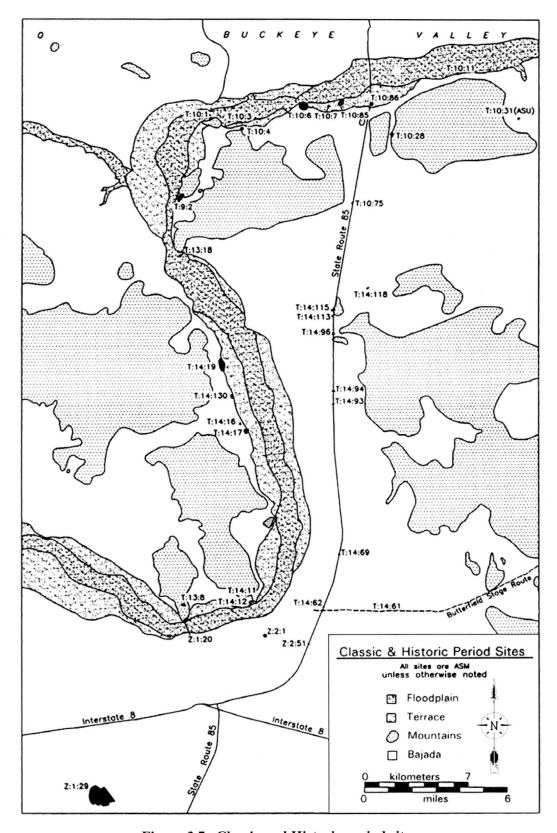

Figure 3.7. Classic and Historic period sites.

Table 3.8. Classic Period Sites

Sites/ Names	Quad	Land-form	Type	Size	Period/ Phase	Features	Assem-blage	Diagnostics
ASM								
T:9:2	Arlington	bajada	habitations	100m x 100m	Sedentary-Classic periods	room block (1), trash mounds (2)	C, GS	Gila plain, Sacaton R/B, Gila and Salt red
T:10:1	Hassa-yampa	Gila River floodplain	activity area	20m x 50m	Classic period	artifact scatter (1)	C, M	redware, Gila plain, PW
T:10:3	Hassa-yampa	Gila River floodplain	activity area	50m x 50m	Classic period	artifact scatter (1)	C, FS, S	Gila plain, PW, olivella bead
T:10:4	Hassa-yampa	bajada	activity area	25m x 25m	Classic period	artifact scatter (1)	C	Gila plain, plain smudged, PW
T:10:6	Hassa-yampa	Robbins Butte	village	510m x 500m	Classic period	stone walls, artifact scatters	C, FS, GS, S	Hohokam R/B
T:10:7	Hassa-yampa	terrace	activity area	100m x 200m	Classic period	artifact scatter (1)	C, FS, GS	Gila plain, red-on-buff, Classic reds, PW
T:10:11	Buckeye	Gila River floodplain	habitation	150m x 150m	Classic period	depression (1), trash mound (1)	C	Classic redware, PW, R/B
T:10:75	Hassa-yampa	bajada	activity area	60m x 45m	Patayan II&III, Classic Period	rock piles (6), surface scatter (1)	C	Palomas, Tumco, and Hohokam buff, Salt red, Gila plain
T:10:85	Hassa-yampa	terrace	activity area	not recorded	Santa Cruz through Polvoron phases	canals (2), artifact scatter (2), roasting pit (1)	C, FS, S, GS, FA, FCR, MB	Santa Cruz R/B, Sacaton R/B
T:10:86	Buckeye	terrace	activity area	230m x 246m	Classic period	ash stains (11), artifact scatters	C, FS, GS	Salt red, Gila plain, Hohokam buff, Hohokam R/B
T:13:8 Fortified Hill Site	Citrus Valley East	bajada	village	2 acres	Sells Phase	artifact scatters, rooms (57), petroglyphs (200)	C, FS, GS, S, FA	PW, redware, Tanque Verde red-on-brown, Gila Plain (Gila)
T:13:18	Spring Mountain	floodplain	village	600m x 800m	Classic period	burials (3), ramada (1), artifact scatters, canals	C, FS, GS, S, FA, G	PW, Classic R/B
T:14:10	Cotton Center	terrace	activity area (part of T:14:11)	not recorded	Classic period	cremation	C	Gila plain, Gila red, Tanque Verde red-on-brown, Gila smudged, LC Buff

Continued

Table 3.8. Classic Period Sites *(Continued)*

Sites/ Names	Quad	Land-form	Type	Size	Period/ Phase	Features	Assem-blage	Diagnostics
T:14:11 Bartley Site	Cotton Center	terrace	village	not recorded	Classic period	artifact scatter, trash mound, burials, cremation	C, FS, GS, S	Casa Grande R/B, Tanque Verde red-on-brown, Gila Red, BW, Gila Plain (Gila)
T:14:12	Cotton Center	terrace	habitation	50m x 60m	Classic period	artifact scatters, perimeter wall, structure, trash mound, burial	C, FS, GS, S	Casa Grande R/B, Tanque Verde red-on-brown, Gila Red, BW, Gila Plain (Gila)
T:14:16 Hi-Vu Ranch	Cotton Center	terrace	village	258m x 288m	Late Sedentary-Early Classic periods	ball courts (2), trash mounds (4), artifact scatters (5), rock feature (3)	C, FS, S, G, GS, FCR, M	Gila plain
T:14:17 Enter-prise South	Cotton Center	terrace	village	273m x 369m	Colonial-Early Classic periods	trash mounds (10), depressions (5), rock features (2), artifact scatter (1)	C, FS, S, GS, FCR	Gila plain, Gila Butte R/B, Casa Grande R/B, Sacaton red, Tanque Verde red-on-brown
T:14:19 Enter-prise Ranch	Cotton Center NW	bajada	village	388m x 866m	Sedentary-Early Classic periods	ball courts (2), trash mounds (16), architecture	C, FS, S, G, GS, FCR, M, W	Sacaton R/B, Gila plain, Sacaton red, Classic red
T:14:62	Cotton Center	bajada	trails w/ campsite	275m x 335m	Classic period	trails (7), artifact scatters	FCR, C	Hohokam buff and R/B, Salt red
T:14:69	Cotton Center	bajada	trails w/ campsite	305m x 490m	Patayan I and Classic period	trails (13), rock features (3), roast pit (1), lithic scatter (2)	C, FS, FCR	LC buff, Salt red, Hohokam buff
T:14:93	Cotton Center NW	bajada	trails w/ campsite	410m x 460m	Patayan II-III	trails (3), rock features (18)	C, FS	Palomas buff
T:14:94	Cotton Center NW	bajada	trails w/ activity area	60m x 365m	Patayan I and Classic period	trails (3), rock features (8)	C, FS	Colorado red, Colorado beige, Gila plain (Salt), Salt red
T:14:115	Cotton Center NW	bajada	activity area	40m x 91m	Preclassic to Classic periods	petroglyphs (6)	none	N/A
T:14:118	Margies Peak	bajada	activity area	60m x 82m	Patayan I and Classic period	artifact scatter (1)	C, FS	Gila plain (Salt), Gila plain (Gila), Salt red, LC buff, LC red, Wingfield plain, Wingfield red

Continued

Table 3.8. Classic Period Sites *(Continued)*

Sites/ Names	Quad	Land-form	Type	Size	Period/ Phase	Features	Assem-blage	Diagnostics
T:14:130	Cotton Center NW	bajada	village	164 m x 333 m	Colonial to Classic periods	ball courts (2), rooms (2), trash mound (1), artifact scatter (1)	C, FS, S, GS, FCR	Gila plain (Gila & Salt), Sacaton R/B, Sacaton red, Gila Butte R/B
Z:1:20	Smurr	rock outcrop	activity area (quarry)	200 m x 250 m	Archaic through Hohokam	lithic quarry (1), petroglyph panels (7)	FS, GS	Archaic and Gila style petroglyphs
Z:1:29 Mobak/ Aux 6 Site	Smurr	bajada	agriculture activity area	1100 m x 1300 m	Sedentary-Classic periods	artifact scatters, rock piles, rock features	C, FS, GS, S, FCR, G, W, M	red-on-buffs, Gila plain
Z:2:51	Gila Bend	bajada	trails w/activity area	365-m diameter	Classic period	trails (6), rock features (4)	C, FS	Hohokam buff, Salt red
ASU								
T:10:28	Buckeye	Buckeye Hills	activity area	3 m x 6 m	Classic period	rock platforms (2)	FS	none
T:10:31	Buckeye	bajada	activity area	1 m x 1 m	Classic period	rock ring (1)	none	N/A
Z:2:1 Gila Bend	Gila Bend	terrace	activity area: ceremonial	40 m x 80 m	Classic period	platform mound (1)	none	N/A
Other								
Pier-pont	Cotton Center	Gila Bend Mountains foothills	village	unknown	Classic period	unknown	unknown	unknown

Key: C - ceramics FS - flaked stone L - lithics S - shell
FA - faunal remains G - glass M - metal W - wood
FCR - fire-cracked GS - ground stone MB - macrobotanical remains PW- plainware
LC- Lower Colorado R/B- red-on-buff BW- buffware

Not all villages relocated to fortified hilltop locations. Some villages moved closer to the Gila River. Wasley and Johnson (1965:80) suggest that relocation away from the second-terrace sites, favored during the Colonial and Sedentary periods, to first-terrace sites during the Classic period indicates abandonment of the canal system in use during the earlier periods. This disruption may account for the apparent increased presence of sites on the bajada and in the mountains compared to the Sedentary period, as the need to supplement agricultural resources with wild subsistence resources spiked upward.

The ballcourt complex fell out of use, and though replaced by platform mound complexes in other Hohokam areas, this was not the case in the Gila Bend area. The Gatlin site's Sedentary period platform mound, the only mound in the Gila Bend area, was abandoned at the end of the Sedentary period along with the area's ball courts (Doyel 2000; Wasley and Johnson 1965).

The changes to the Hohokam settlement pattern at the Sedentary-Classic transition, and indeed, ultimate Hohokam depopulation of the Gila Bend area, have been attributed to the decrease in the amount of water available for irrigation agriculture. Schroeder (1961:24) accounts for the decrease by citing withdrawals upstream for irrigation purposes and desiccation, while others (e.g., Wilcox 1979) attribute the decrease to area desiccation alone.

The occupation of defensive sites suggests a period of conflict. The conflict need only have been intense enough to disrupt the agricultural cycle and the maintenance of irrigation systems to create the conditions that would cause the depopulation of the area. Whether one or a combination of these factors induced hardships, the Gila Bend region, after suffering serious population losses throughout the (dessication or violence) Classic period, was abandoned at the end of the period, and the area was not reoccupied until the Protohistoric period.

Protohistoric and Historic Period

No sites in the examined data bases were attributed to the Protohistoric Period, following the end of the Hohokam Tradition up to the arrival of Spanish explorers and Catholic missionaries on the Middle and Lower Gila. We know however that in the 17th century Father Kino recorded a string of mixed Pima and Cocomaricopa villages located on the Lower Gila from the area north of Gila Bend downstream to the vicinity of Agua Caliente (Bolton 1919), so there is the potential that protohistoric sites occur but remain undocumented in the area covered by the overview.

Two historic period sites that appear on Figure 3.7 are the Warner Goode Homestead (AZ T:14:96 [ASM]) and the Butterfield Stage Route (AZ T:14:61[ASM]). The Warner Goode homestead offers a look at an African-American family homesteading in Gila Bend area during the Great Depression of the late 1920s and 1930 and is fully discussed in Chapter 10. The Butterfield Stage Route played an important role in the exploration and settlement of the Southwest during the second half of the 19th century, and is discussed in Chapter 11.

CHAPTER 4

GEOARCHAEOLOGICAL INVESTIGATIONS

Michael R. Waters

INTRODUCTION

Five days were spent examining the landforms along State Route 85 as part of the archaeological investigations along this roadway. A map showing the geomorphic landforms along the corridor adjacent to the road was constructed. This map shows the distribution of landforms of different age and origin. The map was constructed in an effort to understand the distribution of trail segments that cross State Route 85. In addition to these field studies, a discussion of methodologies to determine the difference between animal and prehistoric human trails is included.

THE GEOMORPHIC MAP

Along the corridor, six major geomorphic surfaces are defined (Figures 4.1 through 4.4). These include: the terraces along the Gila River (T-0 and T-2), Holocene and Pleistocene bajada surfaces (Hf and Pf, respectively), and bedrock and bedrock pediment (Br and Brped, respectively).

BEDROCK AND BEDROCK PEDIMENTS

The Buckeye Hills and Maricopa Mountains are mapped as "granite and related crystalline rocks" on the *Geologic Map of Maricopa County, Arizona* (Wilson et al. 1957). Bedrock is found in the northern portion of the corridor where State Route 85 crosses the Buckeye Hills. Granitic rocks are also present in the middle of the study corridor where the road crosses an inselberg of the Maricopa Mountains.

Adjacent to the bedrock outcrops are bedrock pediments. These are highly weathered areas of bedrock. In these areas, the granitic bedrock had been physically and chemically weathered to form a low sloping platform that extends from the mountain front. These are extremely ancient and stable surfaces. Pediments are confined to the northern part of the study area, adjacent to the bedrock outcrops that make up the Buckeye Hills.

The pediment surfaces typically have a loose gravel lag on the surface. Desert varnish covers many of the angular rocks at the surface. In some places the surface is covered with a loose veneer of grus (weathered granitic bedrock).

GILA RIVER TERRACES

In the northern portion of the study area, State Route 85 crosses the Gila River. Much of the area is taken up with the active channel of the river and its associated floodplain (T-0). Adjacent to T-0 is a late Quaternary terrace of the Gila River. This terrace is likely T-2 as defined by Waters and Ravesloot (2000). The sediment underlying this surface ranges from the late Pleistocene to the historic time period.

ALLUVIAL PIEDMONT

The most common landforms in the study area are the alluvial piedmonts (bajadas) emanating from the Buckeye Hills and Maricopa Mountains. These are both of Pleistocene and Holocene age.

Pleistocene age alluvial piedmonts (bajadas) are common in the study area, but are most prevalent in the southern half of the study area. These sediments were deposited in alluvial fan environments during the Pleistocene and eventually coalesced into a broad alluvial apron across the mountain front. While there are several different ages of Pleistocene fans and they originate from several sources, they are grouped together in this study.

The Pleistocene piedmont is typically covered by a well-developed desert pavement of angular to subangular gravel size clasts of granite (Hayden 1965). The stones in the pavement are typically coated with a dark brown to black desert varnish. These surfaces are usually the highest on the landscape and are heavily dissected by Holocene drainages. Because these surfaces have been stable for hundreds of thousands of years, a well-developed soil has formed beneath them. For the most part, 0.5 to 1m thick petrocalcic horizons are present. In most cases these petrocalcic horizons were close to the surface, and the overlying A and B horizons had been eroded. In some places a thin accumulation of silicate clay and visible pedogenic calcium carbonate (Btk horizon, or clay enriched with calcium carbonate) was noted overlying the petrocalcic horizon. The pavements in the southern half of the study area are better preserved and flatter, while those to the north are undergoing greater destruction by erosion.

The Holocene age alluvial piedmonts were active during the early, middle, or late Holocene, or are active today. These surfaces are covered with a loose gravel lag of unvarnished gravel size clasts of granite. Because these surfaces are recent, they have undergone minimal dissection. Soil development below the surface is minimal with a weak A–C profile. Holocene fan activity appears to have been heavier to the north. Holocene erosion and sedimentation is confined to incised channels in the southern part of the study area.

TRAILS AND GEOMORPHIC SURFACES

In this section, trail segments are compared to the geomorphic map. First the potential for trail preservation on each surface type will be considered. Then, this understanding is used to explain the location of trails in the study area.

Trail segments will not be found on the bedrock and it is unlikely that they will be encountered on the pediment surfaces in the study area. If tightly packed desert pavements with desert varnish are present on pediments, these would be excellent places for trail preservation. However, in the study area the pavements on the pediments are poorly preserved and composed of a loose gravel lag. Thus, trails would likely not be preserved or only very short segments could be encountered where pavements are well developed.

Trails will not be encountered on the terraces along the Gila River. These are composed of fine-grained sediments and thus would not be conducive to trail preservation. Further, these surfaces are sometimes covered by historic floodwaters.

Holocene alluvial piedmont surfaces would likewise be poor localities for the preservation of trail segments. These surfaces were deposited during the Holocene and have yet to develop desert pavement surfaces. Thus, modern sheetwash would eradicate any trail segments that may have existed.

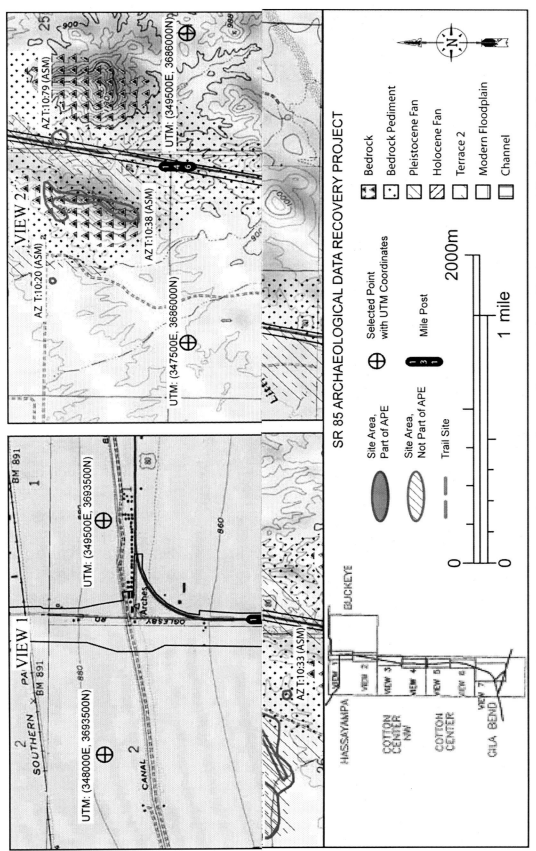

Figure 4.1. Sites, trails, and geomorphology in the APE for the SR-85 Project, Hasayampa and Buckeye Quadrangles.

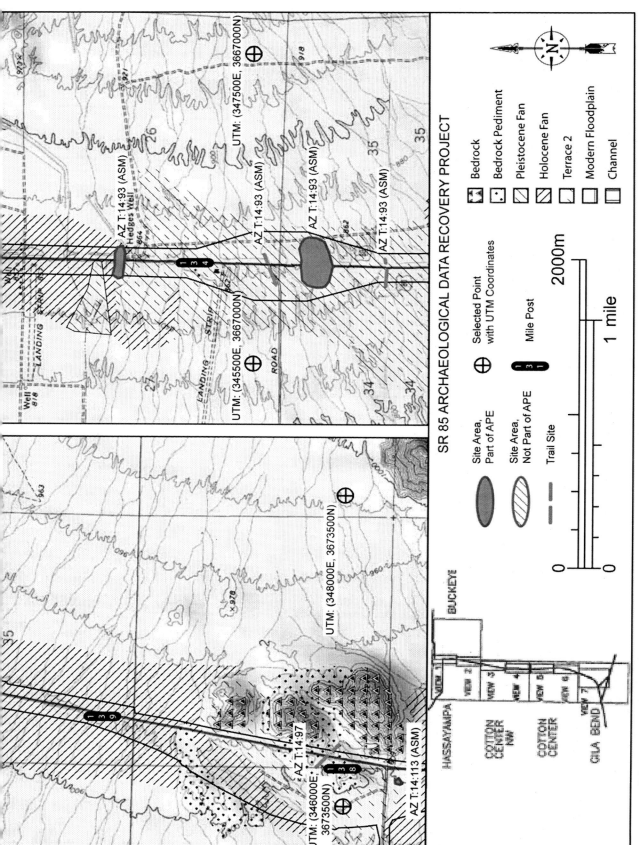

Figure 4.2. Sites, trails, and geomorphology in the APE for the SR-85 Project, Cotton Center NW Quadrangle

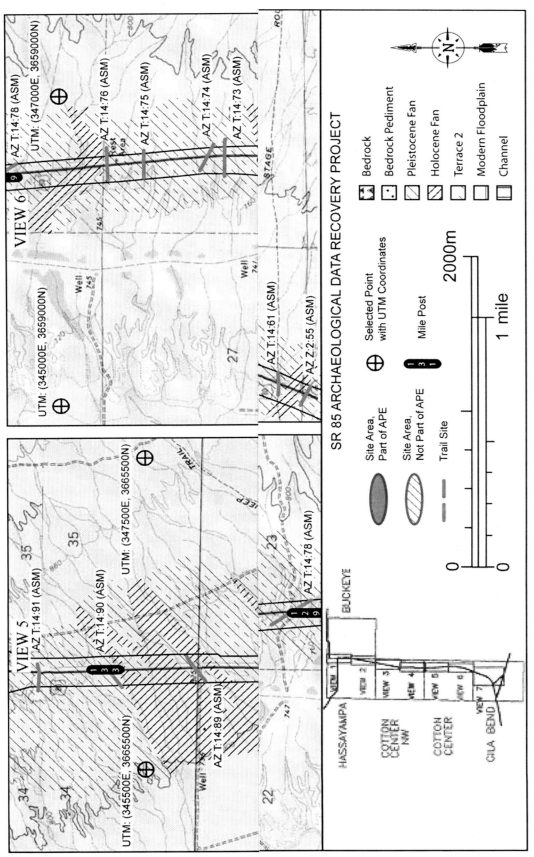

Figure 4.3. Sites, trails, and geomorphology in the APE for the SR-85 Project. Cotton Center Quadrangle.

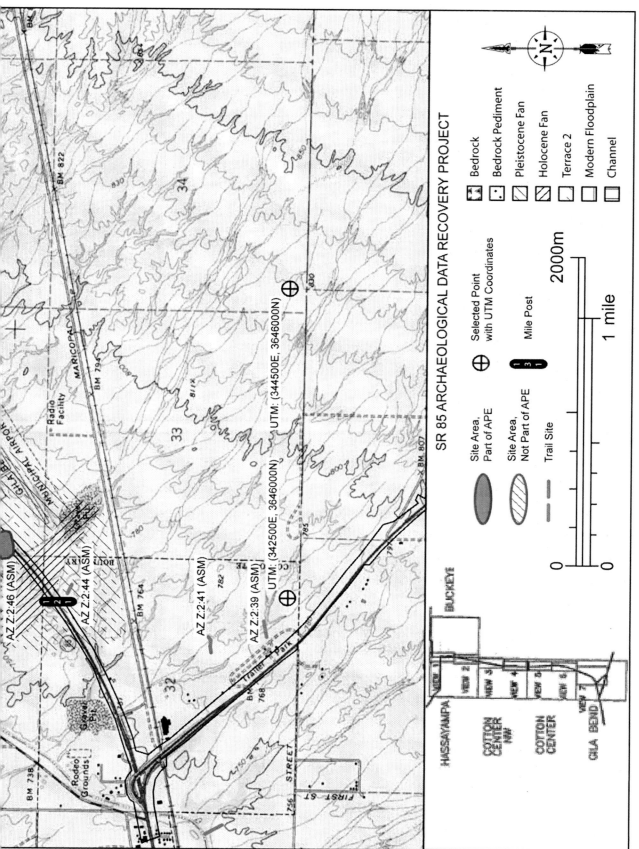

Figure 4.4. Sites, trails, and geomorphology in the APE for the SR-85 Project, Gila Bend Quadrangle.

Trail segments will be best preserved on the desert pavements that cover the Pleistocene alluvial piedmont. Here, the pavements are tightly packed mosaics of stones and will show any modification to them—such as human traffic along a trail (Hayden 1965). These prehistoric trails will be well preserved and will not be obliterated by later sheetwash.

Most of the trail segments are found in the southern portion of the study area. This distribution is likely a result of geologic preservation. Older geomorphic surfaces (especially Pf) are well preserved in the southern portion of the study area. Trail segments are easily detected and preserved because desert-pavement-covered Pleistocene surfaces are very extensive to the south. In the northern portion of the study area, Holocene erosion and deposition have destroyed the older desert pavement surfaces and dominate this area. Thus, trail preservation in this area is poor.

DISCRIMINATING BETWEEN HUMAN AND NON-HUMAN TRAILS

One problem facing the archaeologist in the field is distinguishing between human and non-human made trails. Several archaeological and geological criteria should be applied to trails to determine if they are of prehistoric human origin.

1) Destinations: Prehistoric trails are located for travel from one important location to another, such as from one site to another site, or from one water tank to another water tank.

2) Artifacts and features: Prehistoric trails will typically have artifacts associated with them, such as pot breaks or lithics. Likewise, trails will commonly have rock cairns or other features such as rock alignments or sleeping circles close by.

3) Geomorphic surfaces: Prehistoric trails will be best preserved on older stable surfaces, not surfaces that are geologically active. Trails will be best preserved on Pleistocene and Holocene surfaces covered with desert pavements and desert varnish where they will be preserved and recognizable.

Although animals may reuse old prehistoric trails, the trails will still have the characteristics listed above. Modern animal trails may be distinguished from prehistoric trails because they will have different destinations, such as stock tanks and feeding areas. They may also follow modern barriers such as fence lines. If one finds a trail on a modern Holocene surface that continues onto an older surface, one must consider whether this is an animal trail or reused prehistoric human trail. In some cases, determining the age and origin of some trails may not be possible.

CHAPTER 5

ARCHAEOLOGICAL DATA RECOVERY

John Czarzasty

STAGES OF DATA RECOVERY

The data recovery conducted at six sites (Table 5.1) within the right-of-way corridor of State Route 85 exploited an array of surface and subsurface methods and analytical techniques.

Table 5.1. Project Sites [All Site Numbers Followed by (ASM)]

Sites/ Names	Quad	Land- form	Type	Size	Period/ Phase	Features	Assem- blage	Diagnostics
T:10:86	Buckeye	terrace	Agricultural fields on alluvial terraces	230m x 246m	Pioneer- Classic periods	Ash and charcoal lenses(3), scattered artifacts	ceramics, flaked stone, ground stone	Salt red, Gila plain, Hohokam buff, Hohokam red- on-buff
T:14:92	Cotton Center NW	bajada	Trails with rock cairn and rock circle features	170m x 425m	Patayan II- III and Colonial- Sedentary Periods	Trails (3), rock features (9)	ceramics, flaked stone	Hohokam buff, plainware, Lower Colorado buff
T:14:94	Cotton Center NW	bajada	Trails with rock cairn and rock circle features	60m x 365m	Patayan II- III and Sedentary- Classic period	trails (3), rock features (8)	ceramics, flaked stone	Colorado red, Colorado beige, Gila plain (Salt), Salt red
T:14:96	Cotton Center NW	bajada	Depression era Goode homestead (African American family)	170m x 200m	Historic: Depression era	Multiple artifact scatters, animal pens (2), concrete foundation	metal, glass, wood	N/A
T:14:113	Cotton Center NW	bajada	Rock cairn feature	6m x 8m	Patayan II- III	Rock feature (1), artifact scatter (1)	ceramics	Lower Colorado buff
Z:2:46	Gila Bend	bajada	Thermal feature with fire-cracked rock	140m x 215m	Pioneer period	Roasting pit (1), Fire- cracked rock scatters (3), trails (2), rock features (5)	none	N/A

The data recovery program was organized into the following three stages with seven tasks:

Stage I (Surface)
Task 1. Feature photography.
Task 2. Surface mapping.
Task 3. Surface artifact collection.

Stage II (Subsurface)
Task 4. Subsurface testing/recording.
Task 5. Feature excavation/recording.
Task 6. Excavated feature mapping and photography.

Stage III
Task 7. Backfill and clean-up.

The data recovery program was structured so as to proceed with different tasks being executed at different sites simultaneously, allowing for the efficient use of time, personnel, and equipment resources. On any single site, however, data recovery adhered to the stage and task sequence delineated above in order to ensure thoroughness and completeness, unless actual site conditions deviated appreciably from expected conditions.

STAGE I (SURFACE)

Feature Photography

All known features within the six sites (identified in Harmon and Beyer 1995) were photographed before any surface collecting or excavation took place, so that the condition of each feature was recorded in its "undisturbed" state. Photography preceded surface mapping to avoid the presence of flag pins, crew footprints, etc., in the photographic record.

Surface Mapping

All sites were mapped before any collection or excavation took place. A Global Positioning System (GPS) was used to collect data for map production. Point provenience was recorded for each artifact. The GPS was also used to record trail locations. Using the continuous mode, the GPS was used to trace a sample of trail segments by simply having the operator walk the trail.

Surface Artifact Collection

Once surface mapping was completed, surface artifacts were collected. Individual artifacts and sets of artifacts lying within 30 cm of each were placed in their own specimen bags and assigned a unique specimen number. Artifacts density was not sufficiently great at any site to require collection in 1m by 1m units. A specimen log was kept in the field.

STAGE II (SUBSURFACE)

Subsurface Testing and Recording

All prehistoric sites received subsurface testing in the form of systematic trenching to determine the nature, frequency, diversity, and degree of preservation of subsurface cultural features and deposits. Site AZ T:14:96 (ASM), the historic site, received no subsurface investigation, per instructions in the ADOT

Request For Proposal (2001). At four of the six sites expectations were for shallow soil overlying bedrock, caliche or indurated cobbles; at these four sites the trenches were excavated with hand tools rather than a backhoe. Mechanical equipment was used to excavate trenches at site AZ T:10:86 (ASM). Trenches did not disturb trail features. Mechanical trenches were approximately 0.6 m (2 ft) wide and no more than 1.52 m (5 ft) deep, though investigators were prepared to go deeper to more fully explore any cultural features discovered. One end of each mechanical trench was ramped for access and egress. All appropriate OSHA safety precautions were taken regarding the use of the backhoe and trench depth.

Artifact collecting continued during mechanical subsurface testing from two general contexts: trench back dirt and trench wall. An archaeologist monitored backhoe excavation and collected artifacts discovered in the back dirt. Unless artifacts found in back dirt were clearly associated with a feature visible either in plan view or in the trench profile, they were collected in bulk from each trench.

After the trenches were excavated, the walls of the trenches were faced by hand and allowed to dry sufficiently (which did not take long in the 110° (F) heat) before being examined for the presence of subsurface cultural features or deposits. Locations of all trenches dug during subsurface testing were recorded using the GPS, and the trenches were included on site maps. Additionally, all cultural features identified during subsurface testing were profiled and representative profiles of trench walls were made from selected trenches.

AZ T:10:86 (ASM) had no surface features. Testing consisted of 20-meter long backhoe trenches in a patterned sample with enough coverage to expose at least two percent of the site within the right-of-way. All of the other sites contained surface features. Unlike AZ T:10:86 (ASM) which was on the terrace, these sites were on the bajada and had no alluvial deposits. Hand-dug trenches sufficed to expose the nature of the deposition and soil formation. No burials were encountered at any of the sites. Plans for the recording and treatment of human remains were not implemented.

Feature Excavation and Recording

On sites with features, the first step taken during feature excavation and recording was to make a determination concerning whether the features were natural or cultural (to include natural formations that were used by humans and may have stratified cultural deposits). Once the determination was made, all cultural features were excavated.

No structural features or burials were found. Plans for the excavation and recording of structural features and for the recording and treatment of human remains were not implemented.

Plans originally called for non-burial cultural features to be bisected and one half to be excavated while the other half of the feature remained undisturbed. Small thermal features were to be excavated beyond 50 percent (up to 100 percent) in order to obtain a sample of sufficient size (4 liters) for flotation. Large features such as trash middens or borrow pits were to be sampled by using a 1–m by 2–m unit. However, features were so scant and so shallow that all features were excavated, and only those features devoid of artifacts and subsurface components were excavated to less than 100 percent. Detailed information on each excavated feature, including a plan view and cross section, was recorded.

In addition to artifact recovery during excavation, pollen and flotation samples were taken from appropriate surface and subsurface contexts. Examples of such contexts included, but were not limited to, rock circles for pollen samples and roasting pits for flotation samples where the integrity and discrete nature of the deposits would provide material for reliable interpretation of the samples. Pollen and flotation samples were recorded in the specimen log. No canals were encountered. Plans for excavating and recording of canals were not used.

Excavated Feature Mapping and Photography

Locations of excavated features and trenches dug during feature excavation were recorded using the GPS device, and the trenches were included on site maps. Excavated features were also mapped. All feature locations, both horizontal and vertical, were recorded. All excavated features were photographed.

STAGE III (BACKFILL AND CLEAN UP)

The final step before concluding the investigation of all sites was backfilling excavations, removing fencing, and cleaning up the site. All sites were left in a condition as close as possible to the condition in which they were found at the beginning of data recovery.

SITE DESCRIPTIONS

Physical descriptions of the five prehistoric sites and one historic site in the State Route (SR) 85 project, explanations of the data recovery steps taken, and the results of the data recovery investigations are provided in the remainder of this chapter. Any diversion from the work plan was due to differences between actual and anticipated conditions in the field. Such departures are covered in the accounts of the site investigations. Descriptions of the features are presented and artifact summaries are included for each site. More detailed information on ceramic and lithic artifacts appears in subsequent chapters of this volume. Table 5.1 gives brief descriptions of the five prehistoric sites and one historic site in the project. Their locations are shown in Figures 3.1 and 3.2.

AZ T:10:86 (ASM), Prehistoric Agricultural Fields on the Gila Floodplain

Site AZ T:10:86 (ASM) was a prehistoric agricultural area in the Gila River floodplain, and appeared on the surface as a large but light density Hohokam artifact scatter (see Figure 3.1). The features at the site consist of buried lenses of burned field stubble on the Holocene river terraces. The burned remains of the stubble would accumulate in low spots in the fields, and during overbank flooding would be buried by sediments. The lenses thus provide a chronologic record of plants grown on the flood plain from the Pioneer through the Classic Period. In general these features were not roasting pits because there was an absence of fire-cracked rock and pit outlines, although roasting pits can also occur in these contexts (Wright 1995). The entire site was approximately 230 m (750 ft) E–W by 246 m (800 ft) N–S. The portion of the site in the SR 85 right-of-way, and the only portion of the site investigated in this project, was 70 m (228 ft) E–W by 200 m (650 ft) N–S. Site AZ T:10:86 (ASM) was located in the SW ¼ of the SW ¼ of Section 24, and the NW ¼ of the NW ¼ of Section 25, Township 1 South, Range 4 West (USGS Buckeye, AZ 7.5'/1958, photo revised 1971) (see Figure 3.1).

The work plan for the investigation of the site (Office of Cultural Resource Management 2002:25–27) called for the following tasks:

1) Site photography.
2) Surface mapping.
3) Collect surface artifacts.
4) Excavation of 16 trenches (each 20 m long).
5) Excavation of features.

The field crew walked the entire site area within the SR 85 right-of-way in parallel transects spaced 2 meters apart and marked all surface artifacts with pin flags. The provenience of each flagged artifact was mapped using a theodolite, and the artifacts (or sets of artifacts of the same class within 30 cm of each other) were collected in individual bags and assigned specimen numbers. A total of 295 sherds (or closely spaced clusters), 149 lithic artifacts (two of which were ground stone), and one shell artifact were mapped and collected. The southern half of the portion of the site within the project area had been leveled for modern agricultural use resulting in the addition of fill dirt over the original surface. The artifacts found on the surface in this area had likely been subjected to significant displacement from their original discard locations. The surface in the northern part of the site was a Holocene terrace of the Gila River.

The subsurface exploration consisted of the excavation of 18 backhoe trenches, each trench 20 meters in length. Nine trenches were dug in the Holecene terrace and nine trenches were dug in the portion of the site covered with fill dirt. The actual trenches were in excess of the 16 trenches called for in the work plan, and exceeded two percent of the site within the right-of-way. Two trenches were added to investigate areas of particularly dense surface artifact concentrations. During excavation, backdirt was monitored for artifacts. Eight of the 18 trenches produced additional artifacts: a total of eight sherds and four lithic artifacts. The walls of the trenches were cleaned and examined for artifacts and features. Representative samples of the trench walls, in addition to the locations containing features, were profiled. A map of the surface artifact distribution, trench and feature locations, and excavation units is shown in Figure 5.1.

Three features were discovered in the trench walls: Feature 1 in Trench 18 (Figure 5.2), and Feature 2 and Feature 3 (Figures 5.3 and 5.4) in Trench 6. All three appeared as ashy or organic lenses, or small pit-like features, in trench profiles, likely formed from the collection of the products of field burning in slight depressions during prehistoric times. The backhoe removed the overburden above Feature 1 and the feature itself was excavated by hand. The overburden above Feature 3 was removed by hand as part of the hand excavation of Feature 3. Both features were excavated in 1 x 1 m units. Feature 2 was in close proximity to Feature 3, and appeared to be identical. It was not excavated. Feature descriptions are summarized in Table 5.2

Feature Descriptions

Feature 1 had approximately 0.80 m of overburden and had a 0.30-m maximum feature depth. It was roughly circular in shape and had a diameter of approximately 1.40 m. The first 10-centimeter level of the feature contained ceramic and flaked lithic artifacts. The second 10-centimeter level contained ceramic, flaked lithic, and groundstone artifacts. The third 10-centimeter level contained only ceramics. Material suitable for a C-14 sample was also collected from the third level. The excavated material was sifted through a ¼-inch mesh screen. Pollen and flotation samples were taken from each excavation levels. Flotation samples were analyzed and the results are discussed in a subsequent chapter and shown in Table 5.2.

A radiocarbon assay of the charcoal from Feature 1 produced a 2-σ calibrated interval of A.D. 550–980. Two implicit assumptions must be acknowledged before the interval can be used to estimate the dates of use of the agricultural field. The first assumption is that the carbon-based organism producing the sample died during or shortly before the burning event, i.e., the charcoal was not the product of old wood. The second assumption is that the burning of the fields that produced the charcoal was a human-induced event.

Feature 2 (Figure 5.3), a lens of humic soil and charcoal with an oxidized base, was discovered in Trench 6, and was on the west side of the trench, opposite to and in close proximity with Feature 3 (Figure 5.1). It had approximately 0.60 m of overburden and had a 0.26-m maximum feature depth,

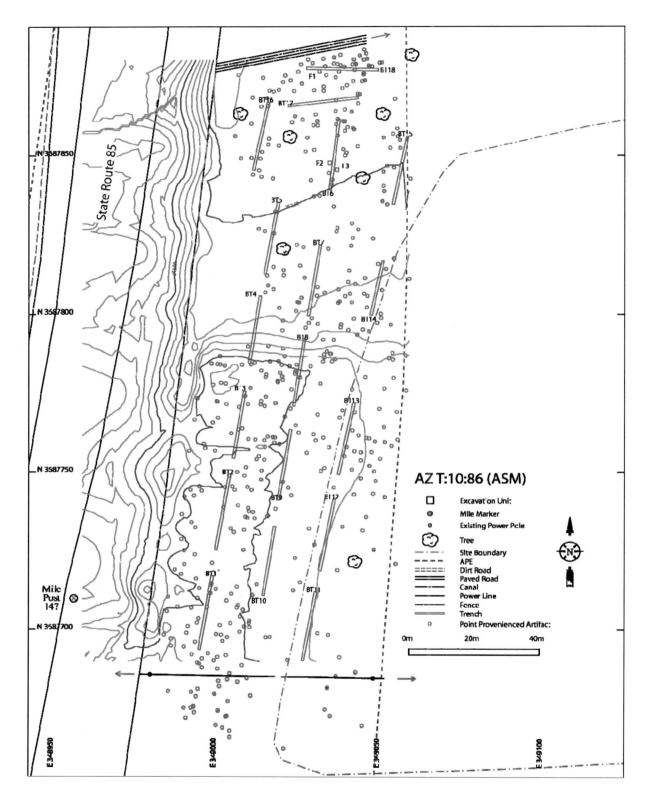

Figure 5.1. Site AZ T:10:86 (ASM) with artifact distribution, trench and feature locations.

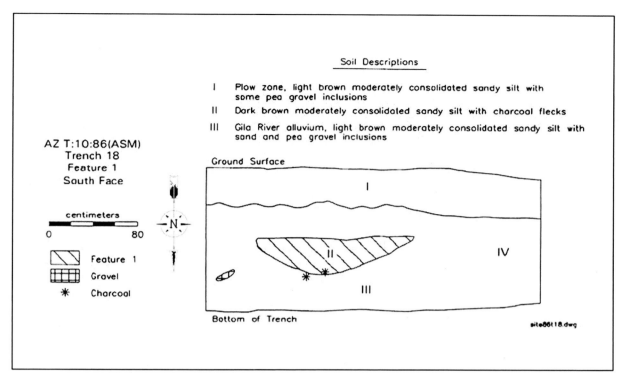

Figure 5.2. Site AZ T:10:86 (ASM) Trench 18 profile, including Feature 1.

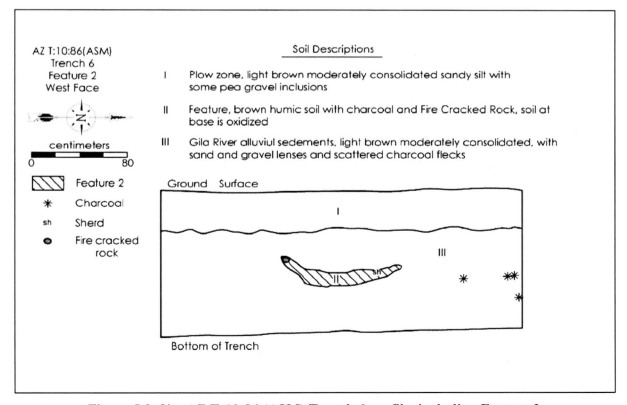

Figure 5.3. Site AZ T:10:86 (ASM) Trench 6 profile, including Feature 2.

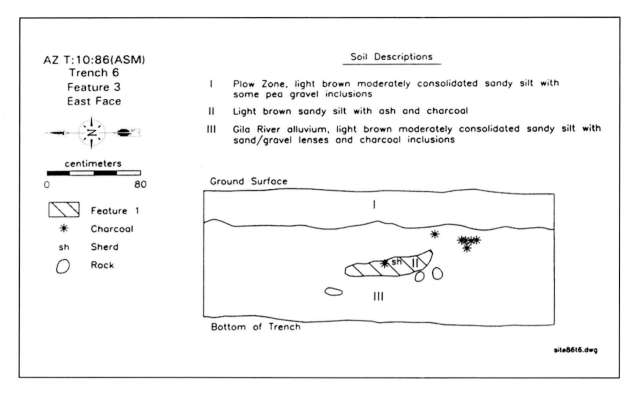

Figure 5.4. Site AZ T:10:86 (ASM) Trench 6 profile, including Feature 3.

Table 5.2. Site AZ T:10:86 (ASM) Excavated Features

Feature Number	1	3
Type	Ashy/organic lens	Ashy/organic lens
Location	Trench 18	Trench 6
Dimensions	1.40-m diameter; 0.30-m thickness	0.76-m diameter; 0.18-m thickness
Depth Below Surface	0.80-m diameter	0.50-m diameter
Artifacts	32 sherds; 1 lithic	5 sherds; 1 lithic
C-14 Samples Analyzed	One C-14: 2 sigma range of A.D. 550–980	None
Flotation Results	Cheno-am Gramineae, Olneya Prosopis, Zea mays, Sphaeralcea Trianthema	Cheno-am Gramineae Olneya Prosopis Sphaeralcea Trianthema
Pollen Results	Not Analyzed	Pinus, Juniperus Cercidium, Celtis, Cheno-am, Cholla, Zea mays, Asteraceae, Liguliflorae Ambrosia, Poaceae, Brassicacea, Sphaeralcea, Boerhaavia, Kallstromia Plantago
ILLUSTRATIONS	Figure 5.2 (profile)	Figure 5.3 (profile)

though 0.14 m feature depth was more typical. Feature length was approximately 1.0 m. Feature 2 was not in the sample of features excavated at site AZ T:10:86 (ASM). No artifacts or samples were recovered from the feature.

The excavation of Feature 3 began with the hand excavation of the 0.50 m of overburden covering the feature. Feature 3 had a maximum thickness of approximately 0.18 m and was roughly circular with a diameter of approximately 0.76 m (Figure 5.4). Five 10-centimeter levels of overburden were removed, three of which contained ceramics and two of which contained lithic artifacts. The excavated material was sifted through a ¼-inch mesh screen. Pollen samples were taken from each level. The feature itself was excavated in two levels of approximately nine centimeters each, varying slightly due to the use of natural levels within the feature. Both levels contained ceramic artifacts. Pollen and flotation samples were taken from both excavation levels within the feature. Results of their analysis are discussed in a subsequent chapter. Summation for Features 1 and 3 are presented in Table 5.2.

Summary

Site AZ T:10:86 (ASM) was a Hohokam agricultural field. Cumulative artifact counts for site AZ T:10:86 (ASM) were 489 ceramic sherds, 196 lithic artifacts (including two ground stone artifacts), and one shell artifact. The results of more detailed examination of these artifacts are presented in subsequent chapters of this report.

One charcoal C-14 sample was taken from Feature 1 at a depth below the surface of approximately 0.80 meters. Testing of the sample resulted in a 1-sigma calibrated result of A.D. 650–870 and a 2-sigma calibrated result of A.D. 530–980. These dates place the site in the range from the Vahki phase of the Pioneer period to the Colonial-Sedentary periods transition. A Pioneer through Sedentary periods Hohokam village, site AZ T:10:128 (ASM), was approximately 2.2 km from AZ T:10:86 (ASM), and occupants of the village may have used the agricultural fields at AZ T:10:86 (ASM) as early as the Pioneer period. Classic period ceramics found at the site indicate that AZ T:10:86 (ASM) was used through the Classic period.

AZ T:14:113 (ASM) – Collapsed Rock Cairn Trail Feature (Patayan)

This feature is very likely the collapsed remains of a rock cairn of the kind associated with trail features in Southern Arizona (Chapter 12). The rocks were associated with an assemblage of Patayan sherds, but there was no subsurface pit feature. The rock feature was located on Holocene soils and there was no evidence of trail immediately next to the feature, although segments of trails were visible on desert pavement in the near vicinity.

Site AZ T:14:113 (ASM) was located in the NE ¼ of the NE ¼ of Section 10, Township 3 South, Range 4 West (USGS Cotton Center NW, Ariz. 7.5'/1973) (see Figure 3.2). The site was on the bajada, and surface evidence of the site consisted of a cluster of about 70 rocks or cobbles and approximately 25 Patayan sherds covering an area approximately 5 m in diameter (Figure 5.5). A summation of site data is presented in Table 5.3. The site was interpreted in the original survey (Harmon and Beyer 1995) as a Patayan activity area, and the request for proposal suggested the site was the location of a roasting pit. The work plan was developed with that in mind. Excavation revealed that there was no roasting pit, and that the site consisted of the cobbles visible on the surface and a shallow (less than 10 cm) deposit containing additional sherds. Based on the excavation results, and the study of similar rock features associated with trails in other parts of the Area of Potential Effect (APE), this feature is interpreted as a collapsed rock cairn.

Figure 5.5. Site AZ T:14:113 (ASM) photo.

Table 5.3. Site AZ T:14:113 (ASM) Single Feature Description

Type	Dimensions	Artifacts	Pollen Results	Illustrations
Rock cluster with artifact scatter	5.00 m diameter 0.10 m depth	102 sherds	Pinus, Juniperus, Prosopis, Cercidium, Cactaceae, Cheno-am, Asteraceae, Ambrosia, Poaceae, Sphaeralcea, Boerhaavia, Eriogonum, Onagraceae, Euphorbiaceae, Plantago	Figure 5.5 (photo) Figure 5.6 (plan view) Figure 5.7 (profile) Figure 5.8 (photo, excavated)

The work plan for the investigation of the site (Office of Cultural Resource Management 2002:28) called for the following tasks:

1) Photograph the feature.
2) Map the site.
3) Collect surface artifacts.
4) Hand-excavate a trench through the site to expose feature profile.
5) Excavate the feature.
6) Excavate a second trench to determine the depth of the artifact-bearing soil.

During the performance of the fieldwork, steps 5 and 6 of this plan were modified to adjust to the discrepancies between the anticipated and the actual natures of the subsurface deposits. The rock feature observed on the surface of the site was photographed and a 6–m x 6–m grid was established over the area of the rock feature.

The field crew walked across the site area in parallel transects spaced two meters apart, marking surface artifacts with pin flags. The surveyed area (a 200-m length of the SR 85 right-of-way) extended beyond the rock feature, but artifacts were found only in the immediate area of the feature. The provenience of each flagged artifact was mapped using a theodolite, and the artifacts were collected in individual bags and assigned specimen numbers. A map of the distribution of rocks was made in the field using marked corners of the grid and measuring tapes; the field map of the rock and cobble distribution was then digitized as an electronic file. Twenty-three individual sherds (or groups of closely spaced sherds) were mapped within the feature (Figure 5.6) and collected.

Feature Description

The subsurface investigation began with the hand excavation of a trench bisecting the approximate center of the rock feature. The trench measured 0.5 m in width and 5 m in length. The trench was excavated in 10-cm levels down to a depth of 60 cm. Sherds were found in the first 10-cm level but not in any of the lower levels. No rocks or cobbles other than those originally visible on the surface were found within the trench. The trench profile showed normal soil development with caliche nodules appearing between 40-and 60-cm depth and a very dense caliche horizon at 58 to 60 cm in depth (Figure 5.7).

The lack of a roasting pit led to a shift in excavation procedures. Given the absence of a pit feature, the entire cluster of rocks and cobbles was defined as the target feature and it was exposed in an excavation with a horizontal emphasis covering an area of 5 m x 5 m. The horizontal exposure was excavated in 1-m x 1-m units (with a few exceptions due to the 0.5-m width of the trench), to a depth of 10 cm. Two of the units measured 1 m x 1.5 m, with the long axis oriented N–S, and one unit measured 0.5 m x 1.5 m and was oriented with the long axis E–W and parallel to the initial hand-excavated trench. The odd-shaped units were next to the trench. The excavated material was sifted through a ¼-inch mesh screen. A total of 17 units, including the hand trench, were excavated. Sherds were recovered from eight of the 17 units, and pollen samples were taken from 16 of the 17 excavated units. Pollen analysis is discussed in a subsequent chapter. Small fragments of charcoal were found in one unit to the south of the initial trench. The exposed feature was photographed (Figure 5.8), and the excavated area was backfilled.

Summary

Total artifact counts for site AZ T:14:113 (ASM) were 102 ceramic sherds. The sherds were Lower Colorado buffware, indicating that site AZ T:14:113 (ASM) was a Patayan site. The results of more detailed examination of the ceramic artifacts are presented in a subsequent chapter of this report.

AZ T:14:96 (ASM) – Early 20th Century Goode Family Homestead

The site was an historic African-American homestead that was erected by the Goode family during the Great Depression era and currently resides atop the Holocene fan. Site AZ T:14:96 (ASM) was located in the NW ¼ of the SW ¼ of the SW ¼, and the SW ¼ of the SW ¼ of the SW ¼ of Section 11, Township 3 South, Range 4 West, and in the NE ¼ of the SE ¼ of the SE ¼, and the SE ¼

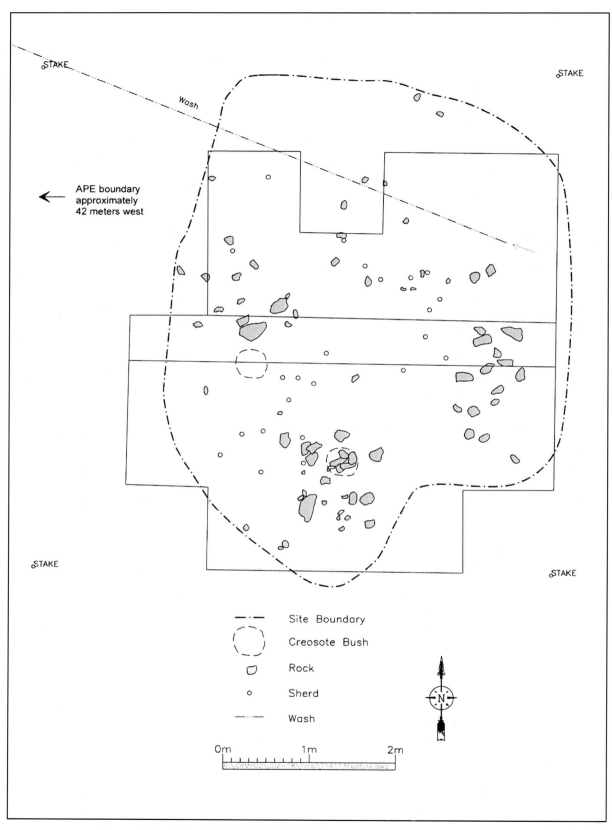

STAKE

STAKE

Wash

APE boundary
approximately
42 meters west

STAKE

STAKE

Site Boundary

Creosote Bush

Rock

o   Sherd

Wash

N

0m   1m   2m

Figure 5.6. Site AZ T:14:113 (ASM) map with artifact distribution.

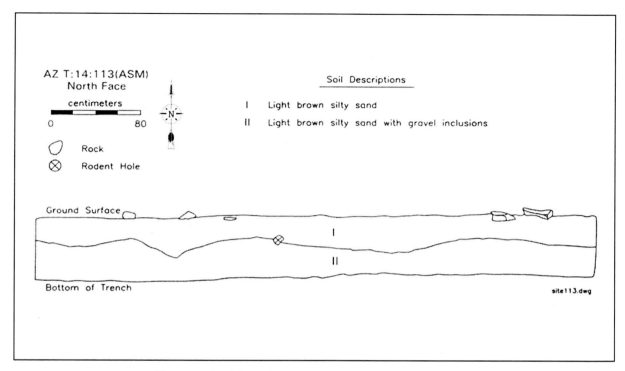

Figure 5.7. Site AZ T:14:113 (ASM) trench profile.

Figure 5.8. Site AZ T:14:113 (ASM) photograph, excavated.

of the SE ¼ of the SE ¼ of Section 10, Township 3 South, Range 4 West (USGS Cotton Center NW, Ariz. 7.5'/1973) (see Figure 3.2). Per the scope of work, the prehistoric component of the site represented by a sparse artifact scatter was not examined. Approximately 4.5 acres of the site were within the highway right-of-way.

The work plan for the investigation of the site (Office of Cultural Resource Management 2002:28) called for the following tasks:

1) Site photography.
2) Surface mapping of historical artifacts.
3) Collect surface historical artifacts.

After initial photography, the field crew walked the site within the right-of-way area in parallel transects spaced two meters apart and marked all surface historic artifacts found with pin flags. The provenience of each flagged artifact was mapped using a theodolite, and artifacts from classes designated for collection (or a sample thereof) were collected in individual bags and assigned specimen numbers. A total of 211 individual metal, glass, or modern ceramic (crockery) artifacts (or groups of closely spaced artifacts of the same class) were identified and mapped. Of the 211 specimens flagged, recorded and mapped, 106 historic artifacts were collected as non-duplicate items with potential for dating. A map of the artifact distribution is shown in Figure 5.9. The surface evidence for the site also consisted of a concrete foundation and animal pens constructed from wood and wire. Figures 5.10 through 5.12 are photographs of the concrete pad and animal pens, and Figure 5.13 is a map of the concrete pad. A summation of site data is presented in Table 5.4.

Artifact samples from three parts of site AZ T:14:96 (ASM) were examined to determine if disposal practices varied over the site. The three parts of the site were designated as the House Cluster, the North Cluster, and the Trash Cluster, and they are shown in Figure 5.9. Figure 5.14 shows the percentages of the artifact types from each cluster.

Artifact Cluster Descriptions

The House Cluster was the area directly surrounding the house. The largest percentage of artifacts in the cluster was auto parts (including a 1938 Maricopa County, Arizona license plate), followed by metal fragments and scraps. The percentage of auto parts was highest in the House Cluster, suggesting that the car was kept at and worked on near the house. There was also a large percentage of cans in the House Cluster, but very few glass shards were found near the house. Cans may have been reused more

Table 5.4. Site AZ T:14:96 (ASM) Description

Type	Dimensions	Artifacts Sampled	Samples Analyzed	Illustrations
Depression Era homestead	150 x 180 m	27 metal 22 cans 59 glass 2 crockery 1 leather	17 glass 2 crockery	Figure 5.9 (site map) Figure 5.10 (concrete pad photo) Figure 5.11 (north pen photo) Figure 5.12 (south pen photo) Figure 5.13 (concrete pad map) Figure 5.14 (artifact cluster contents) Figure 5.15 (datable glass specimens) Figure 5.16 (glass chronology)

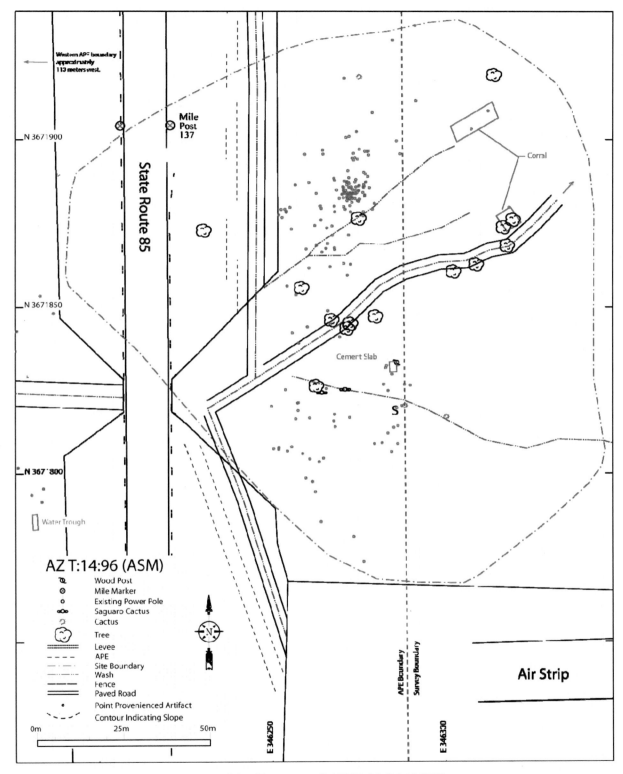

Figure 5.9. Site map of AZ T:14:96 (ASM).

Figure 5.10. Site AZ T:14:96 (ASM) photograph of concrete pad.

often than glass containers, and some cans were found with evidence of reuse, such as a wire strap handle attached to them. The difference in the percentages of can and glass artifacts within the House Cluster may also indicate differential refuse practices, that is, greater efforts may have been made to rid the immediate residential area of the more hazardous glass refuse.

The North Cluster is a sampling area north of the house location and the Trash Cluster. Though the amount of glass increased as one moved away from the House Cluster, sheet metal and cast metal fragments dominated the North Cluster. The North Cluster may be at or near the site of a metal working station on the homestead, rather than an extension of the dumping area, which appears to be within the limits of the Trash Cluster.

The Trash Cluster was where the homesteaders seemed to have deliberately disposed of their refuse. It was far enough removed from the house site so as not to be a nuisance, but still located close enough for convenience. Glass dominated the assemblage.

Figure 5.11. Site AZ T:14:96 (ASM) photograph of north animal pen.

Figure 5.12. Site AZ T:14:96 (ASM) photograph of south animal pen.

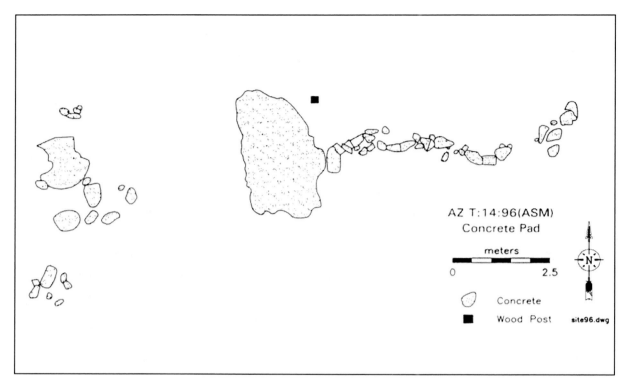

AZ T:14:96(ASM)
Concrete Pad

meters

0   2.5

Concrete

Wood Post   site96.dwg

Figure 5.13. Site AZ T:114:96 (ASM) map of concrete pad.

The presence of glass with identifiable designs, forms, or maker's marks allowed the dates of use or manufacture of the glass to be compared with the known dates of the occupation of the homestead. Thirteen specimens with datable features (Schroeder 2003; see Figure 5.14) were used and Figure 5.16 is a chronology showing the dates of their manufacture compared to the dates of the homestead's occupation. Two of the 13 specimens were manufactured after the abandonment of the homestead. One specimen was manufactured for a brief period before occupation of the homestead, but it may have come from an heirloom, or curated, vessel that was brought to the site by the homesteaders. Even without the possible curated vessel, 10 of 13 of the specimens were of a type manufactured during the occupation of the site, and they represent a good sample of the identifiable glass vessels in use by the site's occupants.

The glassware from which the specimens identified here originated fall into two size categories, soda and medium. The soda category is the smaller of the two, with diameters ranging from 57–86 cm. The two specimens of medium size were 95 cm and 104 cm. The difference in size between the two categories reflects the difference in the size of a vessel from which an individual could comfortably consume the contents directly and the size of a vessel from which contents are usually decanted or transferred into or onto other containers before consumption. Vessel form (e.g., bottle, jar) does not correspond to vessel category. A soda-type vessel could be in the form of a jar, not a bottle. Forms are noted where identifiable.

The following description of the specimens is taken from Schroeder 2003 (dates are inclusive):

Specimen 8 (Figure 5.15) was a clear, round, soda-type vessel manufactured by the Glass Containers Corporation of Fullerton, California beginning in 1945 to the present. (Glass Containers Corporation was located in Vernon, California and San Francisco, California

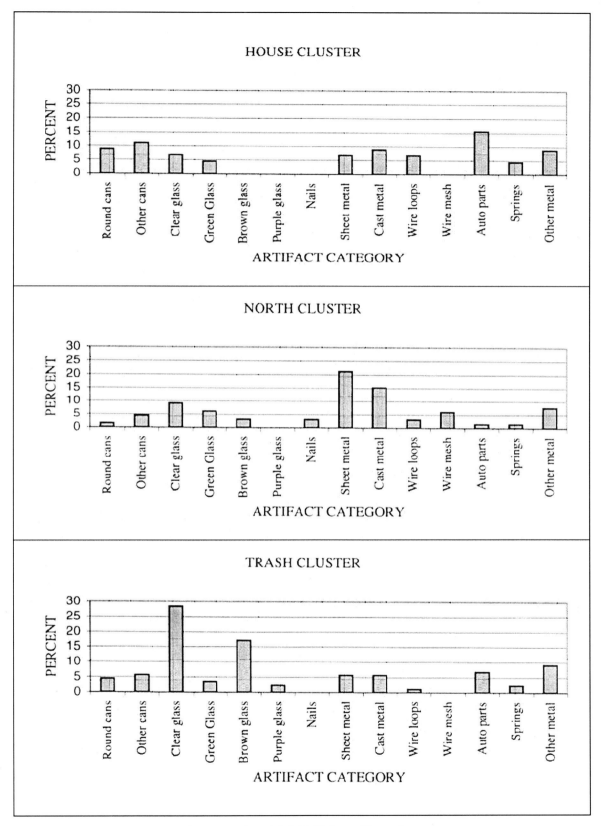

Figure 5.14. Site AZ T:14:96 (ASM) artifact cluster contents.

Figure 5.15. Site AZ T:14:96 (ASM), maker's marks on datable glass vessels.

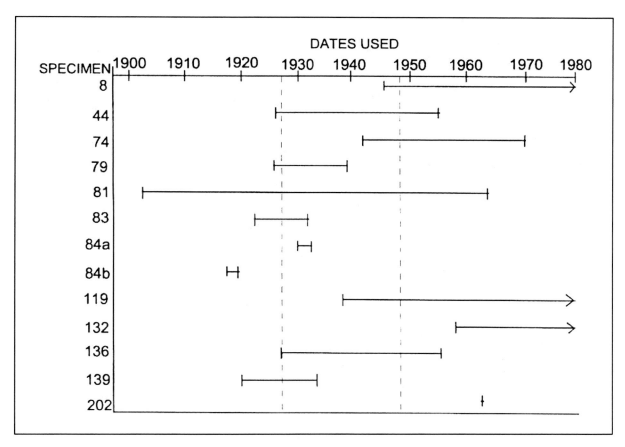

Figure 5.16. Site AZ T:14:96 (ASM) chronology of datable glass.
(Dashed lines represent the limits of the occupation of the Depression era homestead occupying the site).

prior to 1959, and the specimen may have originated at either of these locations, and not Fullerton.) The contents of the original vessel, a bottle 65 mm in diameter, could not be determined. The stamp was embossed on the base of the vessel.

Specimen 44 (see Figure 5.15) was part of a green, round soda-type vessel manufactured by the Reed Glass Company of Rochester, New York between 1927 and 1956 for use by the Cliquot Club of Millis, Massachusetts to bottle their sodas. Contents of the vessel could have been any of the quality ginger ale or flavored sodas produced by Cliquot Club. The diameter of the vessel was 63 mm and the stamp was embossed on the body and base of the bottle.

Specimen 74 (see Figure 5.15) came from a clear-green, round soda-type vessel manufactured by the Owen-Illinois Pacific Coast Company of San Francisco, California between 1943 and 1971. The contents of the original vessel, a bottle 70 mm in diameter, could not be determined. The stamp was embossed on the base of the bottle.

Specimen 79 (see Figure 5.15) came from a clear, round soda-type vessel manufactured by the W.J. Latchford Glass Company of Los Angeles, California between 1925 and 1938, and again after 1957, but 1957 postdates the occupation of the homestead. The contents of the original vessel, a bottle 82 mm in diameter, could not be determined. The stamp was embossed on the base of the vessel.

Specimen 81 (see Figure 5.15) came from a clear, round soda-type vessel manufactured by the Hazel-Atlas Glass Company of Wheeling, West Virginia between 1902 and 1964. The contents of the original vessel, 86 mm in diameter, could be resealed and were either condiments or solvents. The stamp was embossed on the base of the bottle.

Specimen 83 (see Figure 5.15) came from a brown, round soda-type vessel manufactured by the Owen-Illinois Pacific Coast Company of San Francisco, California at their Huntington, West Virginia plant between 1922 and 1932. The contents of the original vessel, a bottle 57 mm in diameter, could not be determined. The stamp was embossed on the base of the bottle.

Specimen 84a (see Figure 5.15) came from a clear, oval medium-type vessel manufactured by the Illinois Pacific Glass Company of San Francisco, California between 1930 and 1932. The contents of the original vessel, a jar measuring 95 mm in diameter, were pickles. The stamp was embossed on the base of the vessel.

Specimen 119 (see Figure 5.15) came from a clear, round soda-type vessel manufactured by the W. J. Latchford Glass Company of Los Angeles, California beginning in 1938 to the present. The vessel was a mustard jar measuring 64 mm in diameter and was embossed on the base.

Specimen 132 (see Figure 5.15) came from a clear, oval medium-type vessel manufactured by the Maywood Glass Company of Compton, California circa 1958. The most likely contents of this vessel, a bottle measuring 104 mm in diameter, were condiments. The vessel does not date to the time of the Goode homestead and is believed to have been introduced to the site after the homestead was abandoned. The stamp was embossed on the body and base of the vessel.

Specimen 136 (see Figure 5.15) came from a brown, round soda-type vessel manufactured by the Reed Glass Company of Rochester, New York between 1927 and 1956. The contents of the original vessel, a bottle of undetermined diameter, could not be determined. The stamp was embossed on the base of the bottle.

Specimen 139 (see Figure 5.15) came from a clear, round soda-type vessel manufactured by the Long Beach Glass Company of Long Beach, California between 1920 and 1933. The contents of the original vessel, a bottle measuring 67 mm in diameter, could not be determined. The stamp was embossed on the base of the vessel.

Specimen 202 (see Figure 5.15) came from a green, round soda-type vessel manufactured by the Owens-Illinois Glass Company of Toledo, Ohio in 1965. The contents of the original vessel, a bottle measuring 72 mm in diameter, could not be determined and was embossed on the base. The vessel does not date to the time of the Goode homestead and is believed to have been introduced to the site after the homestead was abandoned.

Summary

The research significance of site AZ T:14:96 (ASM), in the vicinity of Mile Post 137 of SR 85, was partially realized by the data recovery work in the field. In addition to the site description provided in this chapter, site AZ T:14:96 (ASM) is also addressed in Chapter 10. The chapter is based upon archival research, and also upon oral histories collected from former occupants of the Depression era homestead.

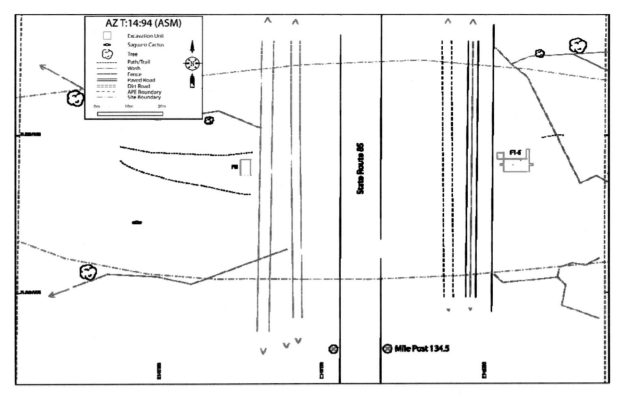

Figure 5.17. Excavated areas on site AZ T:14:94 (ASM).

AZ T:14:94 (ASM) - Collapsed Rock Cairn Trail Feature (Hohokam and Patayan)

This site consists of three rock clusters and three trail segments visible on desert pavement on a Pleistocene Terrace. The rock clusters are interpreted to be collapsed rock cairns of the type frequently observed in southern Arizona in association with trails. Artifacts added to the rock cairns included sherds (both Hohokam and Patayan), flaked stone artifacts and fragments of shell.

Site AZ T:14:94 (ASM) was located in the NE ¼ of the SE ¼ of the NE ¼ of Section 27, and the NW ¼ of the SW ¼ of the NW ¼ of Section 26, Township 3 South, Range 4 West (USGS Cotton Center NW, Ariz. 7.5'/1973) (see Figure 3.2). The surface evidence for the site consisted of three clusters of rocks (assigned six feature numbers in the survey stage) and three trail segments (Figure 5.17). The features as described in the original survey (Harmon and Beyer 1995) were:

1) Two Hohokam buffware ceramic sherds within a scatter of granite and rhyolite cobbles covering a 1.5-m x 2-m area (Figure 5.18).

2) Four Hohokam red-on-buff ceramic sherds within a scatter of granite, rhyolite and schist cobbles covering a 2-m x 3-m area (Figure 5.19).

3) Fifteen Hohokam ceramic sherds within a rock ring and scatter of granite, rhyolite and schist cobbles covering a 1.5-m x 2-m area (Figure 5.20).

4) Ten Hohokam buffware ceramic sherds within a rock ring and rock semicircles of granite, rhyolite, schist and quartzite cobbles covering a 1.5-m x 3-m area (Figure 5.21).

5) A disturbed rock ring consisting of granite and rhyolite cobbles covering a 1.4-m x 1.7-m area (Figure 5.22).

Figure 5.18. Site AZ T:14:94 (ASM) photograph of Feature 1.

Figure 5.19. Site AZ T:14:94 (ASM) photograph of Feature 2.

Figure 5.20. Site AZ T:14:94 (ASM) photograph of Feature 3.

Figure 5.21. Site AZ T:14:94 (ASM) photograph of Feature 4.

Figure 5.22. Site AZ T:14:94 (ASM) photograph of Feature 5.

Figure 5.23. Site AZ T:14:94 (ASM) photograph of Feature 8.

6)   Feature 6 was not in the right-of-way, was not excavated, and is not considered further.

7)   Feature 7 was not in the right-of-way, was not excavated, and is not considered further.

8)   Five Hohokam buffware and Gila Plain ceramic sherds within a rock cluster of granite, rhyolite, schist and quartz cobbles covering a circular area with a diameter of three meters (Figure 5.23).

Features 1 through 5 were found on excavation to be two clusters of rocks buried beneath a slight deposit of Holocene blown sands, with Features 1 through 3 constituting one cluster, and Features 4 and 5 the second cluster. Feature 8 was a spatially distinct cluster of rocks. While excavation revealed additional rocks at a shallow depth, no pit outlines were observed, and the rock features were not associated with buried thermal pits or buried floor features.

Additionally, there were three east-west trails on the site, two trails west of SR 85 and one trail east of SR 85, spanning the entire right-of-way. The trail on the east side appeared to be a continuation of the northernmost trail on the west side. All three trails were between 30 and 50 cm (12–20 in) wide, and they were associated with features and artifacts. A further discussion of trails is presented in Chapter 12.

The work plan for the investigation of the site (Office of Cultural Resource Management 2002:31) called for the following tasks:
1) photograph the features,
2) map the site,
3) collect surface artifacts,
4) excavate a hand trench, and
5) excavate the features.

Feature Descriptions

The field crew walked the entire site area in parallel transects spaced two meters apart and marked surface artifacts with pin flags. The provenience of each artifact was mapped using a theodolite, and the artifacts were collected in individual bags and assigned specimen numbers. Maps of the rock features were made in the field using the marked corners of the grid, measuring tapes, and a 1-m x 1-m frame divided every 10 centimeters with string. One grid was established for Features 1–5 and one grid was established for Feature 8. A total of 113 individual sherds (or groups of closely spaced sherds) and 16 lithic artifacts were mapped and collected.

The subsurface excavation began with the hand excavation of a trench bisecting the approximate center of Feature 1 through 5. Features 1 through 5 (Figure 5.24) were adjacent and their boundaries were virtually indistinguishable; the map in Figure 5.24 shows the approximate feature locations as reported during the surface survey, but the excavated results show that the rocks have a nearly continuous distribution and at best can be divided into two general clusters as shown in Figure 5.24. The trench measured 0.5 m in width and five meters in length. The trench was excavated to a depth below the surface of 40 cm, where a dense caliche layer was encountered. Sherds were found in the first 10-cm level but not in any of the lower levels. One animal bone was found in the 30- to 40-cm level. The trench profile (Figure 5.25) showed normal soil development with a caliche horizon at 40-cm depth. The horizontal exposure of the feature was continued and extended to the caliche layer, with each rock being left on a pedestal. The individual rocks and associated artifacts lay within the top 10 cm of the excavation. The excavated material was sifted through a ¼-inch mesh screen. A total of 35 units, including the hand trench, were excavated.

Twenty-three units were 1 m x 1 m. Eight units were 1 m x 1.5 m. A forty square meter area was exposed. Thirty of the units, including the trench, yielded ceramic sherds. Four of the units yielded shell. Pollen samples were taken from all units and pollen analysis appears in a subsequent chapter. No lithics were recovered during the excavation phase.

Table 5.5. Site AZ T:14:94 (ASM) Feature Descriptions

Feature Number	Type	Dimensions	Pollen Results	Illustrations
1		1.50 m x 2.00 m 0.10 m depth		Figures 5.18 (photo), 5.24 (plan view), and 5.25 (trench profile)
2	Features 1–5 were two rock clusters representing two collapsed cairns. Features 1–3 formed a western cluster, and Features 4 and 5 the eastern cluster. A total of 538 shereds, 17 flaked stone and 4 shell artifacts.	2.00 m x 3.00 m 0.10 m depth	Pinus, Juniperus, Larrea, Prosopis, Cactaceae, Cholla, Cheno-am, Asteraceae, Ambrosia, Poaceae, Brassicaceae, Lamiacea, Boerhaavia Eriogonum Euphorbiaceae Plant	Figures 5.19 (photo), 5.24 (plan view), and 5.25 (trench profile)
3		1.50 m x 2.00 m 0.10 m depth		Figures 5.20 (photo), 5.24 (plan view), and 5.25 (trench profile)
4		1.50 m x 3.00 m 0.10 m depth		Figures 5.21 (photo), 5.24 (plan view), and 5.25 (trench profile)
5		1.40 m x 1.70 m 0.10 m depth		Figures 5.22 (photo), 5.24 (plan view), and 5.25 (trench profile)
8	Rock cairn and artifact scatter with 24 sherds	3.0 m diameter 0.20 m depth	Not analyzed.	Figures 5.23 (photo), 5.26 (plan view), and 5.27 (photo, excavated)

Twenty-three units were 1 m x 1 m. Eight units were 1 m x 1.5 m. A forty square meter area was exposed. Thirty of the units, including the trench, yielded ceramic sherds. Four of the units yielded shell. Pollen samples were taken from all units and pollen analysis appears in a subsequent chapter. No lithics were recovered during the excavation phase.

Subsurface excavation of Feature 8 began with hand excavation of a trench bisecting the center of the feature (Figure 5.27 and 5.28). The trench was 0.5 m wide and 5 m long. The trench was excavated to a depth below the surface of approximately 40 cm, well into the caliche layer underlying the feature. Sherds were found in the first and second 10-centimeter levels but no lower. The excavation was then continued with the horizontal exposure of the feature to depths of 10 cm to 40 cm, with rock left on pedestals. The rocks occurred in the first 10-cm level, intruding occasionally into the next level. No pit outlines for a thermal feature or architectural structure were observed. The excavated material was sifted through a ¼-inch mesh screen. A total of 14 units, including the hand trench, were excavated (Figure 5.27). Five units were 1 m x 1 m. Five units were 1 m x 1.5 m. The remaining units, 0.5 m x 5 m, formed the trench. A fifteen square meter area was exposed. Five of the units, including the trench, yielded ceramic sherds. Pollen samples were taken from all units, and pollen analysis is discussed in a subsequent chapter. The exposed feature was photographed and the excavation was backfilled. Summations for all features excavated at site AZ T:14:94 (ASM) are presented in Table 5.5.

Summary

Site AZ T:14:92 (ASM) consisted of the collapsed remains of possibly up to three rock cairns associated with prehistoric trails, which were associated with both Hohokam and Patayan ceramic sherds. Cumulative artifact counts for site AZ T:14:92 (ASM) were 585 ceramic sherds (includes 23 sherds not associated with a feature), 17 lithic artifacts, and 4 shell artifacts. The results of more detailed examination of the ceramic and lithic artifacts are presented in subsequent chapters of this report.

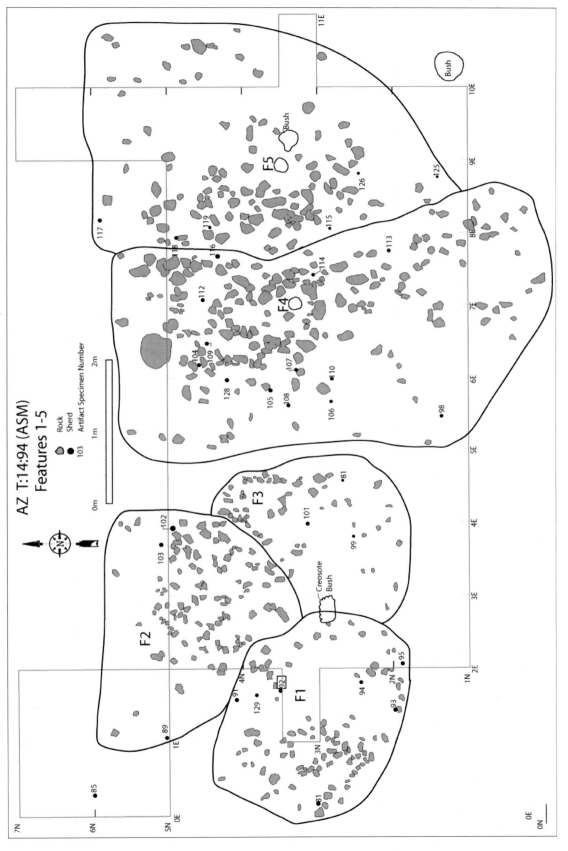

Figure 5.24. Site AZ T:14:94 (ASM) map of Features 1 through 5.

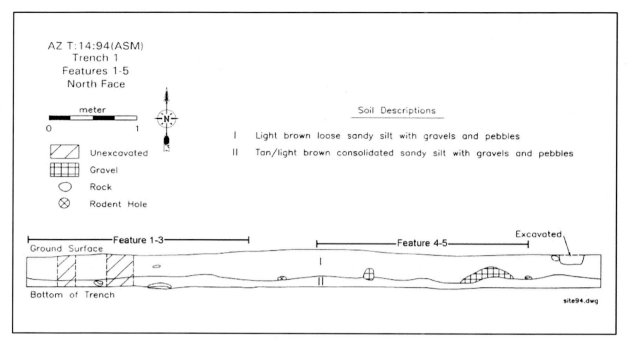

Figure 5.25. Site AZ T:14:94 (ASM) profile of trench through Features 1 to 5.

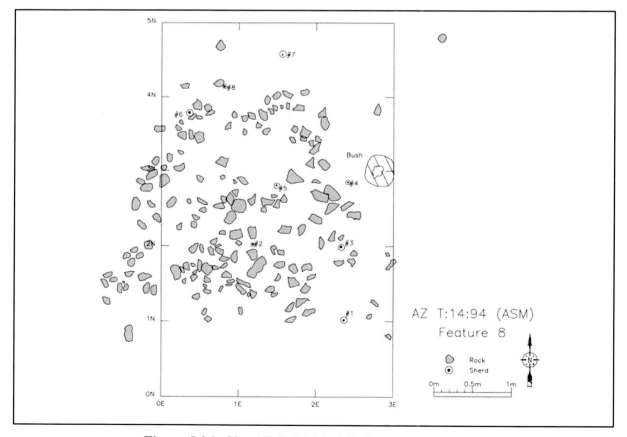

Figure 5.26. Site AZ T:14:94 (ASM) map of Feature 8.

Figure 5.27. Site AZ T:14:94 (ASM) photograph of excavated Feature 8.

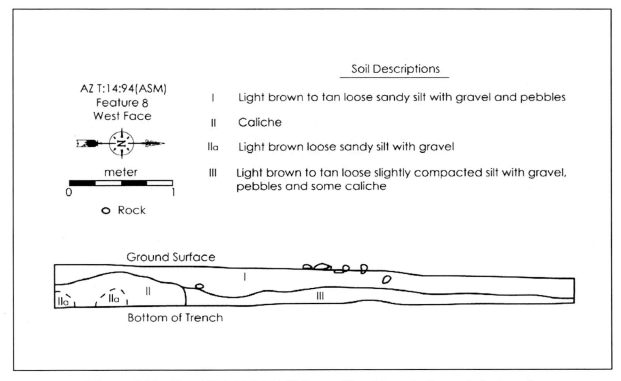

Figure 5.28. Site AZT:14:94 (ASM) profile of trench through feature 8.

AZ T:14:92 (ASM) - Collapsed Rock Cairn Trail Feature (Hohokam)

Eight rock features are the collapsed remains of rock cairns associated with three trail segments on the Pleistocene surface. The site also includes two rock circles. The rock features were not associated with subsurface pit outlines, and were not part of buried thermal features or architectural structures. Only Hohokam sherds were recovered at this site, and all were associated with Feature 1.

Site AZ T:14:92 (ASM) was located in the SE ¼ of the NW ¼ of the NW ¼ of Section 35, and the SE ¼ of the NE ¼ of the NE ¼ of Section 34, Township 3 South, Range 4 West (USGS Cotton Center NW, Ariz. 7.5'/1973) (see Figure 3.2). Figure 5.29 shows the locations of the surface evidence for the site, which consisted of nine rock features and three trail segments. The features as described in the original survey (Harmon and Beyer 1995) were:

1) Approximately 30 Hohokam buffware ceramic sherds scattered within a granite cobble cluster in a 2-m x 3-m area (Figure 5.30).

2) Feature 2 was not in the right-of-way, was not excavated and is not considered further.

3) Feature 3 was not in the right-of-way, was not excavated and is not considered further.

4) Feature 4 was not in the right-of-way, was not excavated and is not considered further.

5) Three granite boulders and one quartz cobble adjacent to a trail, 20 cm x 45 cm, as a possible marker (Figure 5.31).

6) One large boulder surrounded by a diffuse scatter of smaller cobbles covering a 1.5-m x 1.8-m area (Figure 5.32).

7) A rock cluster of small granite cobbles in a 0.5-m x 0.6-m area (Figure 5.33).

8) A rough semicircle of six granite cobbles, each approximately 10 cm in diameter, covering a 0.6-m x 0.75-m area (Figure 5.34).

9) A diffuse scatter of granite and quartz cobbles in a 2.7-m x 3-m area (Figure 5.35).

10) Feature 10 was discovered during the field investigation. It was an ellipsoid alignment of rocks, 1m x 1.2 m along short and long axes of the ellipsoid (Figure 5.42).

Three trail segments, oriented east–west, were located within the site and continued beyond the limits of the right-of-way. On the west side of SR 85, two of the segments intersected. They both may have aligned with two segments on the east side that merged into one trail. All trail segments were between 30 and 50 cm (12–20 in) wide, and they were all associated with features. Trails are covered separately in a subsequent chapter.

The work plan for the investigation of the site (Office of Cultural Resource Management 2002:36) called for the following tasks:

1) Photograph the features.

2) Map the site.

3) Collect surface artifacts.

4) Excavate the features.

The rock features within the right-of-way were photographed. Individual grids were established for each feature to be excavated.

The crew walked the entire site area in parallel transects spaced two meters apart and marked surface artifacts with pin flags. The provenience of each artifact was mapped with a theodolite. Artifacts were collected in individual bags and assigned specimen numbers.

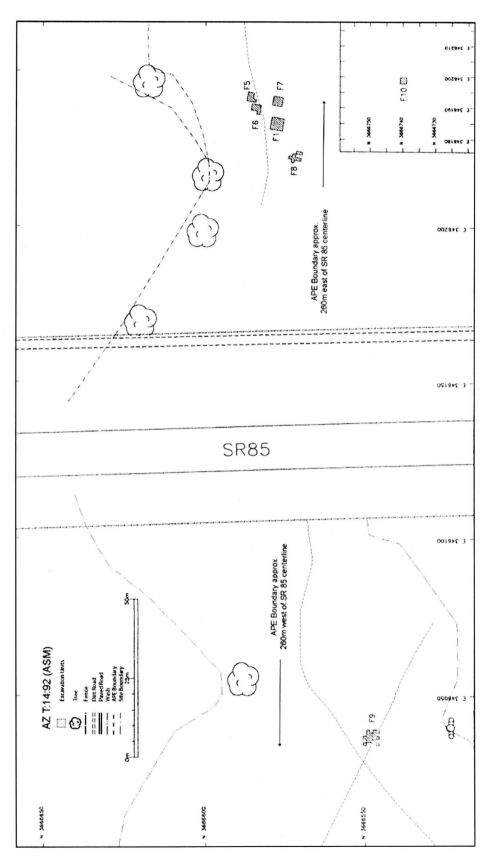

Figure 5.29. Site AZ T:14:92 (ASM) site map.

Figure 5.30. Site AZ T:14:92 (ASM) photograph of Feature 1.

Figure 5.31. Site AZ T:14:92 (ASM) photograph of Feature 5.

Figure 5.32. Site AZ T:14:92 (ASM) photograph of Feature 6.

Figure 5.33. Site AZ T:14:92 (ASM) photograph of Feature 7.

Figure 5.34. Site AZ T:14:92 (ASM) photograph of Feature 8.

Figure 5.35. Site AZ T:14:92 (ASM) photograph of Feature 9.

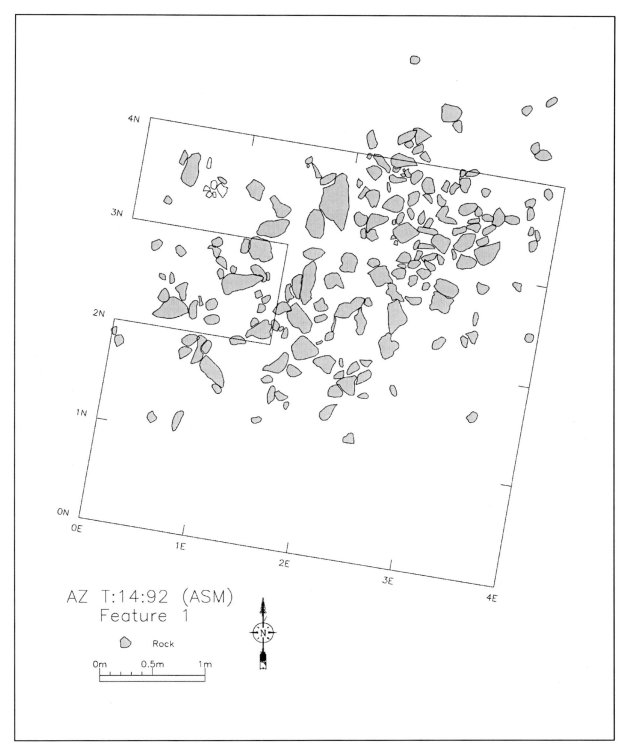

Figure 5.36. Site AZ T:14:92 (ASM) map of Feature 1.

Maps of the rock features (Figures 5.36–42) were made in the field using the marked corners of the grid, measuring tapes, and a 1-m x 1-m frame gridded every 10 cm with string. Thirty-three individual sherds (or groups of closely spaced sherds) and 10 lithic artifacts were mapped and collected.

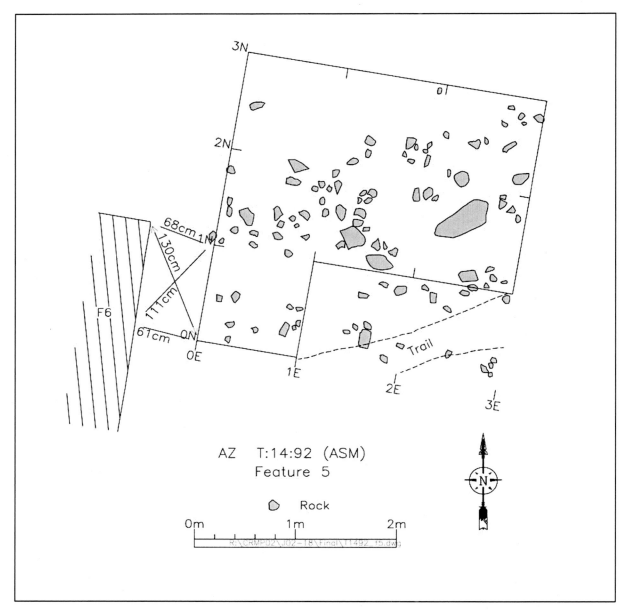

Figure 5.37. Site AZ T:14:92 (ASM) map of Feature 5.

Feature Descriptions

Subsurface excavation began with hand excavation of a trench bisecting the center of Feature 1 (see Figure 5.36). The trench measured 0.5 m in width and 4 m in length. The plan was to excavate the feature in 10-cm levels, but a dense caliche layer appeared within 3–8 cm of the surface.

Horizontal exposure of the caliche layer was continued. The excavated material was sifted through a ¼-inch mesh screen. A total of 13 units, including the "hand trench," were excavated. Eight units were 1 m x 1 m. Four units were 1 m x 1.5 m. A sixteen square meter area was exposed. Twelve of the units, including the trench, yielded ceramic sherds. Pollen samples were taken from all units. The results of pollen analysis appear in a subsequent chapter.

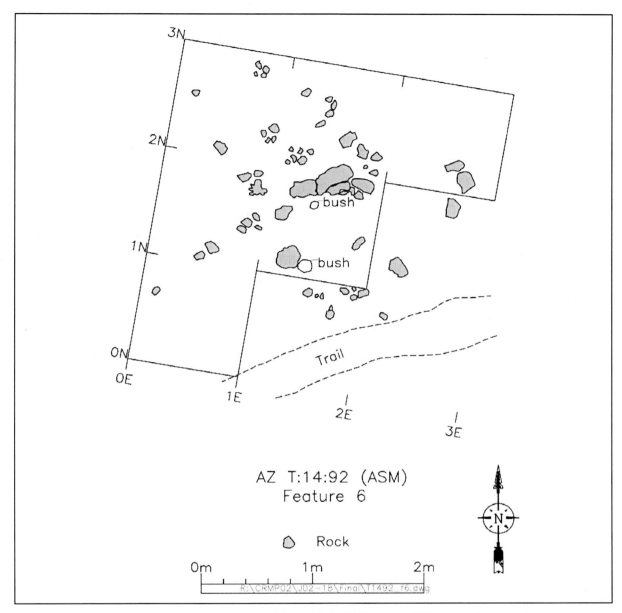

AZ T:14:92 (ASM)
Feature 6

◊ Rock

0m   1m   2m

R:\CRMP02\J02-18\Final\T1492_f6.dwg

Figure 5.38. Site AZ T:14:92 (ASM) map of Feature 6.

Feature 5 (Figure 5.37) yielded no artifacts. The plan was to excavate the feature in 10-cm levels, but a dense caliche layer appeared within 10 cm of the surface. Horizontal exposure of the caliche layer was continued. Excavated material was sifted through a ¼- inch mesh screen. A total of seven units were excavated. A seven square meter area was exposed. All units were 1 m x 1 m, and all units were sampled for pollen.

Feature 6 (Figure 5.38) yielded no artifacts. The plan was to excavate the feature in 10-cm levels, but a dense caliche layer appeared within eight centimeters of the surface. Horizontal exposure of the caliche layer was continued. Excavated material was sifted through a ¼-inch mesh screen. A total of seven units were excavated. A seven square meter area was exposed. All units were 1 m x 1 m, and all units were sampled for pollen.

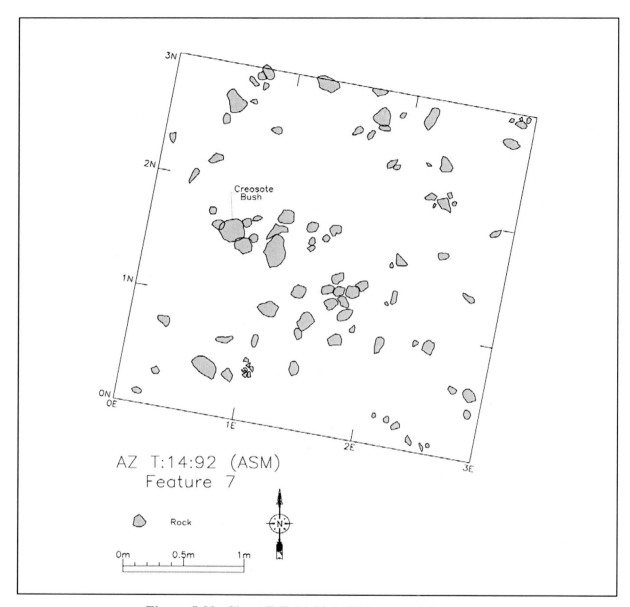

Figure 5.39. Site AZ T:14:92 (ASM) map of Feature 7.

Feature 7 (Figure 5.39) yielded no artifacts. The plan was to excavate the feature in 10-centimeter levels, but a dense, undulating caliche layer appeared between 0–20 cm below the surface, and on one occasion both extremes occurred within the same 1-m x 1-m unit. Horizontal exposure of the caliche layer was continued. Excavated material was sifted through a ¼-inch mesh screen. A total of nine units were excavated. A nine square meter area was exposed. All units were 1 m x 1 m, and all units were sampled for pollen.

Feature 8 (Figure 5.40) yielded no artifacts. The plan was to excavate in 10-centimeter levels, but a dense caliche layer appeared within eight centimeters of the surface. Horizontal exposure of the caliche layer was continued. Excavated material was sifted through a ¼-inch mesh screen. A total of eight units were excavated. An eight square meter area was exposed. All units were 1 m x 1 m, and all units were sampled for pollen.

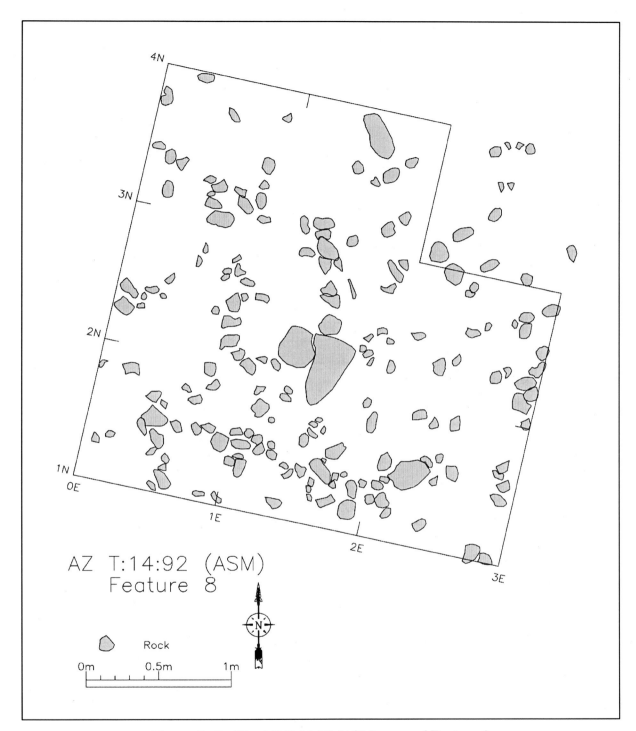

Figure 5.40. Site AZ T:14:92 (ASM) map of Feature 8.

Feature 9 (Figure 5.41) yielded one sherd artifact. The plan was to excavate in 10-centimeter levels, but a dense undulating caliche layer appeared between 1–13 cm below the surface, and on one occasion both extremes occurred within the same 1-m x 1-m unit. Horizontal exposure of the caliche layer was continued. Excavated material was sifted through a ¼-inch mesh screen. A total of 15 units were excavated. A fifteen square meter area was exposed. All units were 1 m x 1 m, and all units were sampled for pollen.

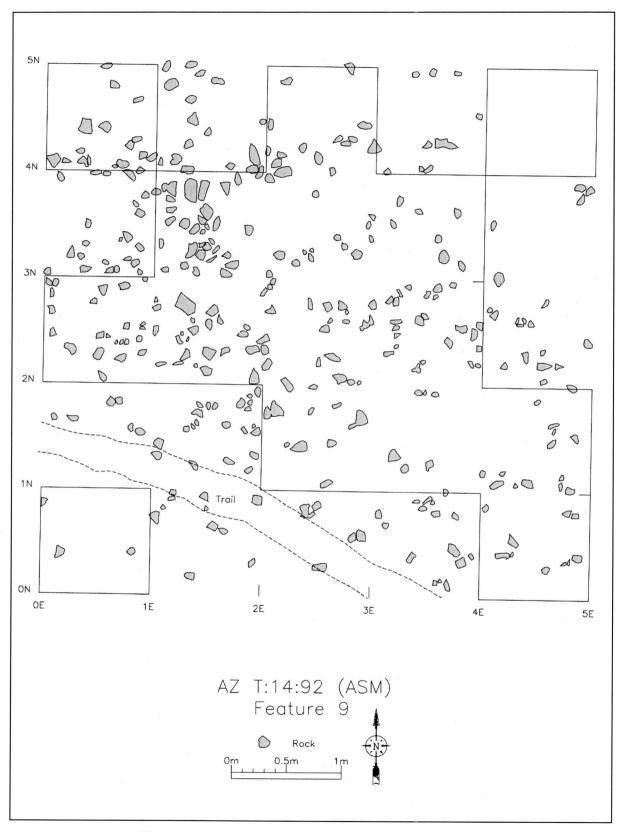

Figure 5.41. Site AZ T:14:92 (ASM) map of Feature 9.

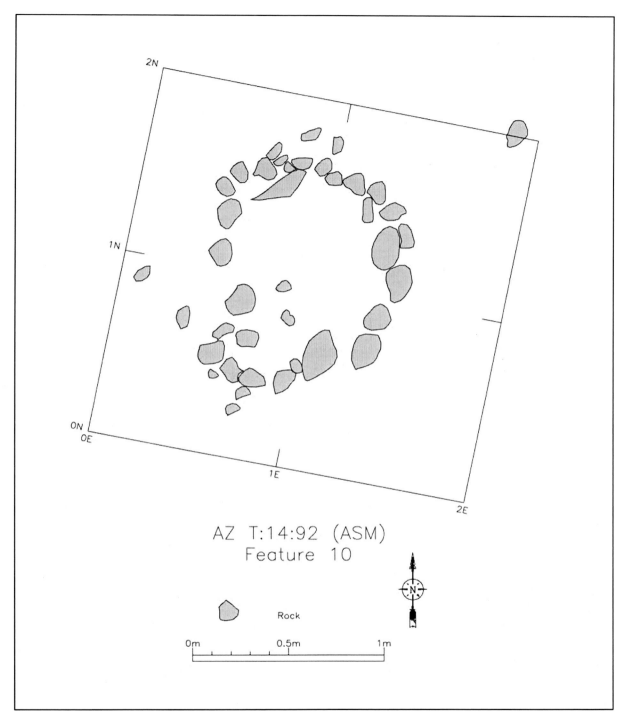

AZ T:14:92 (ASM)
Feature 10

Rock

0m   0.5m   1m

Figure 5.42. Site AZ T:14:92 (ASM) map of Feature 10.

Feature 10 (Figure 5.42) was also bereft of artifacts. The plan was to excavate the unit in 10-centimeter levels, but a dense caliche layer appeared between 2–6 cm below the surface. Horizontal exposure of the caliche layer was continued. Excavated material was sifted through a ¼-inch mesh screen. A total of four units were excavated. A four square meter area was exposed. Four pollen samples were taken from Feature 10.

Table 5.6. Site AZ T:14:92 (ASM) Feature Descriptions

Feature Number	Type	Dimensions	Artifacts	Pollen Results	Illustrations
1	Rock cluster & artifact scatter	2.00 m x 3.00 m 3–8 cm depth	145 sherds; 1 lithic	Pinus, Pinus edulis, Juniperus, Larrea, Prosopis, Cactaceae, Cholla, Cheno-am, Asteraceae, Ambrosia, Poaceae, Brassicaceae, Lamiacea, Boerhaavia, Eriogonum, Euphorb	Figs. 5.30 (photo) & 5.36 (plan view)
5	Rock cluster	0.20 m x 0.45 m 10 cm depth	None	Not analyzed	Figs. 5.31 (photo) & 5.37 (plan view)
6	Rock cluster	1.50 m x 1.80 m 8 cm depth	None	Not analyzed	Figs. 5.32 (photo) & 5.38 (plan view)
7	Rock cluster	0.50 m x 0.60 m 0–20 cm depth	None	Not analyzed	Figs. 5.33 (photo) & 5.39 (plan view)
8	Rock cluster	0.60 m x 0.75 m 3–8 cm depth	None	Not analyzed	Figs. 5.34 (photo) & 5.40 (plan view)
9	Rock cluster		None	Not analyzed	Figs. 5.35 (photo) & 5.41 (plan view)
10	Rock ellipsoid		None	Not analyzed	Fig.5.42 (plan view)

Site AZ T:14:92 (ASM) was an activity area associated with prehistoric trails. Ceramic sherds indicated Hohokam use of the site. Summations for all excavated features are presented in Table 5.6. Cumulative artifact counts for site AZ T:14:92 (ASM) were 305 ceramic sherds and 28 lithic artifacts (including 160 sherds and 27 lithics not associated with a feature). The results of more detailed examination of the ceramic and lithic artifacts are presented in subsequent chapters of this report.

AZ Z:2:46 (ASM) – Thermal Feature (Pioneer Period Date)

The cultural rock features consisted of a Pioneer period roasting pit (Feature 3) associated with three clusters of fire-cracked rock (Features 1, 2 and 6) that possibly represent cleaning episodes of the oven. The oven and fire cracked rock were located on Holocene sediments in a small wash bordered by Pleistocene sediments with desert pavement. The roasting pit included pollen of Zea Mays and radiocarbon assay dated the feature to the Pioneer Period. No sherds or flaked stone artifacts were found at the site. A possible rock mulch pile (Feature 9) was located some distance away on the Pleistocene surface. Features 4, 5, 7 and 8 may not be cultural in origin, or they may represent manuports.

Site AZ Z:2:46 (ASM) was located in the NW ¼ of the NE ¼ of the SW ¼ of Section 28, Township 5 South, Range 4 West (USGS Gila Bend, Ariz. 7.5'/1973) (Figure 3.3). The surface evidence for the site consisted of nine rock features and two trail segments (Figure 5.43). The features as described in the original survey (Harmon and Beyer 1995) were:

1) Approximately 30 fire-cracked and spalled quartzite, rhyolite, and vesicular basalt cobbles concentrated in a 1-m x 2-m area (Figure 5.44).

2) Feature 2 is identical to Feature 1 in size and component rocks (Figure 5.45).

3) Approximately 50 fire-cracked and spalled granite, quartzite, rhyolite and vesicular basalt cobbles concentrated in a circular area with a 1.5-m diameter, which upon excavation increased to a maximum diameter of 2.2 m (Figure 5.46).

4) Approximately 20 quartzite, rhyolite, and vesicular basalt cobbles scattered in a 1-m x 3-m area (Figure 5.47).

5) A rock alignment of six granite, basalt and quartzite cobbles spanning approximately 0.8 m (Figure 5.48).

6) Approximately 30 fire-cracked and spalled rhyolite and granite cobble fragments concentrated in a 1-m x 2-m area (Figure 5.49).

7) A sparse scatter of three rhyolite cobbles and four large granite cobbles in a 2-m x 3-m area (Figure 5.50).

8) A scatter of 15 quartzite cobbles and granite alluvial cobbles in a 1.3-m x 2.5-m area (Figure 5.51).

9) Approximately 100 granite, rhyolite and quartzite cobbles scattered in a circular area with a 4 meter diameter (Figure 5.52).

Additionally, there were two segments of trails approximately 120 m (400 ft) long and 0.3–0.5 m (12–20 in) wide, oriented NE–SW parallel to the right-of-way boundary. Both were on the northwest side of SR 85, but only one was within the right-of-way.

The work plan for the investigation of the site (Office of Cultural Resource Management 2002:36) called for the following tasks:

1) Photograph the features.

2) Map the site.

3) Collect surface artifacts.

4) Excavate the features.

The rock features observed on the surface of the site were photographed. A grid was established that covered Features 1–6. Features 7–9 were isolated from the main cluster of features. Individual grids were established for each of them.

The field crew walked the entire site area in parallel transects spaced two meters apart and marked the sole surface artifact found, a lithic, with a pin flag. The provenience of the flagged artifact was mapped with a theodolite, and the artifact was bagged, collected, and assigned a specimen number. Maps of the rock features were made in the field using marked corners of the grid and measuring tapes.

Feature Descriptions

Feature 1 (Figure 5.55) contained 610 pieces of fire-cracked rock, but had no associated pit. Excavated material was sifted through a ¼-inch mesh screen. No artifacts were recovered. Units were excavated in 10-cm levels. All units were 1 m x 1 m, and all units were sampled for pollen. A

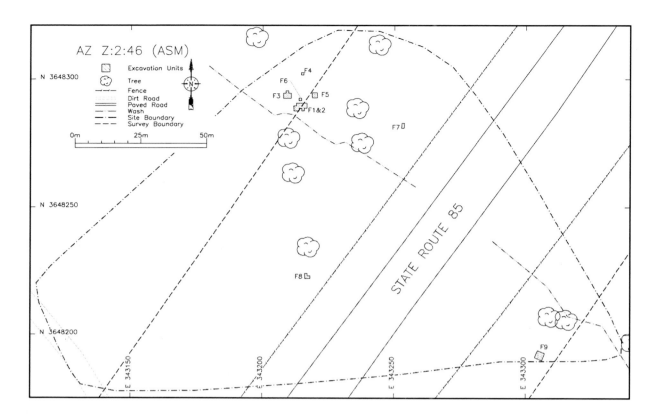

Figure 5.43. Site map of AZ Z:2:46 (ASM).

Figure 5.44. Site AZ Z:2:46 (ASM) photograph of Feature 1.

Figure 5.45. Site AZ Z:2:46 (ASM) photograph of Feature 2.

Figure 5.46. Site AZ Z:2:46 (ASM) photograph of Feature 3.

Figure 5.47. Site AZ Z:2:46 (ASM) photograph of Feature 4.

Figure 5.48. Site AZ Z:2:46 (ASM) photograph of Feature 5.

Figure 5.49. Site AZ Z:2:46 (ASM) photograph of Feature 6.

Figure 5.50. Site AZ Z:2:46 (ASM) photograph of Feature 7.

Figure 5.51. Site AZ Z:2:46 (ASM) photograph of Feature 8.

Figure 5.52. Site AZ Z:2:46 (ASM) photograph of Feature 9.

total of nine units were excavated, exposing an area of five square meters. Maximum depth reached below the surface was 30 centimeters.

Feature 2 (Figure 5.55) contained 613 pieces of fire-cracked rock, but had no associated pit. Excavated material was sifted through a ¼-inch mesh screen. One unit yielded a charcoal sample. No artifacts were recovered. Units were excavated in 10-cm levels. All units were 1 m x 1 m, and all units were sampled for pollen. A total of 11 units were excavated, exposing a seven square meter area. Maximum depth reached below the surface was 30 cm.

Subsurface excavation began with Feature 3 (Figure 5.53). Excavators dug a hand trench bisecting Feature 3. The trench was 1 m wide and 3 m long. The trench was excavated in 10-cm levels down to depth of 50 centimeters below the surface. Caliche nodules appeared between 30 and 40 cm, with a dense caliche layer appearing at 50 cm. The trench profile is shown in Figure 5.54. No sherds or flaked stone artifacts were encountered in this feature, or at any other feature. Despite the presence of fire-cracked rock at four features, Feature 3 was the only feature with a pit. Excavated material was sifted through a ¼-inch mesh screen. A total of 15 units, including the hand trench, were excavated. All units were 1 m x 1 m. A seven square meter area was exposed to cover the maximum dispersal of fire-cracked rock around the periphery of the pit. Pollen samples were taken from all units. One flotation sample was taken from the pit. Pollen and flotation sample analysis are discussed in a subsequent chapter. Charcoal samples were taken from three units. One unit yielded a shell sample. A total of 144 pieces of fire-cracked rock were present.

Feature 4 (Figure 5.56) was determined not to be a cultural feature. Excavated material was sifted through a ¼-inch mesh screen. No fire-cracked rock or artifacts were recovered. One unit, 1 m x 1 m, was excavated and sampled for pollen. The feature was directly on the Pleistocene surface. The trace deposits of soil on the surface were excavated to a maximum depth of two centimeters.

Feature 5 (Figure 5.57) contained no artifacts or fire-cracked rock. Excavated material was sifted through a ¼-inch mesh screen. Units were excavated in 20-cm levels. All units were 1 m x 1 m, and all units were sampled for pollen. A total of four units were excavated, exposing four square meters. Maximum depth reached below the surface was 20 cm.

Feature 6 (Figure 5.58) contained approximately 16 pieces of fire-cracked rock, but had no associated pit. Excavated material was sifted through a ¼-inch mesh screen. No artifacts were recovered. Units were excavated in 10-centimeter levels. A total of two units were excavated, exposing a one square meter area. Both units were 1 m x 1 m, and both units were sampled for pollen. Maximum depth reached below the surface was 20 cm.

Feature 7 (Figure 5.59) contained no artifacts or fire-cracked rock, but may have been a cluster of manuports because it was atop the alluvium and was bereft of subsurface artifacts.

Excavated material was sifted through a ¼-inch mesh screen. Units were excavated from the surface to the caliche layer in one natural level, with the undulating caliche surface at depths between 10 and 30 cm. A total of 2 units were excavated, exposing a two square meter area. Both units were 1 , x 1 m, and both units were sampled for pollen.

Feature 8 (Figure 5.60) contained no artifacts or fire-cracked rock. Excavated material was sifted through a ¼-inch mesh screen. Units were excavated from the surface to the undulating caliche layer in one natural level at depths between 0.0 cm and 12 cm. All units were 1 m x 1 m, and all units were sampled for pollen. A total of 3 units were excavated, exposing an area of three square meters.

Feature 9 contained no artifacts or fire-cracked rock, and may have been a possible agricultural feature since it was a small rock cluster atop desert pavement, but was not part of a larger pattern. Excavated material was sifted through a ¼-inch mesh screen. Units were excavated to the undulating caliche layer in one natural level at depths between 0.0 cm and 16 cm. All units were 1 m x 1 m, and all units were sampled for pollen. A total of 10 units were excavated, exposing an area of nine square meters.

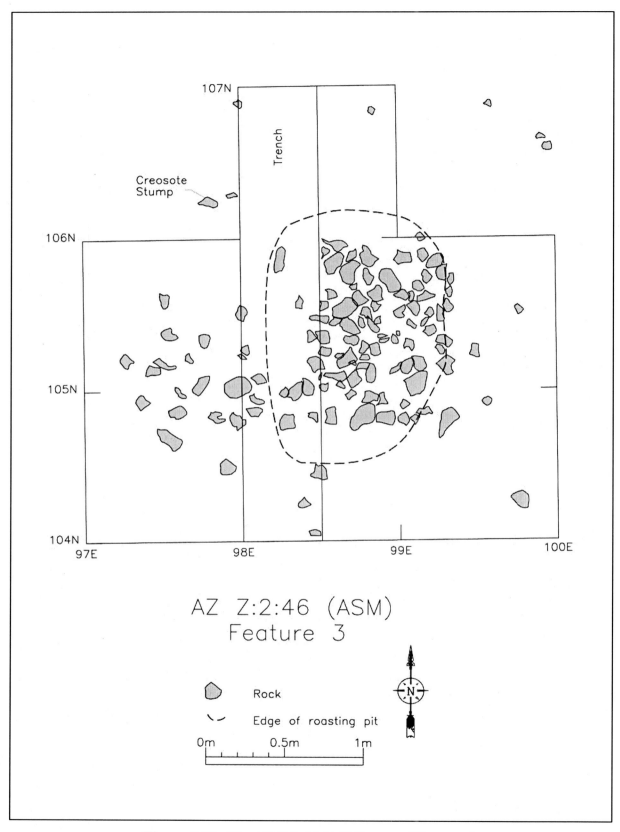

Figure 5.53. Site AZ Z:2:46 (ASM) map of Feature 3.

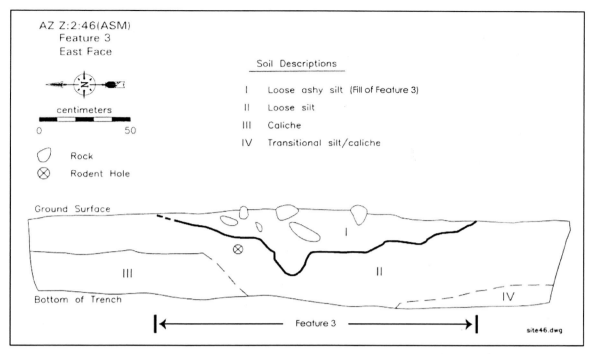

Figure 5.54. Site AZ Z:2:46 (ASM) profile of trench through Feature 3.

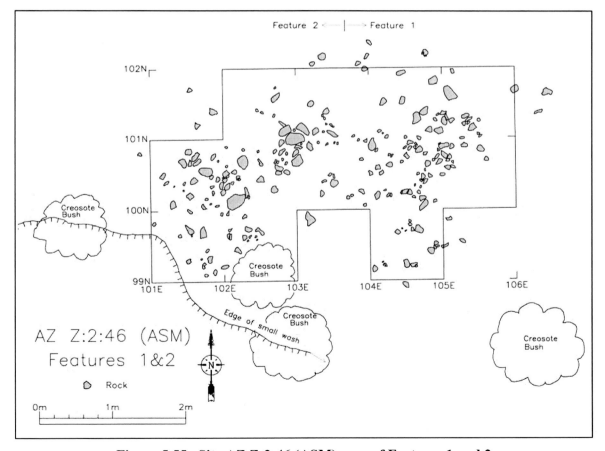

Figure 5.55. Site AZ Z:2:46 (ASM) map of Features 1 and 2.

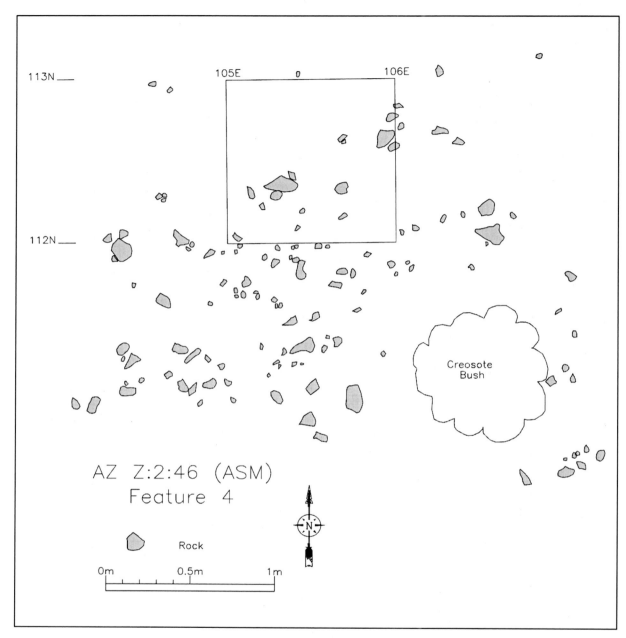

Figure 5.56. Site AZ Z:2:46 (ASM) map of Feature 4.

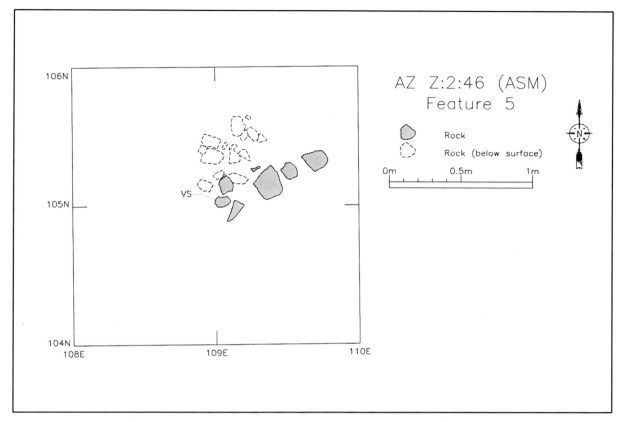

Figure 5.57. Site AZ Z:2:46 (ASM) map of Feature 5.

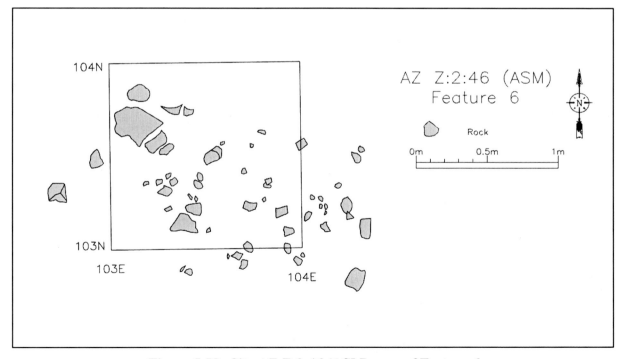

Figure 5.58. Site AZ Z:2:46 (ASM) map of Feature 6.

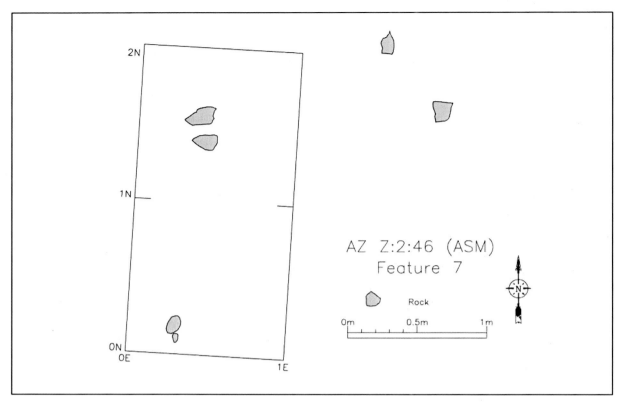

Figure 5.59. Site AZ Z:2:46 (ASM) map of Feature 7.

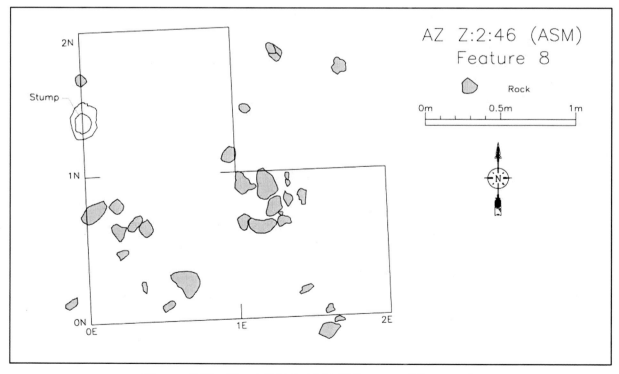

Figure 5.60. Site AZ Z:2:46 (ASM) map of Feature 8.

Summary

Site AZ Z:2:46 (ASM) was an activity area associated with a prehistoric trail segments. Summations for all excavated features are presented in Table 5.7. Cumulative artifact counts for site AZ Z:2:46 (ASM) were 1383 pieces of fire cracked rock weighing 233.5 kg, and 1 lithic artifact. The lithic artifact was not associated with a feature. Three charcoal samples were collected from Feature 3 and one charcoal sample was collected from Feature 2 and analyzed. Calibrated 2-sigma dates clustered around A.D. 550–620, placing the site firmly within the Pioneer period.

Table 5.7. Site AZ Z:2:46 (ASM) Feature Descriptions.
(FCR = fire-cracked rock)

Feature Number	Type	Dimensions	Artifacts	C-14 Samples Analyzed	Flotation Results	Pollen Results	Illustrations
1	Rock cluster	1.0 m x 2.0 m 20-cm depth	610 pieces (71 kg) FCR	None	None	None	Figs. 5.44 (photo) & 5.55 (plan view)
2	Rock cluster	1.0 m x 2.0 m 25-cm depth	613 pieces (110 kg) FCR	One C-14: 2 sigma range, A.D. 530–780	None	None	Figs. 5.45 (photo) & 5.55 (plan view)
3	Circular rock cluster	1.5-m dia 40-cm depth	144 pieces (48 kg) FCR	Three C-14: 2 sigma ranges, A.D. 230–620, A.D. 390–630, A.D. 550–710	Gramineae Prosopis	See Below*	Figs. 5.46 (photo), 5.53 (plan view) & 5.54 (profile)
4	Rock cluster	1.0 m x 3.0 m 2-cm depth	1.0 x 3.0 m 2 cm depth	None	None	None	Figs. 5.47 (photo) & 5.56 (plan view)
5	Rock Align-ment	0.8-m length 20-cm depth	None	None	None	None	Figs. 5.48 (photo) & 5.57 (plan view)
6	Rock cluster	1.0 m x 2.0 m 20-cm depth	16 pieces (5 kg) FCR	None	None	None	Figs. 5.49 (photo) & 5.58 (plan view)
7	Rock cluster	2.0 m x 3.0 m 27-cm depth	None	None	None	None	Figs. 5.50 (photo) & 5.59 (plan view)
8	Rock cluster	1.3 m x 2.5 m No depth	None	None	None	None	Figs. 5.51 (photo) & 5.60 (plan view)
9	Circular rock cluster	4.0-m dia 30-cm depth	None	None	None	None	Figs. 5.52 (photo)

* Feature 3 Pollen Results: Pinus, Juniperus, Quercus, Larrea, Prosopis, Ceridium, Cholla, Zea, Cheno-am, Asteraceae, Liguliflorae, Ambrosia, Poaceae, Brassicaceae, Sphaeralcea, Boerhaavia, Kallstroemia, Eriogonum, Euphorbiaceae, Plantago, Sunflower, Grass, Globemallow, Spiderling

CHAPTER 6

PLAIN AND DECORATED CERAMICS

Arleyn Simon, Kathleen Peterson,
Glen E. Rice, and Matthew Chamberlin

INTRODUCTION

The variety of ceramics recovered from the study area raises interesting issues regarding settlement, land use, and communication and trade routes. The study area bisects the uplands that parallel the Gila River as it flows to the south before bending to the southwest at the distinctive Gila Bend, now part of the Painted Rocks Reservoir. The broad swath of Sonoran desert that lies between the Gila River on the west and the Sierra Estrella to the east saw considerable movement of people throughout the prehistoric period as evidenced by the variety of ceramic types and their origins represented in the archaeological collections.

In this section, we present a brief overview of past archaeological ceramic studies for the study area, followed by a discussion of the methods used for the analysis of ceramics collected from sites identified in the current study and the analysis results. As the majority of these artifacts were surface collected, and the few sherds recovered from excavation were small in size, the analysis emphasizes classification and identification of mineral temper. Due to the small sizes of sherds, only a few specimens warranted discussion of vessel morphology.

Even though the total number of sherds is limited (n = 971), the results of the study indicate some temporal variation among the sites and also marked variation in the composition of major ceramic classes. These results indicate that these prehistoric locations were used by a variety of people as they exploited the area's natural resources and also traversed the desert as part of a far-reaching trade and communication network of trails (see Chapter 12).

BACKGROUND

In the early 20th Century, the archaeologists at Gila Pueblo made a concerted effort to define the nature and extent of the "Red-on-buff" cultures of the Gila Basin and Papaguería (Gladwin and Gladwin 1929a, b) as well as to determine both the eastern and western extent of this distinctive ceramic ware (Gladwin and Gladwin 1930a, 1935). They also determined that the buff wares were associated with sites of the Verde Valley (Gladwin and Gladwin 1930b). Haury later defined many of the Hohokam types through detailed study of collections from Snaketown on the Middle Gila River valley (1937, 1976) and noted similarities to other buff, or cream, colored ceramics in west Mexico. The Hohokam went through two major waves of expansion (Haury 1976; Masse 1982:73, 1980a, 1980b), one wave at the end of the Pioneer period (A.D. 500–600) and another at the transition between the Colonial and Sedentary periods (A.D. 850–950), followed by the transition to the Classic period with the decline of buff ware production and the use of ballcourts and the rise of platform mounds and the import of Salado polychrome ceramics (Bayman 2001; Carlson 1982; LeBlanc 1982).

Building on Rogers (1945) descriptions of Yuman pottery, Schroeder (1958, 1975, 1982) postulated that west Mexican influences led to the development of buff ware ceramic technology in southwestern Arizona and that these Hakataya cultural traditions are manifest in the Pioneer phase architectural and ceramic assemblages along the Gila River including those at Snaketown. Euler (1959, 1982) has discussed the distribution of prehistoric ancestral *Pai* groups along the Colorado River and into the deserts of Arizona and California; and denotes the somewhat overlapping concepts of Patayan (upland) and Laguish (Riverine) groups in the context of Schroeder's original concept of the Hakataya cultural area. The Pioneer period Hohokam used sedimentary alluvial clays, similar to such usage by the Riverine groups along the lower Colorado and Southern California (Euler 1959; Meighan 1959), whereas the upland desert groups tended to prefer, or have access to, residual clays, again with some parallels in the Hohokam core area.

Based on a combination of technological and stylistic attributes, a temporal and technological sequence for Lower Colorado Buff Wares was detailed by Waters (1982a, 1982b). Notably, the early types (Black Mesa Red-on-buff and Colorado Red-on-beige) exhibit broad line elements that may form curvilinear patterns with the addition of finger dots. Around A.D. 700 to 900, large narrow necked jars were made that exhibit the high "Colorado shoulder." Other forms include seed jars, and deep and shallow bowls. By A.D. 1000 to 1500, recurved rims were in favor, along with either stucco finish or fine-lined geometric designs. By A.D. 1500, only Colorado buff ware was common.

Spoerl (1979) details the ceramic assemblages of the Agua Fria settlements, including Gila plain, Wingfield plain, and Verde brown, and notes that these types had been spread from the Salt-Gila Basin into the Verde Valley (Breternitz 1960) and also to the south and west (Greenleaf 1975). Others note the presence of such types along the Lower Gila (Gregonis 2000; Masse 1982; Schroeder 1982), although some varieties in the Papagueria may be distinct from the Agua Fria phyllite tempered pottery. Of note, the Aravaipa variant of Red-on-buff from the Big Ditch Site on the Lower San Pedro (Masse 1982:86; Loomis 1980) was tempered with 2- to 3-mm platelets of phyllite, but does not appear to have been widely distributed.

Wasley (1960:259) reported that the platform mound at the Gatlin Site, located near Gila Bend, Arizona, was occupied during the Sacaton phase based on ceramic collections. Of the total sherd count from excavations (n = 20,645), 72 percent were Gila Plain, 14 percent were Sacaton Red-on-buff, and 13 percent were Buff (possibly undecorated portions of Red-on-buff vessels) (Wasley 1960:259). Of the remaining 1 percent of the sherds (Wasley 1960:259), a variety of wares and types were noted, including: Sacaton Smudged and Sacaton Red, and from earlier phases: Gila Butte Red-on-buff, Santa Cruz Red-on-buff and Rillito Red-on-brown. Intrusive trade wares included Valshni Red, Lower Colorado Buff Ware, Wingfield Plain, Deadmans Fugitive Red, Holbrook Black-on-white, Black Mesa Black-on-white, Deadmans Black-on-red, and (possibly) Tusayan Black-on-red. Variation within Sacaton Red-on-buff was noted with approximately 50 percent of the samples exhibiting a very thin white slip, rather than the usual buff wash. Polishing over the decoration, similar to the technique used on Rillito Red-on-brown sherds from the Tucson Basin, was noted on 13% of the Sacaton Red-on-buff sherds (Wasley 1960:259).

In a recent survey of the central Sauceda Valley (Gregonis 2000), a total of 599 sherds were collected as samples from over 14,000 acres. However, 159 of these were from a single Sacaton Red-on-buff vessel (partially reconstructible). The collection includes types that span the late Pioneer phase to the late 1800's and are indicative of Hohokam, Trincheras, and Patayan-Yuman connections to activities in the area. Ceramic types include those of the Gila Basin and the Salt River valley (Salt Red) as well as some from the Tucson Basin (Gregonis 2000:517–518). Mineral temper inclusions were identified using a 10-power lens (Gregonis 2000:521–522) and included the following categories: rounded or angular sand, schist (in buff wares), granitic sands or constituents, volcanic sands or constituents, a mix of granitic-organic (manure and sand), and also a combination of shell, quartz, and feldspar. Of the Gila Basin buff ware sherds, 55 cases had granitic temper and 187 were tempered with schist (including the reconstructible vessel with 159 sherds).

Detailed compositional analyses through petrography (Miksa 2000a, 2000b) and microprobe analysis (Abbott 2000) were undertaken of a subset of the Gila Basin buff ware sherds; 17 from the Sauceda Valley survey (Abbott 2000), 15 from the Gatlin Site, and four from the Gila Bend area; all were either Sacaton or Santa Cruz Red-on-buff. Results of this study (Abbott 2000) indicate that for the Sauceda Valley sherds, six samples are likely from the lower Gila, while nine are from the middle Gila, and two cases were classified as unknown. Distribution of the various buff wares throughout the valley is suggested to have occurred with activities along established shell trade routes spanning from the middle Gila to the lower Gila valley (Abbott 2000).

The archaeological investigations conducted around the Painted Rock Dam and Reservoir near Gila Bend have resulted in discussion of both middle Gila Basin buff wares and those from the Lower Colorado valley (Vogler 1976). Wasley and Johnson (1965) reported an abundance of Gila plain, Gila Bend variety sherds in the area; however, these may otherwise be identified as the Gila Bend series of the Lower Colorado Buff Wares (Schroeder 1967; Vogler 1976).

At the Rock Ball Court Site near Gila Bend (Wasley and Johnson 1965:12–13; Masse 1982:82) considerable variation in ceramic temper was noted. Temper identification noted that 75 percent of the Gila plain sherds exhibited little if any mica. Further, less than 25 percent of the Gila plain outside the core area is tempered with schist. This is especially the case for late Colonial and Sedentary period sites. However, the type description of Gila plain does not differentiate temper variants (Haury 1937; Masse 1982:78, 82). Regional variants of Gila plain likely exist, but have yet to be well defined.

A limited survey was conducted along the lower Gila between the Painted Rocks area and Blaisdell, AZ, by Vivian (1965) and reported the presence of intrusive buff wares from the Gila River along with pottery originating along the lower Colorado. More work is needed to understand the distributions of various wares and the influences of the Hohokam, Patayan (and/or Hakataya) on prehistoric use and movement through this area (Vogler 1976).

In summary, for the current study it is not surprising to find ceramic types and varieties attributable to the Hohokam core area, including a few ceramics from the Agua Fria and Verde Valleys, as well as the presence of Lower Colorado Buff Wares and other varieties of plain wares that were likely produced at villages along the middle Gila, in the Gila Bend area, or beyond in the deserts of Papageria. Indeed, this variety within otherwise sparse ceramic collections is indicative of the mobility of prehistoric groups between the Hohokam core area and the western deserts throughout the ceramic temporal sequence.

ANALYTICAL METHODS

All ceramics collected from the study area were analyzed (refer to Chapter 5 for discussion of sampling and collection strategies); equal emphasis was placed on collecting decorated and undecorated ceramics in the field, therefore the frequencies presented here are representative of what was available for collection at these sites.

In preparation for analysis ceramics were water washed, followed by an acid wash in dilute acetic acid (3–5%) (essentially vinegar, a nondestructive organic acid) to remove surface caliche, and water-rinsed to neutralize the acid wash. Natural bristle brushes were used to reduce damage to delicate painted surfaces. This analysis of all 971 ceramic sherds in the collection was conducted by Kathleen Peterson; the use of a single person removed any concern for recording variability among analysts. The sherds were classified using attributes of surface treatment and paste type and mineral temper (see Tables 6.3 and 6.4 below for complete list of attributes).

A fresh break was made on an edge of each sherd, and the temper constituencies of the sherd were identified using low-power (reflected-light) binocular microscopes. The analysis made use of the Abbott-Schaller temper categories identified for the Phoenix Basin (Abbott 1994; 2000), and temper categories that have proven useful in the analysis of ceramics from the Middle Gila (Peterson et al. 2000; Burton and Simon 2002).

For the ceramic temper analysis, the temper categories present in each sherd were coded using an *ordinal scale* (3 = major, >10%; 2 = minor, <10% and >1%; 1 = trace, <1%, 0 = 0%). Nineteen categories of minerals and rock types were used in the analysis, although some only occurred in a few cases; muscovite mica (n = 12), Phyllite schist (n = 4), Andesite (n = 1), and Rose Quartz (n = 1). These may be abundant in other locations, but were rare within this collection. However, the distinctive phyllite schist sherds may be typed as Wingfield Plain and are intrusive from the Agua Fria or Verde drainages to the north of the Salt River Valley. Several categories were totally absent in this data set (Camelback Granite, Squaw Peak Schist, and Basalt) and were not used in the quantitative analysis.

The categories based on surface treatment and paste differentiated between the Patayan (Lower Colorado Buff Ware) and Hohokam Ceramic Traditions, and the combination of surface treatment, paste and temper categories was used to make additional distinctions among production loci in both traditions.

THE HOHOKAM CERAMIC TRADITION OF THE GILA BEND AREA

The populations in the Gila Bend area produced their own variants of plain ware (Gila Plain, Gila Bend Variety) and Red-on-buff pottery (Abbott 2000b, Lindauer 1988, Teague 1981; Wasley and Johnson 1965) although they also obtained ceramics from other parts of the Hohokam region, especially the Middle Gila.

Plain ware ceramics produced on the Middle Gila are tempered with mica-schist. The plain wares produced in the Gila Bend area tend to have less mica schist pottery than the plain wares from the Middle Gila; this is recognized as a poor basis for differentiating ceramic types (Teague 1981:45; Wasley and Johnson 1965:27), and the assignment of sherds to one or the other variant is far from consistent (Teague 1981:46). However, plain wares produced in the Gila Bend area can be graded on a continuum ranging from Gila Plain (i.e. plain wares with mica-schist tempered pottery) to "an apparently otherwise identical pottery with virtually no mica temper" (Teague 1981:45), and a petrographic analysis shows that Gila Bend plain wares frequently have "small quantities of finely ground sherd temper as well" (Teague 1981:46). Unfortunately, plain wares and red wares in other parts of the Hohokam region, including the Florence area and the Cashion site in western Phoenix, also have sherd tempered plain pottery, so that single attribute is not in itself distinctive (Teague 1981:46).

Given these classificatory difficulties, we did not attempt to differentiate between the Middle Gila and Gila Bend varieties of mica-schist tempered potter (i.e. between the *Gila* and the *Gila Bend* varieties of Gila Plain). However, by recording the actual temper categories that were observed in the sherds, it is likely that the analysis registered some of the variability in the plain wares, such as the presence of sherd temper, and sherds lacking mica temper.

The populations of the Gila Bend area also produced their own variants of Red-on-buff pottery with different stylistic design attributes (Lindauer 1988) and different paste and temper constituents (Abbott 2000b:597). The red-on-buff sherds recovered as part of the State Route 85 project were extremely small in size, and design analyses could not be performed. Petrographic and micro-probe analyses conducted and reported by Abbott (2000b:597) found that the Red-on-buff sherds produced in the Gila Bend area had "glassy mafic volcanics" that were more heavily weathered than the volcanics that might be found in Red-on-buff sherds of the Middle Gila, and the pieces of crushed mica schist were "less foliated, more fine-grained, and richer in cholorite and biotite" than the mica schists of the Middle Gila. Red-on-buff ceramics from the Gila Bend area also tend to have less caliche than the variety made in the Middle Gila. While these findings hold considerable promise for the ability eventually to distinguish between Middle Gila and Gila Bend varieties of Red-on-Buff ceramics at a macroscopic level (without the use of thin sections or micro-probes) we did not attempt to implement such an analysis in this study. However, the modal temper analysis did find and was successful in recording considerable variability in the constituents of Red-on-buff pottery.

THE LOWLAND PATAYAN CERAMIC TRADITION
(LOWER COLORADO BUFF WARE)

Very little field research has been conducted regarding the chronology of the Lowland Patayan tradition, and much of the current temporal placement of Patayan ceramic types is based on surface collections and stylistic parallels to the Hohokam red-on-buff sequence. Malcolm Rogers conducted extensive surveys of Patayan sites in southwestern Arizona but did not publish his findings. Various surveys have been conducted over the years, but the reports tend to be merely descriptive in nature, and have produced only a small amount of data on the history of the Lowland Patayan (McGuire and Schiffer 1982).

The first classification for the typing of Patayan ceramics was developed by Rogers, using data that had been collected from trails, caves and shrines along southeastern California and southwestern Arizona (McGuire and Schiffer 1982). Rogers devised a system of three numbered periods, using intrusive Hohokam sherds to date these periods as Patayan I, A.D. 500–1000; Patayan II, A.D. 1000–1500, and Patayan III, A.D. 1500–1800 (Waters 1982).

Waters identifies five Lower Colorado Buff ware plainware types during the Patayan II period, beginning approximately around A.D. 1000 to 1500, and extending into the Patayan III time period (Waters 1982). In the SR 85 ceramic assemblage we have identified the presence of two types; Palomas Buff and Tumco Buff, both of which were manufactured within the Patayan II period of time.

Palomas Buff pottery was produced using the paddle-and-anvil method for thinning and shaping the vessel (Waters 1982). The paste contains particles of fine, rounded quartz and is usually very pink to tan in color. Often there was no carbon streaking visible in the sherds that we examined. Palomas Buff may or may not have a scum coat treatment applied to the surface.

A scum coat is a surface treatment found on many Patayan, or Lower Colorado ceramics. The cream-to-white colored film often gives a powdery or chalky appearance to the vessel; it is derived from mineral matter that has been brought to the surface during the firing process (Waters 1982). Several sherds of this variety were found at site T:14:113. This type of surface treatment is especially common on Colorado Buff ware from the California deserts (Waters 1982).

Waters (1982) notes that Palomas Buff was produced frequently along the Lower Gila River between Gila Bend and Yuma, although a more specific production area is not known. However, the type can be found as far south as Sierra Pinacate, Sonora and as far north as the Kofa and Little Horn Mountains.

Typically Palomas Buff is found only in Arizona, and is thought to date to the Patayan II and III Periods, from A.D. 1000 to post-1800, and "is common on historic sites" (Waters, 1982:293, also see p. 568).

Tumco Buff ware was also produced using the paddle and anvil method, and typically has a surface color of pink to buff to light gray (Waters 1982). A thin cream-colored scum coat may also have been applied. This scum coat often has a chalky appearance. The specimens in our collection often had a grayish-colored paste that contained unpulverized red-orange clay pellets. Tumco dates to the Patayan II period, between A.D. 1000 and 1500 (Waters 1982:290), placing it in the time range of both the Sedentary and Classic periods of the Hohokam Tradition.

Description of a Partially Reconstructed Vessel from AZ T:14:92 (ASM)

Within the total collected assemblage of 971 sherds, only one partially reconstructible vessel was recovered. It was found during the collection of surface artifacts, and consists of nine conjoinable sherds collected from site AZ T:14:92 forming the neck and upper body of a wide-mouthed jar (Figure 6.1). Two other conjoinable sherds also appear to have come from this same vessel.

The vessel is a large jar, 11.2 cm at the widest portion of the opening, narrowing to a diameter of 9.8 cm at the orifice interior. The paste color is consistent throughout the vessel, a very pink, fine paste with small clay pellets. These clay inclusions are primarily red, with some occasional fine particles of caliche. We have identified this temper type as Palomas Buff, a variety of Lower Colorado buff ware. There is no carbon streak in any of the sherds. The rim of the jar is approximately 6 mm thick and has a slight recurve on its edge, a characteristic of the Patayan II–III period ceramics. Palomas buff dates to both periods, and this vessel could have been produced between A.D. 1000 and the late 1800s.

The surface treatment of the jar is very characteristic of a Lower Colorado Buff ware vessel, undecorated but with distinct wiping marks. It is pink in color and does not have a "scum coat" often found in Lower Colorado buff wares.

The field work recovered nearly the entire ceramic assemblage present at the site; the site was located on a Pleistocene surface of calcite and desert pavement, had essentially little to no depth, all surface artifacts were collected, and the areas around the rock features were fully excavated. Specimen Numbers 3 and 4 comprise the entire collection of sherds that make up the partially reconstructed vessel from this site. No other Lower Colorado Buff ware sherds from this site can be assigned to the same temper categories as Specimens 3 and 4. While there is a possibility that a single vessel could have been made from two different types of pastes or temper varieties, it seems unlikely because there were so few sherds found at the site—far too few to comprise a complete vessel.

From this we surmise that only a portion of the vessel was ever actually at the site, leaving open two possibilities; the parent vessel broke at the site and the bottom portion was taken away, or only the rim portion was brought to the site.

THE ANALYSIS OF THE CERAMIC ASSEMBLAGES

General Ceramic Ware Categories

The total collection of 971 sherds is summarized on a site by site basis in Table 6.1 with respect to the three major ceramic wares; Hohokam Plain Ware (undecorated), Hohokam Buff Ware, and Lower Colorado Buff Ware (LCBW). There are marked differences among the individual site

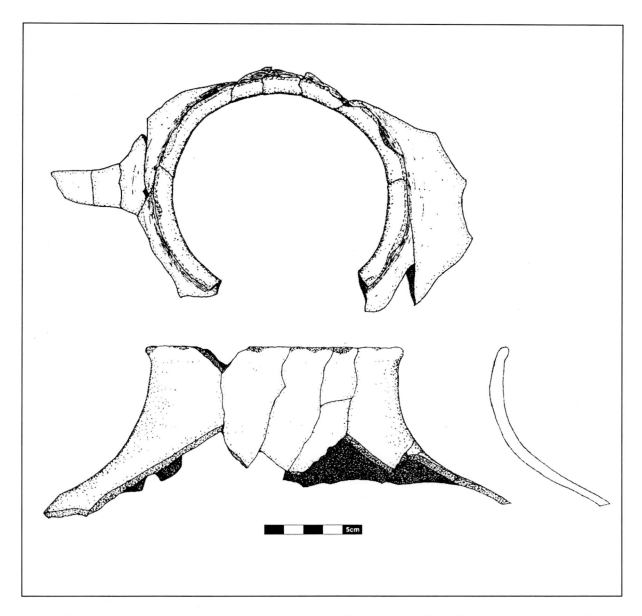

Figure 6.1. Reconstructed rim and neck of a Palomas buff jar from AZ T:14:92 (ASM), specimen numbers 3 and 4. (Drawing by Ryan Peterson.)

collections, which are illustrated when these are ordered by decreasing amounts of undecorated and increasing amounts of Lower Colorado Buff Ware (Table 6.1).

Some of these differences are related to site function. For instance, AZ T:10:86 is a prehistoric agricultural field on the alluvial terrace of the Gila River, and is near several moderate size Hohokam villages, and it is not unexpected that the assemblage has high frequencies of Plain Wares. The other three sites consist of rock features that are either clearly associated with trails visible on the desert pavement (AZ T:14:92) or are interpreted as having once been associated with trails that are no longer visible because the sites were not located on a surface with desert pavement. The function of the rock features is not clear, although it is possible they represent trailside shrines at which travelers occasionally deposited ceramic sherds.

Table 6.1. Frequencies and Percentages of Undecorated Ceramics and Buff Wares by Site

Site Number	Counts				Percentages			
	Un-decorated	Hohokam Buff Ware	Lower Colorado buff Ware	Total	Un-decorated	Hohokam Buff Ware	Lower Colorado buff Ware	Total
T:10:86	149	28	5	182	81.9	15.4	2.7	100.0
T:14:92	115	117	8	240	47.9	48.8	3.3	100.0
T:14:94	108	204	182	494	21.9	41.3	36.8	100.0
T:14:113	2		53	55	3.6		96.4	100.0
Total	374	349	248	971	38.5	35.9	25.5	100.0

Table 6.2. Frequencies and Percentages of Ceramic Class (Surface Treatment) by Site

Site Number	Plain	Plain/ Smudged	Red/ Plain	Buff, plain	Buff, wash	Red-on-buff	LCBW (caliche)	LCBW (clay)	Count Total
T:10:86	130	7	12	8	8	12	2	3	182
T:14:92	109		6	11	82	24	4	4	240
T:14:94	78	4	20	24	86	94	10	172	488
T:14:113	1		1				20	33	55
Total	318	11	39	43	176	130	36	212	965
									Percent Total
T:10:86	71.4	3.8	6.6	4.4	4.4	6.6	1.1	1.6	100.0
T:14:92	45.4		2.5	4.6	34.2	10.0	1.7	1.7	100.0
T:14:94	16.0	0.8	4.1	4.9	17.6	19.3	2.0	35.2	100.0
T:14:113	1.8		1.8				36.4	60.0	100.0
Percent	33.0	1.1	4.0	4.5	18.2	13.5	3.7	22.0	100.0

Note: Site T:4:94 also had 5 sherds of indeterminate surface treatment (badly eroded) and 1 sherd with Red Slipped surface; with these 6 additional sherds, the total count is 971. These six sherds were not included in the tests of association. (Pearson Chi-Square = 587.27, *df* = 21, *p* = .000; Phi = .780, *p* = .000)

The interesting property of these three trail-associated sites is that each is so considerably different from the others. The ceramic assemblage at AZ T:14:92 is split between Hohokam Plain Ware and Hohokam Buff Ware, with only minor frequencies of Lower Colorado Buff Ware.

Site T:14:94, which has the largest sherd count, has substantial numbers of Hohokam Buff Ware, followed by Lower Colorado Buff Ware. This site exhibits associations both with the Hohokam core area to the east and the Lower Colorado to the southwest. In contrast, the Site T:14:113 ceramic collection consists almost completely of Lower Colorado Buff Ware, indicating ties to the Lower Gila and Colorado Rivers to the southwest.

More detail is provided in Table 6.2, where the wares are divided into categories of surface treatment and paste color, and the counts and percentages can be compared on a site-by-site basis. Chi-squared tests of association (Table 6.2) indicated that differences among the site collection proportions are statistically significant.

Among undecorated wares, the majority are Plain wares, although some Plain/Smudged is present at two of the sites. Red/Plain sherds (those with a red but unslipped surface) were present at all four sites, but in small numbers (less than six percent of the total). Only one sherd with a Red slipped surface was recovered from Site T:4:94.

Hohokam Buff Wares are divided between those with an undecorated buff surface, those with a buff wash, and those with red paint decoration on a buff wash (Red-on-buff). Site T:14:94 has slightly more decorated than undecorated Hohokam Buff Wares.

Among Lower Colorado Buff Ware collections, a preliminary distinction was made between sherds with caliche in the temper and those with clay temper. Site T:14:94 had almost exclusive clay tempered Lower Colorado Buff Ware with clay temper and only a few sherds of Lower Colorado Buff Ware with caliche temper. At Site T:14:113 both variants of Lower Colorado Buff Ware occur in appreciable amounts.

The distribution of ceramic classes was next examined by features within sites (Table 6.3). The sherds from Site T:10:86 were all derived from surface collections; several buried ash lens features were excavated but these were not associated with ceramics. The collection is dominated by Plain ware with lesser amounts of Red/Plain and Hohokam Red-on-buff among other less common types. Only a few sherds of Lower Colorado Buff Ware were present.

At Site T:14:92 (Table 6.3), the majority of the assemblage is from the surface collection. Feature 1, a cluster of rocks, was associated with a relatively large number of sherds, the majority of which are Hohokam Buff ware, including Red-on-buff, surface wash, and plain. A second rock feature (Feature 9) produced only one undecorated sherd. Lower Colorado Buff Ware sherds are rare at this site.

The majority of the ceramics from Site T:14:94 (Table 6.3) were recovered from Features 1 through 5; following excavation these features appeared as essentially one large scatter of cobbles and rocks, and we have for that reason treated the associated ceramic assemblage as a single unit. Lower Colorado Buff Ware sherds are the most abundant, followed by Hohokam Buff Ware and Plain Ware. This context has the most variation in ceramic classes of any within the project. Feature 8 had only 23 sherds and most of these were Plain ware, but a few Hohokam Buff Ware and two Lower Colorado Buff Ware are present.

The Site T:14:113 collection (Table 6.3) is overwhelmingly Lower Colorado Buff Ware, although more clay tempered than caliche tempered. Only two other plain ware sherds were recovered.

Geologic Sources of Temper Minerals

Although an exhaustive geological reconnaissance of the broader area was beyond the scope of the present project, analysis of mineral temper constituents of the ceramics collected will provide useful baseline data for further directed studies of potential pottery resources. The mineral temper analysis used in this study is directed with that goal in mind.

Detailed reconnaissance of the area between the Estrella Mountains and Gila Bend and other neighboring mountains will be needed to characterize the various geologic formations and the

Table 6.3. Frequencies and Percentages of Ceramic Class (Surface Treatment) by Site and Feature

Site Number	Feature Number	None (eroded)	Plain	Plain/Smudged	Red Slipped	Red-Plain	HHK Buff, plain	HHK Buff, wash	HHK Red-on-buff	LCBW, (caliche)	LCBW, (clay)	Total
T:10:86	Non Feature		130	7		12	8	8	12	2	3	182
	Total		130	7		12	8	8	12	2	3	182
	Percent	0.0	71.4	3.8	0.0	6.6	4.4	4.4	6.6	1.1	1.6	100.0
T:14:92	Non Feature		86			4	3	23	3	3	4	126
	Feature 1		22			2	8	59	21	1		113
	Feature 9		1									1
	Total		109			6	11	82	24	4	4	240
	Percent	0.0	45.4	0.0	0.0	2.5	4.6	34.2	10.0	1.7	1.7	100.0
T:14:94	Features 1-5	5	65	4	1	20	24	83	89	8	172	471
	Feature 8		13					3	5	2	0	23
	Total	5	78	4	1	20	24	86	94	10	172	494
	Percent	1.0	15.8	0.8	0.2	4.0	4.9	17.4	19.0	2.0	34.8	100.0
T:14:113	Feature 1		1			1				20	33	55
	Total		1			1				20	33	55
	Percent	0.0	1.8	0.0	0.0	1.8	0.0	0.0	0.0	36.4	60.0	100.0
	Total	5	78	4	1	20	24	86	94	10	172	494
	Percent	1.0	15.8	0.8	0.2	4.0	4.9	17.4	19.0	2.0	34.8	100.0

weathered rock fragments and minerals that have washed down from their slopes. An important corresponding analysis of mineral temper in the ceramics from the area will facilitate narrowing the field of possibilities as to what constituents were actually chosen for temper by prehistoric potters and whether these ceramics were made locally or brought into the area from farther afield.

Given the location of the north end of the study area in proximity to the Sierra Estrella, it was expected that the Estrella Gneiss might be an abundant source of temper if pottery were locally made.

Estrella Gneiss is also found at the west end of South Mountain (Abbott 2000; Miksa 2000a, 2000b). However, the identification of Estrella Gneiss as temper does not at this time preclude other possible production locations in the vicinity of the Estrella Mountains, either on the east or west slope.

In a recent geological reconnaissance of the Middle Gila River study area, Burton and Simon (2002) also collected samples from the west side of the Estrella Mountains in the area of Waterman Wash. In this sample, minerals are the result of weathering of the Estrella Gneiss and include abundant slightly rounded quartz and translucent to chalky feldspar with minor amounts of black amphibole and biotite mica, as well as occasional epidote; mafic minerals are a minor constituent. Two other samples from the southwest slope of the Estrella Mountains (Burton and Simon 2002: Estrella 5 and 6) had abundant quartz and feldspar with minor amounts of either biotite, hornblende, magnetite, or a trace of muscovite schist.

Modal Temper Analysis

A modal analysis approach was chosen for the temper analysis of the ceramic collection in which all 971 sherds were characterized by examination of a freshly broken edge through a reflected-light microscope. Modal analysis is used extensively in geological studies and has been successfully applied to large scale archaeological ceramic studies such as those of Roosevelt Platform Mound Study (Simon et al. 1998; Simon 1998) and the Pima-Maricopa Irrigation Project on the Gila River Indian Community (Eiselt and Woodson 2002; Peterson et al. 2002; Burton and Simon 2002).

For the ceramic temper analysis, the sherds were classified by *fine paste* and also the *mineral temper* according to an *ordinal scale* (3 = major, >10%; 2 = minor, <10% and >1%; 1 = trace, <1%, 0 = 0%). Nineteen mineral categories were included (Table 6.4) in the statistical analysis and the number of cases with each constituent summarized. Some free minerals were quite rare in this data set and only occurred in a few cases; muscovite mica (n = 12), Phyllite schist (n = 4), Andesite (n = 1), and Rose Quartz (n = 1). These may be abundant in other locations, but were rare within this collection. However, the distinctive phyllite schist sherds may be typed as Wingfield Plain and are intrusive from the Agua Fria or Verde drainages to the north of the Salt River Valley. The following categories were dropped as they were totally absent in this data set: Camelback Granite, Squaw Peak Schist, and Basalt.

After the initial univariate frequencies and proportions were tabulated and examined (Table 6.4) for each variable, a multivariate approach was used in the next stage of statistical analysis because mineral temper often occurs in combinations and rarely as single categories of minerals or rock fragments. Using SPSS 11.5 statistical software (http://www.spss.com), the data file was used in a Ward's method hierarchical cluster analysis to identify groupings within the data. The first stage of the process was to cluster the variables to discern possible relationships among these. Examination of the resultant dendrogram (Figure 6.2) shows that the least frequent variables are grouped near the top of the diagram, whereas the more frequently occurring variables separate out into pairs and subgroups of minerals in the lower portion of the dendrogram. Interestingly, the South Mountain Granodiorite is closely associated with Quartz-banded with feldspar and also the occurrence of Estrella Gneiss. Sand and mafic minerals share an association as do the occurrence of caliche and clay. Quartz is associated with white feldspar and the fine paste is most closely associated with micaceous schist.

The next step in the multivariate analysis was to conduct a Ward's method hierarchical cluster analysis of the individual ceramic cases (n = 971) again using the variables listed in Table 6.4. The resulting dendrogram (Figure 6.3) illustrates the grouping of the 971 cases into 15 major clusters. Individual cluster assignments for Temper Cluster 15, and a more finely divided version, Temper Cluster 30, are available upon request from the Office of Cultural Resource Managenent,

Table 6.4. Definitions of Mineral Categories Used in Ceramic Temporal Analysis

Label	Definition	Counts					Percent				
		Absent 0% (0)	Trace <1% (1)	Minor <10% (2)	Major >10% (3)	Total	Absent 0% (0)	Trace <1% (1)	Minor <10% (2)	Major >10% (3)	Total
Fine	Fine Paste	673	0	12	286	971	69.3	0.0	1.2	29.5	100.0
Ms	Micaceous Schist	570	66	44	291	971	58.7	6.8	4.5	30.0	100.0
Fw	Feldspar - white	671	89	76	135	971	69.1	9.2	7.8	13.9	100.0
Q	Quartz	368	233	146	224	971	37.9	24.0	15.0	23.1	100.0
Cl	Clay temper	722	53	43	153	971	74.4	5.5	4.4	15.8	100.0
Ca	Caliche	548	207	100	116	971	56.4	21.3	10.3	11.9	100.0
Mf	Mafic minerals (ferro-magnesians)	691	165	52	63	971	71.2	17.0	5.4	6.5	100.0
Sa	Sand	840	21	22	88	971	86.5	2.2	2.3	9.1	100.0
EG	Estrella Gneiss	884	39	12	36	971	91.0	4.0	1.2	3.7	100.0
SM	South Mountain Granodiorite	946	0	0	25	971	97.4	0.0	0.0	2.6	100.0
Qb	Quartz - banded with feldspar	914	11	17	29	971	94.1	1.1	1.8	3.0	100.0
ST	Sherd/Tuff	881	62	17	11	971	90.7	6.4	1.8	1.1	100.0
Is	Indeterminate Schist	947	8	1	15	971	97.5	0.8	0.1	1.5	100.0
Bm	Biotite Mica	893	64	14	0	971	92.0	6.6	1.4	0.0	100.0
Qi	Quartz - iron stained	935	24	4	8	971	96.3	2.5	0.4	0.8	100.0
Fp	Feldspar - pink, tan	946	19	4	2	971	97.4	2.0	0.4	0.2	100.0
Mm	Muscovite mica	959	6	2	4	971	98.8	0.6	0.2	0.4	100.0
Ph	Phyllite schist	967	0	0	4	971	99.6	0.0	0.0	0.4	100.0
An	Andesite	970	0	1	0	971	99.9	0.0	0.1	0.0	100.0
Qr	Quartz - rose	970	1	0	0	971	99.9	0.1	0.0	0.0	100.0

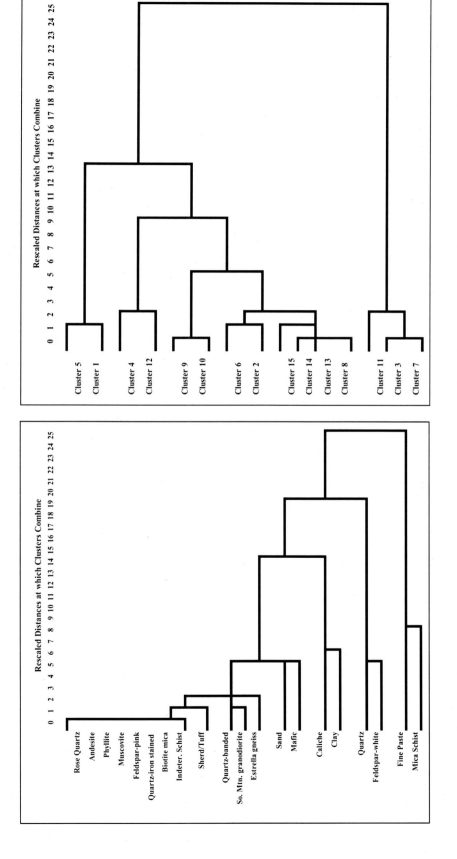

Figure 6.3. **Dendrogram illustrating the results of Ward's method of hierarchical clustering for 971 sherd cases using the temper (and fine paste) categories.**

Figure 6.2. **Dendrogram illustrating the results of Ward's method of hierarchical clustering on ceramic temper variables.**

Arizona State University. The correspondence between the two levels of division is presented as Table 6.12 at the end of this chapter. Given the relatively limited number of sherds in this study, only the Temper Cluster 15 dendrogram will be discussed in detail in this section, recognizing that with other future studies in the area, it may be possible to develop more robust sample sizes for the finer divisions and to develop meaningful inferences as to origination of the classified materials.

Multivariate Analysis of Variance (MANOVA) was conducted to test the validity of differences among the Temper Cluster 15 assignments. Using the full factorial model under General Linear Models (GLM) in SPSS, the results of the MANOVA indicate that differences among the clusters are statistically significant (Pillai's Trace: $F = 37.804$, $df = 280, 13300$; $p = .000$). The observed power of the test is robust given the number of variables and sample size (Observed Power (at alpha = .05) = 1.000).

For further detailed reference, a Multivariate Analysis of Variance (MANOVA) was also conducted to test the validity of differences among the Temper Cluster 30 assignments (data available at Office of Cultural Resource Management, Arizona State University). Using the full factorial model under General Linear Models (GLM) in SPSS, the results of the MANOVA indicate that differences among the clusters are statistically significant (Pillai's Trace: $F = 24.904$, $df = 580, 18820$; $p = .000$). The observed power of the test is robust given the number of variables and sample size (Observed Power (at alpha = .05) = 1.000).

The distribution of the Temper Cluster 15 assignments by ceramic class (surface treatment and paste) is presented in Table 6.5. The Temper Cluster 15 summary statistics are arranged in dendrogram order (refer to Figure 6.2). Percentages were calculated for group membership by Ceramic Class (column totals) and also for Temper Cluster 15 membership within Ceramic Class (row totals).

Based on these summary statistics (Table 6.5), it is apparent that Clusters 5 and 1 are predominantly Lower Colorado Buff Ware, whereas at the opposite end of the dendrogram, Clusters 11, 3, and 7 are predominantly Hohokam Buff Ware. The Cluster groupings in between represent the various combinations of plain and red wares, as well as occasional buff ware sherds.

In order to compare the 15 temper clusters, it is necessary to know the major characteristics of each one. To accomplish this, a series of summary statistics were calculated for the various clusters to measure and rank the abundance of the most common temper variables within each, and the results are given in Table 6.6. The mean value, median value and sum total for each of 20 temper variables were calculated for each of the 15 clusters. All three of these measures were assessed as indicators of abundance of temper. The variables were then ranked using the sum total of sherds possessing each individual temper type (Table 6.6). While this table provides the detailed information on the relative abundances of the variables, a summary of this information is provided in a descriptive format in Table 6.7 where the first two to four highest ranked variables are listed in descending order of abundance. From this description, it can easily be seen how the major paste and temper recipes for different wares breakout out accordingly. The Lower Colorado Buff wares are predominantly clay tempered, although some have abundant quartz and others abundant caliche. The next three large cluster groups (groups 2, 3 and 4) are variations of predominantly undecorated or red ware ceramics having mica schist, sand, or less abundant combinations of temper variables. These groups include such traditional categories as Wingfield, and the Gila Bend and Gila varieties of Gila Plain. The South Mountain Granodiorite and Estrella Gneiss groups separate out well, with the latter closely associated with groups that have weathered individual minerals, rather than composite rock fragments. The clusters (15, 14, 13 and 8) in this group are among the types that traditionally would be called Salt Variety of Gila Plain. The final group is of fine paste wares, that are predominantly tempered with either mica schist, caliche, or quartz and other constituents, and these temper categories are usually associated with Hohokam Buff Ware.

Table 6.5. Frequencies and Percentages of Ceramic Class (Surface Treatment) by Temper

Ceramic Class	Temper Cluster 15 Frequencies															
	5	1	4	12	9	10	6	2	15	14	13	8	11	3	7	Total
None (eroded)	1		2				1						1			5
Plain	2		19	69	23	39	29	24	18	19	25	44	2	1	4	318
Plain/Smudged	1				1		3			2	2	2				11
Red Slipped							1									1
Red/Plain	1		3	1	6	6	6	4	1	2	1	3			5	39
Buff, plain			6	1			1	2		2		1	24	1	5	43
Buff, wash	3		19		2	1	14	6			1	1	86	18	25	176
Red-on-buff	2		22	2	2	3	7	4				2	56	17	13	130
LCBW						2	3	10				1			20	36
LCBW (clay)	103	66	6		1		9	8				3		4	12	212
Total	113	66	77	73	34	52	74	58	19	25	29	57	169	41	84	971

Ceramic Class	Temper Cluster 15 Percentages by Ceramic Class (Row Percentages)															
	5	1	4	12	9	10	6	2	15	14	13	8	11	3	7	Total
None (eroded)	20.0		40.0				20.0						20.0			100.0
Plain	0.3		6.0	21.8	7.3	12.3	9.1	7.6	5.7	6.0	7.9	13.9	0.6	0.3	1.3	100.0
Plain/Smudged	9.1				9.1		27.3			18.2	18.2	18.2				100.0
Red Slipped							100.0									100.0
Red/Plain	2.6		7.7	2.6	15.4	15.4	15.4	10.3	2.6	5.1	2.6	7.7			12.8	100.0
Buff, plain			14.0	2.3			2.3	4.7		4.7		2.3	55.8	2.3	11.6	100.0
Buff, wash	1.7		10.8		1.1	0.6	8.0	3.4			0.6	0.6	48.9	10.2	14.2	100.0
Red-on-buff	1.5		16.9	1.5	1.5	2.3	5.4	3.1				1.5	43.1	13.1	10.0	100.0
LCBW						5.6	8.3	27.8				2.8			55.6	100.0
LCBW (clay)	48.6	31.1	2.8		0.5		4.2	3.8				1.4		1.9	5.7	100.0
Total	11.6	6.8	7.9	7.5	3.5	5.4	7.6	6.0	2.0	2.6	3.0	5.9	17.4	4.2	8.7	100.0

Ceramic Class	Temper Cluster 15 Percentages by Cluster (Column Percentages)															
	5	1	4	12	9	10	6	2	15	14	13	8	11	3	7	Total
None (eroded)	0.9		2.6				1.4						0.6			0.5
Plain	0.9		24.7	94.5	67.6	75.0	39.2	41.4	94.7	76.0	86.2	77.2	1.2	2.4	4.8	32.7
Plain/Smudged	0.9					1.9	4.1			8.0	6.9	3.5				1.1
Red Slipped							1.4									0.1
Red/Plain	0.9		3.9	1.4	17.6	11.5	8.1	6.9	5.3	8.0	3.4	5.3			6.0	4.0
Buff, plain	0.0		7.8	1.4			1.4	3.4		8.0		1.8	14.2	2.4	6.0	4.4
Buff, wash	2.7		24.7		5.9	1.9	18.9	10.3			3.4	1.8	50.9	43.9	29.8	18.1
Red-on-buff	1.8		28.6	2.7	5.9	5.8	9.5	6.9				3.5	33.1	41.5	15.5	13.4
LCBW						3.8	4.1	17.2				1.8			23.8	3.7
LCBW (clay)	92.0	100.0	7.8		2.9		12.2	13.8				5.3		9.8	14.3	21.9
Total	100	100	100	100	100	100	100	100	100	100	100	100	100	100	100	100

Table 6.6. Summary Statistics for the Temper Cluster 15 Assignments

Clus15	Measure	Fine	Ms	Fw	Q	Cl	Ca	Mf	Sa	EG	SM	Qb	ST	Is	Bm	Qi	Fp	Mm	Ph	An	Qr	Count
5	mean	0.0	0.1	0.3	1.0	2.7	0.5	0.2	0.0	0.0	0.0	0.0	0.0	0.1	0.1	0.0	0.0	0.0	0.0	0.0	0.0	
5	median	0.0	0.0	0.0	1.0	3.0	0.0	0.0	0.0	0.0	0.0	0.0	0.0	0.0	0.0	0.0	0.0	0.0	0.0	0.0	0.0	
5	sum	0	7	29	97	277	47	22	4	0	0	0	0	6	13	2	2	1	0	0	0	113
5	rank			4	2	1	3															
1	mean	0.0	0.0	0.0	1.5	2.9	2.5	1.3	0.0	0.0	0.0	0.0	0.1	0.0	0.1	0.1	0.0	0.0	0.0	0.0	0.0	
1	median	0.0	0.0	0.0	1.0	3.0	3.0	1.0	0.0	0.0	0.0	0.0	0.0	0.0	0.0	0.0	0.0	0.0	0.0	0.0	0.0	
1	sum	0	1	3	92	183	156	81	0	0	0	0	8	0	6	4	3	0	0	0	0	66
1	rank				3	1	2	4														
4	mean	0.2	2.9	0.2	0.8	0.3	0.7	0.3	0.1	0.1	0.0	0.1	0.1	0.0	0.0	0.1	0.0	0.0	0.0	0.0	0.0	
4	median	0.0	3.0	0.0	1.0	0.0	0.0	0.0	0.0	0.0	0.0	0.0	0.0	0.0	0.0	0.0	0.0	0.0	0.0	0.0	0.0	
4	sum	12	223	12	63	25	54	21	5	6	0	5	11	1	3	6	2	0	0	0	0	77
4	rank		1		2	4	3															
12	mean	0.0	3.0	2.3	2.5	0.0	0.2	0.4	0.0	0.6	0.0	0.0	0.0	0.2	0.0	0.0	0.1	0.0	0.0	0.0	0.0	
12	median	0.0	3.0	3.0	3.0	0.0	0.0	0.0	0.0	0.0	0.0	0.0	0.0	0.0	0.0	0.0	0.0	0.0	0.0	0.0	0.0	
12	sum	0	219	167	186	0	11	28	0	42	0	0	0	15	3	0	4	0	0	2	0	73
12	rank		1	3	2					4												
9	mean	0.0	0.1	0.1	1.8	0.1	0.2	0.4	2.8	0.1	0.0	0.1	0.0	0.0	0.2	0.0	0.2	0.0	0.0	0.0	0.0	
9	median	0.0	0.0	0.0	2.0	0.0	0.0	0.0	3.0	0.0	0.0	0.0	0.0	0.0	0.0	0.0	0.0	0.0	0.0	0.0	0.0	
9	sum	0	5	5	62	2	6	15	94	3	0	2	0	1	8	1	6	1	0	0	0	34
9	rank				2			3	1													
10	mean	0.0	0.4	2.5	2.6	0.0	0.4	0.3	2.8	0.0	0.1	0.8	0.0	0.1	0.2	0.3	0.0	0.0	0.0	0.0	0.0	
10	median	0.0	0.0	3.0	3.0	0.0	0.0	0.0	3.0	0.0	0.0	0.0	0.0	0.0	0.0	0.0	0.0	0.0	0.0	0.0	0.0	
10	sum	0	20	128	135	1	23	15	147	2	3	44	0	3	10	15	2	1	0	0	0	52
10	rank			3	2				1			4										
6	mean	0.0	0.3	0.1	0.6	0.2	0.5	0.2	0.2	0.0	0.2	0.3	0.4	0.3	0.1	0.0	0.0	0.2	0.2	0.0	0.0	
6	median	0.0	0.0	0.0	0.5	0.0	0.0	0.0	0.0	0.0	0.0	0.0	0.0	0.0	0.0	0.0	0.0	0.0	0.0	0.0	0.0	
6	sum	0	19	10	47	13	38	15	13	0	15	22	27	19	6	3	1	13	12	0	0	74
6	rank				1		2					4	3									

Continued

Table 6.6. Summary Statistics for the Temper Cluster 15 Assignments *(Continued).*

Clus15	Measure	Fine	Ms	Fw	Q	Cl	Ca	Mf	Sa	EG	SM	Qb	ST	Is	Bm	Qi	Fp	Mm	Ph	An	Qr	Count
2	mean	0.0	0.0	0.7	1.6	0.2	2.7	0.9	0.4	0.0	0.0	0.1	0.1	0.1	0.2	0.1	0.0	0.0	0.0	0.0	0.0	
2	median	0.0	0.0	0.0	1.5	0.0	3.0	0.0	0.0	0.0	0.0	0.0	0.0	0.0	0.0	0.0	0.0	0.0	0.0	0.0	0.0	
2	sum	0	2	42	90	14	154	54	23	2	0	3	7	4	9	5	2	0	0	0	1	58
2	rank			4	2		1	3								5						
15	mean	0.0	0.0	2.2	2.9	0.0	0.1	0.7	0.0	0.0	3.0	1.9	0.0	0.0	0.1	0.1	0.0	0.0	0.0	0.0	0.0	
15	median	0.0	0.0	3.0	3.0	0.0	0.0	1.0	0.0	0.0	3.0	2.0	0.0	0.0	0.0	0.0	0.0	0.0	0.0	0.0	0.0	
15	sum	0	0	42	55	0	1	14	0	0	57	37	0	0	1	1	0	0	0	0	0	19
15	rank			3	2			3			1	4										
14	mean	0.0	0.0	1.4	1.5	0.1	0.4	0.0	0.0	2.8	0.0	0.2	0.0	0.0	0.0	0.0	0.0	0.0	0.0	0.0	0.0	
14	median	0.0	0.0	1.0	2.0	0.0	0.0	0.0	0.0	3.0	0.0	0.0	0.0	0.0	0.0	0.0	0.0	0.0	0.0	0.0	0.0	
14	sum	0	1	34	38	3	11	0	0	69	0	6	0	0	1	0	0	0	0	0	0	25
14	rank			3	2					1												
13	mean	0.0	1.0	2.1	2.7	0.0	0.5	2.9	0.0	1.0	0.0	0.2	0.0	0.1	0.1	0.1	0.0	0.0	0.0	0.0	0.0	
13	median	0.0	0.0	3.0	3.0	0.0	0.0	3.0	0.0	0.0	0.0	0.0	0.0	0.0	0.0	0.0	0.0	0.0	0.0	0.0	0.0	
13	sum	0	29	62	77	0	15	85	1	30	0	5	1	3	2	2	0	0	0	0	0	29
13	rank		4	3	2			1		4												
8	mean	0.0	0.2	1.4	2.2	0.1	0.1	0.8	0.1	0.0	0.0	0.1	0.0	0.0	0.2	0.3	0.1	0.0	0.0	0.0	0.0	
8	median	0.0	0.0	1.0	2.0	0.0	0.0	0.0	0.0	0.0	0.0	0.0	0.0	0.0	0.0	0.0	0.0	0.0	0.0	0.0	0.0	
8	sum	0	10	80	128	8	5	45	4	2	0	6	0	2	9	15	4	0	0	0	0	57
8	rank			2	1			3														
11	mean	3.0	2.8	0.1	0.4	0.0	0.6	0.1	0.0	0.0	0.0	0.0	0.2	0.0	0.0	0.0	0.0	0.0	0.0	0.0	0.0	
11	median	3.0	3.0	0.0	0.0	0.0	0.0	0.0	0.0	0.0	0.0	0.0	0.0	0.0	0.0	0.0	0.0	0.0	0.0	0.0	0.0	
11	sum	500	465	14	73	3	102	20	0	6	0	0	27	1	3	2	5	3	0	0	0	169
11	rank	1	2		4		3															
3	mean	3.0	0.4	0.1	0.4	0.2	2.3	0.1	0.0	0.0	0.0	0.0	0.1	0.0	0.1	0.0	0.0	0.0	0.0	0.0	0.0	
3	median	3.0	0.0	0.0	0.0	0.0	2.0	0.0	0.0	0.0	0.0	0.0	0.0	0.0	0.0	0.0	0.0	0.0	0.0	0.0	0.0	
3	sum	121	16	3	18	10	94	3	0	1	0	2	3	0	3	0	0	0	0	0	0	41
3	rank	1	4		3		2															
7	mean	3.0	0.1	0.2	0.5	0.2	0.3	0.3	0.2	0.1	0.0	0.0	0.5	0.0	0.2	0.0	0.0	0.0	0.0	0.0	0.0	
7	median	3.0	0.0	0.0	0.0	0.0	0.0	0.0	0.0	0.0	0.0	0.0	0.0	0.0	0.0	0.0	0.0	0.0	0.0	0.0	0.0	
7	sum	204	10	14	34	14	21	21	11	8	0	0	32	0	12	0	2	3	0	0	0	84
7	rank	1			2		4	5					3									

Table 6.7. Summary Descriptions of Temper Cluster 15 Mineral Constituents

GROUP 1	Lower Colorado Buff Ware
Cluster 5	Clay + Quartz + Caliche
Cluster 1	Clay + Caliche + Quartz + Mafic

GROUP 2	Undecorated or Red Ware Ceramics
Cluster 4	Mica Schist + Quartz + Caliche + (Mafic - minor)
Cluster 12	Mica Schist + Quartz + White Feldspar (Estrella Gneiss or Mafic – minor)
GROUP 3	
Cluster 9	Sand + Quartz + (Mafic – minor)
Cluster 10	Sand + Quartz + White Feldspar
GROUP 4	
Cluster 6	Minor amounts of temper, but several subgroups represented
Cluster 2	Caliche + Quartz + Mafic + White Feldspar

GROUP 5	South Mountain and Estrella Gneiss group
Cluster 15	South Mountain Granodiorite + Quartz + White Feldspar + Mafic
Cluster 14	Estrella Gneiss + Quartz + White Feldspar
Cluster 13	Mafic + Quartz + White Feldspar + (EG - minor)
Cluster 8	Quartz + White Feldspar + Mafic

GROUP 6	Hohokam Buff Ware
Cluster 11	Fine Paste + Mica Schist + Caliche
Cluster 3	Fine Paste + Caliche + Mica Schist + Quartz
Cluster 7	Fine Paste + Quartz + Sherd/Tuff

RESULTS

The results of the ceramic analysis are presented for the individual features and sites in Table 6.8; each feature or part of a site is represented by a matrix that compares the surface/paste categories, or Ceramic Classes (on the vertical axis), to the 15 Temper Groups (on the horizontal axis); the numbers in the matrix refer to the counts of sherds representing that particular combination of surface treatment and temper group. The co-occurrence of particular Ceramic Classes with particular clusters is apparent, as previously discussed.

Those collections with substantial amounts of Lower Colorado Buff Ware have high frequencies for Clusters 5 and 1; this is particular strong in Features 1 through 5 at Site T:14:94. Those sites with Hohokam buff wares have substantial amounts of Clusters 11, 3, and 7; notice in particular, Site T:14:94, Features 1 through 5, and also Site T:14:92, Feature 1.

Table 6.8. Frequencies of Ceramic Class by Temper Cluster 15 for Site and Feature Numbers.

Site Number	Feat. No.	Ceramic Class	LCBW		Unk Sand				Lower Salt River				Middle Gila River					Total	Percent
			5	1	9	10	6	2	15	14	13	8	4	12	11	3	7	Total	Percent
T:10:86	0	Plain	1		11	2	21	22		19	12	34	4	1		1	2	130	71.4
		Plain/Smudged	1			1	1				2	2						7	3.8
		Red-Plain	1		4		1	1		2	1		1				1	12	6.6
		Plain Buff					1			1			2		3	1		8	4.4
		Buff, wash	1					1					2	1	2	1		8	4.4
		Red-on-buff						1					4	4	1	2		12	6.6
		LCBW, no clay						1				1						2	1.1
		LCBW, clay	2	1														3	1.6
		Total	6	1	15	3	24	26		22	15	37	13	1	8	4	7	182	100.0
		Percent	3.3	0.5	8.2	1.6	13.2	14.3		12.1	8.2	20.3	7.1	0.5	4.4	2.2	3.8	100.0	
T:14:92	0	Plain			3	1				6	1		13	60			2	86	68.3
		Red-Plain															4	4	3.2
		Plain buff							1					1	1			3	2.4
		Buff, wash													18		5	23	18.3
		Red-on-buff									1			2				3	2.4
		LCBW, no clay					3											3	2.4
		LCBW, clay	4															4	3.2
		Total	4		3	1	3		1	6	2		13	61	21		11	126	100.0
		Percent	3.2	0.0	2.4	0.8	2.4		0.8	4.8	1.6		10.3	48.4	16.7		8.7	100.0	
	1	Plain			5	14	2	1										22	19.5
		Red-Plain			1	1												2	1.8
		Plain buff						1					1		4		2	8	7.1
		Buff, wash			2	1	4	4				1	5		10	14	18	59	52.2
		Red-on-buff				1	1	1					1		3	10	4	21	18.6
		LCBW, no clay						1										1	0.9
		Total			8	17	7	8				1	7		17	24	24	113	100.0
		Percent			7.1	15.0	6.2	7.1				0.9	6.2		15.0	21.2	21.2	100.0	
	9	Plain												1				1	100.0
		Total												1				1	100.0
		Percent												100.0				100.0	
T:14:94	1-5	Not Recorded	1				1						2		1			5	1.1
		Plain	1		7	18	4	1	14		5	9	2	2	2			65	13.8
		Plain/smudged				2				2								4	0.8
		Red slipped				1												1	0.2
		Red-Plain			1	5	4	3	1			3	2	1				20	4.2
		Plain buff					1					1	3		16	1	2	24	5.1
		Buff, wash	2			10	1					1	12		54	2	1	83	17.6
		Red-on-buff	2		2	2	6	2				1	17	2	43	5	7	89	18.9
		LCBW, no clay				3		5										8	1.7
		LCBW, clay	91	62	1		1	7				2	6			2		172	36.5
		Total	97	62	11	25	32	20	15	2	6	16	44	5	116	10	10	471	100.0
		Percent	20.6	13.2	2.3	5.3	6.8	4.2	3.2	0.4	1.3	3.4	9.3	1.1	24.6	2.1	2.1	100.0	
	8	Plain				2			4		2		5					13	56.5
		Buff, wash													3			3	13.0
		Red-on-buff													4	1		5	21.7
		LCBW, no clay				2												2	8.7
		Total				4			4		2		5		7	1		23	100.0
		percent			0.0	17.4			17.4		8.7		21.7		30.4	4.3		100.0	
T:14:113	1	Plain					1											1	1.8
		Red-Plain					1											1	1.8
		LCBW, no clay															20	20	36.4
		LCBW, clay	6	3			8	1				1				2	12	33	60.0
		Total	6	3			10	1				1				2	32	55	100.0
		Percent	10.9	5.5			18.2	1.8				1.8				3.6	58.2	100.0	

The South Mountain Granodiorite (Cluster 15) was only identified in the T:10:94 collection, particularly the assemblage associated with Features 1–5. The Estrella Gneiss group (Clusters 14, 13, and 8) are most common at Site T:10:86, Site T:14:94, particularly Features 1–5, and Site T:14:92.

Undecorated wares exhibit considerable variation in temper cluster assignment. Clusters 6 and 2 are the most common at T:10:86. At Site T:14:92, Cluster 12 is the most common among surface collected samples, but in contrast, ceramics from Feature 1 are most commonly assigned to Cluster 10.

The undecorated ceramics from Site T:14:94, Features 1–5, exhibit a variety of temper assignments. However, Cluster 4 has the highest frequency. Sherds from Feature 8 are divided between Clusters 12 and 10.

The collection from Site T:14:113 is predominantly Lower Colorado Buff Ware, but has a number of compositional groups represented, reflecting that these types have several points of origin. The sherds without clay temper exhibit less variation than those with clay temper. Most interesting is that a large number of these samples are assigned to Cluster 7, which has a large number of Hohokam Buff Ware sherds at other sites. It could be that similar materials were used for these different types of buff ware in addition to the commonality of fine paste, but further differentiation of the clusters may separate these groups based on secondary temper constituents.

Several variations were noted in the surface treatment, paste, and temper characteristics of Lower Colorado Buff Wares in the collection. A subset of 115 of these from Site T:14:113 was re-examined. Pink was the second most common paste color and varies from distinctively pink to red colored, especially toward the surface of the sherd. The surfaces of these sherds tend to be tan colored, and occasionally covered with a scum coat.

Among this subset of 115 sherds (Table 6.9), only 24 contained clay inclusions; red, yellow, or yellow-red colored. The red clay inclusions and one yellow-red case occurred in beige paste sherds, whereas the yellow and one yellow-red case occurred in the pink paste sherds.

The two categories of paste color are not strongly patterned with respect to the 15 temper groups, as shown in Table 6.10. As noted earlier, the majority of LCBW sherds are assignable to Clusters 5 and 1, both of which contain added clay temper. The two categories of paste color exhibit some variability in temper cluster membership, but the general patterns are the same. In both the beige and the pink paste categories, Cluster 5 is the most common temper group followed by Cluster 1. The difference in percentages between the groups is not significant given the relatively small sample size.

Further studies of Lower Colorado Buff Ware will be needed to determine whether these differences in paste color and the color of clay temper are normal variations in the firing process or whether these correspond to specific production locales. It should be mentioned that much of the clay temper noted in the larger collection is similar to the paste color. At this time, it is unknown whether contrasting clay temper color is accidental or intentional. Studies in the core area of the lower Colorado drainage may be necessary to have sufficient sample sizes to answer these questions.

DISCUSSION

The results of the ceramic analysis (Table 6.8) are used to discuss two topics concerning the nature of the four prehistoric sites in the State Route 85 project that were associated with ceramic assemblages. The first topic deals with the manner in which the sherds came to be

Table 6.9. Frequencies of LCBW Subsample for Clay Inclusion Temper by Paste Color

Paste Color	Clay Inclusions				Total
	none	red	yellow	yellow-red	
none	1			1	2
beige	52	9		1	62
pink	38		12	1	51
Total	91	9	12	3	115

Table 6.10. Frequencies of LCBW Subsample by Paste Color and Temper Cluster 15 Membership

Paste Color	5	1	4	6	2	8	3	7	Total
None	1		1						2
Beige	32	9	0	4	6	1	2	8	62
Pink	22	16	5	4			2	2	51
Total	55	25	6	8	6	1	4	10	115
Percent	47.8	21.7	5.2	7.0	5.2	0.9	3.5	8.7	100.0

deposited at the sites; are they the remains of vessels that were broken and discarded at the sites, or were they originally transported to the site as sherds? The second topic examines the distances and directions from which the sherds have been transported to these particular sites.

ASSEMBLAGES OF SHERDS OR WHOLE VESSELS?

Did the prehistoric populations who visited and used the four prehistoric sites with ceramic assemblages bring whole vessels or broken sherds to the sites? This may appear to be an odd question, since there might seem to be little point in carrying around the pieces of a ceramic vessel once it had broken. In a recent study Hohokam researchers (Van Buren et al. 1992) have shown that prehistoric populations did apparently just that; they carried sherds rather than whole vessels to the location of an agave roasting pit and used the sherds as tools.

Van Buren and others (1992 in Fish, Fish and Madsen 1992: pp. 92–93) recovered nearly all of the sherds associated with an isolated roasting pit in the Marana. By looking at the combination of surface treatments, temper categories, and paste characteristics, they determined that a minimum of 82 "parent" vessels was represented in the sherds recovered from the site. "Of the 82 fragmented vessels identified, 61 (74.4%) are represented by nine or fewer sherds, and the mean number of sherds per vessel is only 8.7." They then concluded that ceramic sherds, rather than complete vessels, were intentionally brought to the roasting pit site to be used as tools. Some appear to have been used as digging tools, with distinctive forms of edge wear that could not have been produced by weathering or fluvial abrasion (Van Buren 1992). Sherds may also have been used as a protective covering to keep the coals from making direct contact with the agave.

A similar argument can be made for site of T:14:92, which is situated on a Pleistocene bajada and consists primarily of trails and rock features. Since there are essentially no Holocene deposits at the site, (and since humans were not present in the New World during the Pleistocene), cultural deposits can only occur on top of the Pleistocene surfaces. All of the artifacts recovered were found either on the surface or in the first few centimeters of loose sediments that had collected around the rock features above the Pleistocene calcite (caliche) surface. A surface collection was made of the entire site, and the areas around the rock features were completely excavated. Of the total sample of 240 sherds, about 20 percent (47 sherds) were recovered during the excavation of the rock features. This resulted in the recovery of nearly all of the sherds that were located at the site.

The sherd analysis presented in Table 6.8 provides a basis for estimating the minimum number of different vessels represented by the sherds at site AZ T:14:92. There are at least 37 different vessels, having different combinations of surface treatments, paste types and temper group, represented at the site (Table 6.11). Since the analysis did not compare sherds on the criteria of thickness and paste color, the number of actual vessels represented in this assemblage of sherds may be greater. The average vessel is represented by 6.5 sherds, and the maximum is 61 sherds representing a possible plain ware vessel of temper group 12 (mica schist, quartz and feldspar). The second largest possible vessel, a Hohokam Buff with a buff wash in temper group 11 (Mica schist and caliche in a fine paste), consists of 28 sherds. The sherds from the site are small, and even a small vessel would break into several dozen sherds of the size found at the site; at best, it is possible that vessel 19 (plain ware temper group 12) is completely represented in the assemblage as a collection of sherds, but for every other category there are too few sherds in the assemblage to represent a complete vessel. In short, the ceramic assemblage at this site consisted of a minimum of 36 different sherds, and perhaps one plain ware vessel.

The ceramic assemblages from sites T:14:94 and T:14:113 also originally consisted of sherds, rather than whole vessels, although the argument is not as strong as for site T:14:92. Because these two sites are located on Holocene alluvium it is more difficult to claim that the surface collection and excavation recovered nearly the total ceramic assemblages. At both sites only a sample of the area was excavated to a depth of more than 10 centimeters, and although the initial test found that most of the sherds occurred in the first 10 centimeters, there is still the possibility that the excavation missed an unknown portion of the assemblage. (The presence of a Pleistocene surface at T:14:92 made it possible to argue more convincingly that the field work there had recovered almost all of the assemblage.) At site AZ T:14:113 and T:14:94, 47 percent (26 sherds) and 48 percent (236 sherds) of the assemblages respectively were recovered through excavation, which indicates the relative importance of the buried portion of the assemblage.

However, if we accept the argument that the field work recovered almost all of the sherds at these two sites, then there are a minimum of 61 different vessels represented at T:14:94 and 10 vessels at T:14:113. Similarly, the average number of sherds per vessel are 7.7 at T:14:94 and 5.5 at T:14:113. At T:14:113, which had a total assemblage of only 55 sherds, there are no whole vessels are represented in the assemblage, but that leaves 49 percent of the assemblage as having been originally brought to the site as sherds.

Due to the small number of sherds in any single analytical category, and lack of reconstructible vessels, we have concluded that people brought sherds rather than whole vessels to Site T:14:92 and very likely to T:14:94 and T:14:113, possibly to be used as tools. We did not observe any wear

Table 6.11. Minimum Number of Vessels Represented by Sherds at AZ T:14:92 (ASM)

Vessel No.	Vessel Type/ Temper Group	Sherd Count			
		No Feat.	Feat. 1	Feat. 9	Total
1	Buff Plain 11	1	4		5
2	Buff Plain 12	1			1
3	Buff Plain 14	1			1
4	Buff Plain 2	1			1
5	Buff Plain 4	1			1
6	Buff Plain 7	2			2
7	Buff Wash 10	1			1
8	Buff Wash 11	18	10		28
9	Buff Wash 2	4			4
10	Buff Wash 3	14			14
11	Buff Wash 4	5			5
12	Buff Wash 6	4			4
13	Buff Wash 7	5	18		23
14	Buff Wash 8	1			1
15	Buff Wash 9	2			2
16	LCBW 2	3	1		4
17	LCBW 5	4			4
18	Plain 10	3	14		17
19	Plain 12	60		1	61
20	Plain 13	6			6
21	Plain 2	1			1
22	Plain 4	13			13
23	Plain 6	1	2		3
24	Plain 7	2			2
25	Plain 8	1			1
26	Plain 9	5			5
27	Red-on-buf 10	1			1
28	Red-on-Buff 11	2	3		5
29	Red-on-buff 2	1			1
30	Red-on-buff 3	10			10
31	Red-on-buff 4	1			1
32	Red-on-buff 6	1			1
33	Red-on-buff 7	4			4
34	Red-on-Buff 8	1			1
35	Red-Plain 10	1			1
36	Red-Plain 12	1			1
37	Red-Plain 4	4			4
				Total	**240**
				Average	**6.5**
				Total:	**240**

patterns on the sherds, which would have indicated that they had been used to dig pits, and indeed no pit features were found at either site. Sherds could have been used for purposes other than digging. Modified sherd fragments could also have been used as eating utensils, or as platters on hold things. There is also the possibility that sherds may have been deposited as offerings to shrines located along the trails. We can conclude that the ceramic artifacts at these three sites represent the use of sherds rather than vessels at the sites.

WHO USED THE SITES AND WHERE DID THEY COME FROM?

The second topic considers the sherds with respect to the possible location of their production, based on their temper constituents. The rock features associated with the trail sites, in particular, exhibit considerable variability with respect to the provenance of the associated ceramic assemblages. One quite clear implication is that the rock features were constructed and used by travelers originating from very different parts of the region. The sample is sufficiently varied to show there is a benefit in continuing such studies of the ceramics associated with trails, but this particular sample does not allow us to determine if such differences exist between entire trails, or if there is simply a lot of variability in the rock features along any given trail.

The Ceramic Assemblage from AZ T:10:86 (ASM)

Site AZ T:10:86 was an area of agricultural fields used from the Pioneer through Sedentary periods and possibly into the early Classic; the ceramics in this field show that the nearby villages obtained some of their plain ware ceramics from the Phoenix Basin and decorated buff wares from the Middle Gila. The dominant ceramic types at Site AZ T:10:86 are plain wares grouped into a variety of temper categories, but about 40 percent of the plain ware assemblage can be attributed to a production local in the Lower Salt River Valley at the northwest end of South Mountain and just to the east of the confluence of the Salt with the Gila River. In this area Estrella Gneiss (Cluster 14), and two weathered sands of Estrella Gneiss (Clusters 13 and 8) were used as temper additions to the production of plain wares (Abbott 1994; 2000:72). It is possible that the production area using Estrella Gneiss temper extended westward of the Salt-Gila confluence to include villages at the north end of the Estrella Mountain range.

Site AZ T:10:86 is a portion of prehistoric agricultural fields on the terraces of the Gila River that were farmed by people living in the nearby Hohokam villages at sites AZ T:10:74 and AZ T:10:131 (Rice 2000:321); these villages were located about 750 meters (2460 feet) to the west, and the ceramics in the field area were most likely derived from those villages (clearly a small percentage could also be attributed to other processes, such as having been dropped by other people passing through the area). The villages and the agriculture field at AZ T:10:86 are located about 32 kilometers (19.9 miles) downstream and to the west of the Salt-Gila confluence. During the Colonial and Sedentary periods a number of modest size Hohokam villages were located along the 32-kilometer stretch of the Gila and Salt Rivers, and ceramics from the South Mountain and Salt-Gila confluence area could easily have reached the vicinity of the Buckeye Hills by being traded from one village to the next.

It is quite plausible to find that 40 percent of the plain wares at AZ T:10:86 were originally obtained from a group of production centers in the lower Salt River valley 30 kilometers upstream. About 18 percent of the sherd assemblage consists of plain, buff, and red-on-buff wares that were manufactured at Hohokam villages on the Middle Gila River (Temper Clusters 4, 12, 11, 3, and 7, and surface treatments Plain Buff, Buff Wash, and Red-on-Buff) located 70 kilometers (44 miles) upstream on the Gila River.

The Ceramic Assemblage From AZ T:14:92 (ASM)

Site AZ T:14:92 (ASM) includes segments of several trails and rock features, and the associated ceramics suggest the route was used by people traveling from the Gila Bend area to the Middle Gila, but not, for instance, to Hohokam villages in the Phoenix Basin or to an area further west of the Gila Bend.

The ceramics collected from Features 1 and 9 at this site differed somewhat from the assemblage collected from the site in general (see Table 6.8). In the non-feature portion of the site the ceramic assemblage consisted of 23 percent buff wares produced on the Middle Gila and 68 percent plain wares with mica schist temper (Plain surface treatment with temper Clusters 4, 12 and 7) that could have been produced either locally or on the Middle Gila. Teague (1981:45–47) found there was a continuum between Gila Plain produced on the Middle Gila (Gila Plain, Gila variety) and that produced in the area of Gila Bend (Gila Plain, Gila Bend variety). Petrographic analyses showed lower amounts of mica schist in the Gila Bend variety, and often there were "small quantities of finely ground sherd temper as well" (Teague 1981:46); this may be represented in our collection by plain wares with temper Cluster 7 (see Table 6.8, site AZ T:14:92).

The assemblage from Feature 1, interestingly, has no plain ware categories with Mica Schist, and instead the plain wares and a few red-slipped wares (18 percent in combination) are tempered with unknown sands (Clusters 9 and 10). About 58 percent of the feature assemblage consists of Hohokam buff wares produced on the Middle Gila, and 18.6 percent of those sherds are decorated.

The larger ceramic producing villages on the Middle Gila lay about 42 kilometers (38 miles) in a direct line east of the site, but the trails at this site were actually part of an overland route that led from villages in the Gila Bend area through the Maricopa and Estrella Mountains to the Middle Gila. The distance along that route was about 70 kilometers (44 miles) from the site to the ceramic production villages on the Middle Gila. (This route has been reconstructed through field and archival research by Darling and Eiselt, as discussed in Chapter 12.) Thus the high percentage of Hohokam Buff with mica schist temper at this site seems to reflect the trail's importance as an overland travel route between the Gila Bend and Middle Gila areas. The higher occurrence of red-on-buff decorated wares around the Feature 1 (18%) compared to the rest of the site (2.4%) is also interesting, suggesting some specific importance was attached to the rock feature. The variety of plain wares at the site probably represents pottery produced both locally and on the Middle Gila, some 70 kilometers away.

The distance to the plain ware ceramic production centers on the lower Salt was about 58 kilometers, but except for a single sherd of Estrella Gneiss, there is no evidence at this site that plain ware ceramic vessels were transported from the Phoenix Basin.

The Ceramic Assemblage from AZ T:14:94 (ASM)

There are no trails visible at this site because it is located on Holocene alluvium (the surface lacks a covering of desert pavement), but the rock features are very similar to those found at AZ T:14:92 (ASM) and the site is interpreted as part of a travel route. The ceramic assemblages associated with the features suggest travelers using the route came from villages on the Middle Gila and the Phoenix Basin to the east, and from the Lower Colorado river to the west. The route may have covered a total distance of about 250 kilometers (155 miles) from the vicinity of Yuma on the Colorado River to the vicinity of Pima Butte on the Gila River, or to the area along the north flank of the South Mountains in Phoenix.

There are two clusters of rock features at this site; Features 1 through 5 consist of a large scatter of rocks that might consist of two adjacent features. We find it difficult to divide these into the five features as was done by the original survey crews. For our purposes here we will combine the ceramic data from Features 1 through 5. Feature 8 is a discrete rock feature located on the opposite (west) side of the highway from Features 1 through 5. The rock features are located on small areas of Holocene alluvium; faint trail impressions exist on some nearby areas of desert pavement, and it seems likely that these rock features were once associated with trails that are no longer visible. This site is also located a short distance to the north of AZ T:14:94 (ASM), and it may have once been part of the system of trails associated with the overland route through the Maricopa and Estrella Mountains to the Hohokam sites on the Middle Gila.

Middle Gila wares (37.2%) and Lower Colorado Buff Wares (38.2%) are relatively evenly represented in the ceramic assemblage from Features 1 through 5. Ceramics from the Phoenix Basin area occur in considerably lower frequencies (8.3%) and include plain wares tempered with South Mountain Granodiorite and Estrella Gneiss. A variety of other temper categories are also represented in the assemblage.

The Lower Colorado Buff wares at Features 1 to 5 included Palomas Buff (57% of the Lower Colorado Buff wares), with a pink colored paste, and Tumco Buff (43%) with a gray to chalky white colored paste. Although the production areas for Lower Colorado Buff Wares are not at all well established, Palomas Buff is most common along the lower Gila from Gila Bend to the confluence with the Colorado River and may have been manufactured somewhere within that region. Tomco Buff appears to have been produced along the lower reaches of the Colorado River (Waters 1982a:288). The Palomas Buff found at the State Route 85 sites was essentially identical to Palomas Buff collected by Schroeder from AZ T:14:6 and AZ T:14:2 in the Painted Rocks Reservoir area just to the west of the town of Gila Bend. The Palomas Buff sherds (about 22 percent of the total assemblage from Features 1–5) may have been produced anywhere along a 180 kilometer (112 miles) corridor extending from the site downstream to the confluence of the Gila with the Colorado. The Tumco buff (16 percent of the assemblage from Features 1–5) were in all probability transported a distance in excess of 180 kilometers from the Colorado to the site area.

The plain and red wares include sherds tempered with South Mountain Granodiorite (3.2%) and Estrella Gneiss (4%); these production centers were located on the north side of the South Mountains in the Phoenix Basin some 50 to 60 kilometers distance. Plain and red wares tempered with mica schist, which may have been produced either locally or on the Middle Gila, constitute less than two percent of the feature assemblage. Other plain wares (nine percent of the assemblage) are tempered with unknown sands (Clusters 9 and 10, possibly local to the Gila Bend area) and a set of other temper types grouped into Clusters 6 and 2.

Hohokam buff wares produced on the Middle Gila comprise 35 percent of the ceramic assemblage. Red-on-buff sherds with mica schist temper (Clusters 4, 12, 11, 3 and 7) form 15.7 percent of the assemblage while another 3.2 percent of the red-on-buff sherds were made using a variety of other temper groups. The large villages that produced Hohokam buff wares on the Middle Gila lay about 70 kilometers away using the overland route through the Maricopa and Estrella Mountains.

The ceramic assemblage from Feature 8 reflects, in considerably smaller numbers, the general patterns observed in Features 1 through 5. The assemblage includes Lower Colorado Buff Wares, Hohokam Buff wares, and Phoenix Basin plain wares.

In combination, the assemblages from these two neighboring sets of features include ceramics that were transported 180 miles from the west along the Gila River, and 70 miles from the East using a route that traveled down the Gila River and then cut overland using passes in the Estrella and Maricopa mountains.

The Ceramic Assemblage from AZ T:14:113

As was the case with AZ T:14:94, the rock features at this site are interpreted as having once been associated with a prehistoric trail that is no longer visible on the Holocene alluvium. The rock feature is similar to those excavated at AZ T:14:92 and AZ T:14:94; the site however is located to the north of those sites and very likely was not associated with the same route as those sites. The associated ceramics are strikingly different, consisting essentially of only Lower Colorado Buff Wares, and about 80 percent of the assemblage has the chalky white colored paste characteristic of Tomco Buff. This suggests that a large part of the assemblage was transported from sites 180 kilometers to the west.

The assemblage includes no evidence of ceramics from either the Phoenix Basin or the Hohokam centers on the Middle Gila. The assemblage would not be unusual if the site lay further to the west, so it was situated between the Lower Colorado River and the villages in the Gila Bend area; that would be consistent with a route that linked the Gila Bend to the Lower Colorado region. As it is, however, the site is situated to the east of the Gila Bend area, suggesting it is being used by people who had traveled from the Lower Colorado past the Gila Bend area and were on their way to the Lower Salt and Middle Gila valleys.

The absence of Hohokam Red-on-buff suggests the site may post-date the collapse of the Hohokam tradition, or at least the end of the Sedentary period when there was a major decline in the production of Red-on-buff. Unfortunately, no charcoal samples were recovered during the excavation of the site to enable radiocarbon dating of the occupation.

CONCLUSION

The modal analysis of the ceramic assemblage recorded the temper constituents, surface treatment, and paste characteristics of 971 sherds. A set of statistical analyses identified 15 major temper groups in the assemblages, and these were combined with the 10 categories of wares and surface treatment to generate the units of the analysis.

The ceramic data have been used to draw two basic conclusions. First, at the three bajada sites associated with rock features and trails, the ceramic artifacts were brought to the sites largely as sherds, not as whole vessels. That is, the ceramics at these sites do not represent the accidental breakage of vessels that were then discarded. It was not possible to determine in what manner the sherds were used, and indeed it has also not been possible to determine the function of the rock features. However, the rock features are consistent with the appearance of ethnographic period shrines, and the presence of sherds at the rock features is consistent with offerings deposited at shrines.

The second finding is that the ceramics associated with rock features came from very different production loci, with considerable variability between features. Since rock features tend to be associated with trails, they are very useful tools for examining the issue of who used the trails and the distances over which they may have traveled. The current study established that rock features on separate trails had very different ceramic signatures; the study could not determine, however, the level of variability that might exist on a single trail. That is, the nature of the project area was such that it cut across a number of different trails, rather than intersecting the same trail at a series of different locations. The current evidence gathered in this study showed that ceramics found on the trails were transported over distances well in excess of 100 kilometers, and came from the Middle Gila and Phoenix basins to the east and the Lower Colorado River on the west.

Table 6.12. Crosstabulation of Temper Cluster 15 by Cluster 30 for Highway 85 Ceramics.
(See page 128.)

Cluster 30	5	1	4	12	9	10	6	2	15	14	13	8	11	3	7	Total
7	84	.	.	.	.	.	.	.	.	.	.	.	.	.	.	84
8	28	.	.	.	.	.	.	.	.	.	.	.	.	.	.	28
3	.	26	.	.	.	.	.	.	.	.	.	.	.	.	.	26
1	.	40	.	.	.	.	.	.	.	.	.	.	.	.	.	40
6	.	.	8	.	.	.	.	.	.	.	.	.	.	.	.	8
15	.	.	69	.	.	.	.	.	.	.	.	.	.	.	.	69
22	.	.	.	24	.	.	.	.	.	.	.	.	.	.	.	24
21	.	.	.	49	.	.	.	.	.	.	.	.	.	.	.	49
16	.	.	.	.	34	.	.	.	.	.	.	.	.	.	.	34
24	.	.	.	.	.	15	.	.	.	.	.	.	.	.	.	15
17	.	.	.	.	.	37	.	.	.	.	.	.	.	.	.	37
26	.	.	.	.	.	.	9	.	.	.	.	.	.	.	.	9
18	.	.	.	.	.	.	6	.	.	.	.	.	.	.	.	6
11	.	.	.	.	.	.	59	.	.	.	.	.	.	.	.	59
2	.	.	.	.	.	.	.	12	.	.	.	.	.	.	.	12
10	.	.	.	.	.	.	.	15	.	.	.	.	.	.	.	15
5	.	.	.	.	.	.	.	16	.	.	.	.	.	.	.	16
9	.	.	.	.	.	.	.	15	.	.	.	.	.	.	.	15
28	.	.	.	.	.	.	.	.	19	.	.	.	.	.	.	19
27	.	.	.	.	.	.	.	.	.	25	.	.	.	.	.	25
29	.	.	.	.	.	.	.	.	.	.	9	.	.	.	.	9
25	.	.	.	.	.	.	.	.	.	.	9	.	.	.	.	9
30	.	.	.	.	.	.	.	.	.	.	11	.	.	.	.	11
13	.	.	.	.	.	.	.	.	.	.	.	30	.	.	.	30
14	.	.	.	.	.	.	.	.	.	.	.	27	.	.	.	27
20	.	.	.	.	.	.	.	.	.	.	.	.	53	.	.	53
19	.	.	.	.	.	.	.	.	.	.	.	.	116	.	.	116
4	.	.	.	.	.	.	.	.	.	.	.	.	.	41	.	41
23	.	.	.	.	.	.	.	.	.	.	.	.	.	.	7	7
12	.	.	.	.	.	.	.	.	.	.	.	.	.	.	77	77
Total	112	66	77	73	34	52	74	58	19	25	29	57	169	41	84	970

CHAPTER 7

LITHIC AND SHELL ARTIFACTS
Glen E. Rice

INTRODUCTION

A total of 80 lithic artifacts and four fragments of marine shell were analyzed. The lithic artifacts were all classified as flaked stone and no ground-stone artifacts were recovered. Flaked-stone artifacts occurred in considerably lower numbers than sherds (80 flaked-stone artifacts compared to 971 sherds) at the sites on State Route 85. Flaked-stone artifacts were most abundant in the assemblage from site AZ T:10:86, located on the Gila River terrace, where they occurred at the ratio of one lithic for every five sherds. This ratio dropped considerably at sites with rock cairns located on the bajada, where flaked-stone artifacts were outnumbered by sherds 1 to 9 at AZ T:14:92, 1 to 34 at AZ T:14:94 and were completely absent at AZ T:4:113 (with an assemblage of 55 sherds). A single lithic core and no sherds were found in association with the roasting pits at AZ Z:2:46, also on the bajada. Most of the materials used for the lithic artifacts were available in the immediate vicinity of the sites. The results of the analysis indicate that at all of these sites, which were specialized activity areas and not residential settlements, the need for lithic tools arose only occasionally and was met expeditiously with the materials closest at hand.

ANALYSIS

The assemblage of 80 lithic artifacts was classified by artifact type and material category; the definitions of the lithic artifact types are given in Table 7.1. The results of the analysis are presented in Tables 7.2 and 7.3. Three of the sites (AZ T:10:86, T:14:92, and T:14:94) had assemblages of 14 to 34 lithic artifacts, one (AZ Z:2:46) had a single lithic artifact, and one (AZ T:14:113) had no lithic artifacts. Inter-site comparisons are made among the three sites with assemblages of multiple lithic artifacts.

LITHIC ARTIFACTS BY MATERIAL CATEGORY

The three most common material categories in the assemblage were quartz, greenstone and rhyolite (Table 7.2) and the most abundant artifact types were the two variants of secondary flakes (37%), tertiary flakes (19%) and shatter (13%) (Table 7.3). There are two noteworthy patterns in the relationship of artifact types to material types.

First, the category of secondary flakes, variant b, occurs almost exclusively on greenstone. This flake type has cortex only on the striking platform, with the dorsal surface covered by previous flake scars. The flakes are generated by a specific technology in which the lithic knapper selected elongated cobbles and struck flakes repeatedly from one end of the cobble using the natural surface of the cobble as the striking platform. This allowed for the rapid production of a succession of similar size flakes without necessitating the preparation of a striking platform. The association of this flake category with greenstone is probably fortuitous; it is likely that the cobbles of the necessary size and shape for this flaking technology happened frequently to be of greenstone material.

The second pattern is that about 60 percent of the shatter is of quartz material. This is a function of the unusual toughness of the quartz material which makes it difficult to work, and requires

Table 7.1. Definitions for Lithic Categories Used in the Analysis

Primary Flake – The dorsal surface and striking platform of the flake are completely covered with cortex.

Secondary Flake – The dorsal surface is covered partially with cortex and flake scars; the platform mound may or may not have cortex.

Secondary Flake Variant b – Cortex occurs only on the striking platform, but not on the remainder of the dorsal surface.

Shatter – An angular fragment of a broken flake, lacking a complete bulb of percussion.

Core – A flaked object that possesses only negative bulbs of percussion, from which flakes have been struck.

Hammer Stone – A lithic object with pecking wear patterns on convex edges and ridges; frequently also a core.

Biface – A bifacially shaped tool, including projectile points and large knives.

Mano – A grinding implement with polish wear and abrasion wear on a convex surface.

Metate – A grinding implement with polish and abrasion wear on a concave surface.

Raw Material, Not Worked – A lithic object that has not been altered by human activity except that human beings have transported it to the site from its natural geological context.

Split Cobble Core Tool – A cobble from which several flakes have been struck on one end, leaving much of the object still covered in cortex.

Table 7.2. Flaked Stone Material Types, SR 85 Archaeological Project Sites

Site No.	Feature No.	Basalt	Chert	Green-stone	Quartz	Rhyo-lite	Vesicular Basalt	Meta-volcanic	Slate/ Shale	Grand Total
T:10:86	Surface		1	16	2	9		5	1	34
T:10:86	Feature 1			2			1			3
T:10:86	Feature 3			1		1				2
T:14:92	Surface	1		1	21	1		1	1	26
T:14:94	1 to 5			6	5	2		1		14
Z:2:46	Surface			1						1
Grand Total		1	1	27	28	13	1	7	2	80
T:10:86	Surface	0.0%	2.9%	47.1%	5.9%	26.5%	0.0%	14.7%	2.9%	100.0%
T:10:86	Feature 1	0.0%	0.0%	66.7%	0.0%	0.0%	33.3%	0.0%	0.0%	100.0%
T:10:86	Feature 3	0.0%	0.0%	50.0%	0.0%	50.0%	0.0%	0.0%	0.0%	100.0%
T:14:92	Surface	3.8%	0.0%	3.8%	80.8%	3.8%	0.0%	3.8%	3.8%	100.0%
T:14:94	1 to 5	0.0%	0.0%	42.9%	35.7%	14.3%	0.0%	7.1%	0.0%	100.0%
Z:2:46	Surface	0.0%	0.0%	100.0%	0.0%	0.0%	0.0%	0.0%	0.0%	100.0%
Grand Total		1.3%	1.3%	33.8%	35.0%	16.3%	1.3%	8.8%	2.5%	100.0%

Table 7.3. Flaked Stone Artifact Categories by Site and Features

Site No.	Feature No.	Primary Flake	Secondary Flake	Secondary Flake var. b	Tertiary Flake	Shatter	Core	Hammer Stone	Raw Material	Split Cobble	Grand Total
T:10:86	Surface	1	11	8	7	4	1	1		1	34
T:10:86	Feature 1		1	1					1		3
T:10:86	Feature 3	1	1								2
T:14:92	Surface	2	2	1	6	6	1		5	3	26
T:14:94	Features 1-5	3	2	3	2		1	1		2	14
Z:2:46	Surface						1				1
Total		7	17	13	15	10	4	2	6	6	80
T:10:86	Surface	2.9%	32.4%	23.5%	20.6%	11.8%	2.9%	2.9%	0.0%	2.9%	100.0%
T:10:86	Feature 1	0.0%	33.3%	33.3%	0.0%	0.0%	0.0%	0.0%	33.3%	0.0%	100.0%
T:10:86	Feature 3	50.0%	50.0%	0.0%	0.0%	0.0%	0.0%	0.0%	0.0%	0.0%	100.0%
T:14:92	Surface	7.7%	7.7%	3.8%	23.1%	23.1%	3.8%	0.0%	19.2%	11.5%	100.0%
T:14:94	Features 1-5	21.4%	14.3%	21.4%	14.3%	0.0%	7.1%	7.1%	0.0%	14.3%	100.0%
Z:2:46	Surface	0.0%	0.0%	0.0%	0.0%	0.0%	100.0%	0.0%	0.0%	0.0%	100.0%
Total		8.8%	21.3%	16.3%	18.8%	12.5%	5.0%	2.5%	7.5%	7.5%	100.0%

the use of strong force in the striking of flakes. The heavy blows occasionally tend to shatter the flake as it is being removed from the core, resulting in a collection of angular pieces of which only a few have evidence of the positive bulb of percussion. By definition, the difference between the shatter and flake categories is that flakes bear a positive bulb of percussion on the ventral surface while shatter fragments do not.

These two patterns in the technological relationship between material type and artifact type are responsible for the strongest spatial patterns observed in the inter-site comparisons. That is, the site with a high frequency of the variant b of secondary flakes, also has large quantities of greenstone material, and the sites with a high frequency of shatter have large quantities of quartz.

No ground stone implements were recovered in the project area. The one piece of vesicular basalt in Feature 1 of site AZ T:10:86 (ASM) was unworked, and was classified as raw material (Table 7.3). The material classified as slate/shale in the Hohokam region is, despite the implications of the name, not prone to tabular fractures and is indeed well suited for flaking.

INTER-SITE VARIABILITY IN MATERIAL AND ARTIFACT CATEGORIES

The most notable differences in material type is in the use of quartz, which is common at the two sites on the bajada (AZ T:14:92 and T:14:94) and rare at the site on the Gila River alluvial terrace (AZ T:10:86). Quartz occurred as cobbles and natural outcrops on the Pleistocene pediment near AZ T:14:92 and 94, and was rare along the Gila river terrace in the area of AZ T:10:86. At site AZ T:14:92, 80 percent of the flakes were struck from quartz cores (Table 7.2), and it is not surprising therefore that the site assemblage also has the highest frequency of shatter at about 23 percent (Table 7.3). What is somewhat surprising is that site AZ T:14:94, which has the second highest quantity of quartz (five pieces constituting 35 percent of the assemblage) actually has no pieces of shatter. AZ T:10:86 has the second highest incidence of shatter (four pieces constituting about 12 percent of the assemblage) has very low quantities of quartz (two pieces or 5.9 percent of the assemblage). If the sample sizes from these sites were larger, and shatter continued to be absent at site AZ T:10:86, one interpretation could be that the quartz artifacts at AZ T:10:86 had been produced somewhere else, and that only large flakes had been transported into the site (the shattered flakes are not particularly useful as tools). However, the very small sample sizes from these sites, particularly the assemblage of only 14 lithics from AZ T:14:94, preclude making such an interpretation since the patterns may have occurred simply by chance in a very small population.

Greenstone and a fine-grained rhyolite are the two most common materials on the river terrace, but rhyolite is rare at both sites on the bajada, and greenstone is common at only one of the bajada sites (AZ T:14:94). In addition to the rhyolite, other fine-grained material types that occur are chert and slate/shale, but these latter are rare at all of the sites.

Secondary flakes with cortex only on the striking platform (variant b) occur in highest frequencies as AZ T:10:86 (count of 8, 23.5 percent) and AZ T:14:94 (count of 3, 21.4 percent). These two sites also have the highest occurrences of greenstone material (count of 16 and 47.1 percent at AZ T:10:86, and a count of 6 and 42.9 percent at AZ T:14:94). Again, given the interrelatedness of greenstone material and the variant b of secondary flakes, these patterns can be attributed to the lithic materials used at the site.

The one unusual part of this pattern is the relatively high proportion of river worn greenstone cobbles at AZ T:14:94. To the best of our knowledge these cobbles were not available on the bajada, and were probably obtained from the river gravels of the Gila River. Nonetheless, only a very small quantity of greenstone, six flakes, occurs at the site, and these could easily have been carried to the location by a single individual. The single core associated with the roasting pits at Z:2:46 was also of greenstone. These patterns are consistent with the use of the bajada for the collection of resources by people living in settlements on the flood plains of the Gila River.

SHELL ARTIFACTS

Four fragments of marine shell were found, all from the excavation of features at site AZ T:14:94. Three were small fragments of *Laevicardium* species and one was a fragment of a *Glycymeris* bracelet. The artifacts were distributed as follows:

Spec. No. 156	Features 1-5, 2 North / 9 East, Level 1	Laevicardium fragment
Spec. No. 162	Features 1-5, 2 North / 4 East, Level 1	Laevicardium fragment
Spec. No. 199	Features 1-5, 6 North / 9 East, Level 1	Glycymeris bracelet fragment
Spec No. 179	Feature 3, 3.5 North / 4 East, Level 1	Laevicardium fragment

An argument comparable to that made for the ceramic artifacts can also be made for the shell artifacts. Nearly the entire artifact assemblage was collected or excavated from Site AZ T:14:94. It seems quite likely that these small pieces of shell were transported to the site as fragments, and not as raw material to be used in the manufacture of shell jewelry or as whole items of jewelry that were broken and discarded at the site. This pattern is consistent with the interpretation that small pieces of artifacts were deposited at the rock features as offerings or contributions, although the ideology underlying such practices is unknown.

CHAPTER 8

POLLEN RESULTS FROM FIVE SITES:
AZ Z:2:46, AZ T:14:113, AZ T:14:92,
AZ T:14:94, AND AZ T:10:86

Susan Smith

INTRODUCTION

The analysis results from 12 pollen samples from five archaeological sites in central Arizona along State Route 85 are presented in this report. The samples were collected from extramural features, including three rock clusters and two basin-shaped depressions. Pollen evidence of cultural activities is often difficult to recover from extramural contexts because these features are open to atmospheric pollen rain and geomorphic processes. Maize pollen was recovered from two of the sites, and there is some evidence for past use of native plant resources.

LIMITATIONS OF POLLEN ANALYSIS

Pollen is a more difficult botanical artifact to interpret than macrobotanical remains. A seed recovered from an archaeological context will have originated from plants at the site or been imported by people, but pollen can be transported long distances by air, water, and other vectors (Faegri and Iversen 1989). The pollination ecology of plant taxa fall into two main systems, wind- and insect-pollinated. Grass, sagebrush, trees, and some shrubs are wind-pollinated and tend to be over-represented in pollen assemblages because these plants produce abundant aerodynamic pollen that can disperse 100's of kilometers. Insect-pollinated plants (the cacti and majority of herb species) produce small amounts of poorly dispersed pollen and are generally under-represented. The recognition of ethnobotanic pollen from archaeological contexts is tempered by consideration of human behavior, ethnobotanical information, the complexity and dynamics of pollination ecology (Faegri and van der Pijl 1979), and the probability that pollen from a processed plant part would become part of the archaeological record.

Methods

Subsamples (20 cc volume) from the sample bags were spiked with a known concentration (25,084 grains) of exotic spores (*Lycopodium*) to monitor any degradation from the chemical extraction procedure and to allow pollen concentration calculations. Processing steps included overnight hydrochloric and hydrofluoric acid treatments, followed by a density separation in a heavy liquid (lithium polytungstate, 1.9 specific gravity).

Pollen assemblages were identified by counting slide transects at 400x magnification to a 200 grain sum, if possible, then scanning the entire slide at 100x magnification to record additional taxa. Aggregates (clumps of the same pollen type) were counted as one grain per occurrence, and the taxon and size recorded separately. Numerous large aggregates in protected archaeological contexts can reflect plant processing.

Four numerical measures were calculated: sample frequency, pollen percentages, taxa richness, and pollen concentration. Pollen percentages or concentrations help smooth statistical display of the wind-pollinated taxa, and the under-represented, insect-pollinated taxa are interpreted with sample frequency measures. Sample frequency is the number of samples recording a particular pollen type or attribute usually calculated as the percent of samples. Pollen percentages represent the relative importance of each taxon in a sample ([pollen counted/pollen sum]*100), and taxa richness is the number of different pollen types identified in a sample. Pollen concentration was estimated by calculating the ratio of the pollen count to the tracer count and multiplying by the initial tracer concentration. Dividing this result by the sample volume yields the number of pollen grains per cubic centimeter of sample sediment, abbreviated gr/cc.

RESULTS AND INTERPRETATIONS

The sample set was productive and all 12 samples yielded significant counts of 100 grains or more. Pollen preservation was moderate to excellent with an average of eight percent degraded pollen. Pollen concentration was moderate to high with a range of 1995 to 36,894 gr/cc. Twenty-eight pollen types were identified and are listed in Table 1 by common and scientific name with sample frequency for each taxon also included. Pollen aggregates were recovered from 9 taxa, and the sample frequency for aggregates is listed in Table 8.1.

Native desert plants are well represented in the results by creosote, paloverde, and mesquite with hackberry and a variety of herb and weed types. A suite of pollen types co-dominate the assemblages including Cheno-Am, sunflower family, ragweed/bursage type, and grass, and in some samples, there are spikes in the representation of native trees and shrubs, such as mesquite and paloverde.

Cheno-Am is a catch-all category that subsumes a variety of plant species (Table 8.1), including saltbush, goosefoot, and tumbleweed. Many Cheno-Am plants are weeds that thrive in disturbed soil, such as would exist around sites, but this group also includes important food plants that for some Indian tribes were staples (Moerman 1998; Rea 1997). Sunflower family and grass are two other broad pollen categories that encompass a range of valued plant species.

All 28 pollen types represent plants with known ethnobotanical uses for food, medicine, fuel, construction, tools, and textiles, but the majority of pollen recovered likely reflects natural deposition from atmospheric pollen rain. Three pollen types stand out as probable economics—maize, cholla, and the cacti category, which subsumes hedgehog, saguaro, barrel, and other cacti.

The results are summarized in Table 8.2, which lists, for each site, the presence of pollen types interpreted to reflect possible cultural use. All of the data are documented in Table 8.3. Maize was recovered only from the basin-shaped depressions at two sites, AZ A:2:46 and AZ T:10:86. High Cheno-Am representation at AZ T:10:86 could reflect the Gila River floodplain setting of this site, agricultural weeds, or use of Cheno-Am taxa. Cotton pollen was identified from a rock cluster sample at AZ T:14:92. Cotton may have been farmed prehistorically in the project region along the Gila River, or cotton pollen or flowers used in some ceremonial way at AZ T:14:92, but the recovered cotton pollen could also reflect modern agriculture.

Cacti pollen was identified from all three rock clusters sampled (see Table 8.2), but was not documented from the two basins. One rock cluster sample (number 143) from AZ T:14:94 yielded 11% cacti and cacti pollen aggregates, which is an exceptional representation. This could be a cultural signature of processing cacti flowers or fruits, such as saguaro and hedgehog, both of which

Table 8.1. Pollen Types Identified and Sample Frequency

		Taxa	Common Name	Sample Frequency as % 12 samples
Local Desert Trees and Shrubs	1	Larrea	Creosote	50
	2	Prosopis	Mesquite	33
	3	Cercidium	Paloverde	33
	4	Celtis	Hackberry	17
		Mesquite Aggregates		8
	5	Ambrosia	Ragweed/Bursage type	92
		Ragweed/Bursage Aggregates		0
Subsistence Resources and Cultigens	6	Cactaceae	Cactus includes sagauro, hedgehog & others	42
	7	Cactus Aggregates		8
	8	Cholla	Cholla	33
	9	Zea	Maize	17
	10	Gossypium	Cotton	8
	11	Cheno-Am	Cheno-Am includes saltbush, goosefoot, tumbleweed, & others	100
		Cheno-Am Aggregates		58
	12	Asteraceae	Sunflower Family	100
		Sunflower Family Aggregates		25
	13	Poaceae	Grass	100
		Grass Aggregates		8
	14	Plantago	Plantain	83
Native Herbs, Weeds, and Subsistence Plants	15	Brassicaceae	Mustard	25
	16	Lamiaceae	Mint	8
	17	Eriogonum	Buckwheat	42
		Buckwheat Aggregates		8
	18	Sphaeralcea	Globemallow	58
		Globemallow Aggregates		17
	19	Boerhaavia	Spiderling	50
		Spiderling Aggregates		17
	20	Kallstroemia	Summer Poppy	17
	21	Onagraceae	Evening Primrose	17
	22	Euphorbiaceae	Spurge	67
	23	Liguliflorae	Chicory tribe includes prickly lettuce (Lactua), dandelion, & others	17
Regional Trees and Shrubs	24	Pinus	Pine	75
	25	Pinus edulis type	Pinyon	25
	26	Juniperus	Juniper	58
	27	Ephedra	Mormon Tea	17
	28	Quercus	Oak	8

Table 8.2. Summary Pollen Result

Site	No. of Samples	Feature No.	Context	Pollen Concentration gr/cc	Maize	Cholla	Cacti	Other
Z:2:46	3	3	basin-shaped depression	3162-19283	1 sample	1 sample	-	19% paloverde pollen in fill at 50 cm, decreasing Cheno-Am & increasing sunflower family with depth, 11% plantain beneath surface rocks
T:14:113	2	-	rock cluster & sherds	17116-21164	-	-	2 samples	high frequencies of grass (11 & 17%) & plantain (15 & 38%)
T:14:92	2	1	rock cluster & sherds	6595-36894	-	-	1 sample	cotton in sample 72, at 30 cm depth, 11% plantain at 30 cm
T:14:94	3	-	rock cluster & sherds	1995-29975	-	1 sample	2 samples (11% at 40 cm depth)	20% creosote at 40 cm depth, 17% mesquite at 20 cm depth, 19% plantain at 40 cm
T:10:86	2	3	basin-shaped depression	21500-25920	1 sample	2 samples	-	maximum Cheno-Am (>80%)

Table 8.3. Pollen Data Raw Counts

Site	Z:2:46	Z:2:46	Z:2:46	T:14:113	T:14:113	T:14:92	T:14:92	T:14:94	T:14:94	T:14:94	T:10:86	T:10:86
Sample	2	7	9	25	27	71	72	132	143	147	484	494
Feature	3	3	3	-	-	1	1	-	-	-	3	3
Context	beneath surface rocks	feature contents at 50 cm depth	feature contents at 60 cm depth	from beneath surface rocks	Control	beneath surface rocks	trench at approx. 30 cm depth	trench through Features 1-5 at 20 cm depth	trench through Features 1-5 at 40 cm depth	Features 1-5 beneath surface rocks	fill at 60 cm depth	feature contents at 80 cm depth
Tracer	24	94	94	16	17	58	12	105	66	10	14	9
Pollen Sum	369	237	315	270	232	305	353	167	128	239	240	186
Concentration[a]	19283.3	3162.2	4202.9	21164.6	17116.1	6595.4	36894.4	1994.8	2432.4	29975.4	21500.6	25920.1
Taxa Richness[b]	14.0	8.0	12.0	13.0	12.0	12.0	17.0	11.0	11.0	12.0	11.0	10.0
Degraded	48	28	52	16	4	8	14	8	24	28	3	2
Unknown	14	2	5	2	8	8	2	16	7	4	1	0
Pinus	14	X[c]	0	20	12	10	8	2	0	2	3	0
Pinus edulis type	0	0	0	0	0	4	2	0	0	2	0	0
Juniperus	4	0	0	4	0	4	22	8	0	14	1	0
Ephedra	0	0	0	0	0	2	X	0	0	0	0	0
Quercus	1	0	0	0	0	0	0	0	0	0	0	0
Larrea	31	0	10	0	0	0	14	10	25	10	0	0
Prosopis	0	0	18	0	6	0	0	29	0	2	0	0
Cercidium	0	45	0	6	0	0	8	0	0	0	1	0
Celtis	0	0	0	0	0	0	2	0	0	0	1	0
Cactaceae	0	0	0	X	X	0	X	X	14	0	0	0
Cholla	0	0	X	0	0	0	0	0	X	0	1	X
Zea	0	0	0	0	0	0	0	0	0	0	X	0
Gossypium	0	0	0	0	0	0	X	0	0	0	0	0
Cheno-Am	26	66	4	22	2	58	44	20	6	36	201	164
Asteraceae	20	66	142	48	8	32	52	16	14	24	10	6
Liguliflorae	0	2	0	0	0	0	0	0	0	0	0	X
Ambrosia	110	48	26	50	66	134	124	16	16	62	0	1
Poaceae	32	20	10	47	25	22	6	2	4	25	1	3

Continued

Table 8.3. Pollen Data Raw Counts (Continued)

Site	Z:2:46	Z:2:46	Z:2:46	T:14:113	T:14:113	T:14:92	T:14:92	T:14:94	T:14:94	T:14:94	T:10:86	T:10:86
Sample	2	7	9	25	27	71	72	132	143	147	484	494
Brassicaceae	4	0	0	0	0	0	0	0	0	6	0	1
Lamiaceae	0	0	0	0	0	0	3	0	0	0	0	0
Sphaeralcea	10	0	6	0	X	X	2	0	0	0	10	5
Boerhaavia	2	0	27	2	2	0	0	0	2	0	0	X
Kallstroemia	0	0	2	0	0	0	0	0	0	0	0	X
Eriogonum	8	0	0	1	0	1	4	0	8	0	0	0
Onagraceae	0	0	0	X	X	0	0	0	0	0	0	0
Euphorbiaceae	6	0	8	12	8	2	10	0	2	12	0	0
Plantago	39	6	0	40	89	16	38	32	4	12	1	0
Total Aggregates[d]	0	0	4	0	2	4	1	5	2	0	6	4
Cheno-Am Aggregates	0	0	0	X(100+)	1(6)	1(6)	0	2(10+)	1(12)	0	6(50+)	4(50+)
Sunflower Family Aggregates	0	0	2(6)	0	1(100+)	1(8)	0	0	0	0	0	0
Ragweed/Bursage Aggregates	0	0	0	0	0	0	1(12)	3(20+)	0	0	0	0
Grass Aggregates	0	0	2(8)	0	0	0	0	0	0	0	0	0
Buckwheat Aggregates	0	0	0	0	0	0	0	0	1(12)	0	0	0
Globemallow Aggregates	X(10)	0	0	0	X(8)	0	0	0	0	0	0	0
Spiderling Aggregates	X(12)	0	0	0	X(6)	0	0	0	0	0	0	0
Cactus Aggregates	0	0	0	0	0	0	0	0	X(8)	0	0	0
Mesquite Aggregates	0	0	0	0	0	0	0	X(10+)	0	0	0	0

a. Taxa richness is the number of pollen types identified in a sample out of a total of 27 pollen types.
b. Concentration is an estimate of the number of pollen grains contained in a cubic centimeter of sample sediment (gr/cc), based on an initial tracer concentration of 25,084 Lycopodium spores and a sample size of 20 cc.
c. X notes taxa identified during 100x scans or taxa presence in sterile samples.
d. Pollen Aggregate notation shows the number of aggregates and the size of the largest aggregate in ( ).

are well represented in the southern Arizona archaeobotanical record (Gasser and Kwiatkowski 1991) and the ethnographic record (Felger and Moser 1985; Moerman 1998; Rea 1997).

Other types that appear enriched in specific features include grass (AZ T:14:113), plantain (all sites except AZ T:10:86), paloverde (AZ Z:2:46), and mesquite (AZ T:14:94). These taxa represent important economic plants. Plantain is an early spring annual harvested for seed, paloverde flowers, beans, and pods were utilized, mesquite pods were a staple for several groups, and grasses were valued for both food and fiber (Doebley 1984; Felger and Moser 1985; Moerman 1998). Globemallow pollen is enhanced at the two sites where maize pollen was recovered (AZ Z:2:46 and AZ T:10:86), which could reflect a possible field weed.

CONCLUSIONS

Maize pollen and a single maize cupule from AZ T:10:86 are evidence for maize agriculture along the Gila River. The pollen and macro results indicate Cheno-Am may have been another economic resource at this site. Maize may have been farmed at AZ Z:2:46. Cacti pollen was associated with the rock clusters at AZ T:14:92, AZ T:14:94, and AZ T:14:113, which could reflect a functional use or a micro-habitat favoring cacti. Another resource associated with the three rock cluster sites and the basin at AZ Z:2:46 is plantain. Mesquite, paloverde, cacti, cholla, and grass representation in the samples reflect the past desert environment that existed when these sites were utilized, and the important resources that were available to people living along the Gila River.

CHAPTER 9

ARCHAEOBOTANICAL REMAINS

Karen R. Adams

INTRODUCTION

Archaeologists collected flotation samples from two prehistoric sites during State Route 85 (SR 85) excavations. The first site (AZ T:10:86) is a large, light-density Hohokam artifact scatter dating to the late Colonial or Sedentary period, situated on the Gila River floodplain and possibly representing an activity area associated with pre-Classic agricultural fields. Previous research at a similar site nearby (Wright 1995) reported subsurface lenses of ash containing plant materials and pollen suggestive of burning maize field rubble (Gish 1995; Kwiatkowski 1995), followed by rapid coverage by over-bank flood deposits. At this site, excavators collected six flotation samples from Features 1 and 3, both basin-shaped depressions. The second site (AZ Z:2:46) on the lower end of the Holocene bajada is an aceramic, possibly Early Agricultural site that includes a basin-shaped depression and some rock features at a location where people were possibly practicing *ak chin* farming. Two flotation samples were gathered from roasting pit Feature 3 that appeared to have some organic content. A pollen report with complementary information on these two sites, plus others (Smith 2003; this volume), has been integrated into the data presented here.

METHODS

A total of eight flotation samples are reported here. The flotation samples, ranging from 0.225 to 4 liters of sediment, were processed in the following manner. Measured sediment was added to a tank of water and agitated, causing the light organic fraction to float to the surface. Water entering the bottom of the tank flowed gently to agitate the tank contents, which then flowed onto a fine mesh screen lined with cheese cloth. The cheese cloth collected the floating light fraction, which was then transferred to a drying rack for at least a day. Heavy fraction was processed and dried separately, after which seeds, plant parts, and charcoal pieces were picked out and saved with the light fraction.

Available light fraction volumes ranged from 5 to 40 ml. Each light fraction was examined in its entirety, and materials were examined for seeds and other reproductive parts. Both charred and uncharred reproductive parts were found in samples, and only the charred items will be further discussed, on the assumption that charred plant materials from archaeological sites usually relate to some intentional or unintentional use of fire in prehistory. Up to 20 pieces of charred wood (charcoal) were identified in flotation samples, or as many as were available having a broad cross-section surface adequate to view anatomical details. All items were identified at magnifications ranging from 8x to 50x using a Zeiss binocular microscope, and in comparison to an extensive modern collection of regional charred and uncharred plant materials backed by herbarium specimens deposited in the University of Arizona herbarium (ARIZ). Identification criteria for the plant parts recovered in southern and central Arizona sites have been previously reported elsewhere (Adams 1994, 1997, 2002, 2003). Full data on all samples are provided in Table 9.2.

RESULTS

A small number of plant parts were recovered from SR 85 sites (Table 9.1). Among these remains was domesticated maize. Wild plants likely gathered for consumption include seeds or fruit of cheno-ams and globemallows, and at least three types of grass grains. The record of wood use for fuelwood and other reasons includes mesquite and ironwood. Use of the word "type" following identifications in Table 9.1 indicates the specimen named has morphological traits identical or very similar to those of the named taxa, but that identification is not absolute because not all reproductive parts of all taxa that occur in the local environment have been examined. For ease of reading, use of the word "type" is implied in the text discussions.

Table 9.1. Plant Taxa and Parts Recovered in Charred Condition from SR 85 Sites

Taxa	Common Name	ID level	Part	Number	ASM Site No	Feat No	Level No
Cheno-am	cheno-am		Seed	2	AZ:T:10:86	1	1
				1	AZ:T:10:86	1	1
				2	AZ:T:10:86	1	3
Gramineae	Grass	type	Caryopsis	1	AZ:T:10:86	1	1
				1	AZ:Z:2:46	3	1
				1	AZ:T:10:86	3	6
Olneya	Ironwood	type	Charcoal	5	AZ:T:10:86	1	1
				3	AZ:T:10:86	1	1
				4	AZ:T:10:86	1	2
				7	AZ:T:10:86	1	3
				3	AZ:T:10:86	3	6
Prosopis	Mesquite	type	Charcoal	15	AZ:T:10:86	1	1
				6	AZ:T:10:86	1	2
				6	AZ:T:10:86	1	3
				20	AZ:Z:2:46	3	1
				20	AZ:Z:2:46	3	1
				12	AZ:T:10:86	3	6
				7	AZ:T:10:86	3	7
Sphaeralcea	globemallow	type	Seed	2	AZ:T:10:86	3	7
Unknown			Tissue	2	AZ:T:10:86	3	7
Zea mays	Maize		Cupule	1	AZ:T:10:86	1	3

Table 9.2. Plant Taxa and Parts Recovered in Flotation Samples from SR 85 Data

ASM Site No	Feat No	Feat Type	Level No	Spec No	Samp No	Taxon	ID level type	Part	Condition	Number	Comments	Avail ml	Exam ml	Orig Samp Vol
AZ:T:10:86	1	basin-shaped depression	1	493-A	1	Cheno-am		seed	charred	2		10	10	4 liters
AZ:T:10:86	1	basin-shaped depression	1	493-A	1	Cheno-am		seed	uncharred		left in sample	10	10	4 liters
AZ:T:10:86	1	basin-shaped depression	1	493-A	1	Gramineae	type	caryopsis	charred	1	type 2	10	10	4 liters
AZ:T:10:86	1	basin-shaped depression	1	493-A	1	Olneya	type	charcoal	charred	5		10	10	4 liters
AZ:T:10:86	1	basin-shaped depression	1	493-A	1	Prosopis	type	charcoal	charred	15		10	10	4 liters
AZ:T:10:86	1	basin-shaped depression	1	493-A	1	Sphaeralcea	type	seed	uncharred		left in sample	10	10	4 liters
AZ:T:10:86	1	basin-shaped depression	1	493-A	1	Trianthema	type	seed	uncharred		left in sample	10	10	4 liters
AZ:T:10:86	1	basin-shaped depression	1	493-B	2	Cheno-am		seed	uncharred		left in sample	5	5	2.85 liters
AZ:T:10:86	1	basin-shaped depression	1	493-B	2	Cheno-am		seed	charred	1	lost	5	5	2.85 liters
AZ:T:10:86	1	basin-shaped depression	1	493-B	2	Olneya	type	charcoal	charred	3		5	5	2.85 liters
AZ:T:10:86	1	basin-shaped depression	1	493-B	2	Soil clumps			uncharred	20+		5	5	2.85 liters
AZ:T:10:86	1	basin-shaped depression	1	493-B	2	Trianthema	type	seed	uncharred		left in sample	5	5	2.85 liters
AZ:T:10:86	1	basin-shaped depression	2	500	1	Cheno-am		seed	uncharred		left in sample	5	5	3.2 liters
AZ:T:10:86	1	basin-shaped depression	2	500	1	Olneya	type	charcoal	charred	4		5	5	3.2 liters
AZ:T:10:86	1	basin-shaped depression	2	500	1	Prosopis	type	charcoal	charred	6		5	5	3.2 liters
AZ:T:10:86	1	basin-shaped depression	3	505	1	Cheno-am		seed	charred	2		5	5	2.8 liters
AZ:T:10:86	1	basin-shaped depression	3	505	1	Olneya	type	charcoal	charred	7		5	5	2.8 liters
AZ:T:10:86	1	basin-shaped depression	3	505	1	Prosopis	type	charcoal	charred	6		5	5	2.8 liters
AZ:T:10:86	1	basin-shaped depression	3	505	1	Zea mays		cupule	charred	1		5	5	2.8 liters
AZ:T:10:86	3	basin-shaped depression	6	none	1	Gramineae	type	caryopsis	charred	1	type 3	10	10	3.5 liters
AZ:T:10:86	3	basin-shaped depression	6	none	1	Olneya	type	charcoal	charred	3		10	10	3.5 liters
AZ:T:10:86	3	basin-shaped depression	6	none	1	Prosopis	type	charcoal	charred	12		10	10	3.5 liters
AZ:T:10:86	3	basin-shaped depression	7	495	1	Cheno-am		seed	uncharred		left in sample	5	5	3.5 liters
AZ:T:10:86	3	basin-shaped depression	7	495	1	Prosopis	type	charcoal	charred	7		5	5	3.5 liters
AZ:T:10:86	3	basin-shaped depression	7	495	1	Sphaeralcea	type	seed	uncharred		left in sample	5	5	3.5 liters
AZ:T:10:86	3	basin-shaped depression	7	495	1	Sphaeralcea	type	seed	charred	2		5	5	3.5 liters
AZ:T:10:86	3	basin-shaped depression	7	495	1	Trianthema	type	seed	uncharred		left in sample	5	5	3.5 liters
AZ:T:10:86	3	basin-shaped depression	7	495	1	Unknown		tissue	charred	2	not charcoal	5	5	3.5 liters
AZ:Z:2:46	3	roasting pit	1	34-A	1	Prosopis	type	charcoal	charred	20		40	30	4 liters
AZ:Z:2:46	3	roasting pit	1	34-A	1	Soil clumps			uncharred	20+		40	30	4 liters
AZ:Z:2:46	3	roasting pit	1	34-B	2	Gramineae	type	caryopsis	charred	1	type 1	10	10	0.225 liters
AZ:Z:2:46	3	roasting pit	1	34-B	2	Prosopis	type	charcoal	charred	20		10	10	0.225 liters

DOMESTICATES

Maize

A single charred maize cupule from Feature 1 at the Floodplain site (AZ T:10:86) is the only evidence of access to a domesticated plant. Cupules are the smallest portions of a maize cob that formerly contained two kernels, and that regularly preserve in recognizable condition. Once the kernels have been removed from the cob, cobs are often used as a source of tinder or fuel for fires. This evidence suggests access to maize ears, rather than only to shelled kernels, which in turn implies that maize was being grown relatively close by.

WILD PLANTS AS POSSIBLE FOODS

Cheno-ams

Charred cheno-am seeds, representing either weedy goosefoot (*Chenopodium*) or pigweed/careless weed (*Amaranthus*) plants, were recovered in three of four flotations samples from Feature 1 at the Gila floodplain site (AZ T:10:86). These plants of disturbed habitats would have been available in gardens to harvest as tender greens in the summer and seeds in the late summer/early fall. People through time have known and appreciated both their productivity and dependable contributions to nutrition and diet. The record of cheno-am pollen at this site is extremely high, and includes pollen aggregates, confirming gathering of the plants when in the flower bud stage, and suggesting usage of this important category of resources in prehistory.

At times, presence of cheno-am seeds and pollen might also reflect gathering of goosefoot and pigweed/careless weed plants to serve as a moist protective layer for other foods being roasted, such as maize. The maize cupule recovered from Feature 1 at AZ T:10:86 provides some support for this suggestion.

Gramineae

Three separate types of grass grains (caryopses) were recognized, one type in each of the three separate features examined for this report. While the evidence is low in numbers, it is suggestive of widespread availability of a variety of grasses. Lacking a more precise level of identification of these grains, it is impossible to say if they represent cool season (spring) or warm season (summer/fall) resources. Grasses have a long history of use in the American Southwest (Doebley 1984), and a strategy to accumulate detailed morphological data on prehistoric grasses aimed to eventually identify them has been suggested (Adams 2001). As with the cheno-am seed evidence, grass presence in these features at SR 85 can relate to human consumption of the grains, or to use of moist grass plants as a protective layer during roasting of larger resources, or possibly even to the burning of fallow agricultural fields prior to re-planting. The pollen record of grasses is enriched in rock cluster site AZ T:14:113.

Sphaeralcea

Two charred globemallow seeds preserved in Feature 3 at the floodplain site (AZ T:10:86). Whether these ancient seeds represent prepared foods or inclusion during burning of field stubble is unknown. Globemallow seeds are reported from a limited number of Hohokam sites, suggesting localized use (Gasser and Kwiatkowski 1991:438). Bohrer reports that globemallow seeds from La

Ciudad in the Phoenix area could represent use of a famine food, or discards from roasting ovens (1987:114). An Arizona species, *Sphaeralcea angustifolia*, has been chewed as gum historically (Castetter 1935:52). The Seri pounded the roots of *Sphaeralcea ambigua* to make a medicinal tea (Felger and Moser 1985:346). Today, showy globemallows are often seen along roadsides in full flower in the springtime, able to produce seeds by the early summer.

WOODS FOR FUELS AND OTHER NEEDS

Olneya

Ironwood charcoal preserved in five of the six flotation samples from the two basin-shaped depressions at the floodplain site (AZ T:10:86). This is suggestive of regular use of ironwood as a fuel source. The dense nature of this wood makes it a fine candidate for long-lasting fires. Ironwood trees prefer to grow in locations with accessible water, such as floodplains. As cold temperature-sensitive trees, they generally indicate locations where frosts and cold-air drainage is less severe, and possibly preferred by agriculturalists looking for fields less vulnerable to freezing. Ironwood pods have edible seeds in the late spring/early summer.

Prosopis

Mesquite charcoal occurred in seven of the eight flotation samples from both sites, including in each of the three separate features examined for this report. Like ironwood, this pattern reflects repeated use of mesquite in roasting pits and other thermal features. Like ironwood, it provides a hot and long-lasting fire. The ethnobotanical record of mesquite use includes extensive references to grinding the pods as a food (Felger 1977). The use of mesquite wood implies access to the dependable pods, available in mid to late summer through the fall, as does the recovery of mesquite pollen in some of the pollen samples, especially a sample at a rock cluster site (AZ T:14:94).

SITE BY SITE DESCRIPTION

AZ T:10:86 (ASM)

The two basin-shaped depressions at this site contain similar wood charcoal records, in that both mesquite and ironwood were regularly burned in prehistory. However, charred reproductive parts differ between these two features. Feature 1 preserved charred cheno-am seeds, a grass grain, and evidence of maize in the form of a cupule. A high concentration of cheno-am pollen grains (>80%) suggests use of these plants as food, which likely grew in abundance in disturbed locations such as agricultural fields. Feature 3 contained a different grass and globemallow seeds, along with maize pollen as evidence of agricultural efforts. The presence of cholla cactus pollen implies people were harvesting cholla flower buds in the late spring/early summer period, perhaps at a time when the maize fields were being planted. Together the seed and pollen records are suggestive of foods processed in the past.

AZ Z:2:46 (ASM)

This aceramic site dates to the Early Agricultural Period or the transition to the Early Ceramic horizon. The roasting pit at this site preserved a charred grass grain, along with mesquite and ironwood charcoal. Evidence may reflect either processing of grass grains for food, or processing a larger product and using moist grass plants to protect the products during the roasting process. Maize pollen in this site suggests possible farming in the lower bajada regions. The presence of plantain (*Plantago* type) pollen and cholla type pollen under surface rocks suggests access to two late spring/early summer resources that people have gathered as food both historically and prehistorically. Plantain seeds are available in the same season as cholla flower buds, and both offer critical foods in the season preceding the availability of agricultural products.

POLLEN FROM OTHER SITES IN THE AREA

Three sites with rock clusters and ceramic sherds (AZ T:14:113, AZ T:14:92 and AZ T:14:94) preserved pollen from cacti other than cholla. This suggests use of one or more fruits of hedgehog, saguaro, barrel or other cactus plants on this landscape. Grass pollen in AZ T:14:113 implies use of grasses, as does the recovery of grass grains in the macrofossil record from basin-shaped depressions in sites AZ T:10:86 and AZ Z:2:46. Mesquite pollen complements the mesquite wood record of fuelwood use, and possibly of mesquite bean use. The pollen record is the only place where evidence of palo verde (*Cercidium*) is recorded.

DISCUSSION

The archaeobotanical seed and charred wood record from eight SR 85 flotation samples is sparse, but informative. Ancient occupants of an activity area associated with agriculture (AZ T:10:86) and a Holocene bajada site (AZ Z:2:46) appear to have been maize farmers, and likely took advantage of weedy wild plants that grew in their agricultural fields and other disturbed places. The broader archaeological record suggests that burning of field stubble may have formed part of their cycle of agricultural tasks. Wood needs for fuel were satisfied by mesquite and ironwood trees that grew nearby, which likely offered edible pods or seeds as well. Roasting events may have required the use of locally abundant weedy plants for use as moist wraps around the products of interest.

PLANTS ON THE LANDSCAPE

The ancient plant record reported here suggests that mesquite and ironwood trees occurred commonly enough in prehistory to regularly be sought as fuel. Mesquite grows along floodplains and the first terrace up, and ironwood does best in areas with both access to water and year-round moderate temperatures. Disturbed ground, likely including agricultural fields, provided prime locations for members of the goosefoot and pigweed/ carelessweed group, as well as globemallow plants, to thrive. At least three separate types of grasses grew in the vicinity, possibly reflecting a more notable presence of grasses on the landscape than at present.

SEASONALITY

The plant record reported here suggests that people were in this region minimally during the late spring/early summer and early fall months. The presence of globemallow seeds, along with cholla pollen, confirms a late spring/early summer presence. Plantain pollen, associated primarily with the rock cluster sites and one basin-shaped depression (AZ Z:2:46) would also be available in the late spring/early summer, before the plants set seed and disperse on the landscape. Cheno-am seeds and pollen, often found in disturbed habitats such as agricultural fields, would have been available from summer through fall. If maize was being grown nearby, agricultural requirements likely had some individuals on the landscape during springtime field preparation through summer or fall harvest of the crop. Grasses offer critical grain products for humans in all seasons from spring through fall. The possibility of double-cropping maize has been suggested for Hohokam groups elsewhere, and might be a possibility in this area as well.

COMPLEMENTARY PLANT RECORDS

Together and separately, the plant macrofossil and the pollen records from these State Route 85 sites reveal information about subsistence activities in prehistory. Evidence of agricultural endeavors is strengthened by recovery of a maize cupule and maize pollen in two sites. Coupled with specimens of garden weeds (cheno-am seeds and pollen, a globemallow seed), it seems reasonable to conclude that people were growing maize and taking advantage of the weeds of their fields. Mesquite and ironwood offered fuels, and most likely foods as well. It seems reasonable that palo verde trees did the same. Grasses likely played an important role as foods, as did plantain seeds and cholla flower buds. Presence on the landscape throughout the agricultural growing season is implied by recovery of late spring/early summer plantain and cholla pollen and globemallow seeds. Summer through fall presence is reflected in the maize and cheno-am record, along with pollen from mesquite, palo verde, and cacti other than cholla. It is unclear if the presence of cotton pollen in one site (AZ T:14:92) clearly belongs to the prehistoric or historic record.

CHAPTER 10

THE HISTORY AND HISTORIC CONTEXT OF SITE AZ T:14:96 (ASM), THE WARNER GOODE HOMESTEAD

Pat H. Stein

INTRODUCTION

A survey conducted by Archaeological Research Services (Harmon and Beyer 1995) during an earlier phase of the State Route (SR) 85 project indicated that site AZ T:14:96 (ASM) marked the remains of a homestead patented by Warner Goode in 1936. Research conducted by Arizona Preservation Consultants for the present data recovery project confirmed that the site was indeed the Warner Goode homestead; the research also quickly discovered that Goode was an African-American sharecropper who had relocated from Oklahoma to the Gila Bend area in the late 1920s to pursue agricultural interests and to build a better future for his family.

This chapter on the Warner Goode homestead is organized in two sections. The first section places the site in historical perspective by describing its historic context. The second section presents archival and oral-historical data that document the site and its inhabitants.

HISTORIC CONTEXT OF THE GOODE HOMESTEAD

The Warner Goode homestead stands at the junction of three important themes in the history of Arizona: (1) the development of homesteading; (2) the movement of African-Americans into the state; and (3) agricultural intensification in the Gila Bend area. The following pages explore these themes to provide an understanding of the world in which site AZ T:14:96 functioned. Each theme is described to approximately 1940, the year when the Goode family sold the homestead and moved off the property.

THEME 1: THE DEVELOPMENT OF HOMESTEADING

Homesteading represents a rich and vital part of our national heritage. From 1862 to about 1940, homesteading played a major part in the transfer of hundreds of millions of acres from the federal government to private ownership (Bureau of Land Management/BLM 1962). It was a significant factor in the settlement of the American frontier (Gates 1968). Homesteading played no less important a role in the development of Arizona. Over three million acres of Arizona land in private ownership today was originally acquired through the process of homesteading (BLM 1962; Stein 1990).

The Homestead Act was enacted during the Civil War under the administration of President Abraham Lincoln. The 1862 act entitled heads of households or persons at least 21 years old to claim up to 160 acres of public land. The homesteader was required to cultivate and improve the tract, build a home, and reside there for five years. The settler who satisfied those requirements could then file a final entry (called a "proof") and receive title (a patent) to the land (BLM 1962).

All federal land was potentially available for homesteading, provided that it was non-saline and non-mineral in character, was not previously withdrawn or reserved, was not occupied for trade or business purposes, and did not lie within an incorporated city or town. The General Land Office (GLO, now the BLM) was the lead agency responsible for tracking homestead applications and for classifying land as suitable or unsuitable for settlement. GLO subdivision surveys—those which divided townships into sections—often served as the catalysts that triggered a wave of homestead applications in a particular locality (Gates 1968).

The homesteader had the right to relinquish (voluntarily surrender) the claim at any time. Alternatively, the homesteader could commute the claim; that is, he or she could purchase the land outright from the government for a nominal price of $1.25 or $2.50 an acre (the price depending on where the land was located in relation to railroads). The government could also cancel the claim if the homesteader was found to be in non-compliance with federal laws and regulations.

In theory, GLO inspectors were supposed to visit homesteads to check for compliance with the law. In practice, inspections rarely occurred because the GLO was understaffed and the distances involved were vast. Therefore, local witnesses played key roles in supporting or refuting a homesteader's word. The GLO published a series of notices of the claimant's intention to "prove up" in a local newspaper; readers were expected to come forward if they knew of deception involving the claim. Also, two witnesses were required to provide testimony in support of the claim at the time of final proof (Stein 1990).

Under the Homestead Act, rich farmlands in the Midwest quickly passed from government to private ownership. Through time, potential homesteaders seeking land to claim were forced to move westward into the mountains and deserts. There, they encountered low rainfall or short growing seasons that defeated many attempts at settlement. Thus, Congress amended the 1862 act many times to try to make homesteading more feasible. Some examples are cited below; a more complete account of changes in homestead law may be found in Gates (1968).

One such change, the Enlarged Homestead Act of 1909, allowed the settler to claim up to 320 acres. The act was often referred to as the Dry Farming Act because it acknowledged that many western lands that were too arid for highly water-dependent crops could be made productive if they were cultivated less intensively and more *ex*tensively, using dry-farming methods.

Another legislative change, adopted in 1912, reduced the homestead residency requirement from five to three years. It also gave settlers the option of being absent from their claims for five months of each year. The passage of this legislation was eagerly awaited by many westerners. It meant that they could legally leave their claims for extended periods, and work elsewhere to raise cash during intemperate seasons on the homestead.

From about 1929 to 1936, new regulations relaxed the requirements regarding residency on, and cultivation of, the claim, provided that the homesteader could prove hardship due to economic or climatic conditions. The new regulations were enacted in response to widespread drought as well as the Great Depression. As a later section of this chapter will show, these changes proved vitally important in the case of Warner Goode's claim (Funk 1936; Stein 1990).

Nationally, more than 270 million acres of land were homesteaded between 1862 and the repeal of enabling legislation in 1976 (BLM 1962). In Arizona, homesteading provided the vehicle for the transfer of more than four million acres from the public domain to private ownership. Over one million of these acres were eventually reacquired by the federal government through the Bankhead-Jones Act, and thus were returned to the public domain. However, over 3 million acres of the Arizona land that was patented through homesteading still remain in private ownership (Stein 1990).

The earliest successful (patented) homestead in Arizona was filed in the 1870s in present-day Mesa; all earlier claims culminated in relinquishments or cancellations. Eventually, more than 21,000 homestead claims in Arizona would be successful, culminating in title patents. However, throughout the history of homesteading in Arizona, unsuccessful claims would far outnumber successful ones. Preliminary figures suggest that, for every claim that culminated in a patent, two would be relinquished or canceled (Stein 1990).

Arizona, like the rest of the nation, experienced a peak in homestead patenting beginning in the 1910s and a steady decline beginning around 1920. The downward trend continued nationally, but reversed sharply in Arizona around 1930. Our state then witnessed its second and final homesteading "boom" from 1930 until about 1936. Little patenting occurred in the state after 1940 (BLM 1962), when new laws and changes in public land policy made it increasingly difficult to find land to homestead.

THEME 2: THE MOVEMENT OF AFRICAN-AMERICANS INTO ARIZONA

African-Americans have a long history in Arizona. The first non-native to enter the area is believed to have been a North African Moor named Estevanico. Estevanico first trekked through what is now Arizona either in 1536, as a survivor of the ill-fated Cabeza de Vaca expedition, or in 1539, as a guide for Marcos de Niza (Officer1987; Wagoner 1975).

The earliest African-Americans to have a sizeable presence in Arizona were soldiers who served in the Ninth and Tenth Cavalry Regiments following the Civil War. They were stationed at several Arizona posts, including Fort Huachuca, during the Indian Wars era. Native American opponents gave the troopers a sobriquet that acknowledged both their fighting tenacity and their dark, curly hair. The "buffalo soldiers" accepted the title and wore it proudly; indeed, the most prominent feature of the regimental crest of the Tenth Cavalry was a buffalo (Leckie 1967).

Other African-Americans followed the buffalo soldiers to Arizona. Many were fleeing the bigotry that persisted in the South after the Civil War. The non-military Black population within Arizona Territory grew from 26 in 1870, to 155 in 1880, to 1357 in 1890 (Harris 1983). These civilians found work in the ranching, mining, agricultural, and retail industries. Some, such as Richard Rosser and William Crump (both of Phoenix), acquired extensive properties, operated successful businesses, and became leaders in their communities (Harris 1983).

The late nineteenth and early twentieth centuries witnessed periodic attempts by African-Americans to establish their own enterprises in Arizona. A prominent example was the Afro Mining Company, founded in 1912 by a group of Tucson citizens led by J. W. Miller. A super-salesman who had started as a cook in a mining camp, Miller sold stock in the operation, located in the Comobabi area. An estimated $250,000 was invested in the mining company before Miller's untimely death in the 1920s (Harris 1983).

Unfortunately, some African-Americans were lured to Arizona by fraudulent schemes. Bouse Wash, located on Highway 60 between the communities of Hope and Brenda, was to be the site of a utopia for some 500 African-American colonizers from Los Angeles. Around 1925, White men approached the Californians, saying they had found some good homestead land along Bouse Wash. The men offered to survey the land, lay out section lines, and dig wells there—all for a dollar an acre. People who bought into the scheme found that they had been victimized by swindlers who disappeared with their money. Many of the families who tried to eke out a living on the land eventually pulled up stakes and returned to California or relocated to Phoenix (Harris 1983).

An African-American community that enjoyed greater success was that of Mobile, Arizona. Founded originally as a stop along the Southern Pacific Railroad, Mobile first began to attract Black homesteaders in 1929–1930. Settlement continued through the 1930s. Most of the settlers came from Oklahoma or Texas, often by way of Phoenix. Many of them succeeded in building homes, residing on the land, and eventually gaining title patents to it. Mobile continued to grow in the 1940s, but then declined in the 1950s as many of its residents sold their holdings and moved back to Phoenix (Swanson 1992).

As African-Americans immigrated to Arizona, so, too, did Euro-Americans, and in far greater numbers. The influx of southern Whites contributed to a tightening of Arizona's race laws in the early 1900s. In 1909 the Territorial Legislature stipulated that school trustees had to segregate pupils of the "African race" from those of the Caucasian race, except in high schools. In cases where 25 or more "Negroes" matriculated in a high school, 15 percent of the district's residents could call an election to decide whether or not to segregate those students. In 1912, the state constitution further codified segregation by prohibiting interracial marriage (Harris 1983; Thul 1990).

Arizona's schools practiced segregation in a variety of ways. Trustees of the Phoenix school system maintained separate facilities for Black and White students at both the elementary and high school levels. When Tucson's Black students finished eighth grade at Dunbar Elementary (as their school was called), they went on to attend segregated classrooms within otherwise-integrated high schools. Prescott, on the other hand, practiced segregation only at the primary level; its high school was fully integrated. In small towns with few Black students, segregation was sometimes ignored entirely, mainly because it was not financially practical to provide separate facilities and teachers. Other small towns set up jim-crow schools at the first sign of African-Americans in any appreciable number. For example, the rural town of McNary in northern Arizona established an elementary class for "colored" students when a lumber company relocated their families there from Louisiana in 1924 (Harris 1983).

It is at this point that the African-American experience in Arizona intersects the history of the Goode homestead. As the Oral History section of this chapter will show, being a person of color and obtaining a secondary education in rural Arizona could prove problematic. The quest for a good education motivated Warner Goode and his family, and played a vital role in the decisions they made about their homestead and future.

THEME 3: AGRICULTURAL INTENSIFICATION IN THE GILA BEND AREA

Gila Bend owes much of its early history to its strategic location along the Gila River at the western end of the "40-mile desert." In prehistoric and historic times, the Gila Bend area served as a watering point along a popular travel corridor that connected the Sonoran Desert and the Pacific coast. Travelers found that they could save miles and time if they avoided the great northern bend of the Gila River and instead took a short-cut across the waterless expanse between (approximately) Sacaton and Gila Bend. The Spanish Overland Route (Anza Trail) of the eighteenth century and the Leach Wagon Road of the nineteenth century each depended on the Gila Bend locality as a watering point and rest stop (Bachman 1941).

In 1857 the Butterfield Overland Mail Company established a stage station in the area. Called Gila Ranch, the station was located on the southern bank of the Gila River about 4.5 miles north of the present town of Gila Bend. A small community—with a post office, a saloon, and a few houses—developed around the station. By 1880, the settlement numbered about 40 residents (Ryden 1999). Most were farmers who used a small irrigation ditch to raise grain for freighters (Granger 1983).

The community near the stage station experienced a relatively short life. A shift in the dominant mode of transportation—from horse to iron horse—resulted in a shift in the location of the town. In

1879, the Southern Pacific Railroad laid tracks through the area. The tracks followed an east–west course about 4.5 miles south of the old station. The community gradually shifted to the south to be closer to the tracks (Ryden 1999).

Construction of the railroad stimulated new forms of development. In 1882, G. W. Webb announced plans to use Gila River water and a large tract of land to create a colony similar to Riverside, California. By 1883 his crews were working to construct the Gila Bend Canal. Although Webb could not complete his plan because of legal entanglements, the scheme nonetheless brought an influx of new settlers to Gila Bend (Ryden 1999).

Subsequent years saw the construction of additional railroad facilities, the establishment of a townsite, and the development of amenities such as a school. The local economy received a further boost when former territorial governor Lewis Wolfley announced plans in 1891 to build a dam across the Gila River. Wolfley predicted that the dam would open a huge tract of the Gila River Valley to agriculture. The construction project poured money into the local economy and attracted new settlers. By 1900, Gila Bend's population numbered about 130 individuals (Ryden 1999).

Plagued by legal and technical problems, Wolfley could never make a paying proposition of his dam and irrigation project (Ryden 1999). Flooding and poor design constantly eroded the dam, situated about 20 mi upstream from Gila Bend. A torrent in January 1895 took out a 400-ft section while the structure was being redesigned and overhauled. By 1905, the damaged section still had not been repaired. Wolfley's dream ended in 1910 when he was killed in a streetcar accident in Los Angeles (Barrios 1989).

Six years after Wolfley's death, Frank A. Gillespie arrived in Arizona. Gillespie had amassed a fortune in the Oklahoma oil fields; in 1916, he was said to be earning up to $20,000 a day in oil revenues. He came to Arizona looking for ways to invest his money. Wolfley's old project became the object of Gillespie's search (Barrios 1989).

With C. F. Ainsworth of Phoenix, Gillespie acquired what was left of Wolfley Dam and its associated Gila Bend Canal. They hired J. B. Girand, a prominent Arizona engineer, to design a new dam on the old damsite. The Gila Water Company, as the new enterprise was called, began building Gillespie Dam in 1919 and completed it in 1921 at a cost of $1.6 million. As part of the project, segments of the old Gila Bend Canal were also modified at a cost of about $300,000 (Barrios 1989).

At the time of its completion, Gillespie Dam was said to be the largest private irrigation enterprise in the United States (Barrios 1989). Agricultural development intensified in the years following its construction. In 1923, about 12,000 acres were farmed using water supplied by the dam. By 1927, the project irrigated some 15,000 acres. Under the direction of Frank's son Bernard, the project would eventually deliver water to about 85,000 acres (MacPherson 1973; Ryden 1999).

Most of the project area was planted in cotton, a labor-intensive crop that required picking by hand. A large seasonal work force was needed. Gillespie therefore hired many laborers, including African-Americans and Mexican-Americans, to harvest his fields. Although most of the cotton-pickers were migrant workers who moved on after each harvest, some stayed, establishing more or less permanent homes in the area and contributing to its population base (Ryden 1999).

To assure an adequate supply of labor for projects like Gillespie, the Arizona Cotton Growers' Association hired contractors to scour the western cotton states and recruit workers. The association:

> ...did not leave labor procurement to chance. To ensure that potential workers had
> the ability to make the trip west, the association transported cotton pickers from the

western cotton states directly to Arizona in trucks and chartered buses and trains, the cost deducted from each worker's wages. By the late 1920s, it distributed gasoline cards throughout Oklahoma, Texas, and New Mexico to rebate transportation costs at the end of the season. Moreover, the association maintained a mailing list to encourage pickers to return each year [Weisiger 1995:46].

Labor recruiters found particularly receptive minds among Oklahoma's sharecroppers (Weisiger 1995). Many had watched their crops wither and die during years of worsening climatic conditions; they were ready to pull up stakes and begin life in a new land. With its large irrigation project and seasonal employment possibilities, Gila Bend must have seemed, to such farmers, a land of greater opportunity.

A HISTORY OF THE GOODE HOMESTEAD

This section presents archival and oral-historical data documenting the Warner Goode homestead. The archival data was collected from repositories including: the State Office of the Bureau of Land Management; the Maricopa County Recorder's Office; Arizona State Library, Archives, and Public Records; the State Historic Preservation Office; and the National Archives and Records Administration in Washington, DC. Oral-historical information and the photographs presented in this section were provided by Calvin C. Goode, son of homesteader Warner Goode, in an interview conducted at the site on 24 January 2003.

The two data sets presented in this section are complementary. The archival data focuses on the period from 1929 to 1936, beginning with the filing of a homestead application and culminating in the conveyance of a patent deed from the federal government to Warner Goode. The oral-historical data documents specific events and activities that occurred on the homestead from 1929 to 1940, when the property was sold. The oral-historical information also provides insight into processes that affected the site after the Goodes moved away in the summer of 1940.

ARCHIVAL DATA

Warner Goode filed his homestead application with the Phoenix branch of the General Land Office on 5 May 1929. He listed his address as Buckeye, AZ, at the time of the application. He stated that he was a native-born citizen of the United States, married, and over 21 years of age. He claimed 160 acres, described as the entire NW ¼ of Section 11 in Township 3 South, Range 4 West. A witness familiar with the land, W. E. Morris of Buckeye, verified the applicant's testimony that the 160 acres contained no known mineral resources, and no spring, waterhole, or other body of water. The General Land Office accepted Goode's filing fee of $16.00, and allowed the claim to go forward (BLM nd; National Archives 1929a).

The next recorded event involving the homestead occurred on 12 November 1929, when Warner Goode amended his application to change its legal description. The new legal description was the SW¼ of the SW¼ of Section 11, Township 3 South, Range 4 West; as well as the NW¼ of the NW¼ and the S½ of the NW¼ of Section 14, in the same township-range. Like the original application, the amended one included 160 acres. The reason for the change was that Warner Goode had discovered that some of the land in his original claim (the NW¼ of Section 11) actually belonged to someone else. Goode reported that old, deteriorated survey markers had made it difficult to describe his claim accurately. According to the claimant, his homestead was situated:

…in a township surveyed in 1883 that was then marked with wood posts for corners, which have wrotted [sic] since then. Therefore I could not tell where the [corners] were located. But since that time a few of the neighbors, one of them cornering with me, having had their land surveyed, has shown me that my land is more taken up by the foot hills than I at first thought…The lay of said land is fairly good and better protected by the mountains from the cold north winds [Warner Goode, cited in National Archives 1929b].

The homesteader's testimony was corroborated by two witnesses. The first was a neighbor, William Eugene Morris, described as a 39-year old carpenter residing in Arlington, AZ. The second witness was John Wesley Jones, described as a 60-year old farmer residing in Phoenix. The General Land Office found the paperwork to be in order, and approved the amended application on 12 February 1930 (BLM nd). Figure 10.1 is a map showing the locations of Goode's original and amended homestead claims.

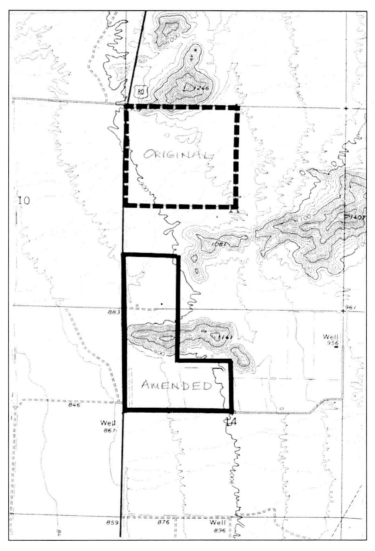

Figure 10.1. Map showing location of Warner Goode's original (broken line) and amended (solid line) homestead claims in Township 3 South, Range 4 West.

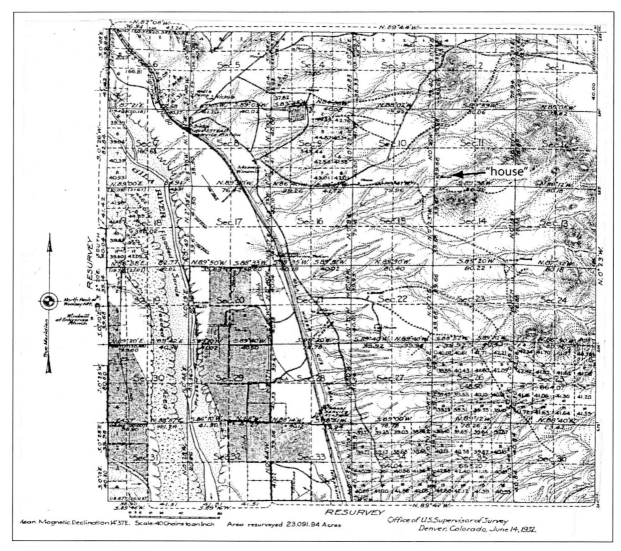

Figure 10.2. 1932 GLO map of Township 3 South, Range 4 West. The "house" shown in the SW ¼ of Section 11 is that of the Goode family. (GLO 1932)

The General Land Office soon rectified the problem encountered by Warner Goode and other nearby settlers by ordering a resurvey of Township 3 South, Range 4 West. The resurvey conducted by Benjamin J. Kinsey in April 1931. Section lines were redrawn, and section corners reestablished during the survey. In his general description of the township, surveyor Kinsey noted that:

> …practically all of the lands along the Gila River are occupied and are being farmed. Most of the land west of U.S. Highway 80 has been taken up under the Homestead Act, and shows much improvement consisting of houses and other buildings, fences, and well. East of the Highway are some scattered settlers, and there are a few wells, one in sec. 5, and one each in secs. 8 and 9. The main canal of the Gila Water Company, close to the highway, paralleling same, conveys irrigation water from the Gillespie Dam to Gila Bend territory [Kinsey 1931].

The General Land Office map (GLO 1932) generated by Kinsey's resurvey (Figure 10.2) provides a glimpse of the physical and cultural setting in which the Goode homestead functioned. On the map, the agricultural development cited by Kinsey west of Highway 80 is particularly apparent in the southwestern quadrant of the township. Highway 80 and the Gila Water Company canal paralleling it are seen traversing Sections 6, 7, 8, 16, 17, 21, 28, and 33. A telephone line also parallels the highway and canal. Along or close to the highway, other signs of development include the "Homestead Service Station" and "Massey's Windmill," both in Section 8, a "Highway Maintenance Station" in Section 16, and the "Woods Service Station" in Section 28. A network of primitive roads is shown radiating from the highway in a generally eastward direction toward the homesteads of the Goodes and other settlers. Although not labeled as such, the Goodes' house is shown in the SW ¼ of Section 11.

The Goode homestead was not recorded again in documentary records until 1935. On February 7th of that year, Warner Goode appeared before officials at the General Land Office in Phoenix, and announced his intention to "prove up" on his homestead, that is, to prove that he had satisfied the requirements of the Homestead Act so that he could gain legal title to the land. Goode indicated that he would be filing a Three-Year Proof (see preceding section for a description of this term). He specified that his witnesses would include two of the following people: Ruben Smith, Winfield Riley, Mrs. Love Jordan, or Moat Grayson, all of Gila Bend. With approval from the General Land Office, Goode set a date of 25 March 1935 for filing his "Final Proof" application (National Archives 1935a).

The notice of Goode's intent to file a final proof was published in the Buckeye Review for a period of five consecutive weeks beginning on 15 February 1935. The notice (Figure 10.3) stated the homesteader's name, the location of his claim, the witnesses to potentially testify, and the date for the Final Proof application. The notice was also posted in the General Land Office from February 7th through March 25th (National Archives 1935b).

Warner Goode appeared before the General Land Office as scheduled on 25 March 1935 to file his Final Proof. He testified that he was married, and had a wife and five children. He stated that in August 1930 he had finished building a residence on the homestead (in the SW¼ of the SW¼ of Section 11) and had moved into it with his family immediately thereafter. Since that time, he had been absent from the land for only four short periods: from 6 June to 3 September 1931, from 8 June to 8 September 1932, from 15 June to 10 September 1933, and from 12 June to 10 September 1934. His improvements to the land consisted of a three-room "box house" (valued at $120), 10 acres fenced with two-strand barbed wire (valued at $20), a chicken house made of lumber (valued at $10), and 21 cleared acres (valued at $100) (Warner Goode, cited in National Archives 1935c).

The cleared acreage was intended to be used for agriculture; however, Warner Goode testified that he experienced little success growing crops. In 1930 he planted five acres in maize, but there was "No harvest. Too dry" (Warner Goode, cited in National Archives 1935c). Similar attempts to plant maize in 1931 and 1932 met with similar failure. In 1933, Goode planted only two acres for a vegetable garden and cotton, but, again there was no harvest because of the lack of water. In 1934 he did not attempt to grow crops at all. In early 1935, he planted a small garden in unspecified crops. As of the date of his testimony on March 25th of that year, the garden had sprouted but not yet matured. The claimant testified that "The reasons I have not cultivated the required areas each year since 1932 was because of the dry conditions, not enough rain to make a crop; it is a waste of seed to plant a crop" (Warner Goode, cited in National Archives 1935c).

Warner Goode paid the customary fee of $7.50 when he filed his Final Proof. In an affidavit, he stated that he had not filed his final proof sooner because, with the Depression and poor economic conditions, he had not had the money to do so (National Archives 1935c).

The two witnesses interviewed by the General Land Office in support of Goode's final proof were Winfield F. Riley and Ruben Smith. The testimony of each man generally corroborated Goode's

NOTICE FOR PUBLICATION

Department of the Interior, General Land Ofice at Phoenix, Arizona, February 7, 1935

NOTICE is hereby given that Warner Goode, of Gila Bend, Arizona, who, on February 12, 1930, made Homestead Entry, Sec. 2289, R. S. U. S., No. 065876, for SW ¼ SW ¼, Section 11 · NW ¼ NW ¼, S ½ NW 1/4, Section 14. Township 3 S., Range 4 W., G. & S. R. B. & Meridian, has filed notice of intention to make Final Three Year Proof to establish claim to the land above described, before Register, Uinted States Land Office, at Phoenix, Arizona, on the 25th day of March, 1935. Claimant names as witnesses: Ruben Smith, Winfield Riley, Mrs. Love Jordan, Moat Grayson, all of Gila Bend, Arizona.

P. J. KEOHANE,
Registe1

First publication February 15, 1935.
Last publication, March 15, 1935.

Figure 10.3. Notice of Publication for the Warner Goode Homestead. (*Buckeye Review* 1935)

statements as to improvements made to the land and the attempts to grow crops there. Concerning the Goode's three-room house, Riley specified that it was built of lumber and had tin roofing (National Archives 1935d). Concerning Goode's brief yearly absences, Smith noted that the homesteader had gone away to pick cotton (National Archives 1935e). Regarding improvements to the land, Smith also stated that Goode had a small shed that functioned as a garage.

The Phoenix official who reviewed Goode's Final Proof was Registrar P. J. Keohane. Keohane noted that the application appeared to be "defective to some degree as to cultivation." The issue was that Goode had never filed a special request that would have allowed him to reduce the number of acres he was required to cultivate. Keohane forwarded his opinion, as well as Goode's Final Proof application, to the Commissioner of the General Land Office for a ruling (Keohane 1935). Warner Goode waited anxiously as the federal government considered his case.

Finally, in February 1936, Washington responded. Commissioner Antoinette Funk noted that an act dated 19 August 1935 (Public Law No. 285) had made it unnecessary for homesteaders in extremely arid lands to cultivate their claims. Applying the 1935 law to the Goode claim, the Commissioner ruled that Goode's Final Proof was satisfactory in all respects, and ordered the Phoenix office to issue a Final Certificate in the homesteader's name (Funk 1936). Registrar Keohane complied with the directive, issued the certificate on 18 February 1936, sent the original to Washington, and mailed a copy to the homesteader (BLM nd; National Archives 1936).

The final step in the process occurred on 12 October 1936 when the federal government issued a Patent Deed to Warner Goode. Signed by President Franklin D. Roosevelt, the deed conveyed 160 acres to the homesteader and specified the legal description of the property (BLM 1936). After seven long years, Warner Goode had gained title to his piece of the Arizona desert.

The present investigation located two additional records pertaining to Warner Goode. A Warranty Deed at the Maricopa County Recorder indicated that Warner and his wife Clara sold the homestead on 5 August 1940 to Mary A. Kinderman. The price paid for the 160-acre tract was $150 (Maricopa County 1940).

The final record pertaining to Warner Goode was his obituary. The obituary indicated that he had been born in Chandler, Oklahoma; had homesteaded near Gila Bend in the 1920s and 1930s; had moved with his family to Phoenix in 1948; had worked variously as a road grader for Maricopa County and as a self-employed cement and rock mason; was a member of the Sky Harbor Congregation of Jehovah's Witnesses; and had most recently resided at 1446 East Jefferson Street in Phoenix. At the time of his death on 24 July 1982, Warner Goode was survived by his wife Clara, three sons (Melvin, Calvin, and Alvin), four daughters (Doretha, Lillie, Iretha, and Evelyn), three brothers, five sisters, 20 grandchildren, and 12 great-grandchildren (*Arizona Republic* 1982).

ORAL HISTORY

Calvin C. Goode, son of homesteader Warner Goode, has for decades been a prominent figure in central Arizona. His accomplishments are legion. He served for 22 years on the Phoenix City Council, where he gained a reputation as a hard-working, reliable politician. As a city councilman, he articulately represented minority neighborhoods and consistently supported programs to benefit young people. Now retired from the council, Mr. Goode continues to lead an active life in public service. He is a founding member and current President of the George Washington Carver Museum and Cultural Center in Phoenix. The "Calvin C. Goode Lifetime Achievement Award" celebrates the accomplishments of Arizona's outstanding African-Americans. A city municipal building is even named in his honor.

Born in 1927, Calvin Goode spent much of his youth—from 1929 to 1940—on the family homestead north of Gila Bend. On 24 January 2003, he accompanied the author on a visit to the site. There, he shared memories and photographs of his family's experiences as homesteaders. The following pages present the information obtained during the on-site interview.

Warner Goode was born in Oklahoma in 1902. He and his wife Clara, a native of Arkansas, spent the early years of their marriage in Depew, Oklahoma, where they gave birth to two sons (Melvin and Calvin) and one daughter (Lena). Warner had an 8th-grade education, Clara a 6th-grade education.

Warner worked as a sharecropper. A hailstorm in Oklahoma destroyed his crop and convinced him that it was time to try to earn a living elsewhere. He looked toward Gila Bend, a promising area of rapid agricultural growth where his wife had relatives living. Thus, in 1927, Warner Goode sent his wife and children by train to Arizona, and set off in his truck to join them.

It should be emphasized that the Goodes relocated to Arizona for economic rather than health reasons. Many immigrants to the state during the 1920s were veterans who had suffered respiratory damage during World War I; they sought relief in southern Arizona's clean, warm climate. This factor did not influence the Goode family. Warner Goode was not a veteran, and neither he nor his young family suffered from respiratory or other chronic ailments. Warner Goode was a hale and hearty 25-year-old when he arrived in the Copper State.

Calvin Goode was 10 months old when his family made the move. He did not recall how his father happened to select an exact spot to homestead. He assumed that his father had found that most of the best land—close to the Gila River or under the Gila Water Company Canal—was already settled, leaving Warner little choice but to select arid land away from readily-available water. One thing seemed clear, however; Warner hoped that he could drill a well, find water, and develop a productive farm on the spot he chose to settle.

The family continued to grow after settling on the land. Two more children would be born to Warner and Clara between 1927 and 1935, and two more between 1935 and 1940. Thus, two adults and seven children would come to reside on the desert homestead (Figures 10.4 through 10.7). In addition, relatives would sometimes come for visits.

The Goodes and their visitors stayed in two small houses south of a small wash in the SW¼ of the SW¼ of Section 11 (all that remains of the structures today are a concrete pad and bits of cement). The more western of the two houses—the one favored by the family as a residence—was of wood frame construction with a tin roof. The other house, used to some extent by the family but also by visiting relatives, had walls built partly of railroad ties and a roof of boards with earth piled on top to keep out the rain.

Clara Goode cooked for her family on a small woodstove. There was no electricity; kerosene lamps provided the only light for night time reading and studying. Except for a homemade evaporative device (made of burlap to keep water cool), the homestead did not have any form of refrigeration. Lacking a reliable way to store food, the family ate a diet consisting largely of fresh and cured meats (see section on livestock below) plus canned goods. Wild cactus fruit sometimes supplemented the diet. Warner and his boys used a .22 to hunt for rabbits and other edible game.

Features of the homestead included pens (north of the aforementioned wash) where livestock was raised. At various times in the homestead's history, such animals included hogs, chickens, up to two horses (a small, wild equine was considered "Melvin's horse"), and even cows. The hogs, chickens, and cows helped meet the family's dietary needs.

Perhaps the most remarkable feature on the property was a well—or more precisely, an *attempted* well. Using a peach tree twig to douse for water, Warner located a promising spot south of the wash in the vicinity of his houses (a shallow depression marks the spot today). He excavated the location using a drilling machine in which he owned part interest (Figure 10.8). The homesteader and his youngsters took turns operating the equipment, eventually reaching a depth of about 100 feet. Alas, no water was found.

The wash through the site rarely flowed. Lacking a well, the Goodes had to haul water to their property. Containers larger than 50-gallon drums were used to carry the liquid (Figure 10.9). The source was usually an irrigation ditch near the Gila River. Other sources included a tank at Arlington and the "Whitfields' Well"; the latter was owned by another African-American family living in the township. The Goodes did not boil or otherwise treat the water to make it more potable. Nonetheless, the family enjoyed relatively good health during its decade on the property.

Attempts to raise crops on the homestead met with little or no success. Calvin Goode remembered that his mother dug rows and planted corn. A family photograph documents that the corn attained a height of at least one foot (Figure 10.10). Mr. Goode did not recall that such crops ever matured to yield food for the family. Dry conditions and the lack of water usually made any harvest impossible. The family purchased necessities in Gila Bend, Phoenix, and occasionally Buckeye. The Goodes paid for such goods and services with money earned through a variety of entrepreneurial

Figure 10.5. Calvin, Lena, Melvin, Lillie, and Doretha Goode at the Goode homestead during the 1930s.
(Photo courtesy of the Goode family.)

Figure 10.4. Warner, Doretha, and Lillie Goode at the Goode homestead during the 1930s.
(Photo courtesy of the Goode family.)

Figure 10.7. Lena, Calvin, and Melvin Goode, on the family truck. (Photo courtesy of the Goode family.)

Figure 10.6. Four of the Goode youngsters at the Goode homestead during the 1930s. (Photo courtesy of the Goode family.)

Figure 10.9. Containers larger than the 50-gallon drum, shown here with Calvin and Melvin Goode, were used to haul water to the Goode Homestead. (Photo courtesy of the Goode family.)

Figure 10.8. Drilling machine digging for water on Warner Goode's homestead during the 1930s. (Photo courtesy of the Goode family.)

Figure 10.10. Clara Goode circa 1935 in a small field of corn on the homestead.
(Photo courtesy of the Goode family.)

activities. A common activity was picking and chopping cotton at commercial farms along the Gila Valley. Warner Goode also found that he could generate a somewhat reliable income by selling fuel wood. He would remove dead ironwood trees from the desert, haul the wood to his property, and saw it into 12-inch logs. His circular saw was metal-toothed, and was driven by a rear wheel of his truck. Today, a small pile of wood chips is all that remains of the activity.

Processing fuel wood was a hazardous activity. Once when Warner was sawing wood into logs, one of the saw-teeth flew off and put a gash in his jaw. He had to make an emergency trip to a hospital in Buckeye to get medical attention. Phoenix provided a ready market for Warner Goode's fuel wood. While visiting Phoenix, he would often use some of the proceeds from the sale of fuel wood to buy fruit and vegetables; these he would sell in Gila Bend to further boost his income. "Sandia" (watermelon) was a particularly popular treat among his Gila Bend clientele.

Another way that Warner Goode earned money was by working for the Works Progress Administration (WPA). As a WPA laborer, he was paid $44 per month—$4 per day, 11 days per month. He also enrolled in WPA programs that provided food and other goods for his family. One such program provided clothing. Calvin Goode recalled that the clothes were often much too large, and hung in folds on him and his siblings.

The children attended school in Gila Bend. Located at the southeast corner of Barnes Avenue and Locke Street, the segregated facility was known as "the colored school." Grades 1 through 8 were taught there. Its student body normally numbered about 25. Enrollment increased during cotton-picking season (fall and early winter), when workers and their families annually migrated to the Gila River Valley from the South. So many teachers—all of them African-American—cycled through the one-room facility that Calvin Goode had four teachers in his eight years of attendance there.

The lack of water, plus the quest for higher education, influenced the Goodes' decision to sell the homestead and move elsewhere. Calvin Goode graduated from the eighth grade in the spring of 1940. He received a certificate entitling him to enroll in high school, but there was no such institution for African-Americans in Gila Bend. Therefore, the Goodes decided to move to Prescott, which had an integrated high school.

The Goodes put their 160-acre homestead up for sale, found a buyer in August 1940 (see preceding section on archival records), and relocated to Prescott. According to Calvin Goode, no one lived on the homestead after his family departed from it. However, other people from the area came onto the property and salvaged useful items and materials.

The history of the Goode family may be summarized as follows. In Prescott, Warner and Clara gave birth to their eighth child, Evelyn. The family purchased five acres for $300. Warner supported his family by doing concrete work and odd jobs. Unfortunately, the high altitude disagreed with Calvin Goode's constitution, and so he transferred to Carver High School in Phoenix. The family joined him in Phoenix some time later. Warner and Clara Goode at first lived in a neighborhood on the west side of Sky Harbor Airport. When the airport eventually expanded and bought them out, they moved to 1446 East Jefferson Street, where they resided for the rest of their lives. Warner Goode retired from Maricopa County as an operator of a road grader. Warner died in 1982 and Clara, a decade later.

Most of the eight Goode children went on to lead long and productive lives. Lena Mae Goode, eldest of the children, first attended high school in Mesa, Arizona—living with grandparents while she did so—and later completed her high school education in Prescott. She died in 1941 at the age of 19. Melvin W. Goode graduated from Prescott Senior High School and worked as an auto mechanic.

He died in 1984. Calvin C. Goode attended Prescott High School for three years and graduated from Carver High in Phoenix in 1945. He graduated from Arizona State College at Tempe with a Bachelor's degree in business and went on to earn a Master's degree in education from Arizona State University (ASU). He was employed for 30 years with the Phoenix Union High School District in various positions. Doretha Goode Cook graduated from high school in Prescott and received a teaching degree from ASU. She taught elementary school for ten years in Phoenix and retired after teaching for 27 years in Stockton, California.

Lillie Mae Goode Sanders graduated from Carver High School and Phoenix College. She was employed for several years with the City of Phoenix, traveled with her military husband, and became homemaker for her husband and three sons. She died in 2001. Iretha Goode Lucky graduated from Carver, attended ASU, and later earned a Registered Nursing degree. She worked as a nurse for many years and recently retired, after 27½ years, from the Veterans' Hospital in Phoenix. Alvin Goode attended Carver High until that school closed in 1954, and then transferred to and graduated from Phoenix Union High School. He attended Phoenix College for a short period of time. He spent six years in the Arizona National Guard, and retired from the City of Phoenix after 32 years of service. He now resides in Prescott. Evelyn Goode Johnson graduated from Phoenix Union High School. Her employment has been in the hotel and retail areas. She presently resides in Prescott.

SUMMARY AND CONCLUSIONS

Site AZ T:14:96 (ASM) marks the remains of a homestead filed by Warner Goode in 1929 and occupied by the Goode family until the summer of 1940. Warner Goode was an Oklahoma sharecropper who moved to Arizona seeking a better life for his wife and children. He hoped that he could drill a well, find water, and develop a productive farm on the land he chose to settle.

Despite his best efforts, he never struck water. Lacking that precious liquid, his crops repeatedly failed. His 160 acres could not support his growing family, and Warner had to work several jobs to make ends meet. He cut fuel wood and sold it in Phoenix, bought fruit and vegetables and sold them in Gila Bend, picked cotton, and worked on projects for the Works Progress Administration to eke out a living. His diligence paid off; in 1936, he received a title patent for his claim. He was one of 511 Arizonans to receive homestead patents during that year (BLM 1962). He succeeded where many others failed: for every one homestead that culminated in a patent, approximately two ended in relinquishment or cancellation (Stein 1990).

Warner Goode's accomplishment appears all the more remarkable in light of the fact that he was African-American. He, his wife Clara, and their many children had to function in a sharply segregated society while they homesteaded their land near Gila Bend. The Goode children attended the local "colored school." The school district offered only an elementary education to Black students. The district did not provide facilities for African-American youngsters—no matter how gifted or bright—to attend high school.

The quest for a higher education for their children and the lack of water on their land led Warner and Clara to sell the homestead and move elsewhere. They chose Prescott, one of the only Arizona cities that had fully-integrated high schools. They sold their 160-acre homestead in 1940 for less than a dollar an acre.

The move helped the Goode children attain the education their parents desired. Warner Goode had an 8th-grade education, and Clara, a 6th-grade education, yet each of their eight children would complete high school. Five went on to attend college. In one generation, the Goodes went from sharecroppers to professionals in education, health care, and public service.

CHAPTER 11

AN OVERVIEW OF HISTORIC TRAILS: THE ANZA AND BUTTERFIELD ROUTES

Pat H. Stein

INTRODUCTION

This chapter presents an overview of two historic highways that crossed the land now traversed by State Route 85. The Juan Bautista de Anza Trail, used principally from 1775 to 1781, and the Butterfield Overland Mail Route, used mainly from 1858 to 1861, played major roles in the exploration and settlement of North America. The following pages trace the development, use, and decline of these important routes. Using historical records, the chapter also reviews what is known about the locations of the two routes in relation to the current SR 85 project area.

THE ANZA TRAIL

Historic Setting

In 1774 and 1775–1776, Captain Juan Bautista de Anza led two expeditions across southern Arizona while journeying to California on behalf of the Spanish crown (Figure 11.1). The expeditions were remarkable for the distances traveled, the difficulties encountered, and the successes achieved. Expedition participants documented the voyages in daily journals. Later scholars (including Bolton 1930; Bowman and Heizer 1967; Garate 1994; and Trafzer 1975) used the diaries and related archives to retrace Anza's steps. Such primary and secondary sources have produced a meticulously detailed account of the expeditions and the events surrounding them. The sources indicate that the journeys occurred as the result of a unique set of political, economic, and religious circumstances.

Nearly two centuries after Christopher Columbus came to the New World, Spain controlled a vast territory that included much of North, Central, and South America. However, by the latter half of the eighteenth century, the crown perceived imminent threats to its imperial grasp. From the east, England and France continued to sponsor voyages of discovery. From the west, Russian ships plied the Northwest Coast while hunting for seal and otter. From within, the crown watched warily as the Society of Jesuits amassed power, wealth, and influence inside the Spanish realm (National Park Service/NPS 1996).

To subordinate the Catholic Church to the Spanish crown, King Carlos III ordered the expulsion of the Jesuits from his domain in 1767. Following their removal in July of that year, the crown entrusted the Southwest missions to the Order of Friars Minor (Franciscans). From their mission bases in Baja (Lower) California, the Franciscans sought to extend the realm of Christendom into Alta (Upper) California (Fontana 1994; Officer 1987).

The Franciscans found a powerful military ally in the person of José de Gàlvez, *Visitor General de Nueva España.* Gàlvez had the task and the will to return the Spanish empire to its former days of wealth and glory. He shared the Franciscans' desire to explore and settle Alta California. Largely at his instigation, the decision was made in 1769 to push the Spanish realm northward from Baja along the Pacific Coast (Fontana 1994).

Figure 11.1. Anza's expeditions of 1774 and 1775–1776.
(Source: National Park Service 1996)

A peaceful assault was launched on Alta California. Expeditions led by Gaspar de Portolá in 1769 and 1771 culminated in the founding of five missions and two presidios: San Diego de Alcalá, San Carlos Borromeo de Carmelo, San Antonio de Padua, San Gabriel Arcángel, San Luis Obispo, San Diego, and Monterey. During the 1769 expedition, a scouting party also arrived at San Francisco Bay (Fontana 1994; NPS 1996).

By the early 1770s, a small force of approximately 60 soldiers and 11 friars manned the five missions and two presidios of Alta California. The seven settlements were highly dependent on outside supplies for their survival. Their occupants were often threatened with starvation. Attempts were made to deliver goods to the struggling settlements by sea, but this proved hazardous and unsuccessful. Prevailing winds and currents along the California coast proved too much for northbound supply ships, blowing many out to sea or hurtling them upon rocky shores. Overland travel from Baja California proved equally long and arduous; besides, the desert peninsula produced little surplus food for export. It became clear to the church and crown that Alta California's feeble settlements could be maintained only if a safe and dependable overland route could be opened from northern Mexico (NPS 1996).

It was at this point that Juan Bautista de Anza entered the California scene. During the 1770s he would unite the Mexican and Pacific frontiers by developing an overland route between Arizpe and Monterey (Bowman and Heizer 1967).

JUAN BAUTISTA DE ANZA: A BRIEF BIOGRAPHICAL SKETCH

In 1772, when Juan Bautista de Anza proposed to find a land route between Mexico and California, he was 36 years old and served as captain of the small Presidio of Tubac in Sonora (now southern Arizona). He had been born in Fronteras, Sonora, in 1736, the son of aristocratic Basques who had emigrated from northern Spain in 1712. Little is known of his early life, although it is generally thought that he attended the College of San Ildefonso in Mexico City, and then the military academy there (Bowman and Heizer 1967; Garate 1994).

In 1752, Anza enlisted as a volunteer in the Fronteras presidio army. He quickly rose in its ranks. After two years of service, he was promoted to lieutenant. In 1760, at the age of 24, he became a captain. The first post under his command was the newly-established Presidio of Tubac. His predecessor there, Juan de Belderrain, had recently died of wounds sustained during a campaign against the Seri (Bowman and Heizer 1967; Garate 1994).

From Tubac, Anza frequently engaged in campaigns against native groups of the Sonoran Desert. His far-reaching maneuvers—south to the Sinaloa border, north to the Gila River, east beyond San Bernardino, and west to the Gulf of Mexico—gave Anza an unexcelled knowledge of native trails, trade routes, watering holes, villages, and pasturage. It was during one such campaign in 1769 that Anza learned through the Gila River Pima that white men (Spaniards from Portolá's expeditions) had been seen in Alta California. Anza realized that it was both timely and feasible to open a supply route to Upper California. In 1772 he petitioned the government to explore such a route. He received permission from Antonio Maria Bucareli y Úrsua, Viceroy of New Spain, in 1773 (Bowman and Heizer 1967; Garate 1994; NPS 1996).

The dream of an overland route was not new. Among Spaniards, the idea dated back to the seventeenth century; Anza's father had even proposed such a route in the 1730s. Anza would literally follow the footsteps of many others in journeying to California. According to Garate (1994:15):

> ...the entire route, in sections, was previously known to various native tribes. Much of it had also been traveled by Spaniards. Juan de Oñate rode down the Gila to the

Colorado 170 years before Anza. Father Eusebio Kino had explored the area between Sonora and the point at which the Rio Colorado empties into the Gulf of California. Melchior Diaz and Padre Francisco Garcés had both crossed the Colorado River, although 230 years apart. Gaspar de Portolá had pushed north from San Diego to Monterey and Pedro Fages had explored the South San Francisco Bay. Anza already knew the country well between Sinaloa and the Gila River.

Anza's accomplishment was in connecting all the pieces and leading a colonizing party safely to its destination across 1,800 miles of wilderness (Garate 1994).

THE EXPLORATORY JOURNEY OF 1774

Anza led two expeditions to Alta California. The first, in 1774, explored the Southwest for the purpose of finding an overland route. The second, in 1775–1776, used the route to convey a party of colonists from Mexico to the Pacific Coast. Anza funded both expeditions, with assistance provided by the Spanish military and the Franciscan order.

The first expedition departed Tubac on 8 January 1774. With Anza were 21 soldiers, five mule packers, an O'odham interpreter, a carpenter, and two personal servants. Juan Bautista Valdéz, a soldier who had served with Portolá, joined the expedition as courier. Fathers Francisco Garcés and Juan Marcelo Díaz accompanied the group to provide spiritual guidance. Sebastián Tarabal, a Baja California Indian who had recently walked to Sonora from Mission San Gabriel, served as guide (Fontana 1994; Garate 1994; NPS 1996).

The group camped the first night near the Camino Real, the long-established road that ran through northern Mexico to San Xavier. However, the following day, instead of going north toward the Gila as originally planned, the party headed in a southwesterly direction toward Caborca (northern Mexico). Apaches had raided Tubac, driving off most of its horse herd; the explorers thus went to Caborca seeking extra mounts. The trip to Caborca put Anza's group on the classic "short route" to the Colorado River (the route approximately parallels the U.S.-Mexican border today). Called *El Camino del Diablo* (the Devil's Highway), the route would prove too rocky, dry, and barren to serve as an overland supply route (Garate 1994; NPS 1996).

The party struggled for more than two weeks on the camino before reaching the confluence of the Colorado and Gila rivers. There, Anza met with Olleyquotequiebe (aka Salvador Palma), chief of the Yuma Indians. The two leaders developed a trusting relationship and became friends. The chief offered his assistance, which Anza would shortly need (Garate 1994).

The Anza party crossed the Colorado River, traveled south, and soon found itself bogged down in the windswept sands of uncharted territory. At the end of two weeks with no discernible progress, animals began to die. Anza made the decision to send seven men and most of the expedition's livestock back to Chief Olleyquotequiebe. The remaining party, stocked with only a month's provisions, turned west and continued the journey (Garate 1994).

Conditions improved after a few more days of hard riding. The party finally arrived at San Gabriel on 22 March 1774. The poverty of that mission did not allow Anza and his men to remain long. Valdéz was dispatched to Mexico City to report on the progress of the expedition. Garcés led a group of seven soldiers to San Diego to obtain supplies. Meanwhile, Anza and a small contingent rode on to Monterey, the final destination for the expedition (Garate 1994; NPS 1996).

On the return trip to Tubac, Anza took a route that avoided *El Camino del Diablo*. After crossing the Colorado at Yuma Crossing, he followed the Gila from its mouth eastward to the Gila River O'odham villages, thence to the Casa Grande ruins. From the ruins, the Anza party turned south/southeast before reaching Tucson, San Xavier del Bac, and finally Tubac. By 27 May 1774, all members of the expedition except Valdéz were back at the presidio. The exploring party had achieved its goal: Mexico and California were now linked by an overland route (Fontana 1994). For his efforts on behalf of the crown, Anza was promoted to the rank of Lieutenant-Colonel (Bowman and Heizer 1967).

THE COLONIZING EXPEDITION OF 1775–1776

The goal of Anza's second expedition to Alta California was defined in a decree by Viceroy Bucareli dated 28 November 1774: to lead a group of colonists from northwestern New Spain overland on the new route "for the reinforcement of the royal presidio of San Carlos de Monterey and for the establishment of the port of San Francisco" (Antonio Maria Bucareli y Ursúa, translated and cited by Bowman and Heizer 1967:38). Additional instructions directed Anza to collect colonists, deliver them to Monterey, and assist the governor in exploring the San Francisco River for the site of a presidio (Bowman and Heizer 1967:38). The establishment of an outpost at San Francisco was intended to protect Spain's interests from incursions by other colonial powers (NPS 1996).

Anza recruited his colonists mainly from Culiacán, Sinaloa, El Fuerte, and Alamos. Each town suffered from abject poverty. Many families there were receptive to the idea of trying their luck in a new land. Thirty-eight families would choose to make the trip. Livestock was purchased from ranchers in Sinaloa and Sonora. Supplies came mainly from Horcasitas and the Sonoran missions (Garate 1994).

For the new expedition, Anza chose as his second in command José Joaquín Moraga; it would eventually be Moraga who would lead the colonists in founding the Presidio of San Francisco. Anza recommended Friar Pedro Font to serve as chaplain, presumably because the Franciscan could read latitudes. Fathers Garcés and Thomas Eixarch would accompany the expedition only as far as Yuma Crossing, where they would continue efforts to missionize the native population (Garate 1994; NPS 1996).

The colonists gathered at Horcasitas, Sonora (about 175 miles south of the current international boundary). In Horcasitas, three colonists died of unknown diseases. On 29 September 1775, the remaining 177 persons left for Tubac. Four births occurred between Horcasitas and Tubac (NPS 1996). Additional people joined the caravan at Tubac. The expedition numbered approximately 240 people (including colonists, soldiers, clergy, scouts, servants, interpreters, muleteers, and cowboys) when it departed Tubac on 23 October 1775 (Garate 1994; NPS 1996).

A woman died in childbirth during the first night. The expedition would record only one additional death (an infant) during the difficult 1200-mile journey from Tubac to Monterey (Garate 1994).

The expedition traveled down the Santa Cruz River toward its junction with the Gila River. At the latter, the travelers rested a day while Anza, Font, and several soldiers visited nearby Casa Grande ruins. The journey then resumed, with the expedition veering westward away from the Gila for several days, and finally rejoining that river at Gila Bend (Garate 1994). (The following section of this chapter provides a detailed view of the expedition's route from Casa Grande to Gila Bend, and describes the route in relation to SR 85).

As the party continued along the river west of Gila Bend, another birth occurred. The expedition rested two days while the mother recuperated, and then resumed the journey. Chief Olleyquotequiebe and his Yuma followers greeted the travelers when they arrived at the Gila-Colorado confluence on 28 November. With help from the Yumas, the expedition crossed the Colorado without serious incident (Garate 1994; NPS 1996).

After leaving Fathers Garcés and Eixarch with the Yuma, Anza led his followers toward known, abundant water at San Sebastián Marsh. He knew water would be scarce between Yuma and the marsh, and so he divided the expedition into four groups—three of colonists and one of livestock. Each would travel a day apart to better secure water from slow-filling desert watering holes. As the lead group, headed by Anza, reached the Santa Rosa Mountains, an unexpected snowstorm held them captive for five nights. Temperatures plummeted, and the travelers began to succumb to the cold. The soldiers worked frenetically to reunite the three groups of colonists. Once reunited, the colonists rejoiced, and continued their journey toward San Sebastián (Garate 1994).

Rains drenched the travelers, but they arrived safely at the marsh, and then continued west toward San Gabriel. At San Carlos Pass, they experienced one of California's first-recorded earthquakes. Snow lingered in the mountains, and the land around them was still a desert, but Anza urged them on, with promises of the lush landscape that awaited them. True to his word, Anza soon delivered them to a land that was lush beyond all expectations (Garate 1994; NPS 1996).

The expedition was delayed for seven weeks at San Gabriel while Anza and a detachment of soldiers attempted to quell an insurrection at the San Diego mission. At San Gabriel, expedition members soon began to experience food shortages. Four disgruntled men abandoned the mission and headed for Sonora, taking 25 horses and two mules. Upon Anza's return, the men were tracked down and taken to confinement at San Gabriel (Garate 1994).

The journey resumed. On 10 March 1776, the expedition reached Monterey. The colonists waited there while Anza continued north to scout San Francisco Bay. After finding a suitable site for a presidio, the leader returned to Monterey in early April. Fernando Rivera y Moncada, captain of the Monterey presidio, did not share Anza's assessment of the bay as a suitable site for settlement. It would be June before Rivera would allow the colonists (under the command of José Joaquín Moraga) to proceed to the northern bay (Bowman and Heizer 1967; Garate 1994).

In the meantime, Anza completed his mission by returning to Sonora. Twenty-eight persons— Font, one commissary, 10 soldiers, 14 muleteers and servants, and a husband and wife who wished to return to their homeland—accompanied him. They left Monterey on 4 April and arrived safely at Horcasitas on 1 June 1776 (Bowman and Heizer 1967). Anza's second and final journey to California was over.

In honor of Anza's exceptional service, the crown appointed him Governor of New Mexico. While serving in that capacity, he opened a route between Santa Fe and Arizpe, led a relief mission to drought-stricken Hopi, and negotiated a peace treaty with the Comanche. He died suddenly in Arizpe on 19 December 1788, at the age of 52 (Bowman and Heizer 1967).

Ironically, Anza outlived the route he had opened to California. On 17 July 1781, following years of strained relations with the Spanish, the Yumas rebelled, bringing an end to foreign rule at Yuma Crossing. Lacking that vital link across the Colorado River, the crown gave up all hope of maintaining its overland route from Sonora to Alta California (Trafzer 1975). The route would not be reopened until Mexico won its independence from Spain.

THE ANZA TRAIL IN RELATION TO THE SR 85 PROJECT

An outstanding set of primary and secondary resources provide a closer look at the overland route that Anza blazed between Sonora and Alta California. In its day, the route was documented in the daily journals of not one but three chroniclers: Anza, Pedro Font, and Francisco Garcés. The original Spanish versions of these journals, plus English translations of them, are available online through the "Web de Anza" (University of Oregon 2000; http://anza.uoregon.edu/). The website also includes maps illustrating the overland route as described by Anza, Font, and Garcés. In addition, the National Park Service has produced a document describing the "Juan Bautista de Anza National Historic Trail" and historic places along that route (NPS 1996).

Such sources make it possible to discern the general trajectory of the Spanish overland (Anza) route. However, they cannot be used to plot that route with pinpoint accuracy, for several reasons. First, it is thought that Anza, as a military man, would have kept the colonists close together and in a defensible line, treading a narrow track, as they journeyed across the desert; however, the livestock accompanying the expedition, as well as livestock accompanying later supply missions, would have cut much wider swaths. Second, Spanish subjects who used the overland route after Anza did not necessarily follow in his exact footsteps. More likely, they cut parallel tracks as they traveled between the campsites described in Anza's journals. Third, the location of the route varied with the seasons; travelers often took a "high road" during wet spells and a "low road" during drier weather. Fourth, Spaniards used the route for a relatively short period, from 1775 to 1781; it is therefore difficult, if not impossible, to distinguish their tracks from those of earlier and later travelers (NPS 1996).

All of the above factors lead to the conclusion that the overland route is better conceptualized as a corridor than as a distinct, well-trodden path (NPS 1996). This realization can be frustrating for the archaeologist or cultural resource manager assigned the task of identifying and protecting "the trail." Does the overland route pass along the north side of a hill or the south side of it? Are these the tracks of the Anza expedition, or are those the tracks, 100 meters away? Such questions usually cannot be answered unless the researcher is fortunate enough to find Spanish Colonial artifacts in association with a suspected segment of the trail. Instances of such discoveries are rare.

Bearing in mind the limitations of the documentary record, scholars have been able to use the Anza, Font, and Garcés journals to determine approximately where the overland route passed. By identifying the points mentioned in the journals, historians have been able to "connect the dots" and generate a plausible reconstruction of the corridor's location. The following paragraphs review what is known about the corridor east of, within, and finally west of the current SR 85 project area.

The three journals state that on 30 and 31 October 1775, the colonizing party camped at a place referred to as La Laguna. La Laguna was situated along the Gila River some three leagues (about 7.8 mi) west–northwest of a well-known ancient landmark, the Casa Grande ruins. Anza and a small contingent visited the archaeological site while the majority of the colonists rested.

The same journals relate that on 1 November, the expedition departed from La Laguna and trekked west-northwest, following the meanders of the Gila for about four leagues (10.4 mi), before arriving at Uturitac (aka Juturitucam), the first village of the Gila River Pima. Anza estimated that Uturitac lies 42 leagues (109.2 mi) from the Tubac Presidio. The party camped at Uturitac for the night, and resumed the journey the next day.

The party got a late start on 2 November because livestock were missing and had to be recovered before the journey could resume. The colonists managed to cover only two leagues (5.2 mi) that day. By nightfall they had reached the Pueblo of Encarnación de Sutaquison (aka Sutaquizon), where they camped for the night. Their journey along the Gila that day had taken them through two other villages, also occupied by the Pima.

On Friday, 3 November, the expedition left the course of the Gila River and veered west-northwest. Anza's objective that day was to reach some lakes that might offer good pasturage. After a distance of two leagues (5.6 mi) from Sutaquison, the party arrived at that destination, and camped for the night.

It was Anza's intention to depart the next day, but fate intervened. The lakes proved to be little more than a pond of bad water. Several travelers, including Font, were made sick by it. The expedition halted for three days while the stricken colonists recuperated. Appropriately, they named the place La Laguna del Hospital. The period spent at "Infirmary Lake" allowed Font time to determine its latitude as 33° 14½'.

The still-ailing party left the contaminated pond on 7 November. Anza led the group west-southwest and then west across the desert, thus avoiding the big, northern bend of the Gila River. Five leagues (13 mi) distant from La Laguna del Hospital, the expedition reached pasturage at an *arroyo seco* (dry wash), and spent the night.

Upon leaving the Arroyo Seco campsite on 8 November, the group headed in a west to southwesterly direction. At a distance of about two leagues (5.2 mi), they entered an area that Anza termed the Pass of the Cocomaricopas. The three-mile pass was likely today's "Butterfield Pass," located in the Maricopa Mountains.

West of the pass, the group began to reach better country. An additional trek of four leagues (10.4 mi) in a west-southwesterly direction brought them to Upasoitac (aka Opasoitac and Uparsuytac), a village of the Opas. At Upasoitac the Opas and Spaniards exchanged gifts, the sick recuperated, livestock fed on abundant pasturage, and Father Garcés preached to nearly 500 persons.

The expedition remained at Upasoitac until 11 November. The colonists then followed the Gila River downstream in a west-southwesterly direction. Rain threatened them after about a league and a half (3.9 mi), and so they make camp amidst Opa arbors and bowers at a place the Spaniards called Rancherías de San Martín. When heavy rains ceased at daybreak, the travelers were able to resume their journey. On 12 November they covered four leagues (10.4 mi) in four hours, and arrived at Ranchería de San Diego, where they made camp for one night.

Figures 11.2 and 11.3, produced by the University of Oregon and the National Park Service respectively, depict the Arizona and Maricopa County portions of Anza's 1775–1776 expedition. The maps indicate that the historic route probably crossed the current SR 85 project area at or near Upasoitac. Upasoitac was situated south of the Gila River, about a mile east of Gila Bend, and very near the junction of SR 85 with Highway 238.

THE OVERLAND (ANZA) ROUTE UNDER MEXICAN RULE

Mexico won its independence from Spain in 1821. According to Officer (1987), one of the most important developments in Arizona in the aftermath of independence was the decision to reopen communications between the Arizona presidios and those in California. Anza had opened the overland route nearly a half-century before, but it had lain dormant for decades following the Yuma uprising.

The Mexican government ordered Captain José de Romero of the Tucson presidio to lead an expedition to California for the purpose of re-establishing the overland trail. The Romero party set out

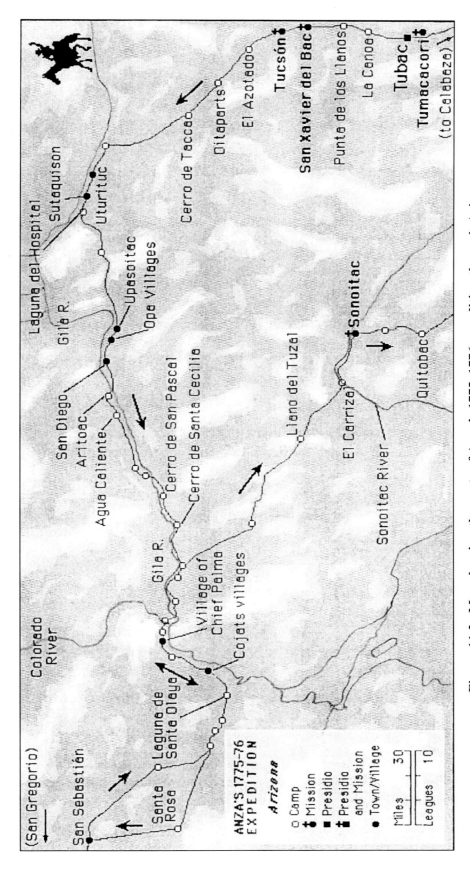

Figure 11.2. Map showing the route of Anza's 1775–1776 expedition through Arizona.
(Source: University of Oregon 2000, drawn by Patrick Witmer and based on maps by Bolton 1930.)

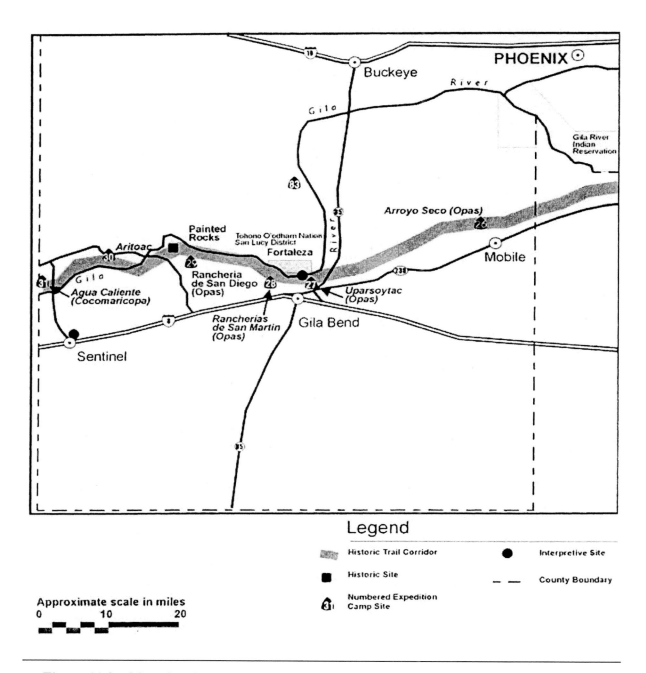

Figure 11.3.   Map showing the Anza Trail Corridor through Maricopa County, Arizona.
(Source: National Park Service – http://www.nps.gov.juba/Maricopa.htm/)

from Tucson on 8 June 1823. Father Félix Caballero, a Franciscan who had made the journey from California to Arizpe during the preceding month, accompanied the group. Not long after Romero left Tucson, rumors surfaced there that the Yumas had killed all the expedition members. Fortunately, the rumor proved false. The Romero party arrived safely at its California destination in mid-July, and the overland route to California was officially reopened (Officer 1987).

The route would play a vital role when the U.S.-Mexican War erupted in 1846. Colonel Stephen Watts Kearny of the United States Army was ordered to establish U.S. control over the vast Southwest.

He assembled his troops (called the Army of the West) at Fort Leavenworth. He marched westward, handily took control of New Mexico, and continued on to California. From the Gila River Pima villages to Yuma, Kearny followed much the same corridor that Anza had taken in 1775–1776. Accompanying Kearny was Lieutenant William H. Emory of the Corps of Topographical Engineers. Emory generated the first relatively accurate map of the trail. In a few more years, scores of civilians would follow Emory's map of the Gila Trail as they journeyed to the California gold fields (Walker and Bufkin 1986).

Reinforcements were dispatched to assist Kearny. They consisted of the Second Missouri Mounted Rifles and a 500-man volunteer infantry. The latter group consisted of Latter-Day Saints and was called the Mormon Battalion. Under the command of Philip St. George Cooke, the battalion was ordered to march to California and build a wagon road as it went (Walker and Bufkin 1986).

The Mormon Battalion followed Kearny's path to southwestern New Mexico. To avoid terrain too rough for wagons, the battalion then changed direction, marching south-southwest to the Peloncillo Mountains (in southeastern Arizona), thence along the San Pedro River to Benson, and then westward to Tucson. From Tucson to Yuma Crossing, the group followed a route similar to that taken by Anza in 1775 (Walker and Bufkin 1986).

The campaigns of Kearny and Cooke contributed to the U.S. victory in the war with Mexico. By the 1848 Treaty of Guadalupe Hidalgo, the United States came to rule most of Mexico's former territory in the Southwest. Excluded from the treaty was a strip of land south of the Gila in Arizona. Six years later, the U.S. would acquire that land through the Gadsden Purchase. Through this historical process, the old overland route to California came into the possession of the United States. The era of the Butterfield Stage was about to begin.

THE BUTTERFIELD OVERLAND MAIL ROUTE

Historic Setting

Through purchase and treaty, the United States experienced rapid territorial growth between 1803 and 1853. By mid-century, the country stretched from the Atlantic to the Pacific oceans. The 1848 discovery of gold in California caused the population of the far west to burgeon. Countless forty-niners followed the trails of Anza and the Mormon Battalion in a rush to the Golden West.

By the mid 1850s, half a million people resided in the State of California, the Oregon Territory, and the gold camps of Nevada. The strident voice of the emergent Pacific Coast raised an affluent cry for better communication with the East. The common route to California—around the southern tip of Cape Horn, measuring more than 15,000 miles from New York to San Francisco—was time-consuming, expensive, and extremely dangerous. The trip remained costly and hazardous even after William Henry Aspinwall completed a railroad across the Panamanian Isthmus in 1855 (Greene 1994).

Congress at first responded to the demand for better communication by sponsoring projects to build roads to California. These projects were fostered by the Department of the Interior and directed by A. H. Campbell of the Pacific Wagon Road office. One such project, approved in February 1857, appropriated $200,000 to construct a wagon road between El Paso and Fort Yuma. Colonel James B. Leach was appointed to supervise the work, and was assisted by Major N. H. Hutton. Their instructions were to undertake no heavy grading or bridging; to prepare a road over which heavy wagons could pass; and to make provisions for collecting and preserving rainfall so that travelers would be assured a supply of drinking water (Conkling and Conkling 1947; Farish 1915; Faulk 1973).

The route selected by Leach corresponded largely with that taken by Cooke in 1846, but led down the San Pedro River to Aravaipa Creek, and thence to the Gila, thus cutting about 40 miles from Cooke's route. Leach divided his laborers into work parties; some drilled wells, others worked eastward from Fort Yuma, while still others worked westward from Texas. Out of this activity grew a primitive roadbed measuring about 18 feet wide on straight stretches and about 25 feet wide on curves. Culverts were installed, grades were reduced, and watering places were developed. Leach and Hutton completed their work by September 1858 (Conkling and Conkling 1947; Faulk 1973). This wagon road not only eased the journey of immigrants and freighters to California, but also paved the way for the Butterfield stage.

Shortly after funds were appropriated for Leach's road, Congress authorized the first mail route between Texas and California. The contract to carry the mail was awarded to James E. Burch on 22 June 1857. The route, called the San Antonio and San Diego Mail Line, was to follow the 32nd parallel. The length of the route was 1,476 miles. Three fully-equipped stations—at San Antonio, El Paso, and San Diego—served the route. Maricopa Wells, in Arizona, was the most important way station between El Paso and San Diego. The contract was intended to run for four years as a semimonthly service at $139,800 per year. However, only 40 trips were ever completed by the San Antonio and San Diego Mail Line. Its contract was terminated in September 1858 when it came in conflict with the new Butterfield contract (Sloane 1958).

THE BUTTERFIELD OVERLAND MAIL

The San Antonio and San Diego Mail Line was intended to carry mail within the Southwest but not to serve as a communication link between eastern and western America. To develop such a link, Congress in March 1857 passed the overland mail bill. The act authorized the Postmaster General "to contract for the conveyance of the entire letter mail from such point on the Mississippi River as the contractors might select, to San Francisco, in the state of California, for six years at a cost not exceeding three hundred thousand dollars per annum for a semi-monthly, four hundred and fifty thousand dollars for weekly, or six hundred thousand dollars for semi-weekly service, to be performed semi-monthly, weekly, or semi-weekly, at the option of the Postmaster General" (Rose nd:31). Sponsors of the bill included Senator Thomas J. Rusk of Texas, Senator W.M. Gwin of California, and Representative John S. Phelps of Missouri (Greene 1994).

A month after the bill's passage, the U.S. Post Office Department advertised for bids from contractors to carry the mail on a route across the barren expanses of the "Great American Desert," as the Southwest was called. The contract required that the service be performed "with good four-horse coaches or spring wagons, suitable for conveyance of passengers, as well as the safety and security of the mails." The successful bidder would be given the right to preempt 320 acres "of any land not then disposed of or reserved, at each point necessary for a station, not to be nearer than ten miles from each other." Service was to be performed "within twenty-five days for each trip" (Greene 1994:11; Rose nd:31).

Nine bids were submitted for "the Great Overland Mail Contract." Keen excitement attended their opening. A bid submitted by John Butterfield and associates won the contract.

John Butterfield was well known in the fields of staging and freighting. His strategy in winning the government contract was to submit three bids: one for a semi-weekly service from St. Louis; a second for a semi-weekly service from Memphis; and the third for a semi-weekly service starting from both St. Louis and Memphis, converging at a mutual point, and thence proceeding on a single route to San Francisco. The third bid, proposing a bifurcated route, was the one selected by the Postmaster General (Rose nd).

The contract, signed on 16 September 1857, called for the two eastern branches of the bifurcated route to converge at Little Rock, to proceed westward to El Paso,

> …and thence along the new road [Leach's wagon road] being opened and constructed…to Fort Yuma, thence through the best passes and along the best valleys for safe and expeditious staging to San Francisco…and back, twice a week…at six hundred thousand dollars a year, during the term of six years, commencing the 16th day of September, 1858 (Rose nd:31).

After considerable discussion, the point of convergence for the two eastern termini was changed from Little Rock to Fort Smith.

Butterfield's Overland Mail Company quickly constructed a chain of stations along the route. Stock was purchased, wagons and coaches were ordered, wells dug, and provisions hauled into each station. Drivers, conductors, station-keepers, blacksmiths, mechanics, hostlers, and herders were hired. By the time service began, the company had hired more than 2,000 people, and built nearly 200 stations along the 3,124-mile bifurcated route (Greene 1994; Sloane 1958).

The first eastbound trip departed from San Francisco on 15 September 1858; the first westbound trip departed from St. Louis a day later. Heeding Butterfield's admonition that "nothing on God's earth must stop the United States mail," (John Butterfield, cited by Rose nd:32), the drivers arrived at the eastern and western termini on schedule. Incredibly, the Butterfield Overland Mail would arrive late at its termini only three times in the 2½ years it would operate over the route (Sloane 1958).

Although its contract allowed 25 days for each journey, the Overland Mail Company found that it could shave hours off this time after the first few trips. To maintain peak efficiency, Butterfield divided the route into seven divisions. Each division was under the direction of a superintendent. Butterfield relied on the superintendents to keep the stages rolling and on schedule. Overall, the stages traveled at an average speed of 5½ miles an hour and covered 110 miles a day. However, the rate of speed varied by division, according to the difficulty of its terrain. For example, the Tucson to Fort Yuma portion of the route was called Division 6, and included 280 miles. The Division 6 superintendent was allotted 71¾ hrs to get the coaches between Tucson and Fort Yuma. Therefore, Division 6 drivers were expected to travel at speeds averaging about 3.9 mi per hour (Farish 1915; Faulk 1973).

The through-fare was originally $200 westbound and $100 eastbound—more people wanted to travel west than east—but when customers protested, the fare in both directions was reset to $150. For shorter distances in either direction, the fare was ten cents per mile. Butterfield's strict schedule called for each coach to make only two meal stops per day; prices of meals at the "scheduled" stations varied from forty cents to a dollar each. In addition to meal stops at scheduled stations, the coaches made ten-minute stops at way stations. When stopped at way stations, passengers stretched their legs or sought the privy, while drivers quickly changed horses and picked up or delivered sacks of mail. Stations ranged from nine to 60 miles apart (Farish 1915; Faulk 1973; Greene 1994).

The coaches rolled both night and day. Opinions varied concerning the level of comfort they provided. Waterman L. Ormsby, the only through-customer on the first westbound stage, wrote upon the conclusion of his trip that "The journey has been by no means as fatiguing to me as might be expected by a continuous ride of such duration, for I feel almost fresh enough to undertake it again" (Waterman L. Ormsby, cited by Greene 1994:26). Still, Ormsby returned from California to the East by boat. Another passenger probably expressed the view of many when he wrote that the Butterfield stage "possesses a wonderful charm, especially in remembrance" (H. D. Burrows, cited by Greene 1994:23).

The Butterfield Overland Mail operated along the southern (Gila) route for less than three years. By 1860, the country was on the brink of civil war. The Southern element, which had influenced the selection of the southern route, no longer controlled Congress. Indications were that the South would secede; it was equally obvious that the overland mail would have to be discontinued or re-routed. Therefore, on 2 March 1861, Congress authorized and required the Overland Mail Company to shift from the southern route to a central route; the latter ran from St. Louis via Salt Lake to Placerville. Service was discontinued over the old Butterfield route on 1 April 1861 and inaugurated over the new route on July 1st of the same year (Farish 1915).

The withdrawal of mail service from the southern route left Arizona without reliable communications with the east and west for much of the 1860s. Any mail received in Arizona during that decade was by the courtesy of private individuals or military travelers (Sloane 1958). It was not until 1869 that stages began to rumble once more along the former Butterfield route; during that year the Southern Overland U.S. Mail and Express initiated service between Tucson, Mesilla, El Paso, and eastward through Texas. The following year the Tucson, Arizona City, and San Diego Stage Company re-established service from Arizona to the West Coast, thereby completing the transcontinental link across the Southwest. These firms, under various reorganizations, would continue to operate until 1881, when completion of the Southern Pacific Railroad rendered such lines obsolete (Faulk 1973).

THE BUTTERFIELD OVERLAND MAIL ROUTE IN RELATION TO THE SR 85 PROJECT AREA

The route of the Butterfield Overland Mail through Arizona has been well studied and is relatively well known, thanks mainly to the work of Roscoe and Margaret Conkling, followed by that of Gerald Ahnert. From the late 1920s through mid 1940s, the Conklings conducted a detailed archival investigation of the route and traveled its entire length. Their three-volume opus (Conkling and Conkling 1947) provided a nearly mile-by-mile account of the trail and a history of every station along the route Decades later, Gerald Ahnert used the Conkling reference to retrace the Butterfield road through Arizona. His travels—from Stein's Peak on the east to the Gila-Colorado junction on the west—were reported in a publication (Ahnert 1973) containing maps of the route and descriptions of its stations.

These sources and others (including Faulk 1973; Greene 1994; and Sloane 1958) indicate that the Butterfield Trail in Arizona was approximately 437 miles long. There were 26 Butterfield stations in Arizona. Not all of them were in operation at the same time. After Butterfield began service on the southern route, the company found that more way stations were needed, and thus built additional stopping points across the desert. All but two of the stations were constructed of adobe. Those at Dragoon Springs and Apache Pass, in southeastern Arizona, were constructed of stone. Virtually all of the stations now lie in ruins or have been obliterated by modern development.

The Arizona portion of the route may briefly be described as follows (before this discussion turns to a more detailed review of the trail near SR 85). From the east, the trail entered Arizona just north of Stein's Peak, went in a generally southwesterly direction to San Simon, and continued through Apache Pass to Ewell's Station, Dragoon Springs, and then the San Pedro River. Upon crossing the San Pedro, the route turned in a generally northwesterly direction and proceeded to Cienega Springs before reaching Tucson. From Tucson, the route followed the Santa Cruz River downstream to the Pointer Mountain Station, and then continued to Picacho Pass, Blue Water, Oneida, and finally Sacaton, south of the Gila River. From Sacaton the route veered away from the Gila; thus avoiding the big, northern bend of the river. The route rejoined the river at Gila Bend, and

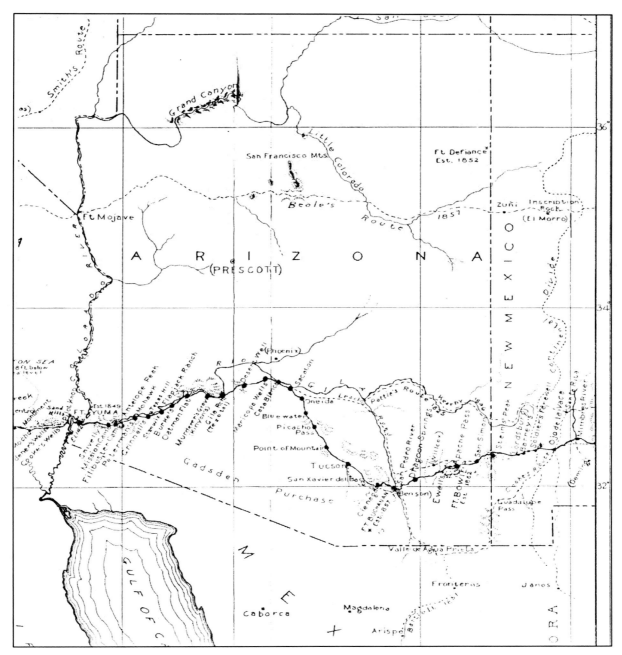

Figure 11.4. The Butterfield Overland Mail Route through Arizona.
(Source: Conkling and Conkling 1947)

followed the river downstream to its junction with the Colorado. The trail left Arizona and entered California at Yuma Crossing Figure 11.4 depicts the Butterfield Route through Arizona.

   This review of the Butterfield Route in relation to the SR 85 project area will begin at a well-known point, Maricopa Wells. Research by the Conklings (1947) and Ahnert (1973) indicates that the wells were located on Santa Cruz Wash, about eight miles north of the present community of Maricopa and about three miles northwest of Pima Butte. Maricopa Wells was located in Section 17, T3S, R3W, now part of the Gila River Indian Reservation. Philip St. George Cooke and the Mormon Battalion are believed to have dug the shallow wells while traversing the area in 1846. Forty-niners frequented the spot, and John Russell Bartlett also visited the place while conducting an international boundary survey in 1852. In 1857, the San Antonio and San Diego Mail Line made the wells a regular stop on its route between California and Texas Thus, by the time Butterfield established its station, Maricopa Wells was known as a reliable desert watering hole (Ahnert 1973; Conkling and Conkling 1947).

Leaving Maricopa Wells, the westbound route turned sharply southwestward. About six miles from the station, the route crossed the southern base of Montezuma's Head at the southern end of the Sierra Estrella. The road then proceeded to the pass between the Sierra Estrella and the Palo Verde Mountains. A mile and a half beyond the pass, the road crossed what is now the boundary line of Pinal and Maricopa counties at a point about one mile north of present Enid on the Southern Pacific Railroad (Ahnert 1973; Conkling and Conkling 1947).

The Butterfield route then continued almost due west to Desert Well, a station approximately 20 mi from Maricopa Wells. Desert Well was an "extra" stopping point established by Butterfield late in 1858 after operations had begun. The station provided relief from the dreaded "Forty Mile Desert" between Maricopa Wells and Gila Bend. Its location was approximately 5.5 mi west/northwest of present Mobile and two miles north of the Southern Pacific Railroad. The Conklings (1947) and Ahnert (1973) each state that the station was on Waterman Wash; however, their maps and descriptions suggest that the station may have been on a tributary to that wash. The site now called Conley's Well on some maps is believed to mark the site of the old Desert Well station.

From Desert Well, the overland route curved slightly southwest and headed for Pima Pass in the Maricopa Mountains (the pass is called Butterfield Pass on some maps today). Along the pass, the Butterfield company constructed a tank and stocked it with water brought from Gila Ranch Station (to the west). The tank site later became known as Happy Camp (Ahnert 1973; Conkling and Conkling 1947).

Leaving Pima/Butterfield Pass and the Maricopa Mountains, the route continued almost due west across the desert toward the next station, Gila Ranch. The route is believed to have crossed the current SR 85 project area at a point about five miles north of Gila Bend. Figure 11.5 shows the Butterfield route in this locality.

West of the current project area, the Butterfield route soon reached Gila Ranch Station. Gila Ranch was situated in T5S, R4W, Section 8, on the south bank of the river and about 4.5 mi north of the present town of Gila Bend. The original Butterfield station at Gila Ranch was built in the summer of 1858 but was destroyed by Native Americans early in 1860. Butterfield immediately rebuilt the station on the same site. Gila Ranch was a "scheduled" (also called time-table) station, meaning that the mail arrived at this point at precise times: on Wednesdays and Saturdays at 9 p.m. on the westbound route, and on Mondays and Thursdays at 7:30 p.m. on the eastbound route. Westward from Gila Ranch, the Butterfield route continued down the Gila River to its junction with the Colorado River, then crossed the Colorado to enter California.

SUMMARY

This chapter has provided an overview of two historic trails in relation to the SR 85 project area. Today, the Anza Trail and the Butterfield Overland Mail Route are ghostly and enigmatic cultural resources that appear and disappear as they cross the Sonoran Desert floor. Their ephemeral nature belies their powerful role in American history. Both resources represent milestones in the fields of exploration, transportation, and communication.

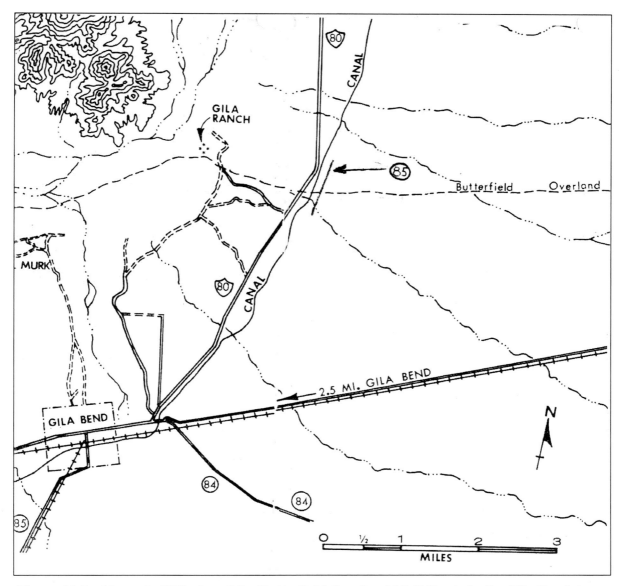

Figure 11.5. Ahnert's 1973 plot of the Butterfield Overland Mail Route in the Gila Bend Area, information has been added (note arrow) to show a portion of the SR 85 Project Area in relation to the trail. (Source: Ahnert 1973)

The significance of Juan Bautista de Anza and the route he opened is widely recognized. According to the National Park Service (1996:7–8):

> Anza displayed remarkable leadership to bring at least 240 people safely over a little-known route in a hostile environment. Anza made contact with the many native peoples along the way and noted locations of water, forage, and fuel which made possible a route of settlement between Sonora and Alta California. Although the route was largely abandoned by the Spanish after an uprising of the Yuma Indians in 1781, it had allowed the passage of enough cattle, settlers, and soldiers to ensure the survival of the existing settlements and to begin the pueblos of San Jose and Los Angeles...The soldiers and families that Anza escorted brought their

language, customs, traditions, and general expressions of Hispanic culture as it existed in the New World. These early settlers of California were a mixed group of European, Native American, and African heritage. They had a significant impact on the cultures of the indigenous peoples they encountered and on the development of California. The diaries of the two expeditions provide a record of the American Indian cultures and of the landscapes encountered by Anza.

In honor of Anza's achievement, the U.S. Department of the Interior designated the "Juan Bautista de Anza National Historic Trail" in 1990. The route received further recognition in 1999 when it became a "National Millennium Trail."

The Butterfield Overland Mail Route through Arizona similarly possesses great historic significance. The trail was an important early highway of the nation. It served as the first mail route linking the eastern and western United States. It blazed a path for later transcontinental connectors, such as the Southern Pacific Railroad. More than 2,000 miles of the overland route traversed a region virtually unknown to the average American citizen; and yet, the company operating the route delivered passengers and mail to their destinations safely and on time. The route gave a sense of order and predictability to a young nation coming to grips with an adolescent growth spurt engendered by its own policy of Manifest Destiny.

Both the Anza and Butterfield trails became like rivers through a landscape lacking naturally navigable routes. The Spaniards and the Euroamericans viewed the Southwest as a land of little value, a region to be crossed as rapidly as possible to get to the West Coast. The Anza and Butterfield trails responded to, and reflected, these periods of history. Over them flowed the people, goods, and eventually mail that bound the east and west.

CHAPTER 12

TRAILS RESEARCH IN THE GILA BEND AREA

J. Andrew Darling and B. Sunday Eiselt

INTRODUCTION

Human beings travel to survive. They travel for food, to visit relatives, to trade, or to make war. Trails are the physical manifestation of routine travel. In recent years, projects such as Route 66, the *Camino Real*, and the Spanish or Santa Fe Trails have memorialized historic routes of travel, which shaped a developing nation. But, what was Native American infrastructure like before the arrival of Euro-Americans?

He'kugam Vo:g is a Pima phrase meaning Ancient Trail. The arid southwest provides us with a unique natural landscape where trail segments, some as old as 10,000 years, are still visible on the desert surface. In connection with data recovery efforts sponsored by the Arizona Department of Transportation (ADOT), the Cultural Resource Management Program of the Gila River Indian Community examined a 30 percent sample of the 47 sites along SR 85 near Gila Bend exhibiting one or more trail segments.

Viewing trails as Native infrastructure is a theme that appeals to concepts of how communities function as collections of interconnecting ideological and material systems. Knowledge of trails—not just of where people were but how they got there—provides an important dimension for understanding the location and distribution of sacred sites and settlements. It also provides insights into the regular flow of resources (energy and information) among traditional communities. These data can be used to structure new research questions about the historic and prehistoric past.

Ultimately, trail studies will provide a greater understanding of how human beings traveled in the past. This includes the variety of journeys undertaken such as routine trips to gather resources, trips between settlements, and ceremonial journeys to gather special resources such as salt or shells, to worship, or to make war.

PROCESSUAL ASPECTS OF TRAILS

Trails are the product of human beings repeatedly traveling across preexisting game trails, natural corridors between resource areas (such as water sources), or along purposefully constructed or established routes of travel. Many trails are created through repeated usage. Other trails are designed and constructed. In some instances trails exhibit characteristics of casual clearing of stones and debris by travelers and intentional or formalized engineering. Geographic and environmental considerations also determine the location, appearance, and duration of trails.

Trails serve as a guide or facility for structuring the movement of people, baggage, and livestock from one location to another. As such they record the movement of individuals across geographic space. Most trails were used repeatedly for long periods of time by differing ethnic groups, and for a variety of functions requiring mobility. These functions might include seasonal mobility, trade, resource acquisition, religious observances, warfare, or other unrelated social obligations.

Becker and Altschul (2003:33–38) present a number of themes that outline certain basic processual aspects of trails research. These include Settlement Pattern and Trail Use, Trade, Territorial Boundaries, and Trail Systems. Each of these themes considers the ways in which economic, sociopolitical, and religious behavior may relate to the structure and use of trail systems over time. The most basic fact underlying all of these behaviors is that mobility or travel is not random. Repeated actions in the social and natural landscape produce trails, which remain visible on stable desert ground surfaces. Trail networks evolve in tandem with other aspects of a society's infrastructure or the ways that information, material culture, and people circulate and interact.

TYPOLOGICAL ASPECTS OF TRAILS

Classification schemes serve to describe and organize information about trails. These can be used to establish relationships between individual trail segments, interconnected trail networks, individual settlements, and settlement systems. Trail typologies normally organize specific trail types in terms of their function, chronology or history, and/or physical characteristics.

Stein (1994:37) provides a typology for historic trails as a guide for managing historic properties. She identifies nine different trail types:

1. Native American Trails
2. Spanish Period Trails and Roads
3. Mexican Period Trails and Roads
4. U.S. Government Trails and Roads of the Early American Period
5. Mormon Trails and Roads
6. Stagecoach, Freight, and Toll Roads
7. Stock Trails
8. Early Automotive Routes
9. Other Historic Trials and Transportation Corridors

Stein's classification scheme favors chronology and function over physical properties, although she does associate certain trail characteristics with specific transport facilities, such as foot traffic, livestock, wagons or automobiles. Stein's typology is useful for identifying and organizing information on trails in historical documents. As she notes, many historically documented trails no longer exist and therefore cannot be considered eligible for the National Register of Historic Places.[3]

Other typologies also serve to describe the physical characteristics and putative function of prehistoric or historic trails as they occur in the field. Outmoded classification schemes utilize familiar categories including hunting trail, war path, and trade trail (Jones 1967:5). Becker and Altschul (2003:28–30) provide a functional scheme based on three trail types—trackways, minor trails, and major trails. We will present a classification scheme that is similar but focuses on the mode of travel (as a human behavior) rather than the trail itself. As noted by Becker and Altschul, among others, the disadvantage of any trail typology is that any one trail could have carried many different kinds of traffic. By focusing on travel in relation to general theories of human mobility, the process becomes one of human decision-making with reference to which trails would best serve the purpose of the trip. This approach acknowledges that certain trails may be used exclusively for certain kinds of travel whereas most trails are multi-functional and the features and artifacts found along them represent a wide range of activities.

---

[3]The physical integrity of a trail is critical for evaluation of a trail's eligibility status including its location, associations, and other materials.

Network analysis offers some compelling avenues for research (see for example Helbing, Keltsch and Molnár 1997, see also Becker and Altschul 2003:38) and incorporates human decision making in models of trail evolution. These studies suggest that trail networks initiate simply as the most direct route between two destinations. As preferred routes of travel become part of the knowledge base of pedestrians they will make small detours to access preferred routes. In time mature trail networks may acquire a configuration that reflects a compromise between constraints of preference (reflecting social and functional choices by travelers) and spatial efficiency. Furthermore, what underlies effective modeling of trail network evolution is the realization that individual travelers receive and process information (or knowledge) as they travel (see for example Kelly 1995:150; Rockman and Steel 2003). Thus, the act of travel goes beyond the simple act of getting from place to place. While research on trail network evolution is beyond the scope of the current study, the unusual degree of trail preservation along SR 85 may provide an opportunity for research in the future.

TRAILS RESEARCH ALONG SR 85

Trails research was conducted along SR 85 to address two primary research questions:

1) What kinds of features and artifacts co-occur with trail sites?

2) Where do the trails go?

Native American trails are as much represented by the trail itself as the artifacts and features scattered along it. These commonly include rock cairns/rock piles, trail markers, shrines, hearths, campsites, and linear artifact scatters (Breternitz 1975; Brown and Stone 1982; Harmon and Beyer 1995; Rodgers 1976, Rogers n.d. [notes on file San Diego Museum of Man], 1966; Stone 1986, 1991; Woodall 1995). Woodall (1995:13–14) notes that the most frequently observed feature adjacent to trails were rock clusters. Rock clusters/piles could represent roasting pits, hearths, or trail markers. Rock piles may also represent trail shrines as noted by Treutlein (1949:228); cited in Ezell 1961:78–79). Ezell (1961:79) noted this trait on a San Dieguito shrine identified in the saddle of the Buckeye Hills northeast of Gila Bend and a similar shrine in the saddle of Gila Butte along the Gila River.

The second question addresses the origin and destination of trails in relation to their characteristics including associated artifacts and features. Prehistoric and historic indigenous trails can be classified in terms of the types of travel conducted along them. This includes travel between settlements (Type I), travel from a settlement to a resource area (Type II), and ritualized travel, from a settlement to a particular location for a specific social-ceremonial function (Type III). As discussed above, the relationship of types or modes of travel will be considered in more detail in relation to the archaeological record of trails in the Gila Bend area.

TRAILS RESEARCH METHODOLOGY

Trail research followed two phases:

I. Background research and review of the trails records of Malcolm Rogers at the San Diego Museum of Man

II. Field Survey along SR 85.

Background research included extensive use of Malcolm Rogers' survey records, located at the San Diego Museum of Man, to contextualize the historic and prehistoric trail networks maintained by the O'odham (Pima) and Pee Posh (Maricopa) Tribes. These data provide important views of how local trail systems are integrated into extra-local networks of travel. Oral histories, creation stories, and other accounts further document the manner in which trails are used. Rogers recorded over 6000 sites, ceramic and preceramic, during several field seasons between 1928 and 1960. Regrettably only a small number of reports were produced, none of which provide a synthesis of over 20 volumes of notes resulting from his regional survey and extensive research (McGuire 1982:440).

We were particularly interested in records related to Rogers' thorough mapping and recording of trails in southwestern Arizona, since further studies of this important data set would help place the SR-85 trails in a regional context. Combined with the research of Stein (1994), Pendleton (1986), Von Werlhof (1988), and Hayden (1965, 1967, 1972), historical accounts of trail use (e.g. Manje 1971; Sedelmeyer 1955), ethnographies describing trail use (e.g. Bean 1974; Jett 2001; Laird 1976) and finally synthetic studies of trail systems (e.g. Davis 1961; Johnston and Johnston 1957; Sample 1950), a clear picture of trail use and Native American infrastructure emerges which incorporates the Gila Bend and extends throughout the arid Southwest (Figure 12.1).

As part of the ADOT archaeological project along SR 85, Arizona State University collaborated with the Gila River Indian Community, Cultural Resource Management Program, in their on-going Traditional Cultural Properties Research project funded by the Pima-Maricopa Irrigation Project and the National Park Service. The immediate goal was to identify previously recorded trails and map them beyond the existing SR 85 right-of-way. A 30 percent sample of 14 sites out of the 47 sites with trail segments reported by Harmon and Beyer (1994) was selected for visual examination in the field. Selection was based on three priorities designated in the research plan. First, survey was conducted to verify the continuation and integrity of the trail as a long linear archaeological feature on the landscape and to distinguish it from other animal trails or recently created vehicle tracks. Second, sites were selected in strategic locations along major routes of travel connecting the Gila Bend region with other known or suspected historic and prehistoric indigenous routes of travel. Third, trails in the vicinity of the Butterfield Stage Route were examined to determine the relationship between them and this long-standing historic Euro-American road.

Field recording focused on following the trails out of the previously recorded site boundaries away from the SR 85 right-of-way in an easterly or westerly direction, or roughly perpendicular to the north-south trending highway. In general, no trails along the bajada of the Gila Bend Valley were shown to travel north-south (a few short north-south tracks were used by cattle). Field crews consisted of 2–4 persons and trail locations were mapped using a GPS unit. Approximately three weeks were spent documenting trails in the field. Intact trail segments could exceed a kilometer in length and waypoints were taken regularly at 50-meter intervals or less when specific features along the trail were identified. Field notes were taken at each waypoint describing the character of the trail, artifacts or features, and where possible, a width measurement was made. Digital photography was used to record specific details of the trails and associated features.

TRAIL IDENTIFICATION

Trails consist of segments, which in turn are composed of one or more tracks or linear artifact scatters. Tracks are the walking surface or the physical representation of the trail on the ground. A track normally consists of a cleared linear area approximately 40–60 centimeters wide with a central walking surface that may be compacted slightly, lowered a few centimeters below ground surface with occasional slight lateral berms or stone-lining marking the edge of the track. In many cases well-used trails may be represented by more than one parallel track. At other times trails may only appear as linear vegetation changes resulting from the accumulation of moisture in the worn walking

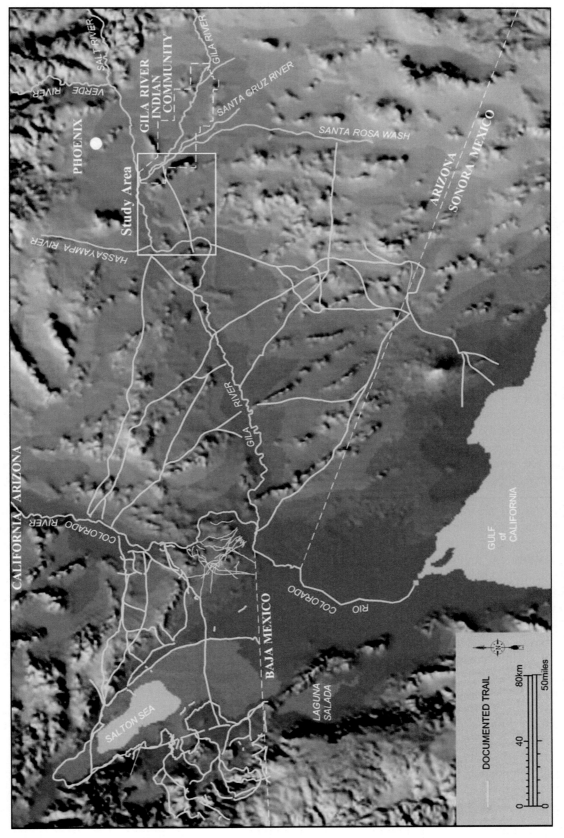

Figure 12.1. Map showing indigenous trails recorded by Malcolm Rodgers.

surface. Tracks occasionally became erosion channels and were downcut sometimes as much as 10-20 cm. The occurrence of multiple tracks is not considered evidence of braiding or branching as the individual parallel tracks of prehistoric trails do not tend to cross back and forth. Instead, these may represent varying chronological stages of a continuously used trail. Each trail segment was of varying length and characteristics and was numbered in the order of its discovery. Segments recorded in the field were mapped and associated with each other to form trails based on field observations and their location.

Trail recording generally focused on attributes useful for testing the validity of a prehistoric or historic trail observed in the field. These included the following (see also Becker and Altschul 2003:46-47 for a similar series of attributes):

1. width, variability in width
2. depth of trail
3. presence of parallel trails or multiple tracks
4. presence or absence of desert pavement
5. compaction in the trail
6. presence of a berm
7. rock border
8. vegetation patterns
9. branching or fading (particularly at the endpoints of a trail segment)
10. location on the geomorphic landscape
11. use or reuse by animals or humans

Trail integrity varied along its length and was subject to natural or geomorphic processes that would greatly modify its appearance including erosion, cross-cutting animal tracks and vegetation cover. Contextual elements include associated features, artifacts, and geomorphology, which were critical for verifying that a trail was generated by humans rather than other domestic or wild animals. In certain cases the only evidence for a trail segment consisted of a linear artifact scatter, which connected visible trail segments or tracks on the ground surface. In these instances, the track or pathway had been entirely removed by erosion or other disturbance.

Waters (this volume) has demonstrated the association of prehistoric trail segments with relic or older geomorphic surfaces. Archaeological survey and geomorphic mapping along the roadway corridor reveals a distinctive pattern of where trails appear and where they do not. Stable Pleistocene alluvial fans are the most likely location for encountering trails and nearly all of them in the project area exhibit probable trails (Figure 12.2). Fragile desert pavement surfaces preserve the effects of regular foot traffic along a trail (Hayden 1965). Artifacts or other features placed along these trails also will not be removed by subsequent erosion.

Historic roads and animal trails at times can be confused with prehistoric trails. In cases where suspected trails cross active Holocene alluvial surfaces and archaeological features or artifacts were not present, it often resulted that these trails led to a modern cattle tank or corral facility for domestic animals. Becker and Altschul (2003:17–18) point out that cattle in particular tend to take a longer, more circuitous route avoiding steep slopes while ascending and a more direct route while descending. They go on to suggest that unlike cattle and burros, it may be more efficient energetically for humans to ascend steep slopes directly, even to the point where the grade requires the cutting of artificial steps (2003:19–20). "Ascent Trails" are a common form of trail often seen rising perpendicular to the slope of small buttes or similar isolated physiographic desert features. In many cases these trails lead to an exposed bedrock promontory that provides a commanding view serving as a lookout and/or rock art site.

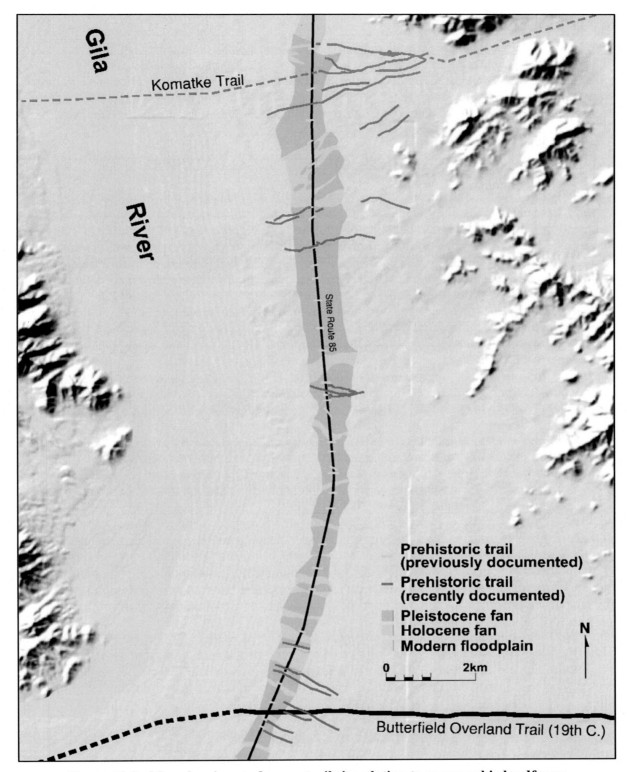

Figure 12.2. Map showing study area trails in relation to geomorphic landforms.

Historic or modern roads also tend to obscure prehistoric trails or in some instances mimic them. However, like animal trails many roads tended to cross-cut both recent and older geomorphic surfaces. Even in the case of the Butterfield stage route, which has been out of use for more than 100 years, the road follows a direct line across both recent arroyo bottoms and older terraces, unlike older indigenous trails found on relic Pleistocene surfaces. It was also observed that roads and trails might coincide in the same location. This is not surprising since the preferred route of travel in the past may continue to be preferred today. In these instances, trails might be found paralleling historic or modern roads and two tracks.

RESULTS OF TRAIL SURVEY ALONG SR 85

A total of 39 trail segments representing 30.3 km of prehistoric and historic indigenous trail directly associated with sites along SR-85 were recorded as part of data recovery. Most trail segments could be linked with other segments to form what were identified as trails. In many cases these linkages were assumed and were not visible on the ground, whereas other direct connections between segments were observed as trail branching. An additional 9.08 km of linear distance may be added to the total distance covered by trail segments to account for these linkages for a total of 39.83 km of trail observed within the Gila Bend portion of the Gila River Valley. Finally, the Oyadaibuic-Komatke Trail is a prehistoric and historical period trail which extends from east of the Estrella Mountains to as far as the painted rocks area beyond the Gila bend, passing through passes in the Estrella Mountains, the Maricopa Mountains east of SR-85, and the Gila Bend Mountains, immediately west of SR-85 across the Gila River. Portions of this trail were observed in each location. Adding the 3.7 km of this trail observed in the Estrellas as well as the 35.41 km of intervening sections of the trail that must have existed in the now eroded valley bottoms yields a grand total of 78.94 km (49 mi) of indigenous trail considered as part of this study.

Trail characteristics and features along trails are an important part of this research. Features observed include linear sherd and lithic scatters, trail markers, trail shrines, rock art (petroglyph boulders and panels), stone circles, and pot-rests. The trails themselves can be linear segments or multiple tracks across the desert landscape, which in some cases are constructed or are the byproduct of constant use for hundreds of years. Other trails may only be seen as long linear scatters of artifacts. A characteristic of many trails in the study area is the prevalence of white quartz or feldspar nodules made into trail markers or lining the trail. Some scholars have remarked on the sacred significance of quartz (Ezzo and Altschul 1993; Rogers 1976; and Stone 1991). However, O'odham (Pima) tradition also records that quartz served to illuminate trails on moonlit nights or when torches were used for night-time travel. An historical account describes one trail as a "river of torches" due to the prevalence of burned-out torches observed along its length (Sedelmayr 1955).

Trail segments appeared as sets representing individual trails or groups of trails crossing the Gila Bend Valley and beyond (Figure 12.3). To describe each individual trail segment would go beyond the scope of this chapter. Each of the eight groups or segment sets will be described below with respect to its particular characteristics. These will be summarized in a discussion that follows.

TRAIL SEGMENT SETS

Segment Set 1

Segment Set 1 consisted of 11 trail segments originating at sites AZ T:14:92-93 in the SR-85 right-of-way. Selected segments were identified and mapped to establish the pattern of trails crossing

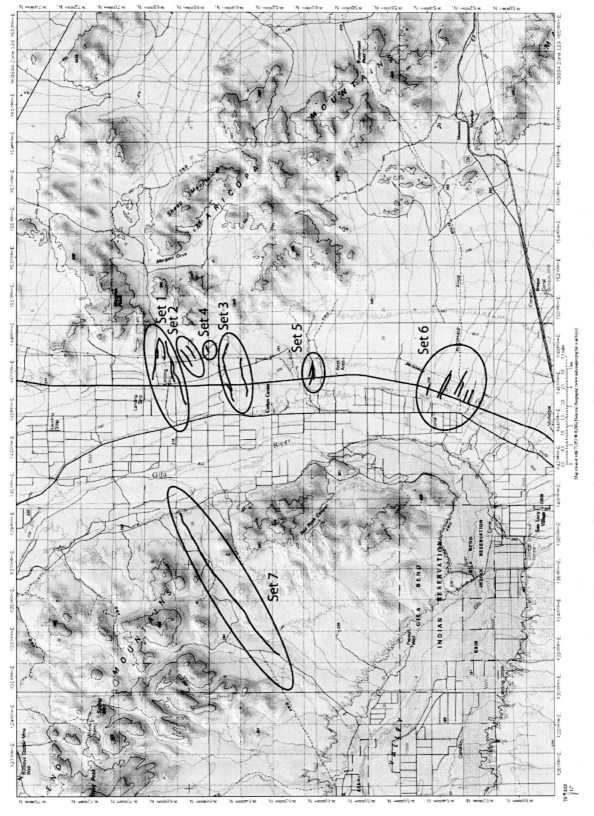

Figure 12.3. Map showing recorded trail segment sets 1 to 7.

this area. Trails were shown to cross the freeway in an east/northeast to west/southwest direction oriented to a pass in the Maricopa Mountains (Figure 12.4). As will be discussed below this complex of trails represents a portion of the Oyadaibuic-Komatke Trail with branching or fanning out towards the west from the pass to access prehistoric and historic sites in the Gila Bend Valley.

Trail features in Segment Set 1 were numerous and included extensive linear artifact scatters consisting of mixed lithic and ceramic artifacts along visible trail segments. Ceramics included primarily non-diagnostic plain or buff pottery, although a minor amount of red-slipped wares and red-on-buff sherds were observed. In all cases, sherds appeared in concentrations many apparently representing potbreaks or drops. Pottery fragments were exclusively from jars and no obvious bowl sherds were observed.

Lithics along the trail consisted of mainly tested river cobbles transported up from the valley bottoms or alluvial terraces. Many of these fall into the category of primary flake tools as described by Haury (1976) for the Hohokam but may pertain to other periods. Quartz and feldspar scatter and shatter along the trail was common and trail segments passed a number of natural outcrops. Even though this material did occur naturally, its occurrence along visible trail segments and in formal features beside the trails seemed to indicate intentional placement.

An unusual shell artifact consisted of an unmodified *glycymeris* shell that was found approximately one meter off a well-defined track (Figure 12.5).

Formal features along Segment Set 1 included rock piles or concentrations, rock circles (Figure 12.6), small cairn like features, and trail markers. Sherd and quartz concentrations tended to associate with these features, which occasionally occurred at trail branches.

Trail segments were of variable length and integrity on the ground. However, the majority of trails were visible as tracks compacted 1–3 centimeters below the surrounding desert pavement (Figure 12.7). Trail width ranged from 39.1–54.3 cm with occasional berms along the side of the trail due to heavy use. Parallel tracks were common, although trails may diminish to differential vegetation growth in tracks and linear artifact scatter only. Visible tracks were confined to an elevation range of 887.2–960.8 feet above sea level (ft asl) characteristic of the Pleistocene terrace/bajada environment where trails are most visible.

The most overwhelming pattern exhibited by Segment Set 1 was its obvious convergence on the pass in the Maricopa Mountains to the east. All trail branching was to the west as the trails leaving the pass fan out to settlements with locations below the interface of the bajadas and lower floodplain. The convergence pattern approximates a 50 percent reduction in visible trails or a decrease from five or six trails at the SR-85 right-of-way to approximately three trails in closest proximity to the pass. Unfortunately, this pattern could not be carried out further below the bajada where the active floodplain has removed any signs of prehistoric trails. Likewise, erosion off the flanks of the Maricopa Mountains has buried the trails as they proceed into the pass.

Segment Set 2

Segment Set 2 consisted of only two probable trails (see Figure 12.4). With similar configuration as those trails in Segment Set 1, these trails also likely represent branches off the Oyadaibuic-Komatke Trail as it proceed to the west from the Maricopa Mountain Pass. Although rather distantly offset to the east, these two trails may have at one time passed through site AZ T:14:90 located at the SR 85 right-of-way.

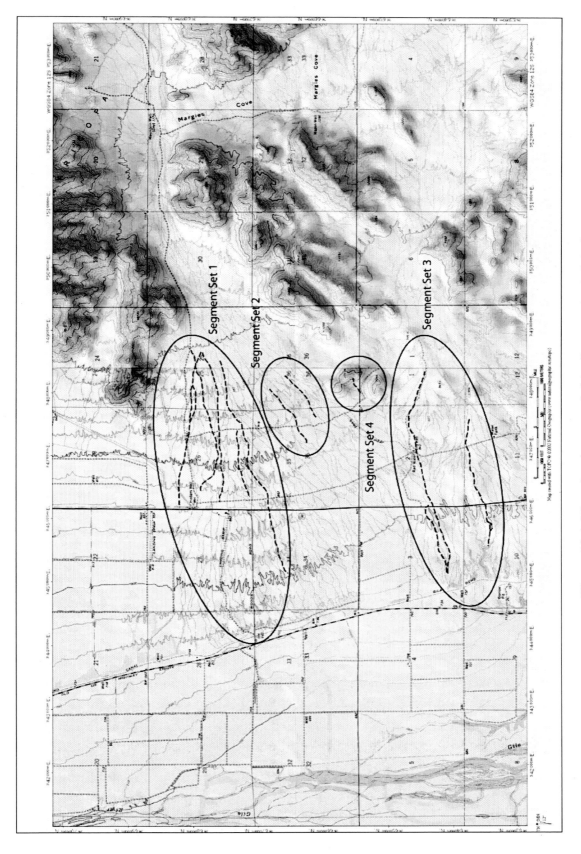

Figure 12.4. Map showing recorded trail segment sets 1 to 4.

Figure 12.5. *Glycymeris* **shell associated with trail.**

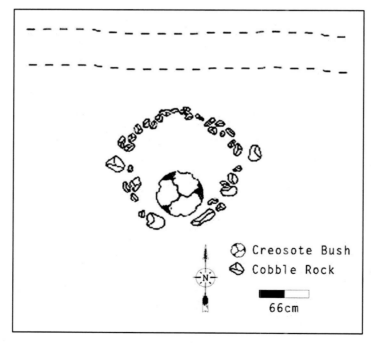

Figure 12.6. Trail TL1-2, Feature 1, rock ring.

Figure 12.7. Two photographs showing branching and parallel tracks as part of a typical trail.

Artifact remains along the trail consisted primarily of non-diagnostic buff, plain, and redware body sherds concentrated into pot drops. Some lithics occur consisting of tested rhyolite river cobbles but quartz and feldspar is less common. Trail characteristics include parallel tracks and well-defined trail segments averaging 35.4 cm in width. Elevation of the trails ranged from 937 to 946 ft. asl. The southernmost trail is obscured in part by recent cattle traffic to access low spots where grass was observed. No formal features or rock concentrations were observed along these trail segments.

Segment Set 3

Segment Set 3 consisted of six trail segments representing two trails. These segments cross SR-85 and appear to associate with sites AZ T:14:86 and AZ T:14:88 located in the right-of-way. Located south of Sets 1 and 2, Segment Set 3 follows a similar east/northeast to west/southwest orientation and may represent a subsidiary route into the Maricopa Mountain pass that passes through a small side canyon identified as Margies Cove (see Figure 12.4).

The northern of the two trails is most similar to the trails described in Segment Sets 1 and 2 consisting of parallel tracks, abundant sherd and lithic scatters, and up to ten formal rock features including rock rings, rock concentrations, and possible trail markers. One petroglyph boulder, as well as chipping stations utilizing locally occurring basalt-rhyolite, was noted as the trail passes to the east toward the base of the mountains. Trail width ranged from 33 to 35 cm, and trail segments were clearly visible as tracks with well defined walking surfaces. Elevation of this trail ranged from 761–926 ft asl.

The southern trail in this segment set was distinctive. Unlike the trail to the north, no ceramic artifacts were encountered, although lithic remains were abundant. A total of nine petroglyph boulders were observed with figures consisting mainly of abstract concentric circles (Figure 12.8). Most of the lithics were found in three chipping stations located either side of the trail in which all stages of lithic reduction were represented, utilizing naturally occurring basalt or other volcanics. Four additional features consisting of rock concentrations were noted. Quartz is also less abundant along this trail but appears in association with rock features. As with previous trails, parallel tracks were observed with well defined walking surfaces and edges. Average elevation of this trail was 812.8 ft asl and trail width averaged 33.4 cm.

Segment Set 4

Trail Segment Set 4 represents a single "ascent" trail located on the west side of a small butte located between Trail Segment Sets 1–2 and 3 (see Figure 12.4). This trail was observed from a distance but on closer inspection appears to conform to a naturally occurring vein of granite or gneiss. While there is some doubt as to the validity of this trail, a width measurement of 30 cm was obtained. Elevation change ranged from 850 ft asl at the trail's base to 1018 ft asl at the summit. Like other ascent trails in the region, this trail approaches the slope at a perpendicular angle and ascends directly without meandering. No artifacts were observed along the trail or on the summit, although a naturally occurring quartz outcrop is present. Two features, a rock concentration and a circular stone structure were observed. The circular feature built of granite boulders is approximately one meter in diameter and about 15 meters from the possible ascent trail (Figure 12.9). Similar features have been observed in the Gila River Indian Community and are described as possible lookouts.

Segment Set 5

Trail Segment Set 5 consists of five trail segments making up three converging trails (Figure 12.10). These trails are oriented east–west, crossing SR 85 and are associated with sites AZ T:14:79-80.

Figure 12.8. Boulder petroglyph associated with trail.

Average elevation ranges from 750–780 ft asl and the individual tracks are highly variable in their integrity and visibility. In general, trail width ranged from 29–35 cm. Ceramic artifacts were non-diagnostic and were concentrated in only a few potdrops. Lithic scatter was more common throughout, although three chipping stations exhibiting all stages of reduction were found along the eastern portion of the trail going towards the mountains. Tested river cobbles appear to have been more common along the western portion of the trails. Four features included rock piles or concentrations and three petroglyph boulders were observed.

Segment Set 6

Segment Set 6 consists of nine trail segments forming eight parallel trails oriented east/southeast to west/northwest (Figure 12.11). Observation of these trails was conducted to establish their relationship with the Butterfield Stage Route, which passes on an east-west trajectory across these clearly earlier trails. These trails are associated with sites recorded along SR 85 including AZ T:14:28, AZ T:14:61-62, AZ T:14:64 and AZ Z:2:54-55.

These trails are very uniform in their characteristics. Average elevation ranges from 770–786 ft asl and average width ranges 35–45.7 cm. Artifact assemblage is dominated by ceramics, while lithics are few and consist of isolated flaked river cobbles primarily. Two worked fragments of *glycymeris* shell were encountered. Quartz or feldspar is largely absent. There are no features present although artifact distribution is continuous and follows the clearly visible trails. Parallel tracks were observed sporadically.

Figure 12.9. Circular feature associated with ascent trail.

Two of the trails were shown to cross the Butterfield stage route which cuts through the preexisting indigenous trail visible on either side of the road. The stage route is a visible cut up to 30 cm or more beneath ground surface with visible berms to either side. At each location where the trails crossed the stage line, historic solder seam, and hole-in-top cans were observed.

Segment Set 7

Segment Set 7 consists of a continuation of the Oyadaibuic-Komatke Trail through a pass in the Gila Bend Mountains into the painted rocks area (Figure 12.12). Actual visible segments were short, located at either end of the segment set with a 6 km segment assumed to connect the two. The trail is oriented northeast-southwest. The northwest portion rises out of the Gila Bend Valley onto the narrow bajada and enters the pass. A later wagon road or two-track dating to the early part of the last century partially obscures the trail. Average elevation on the eastern portion of the trail is 750.1 ft asl, whereas on the western end the elevation is 837.6 ft. asl, where the trail has already crossed the uppermost portion of the pass and is descending into the painted rocks area. Average width of the trail, where visible, was 35 cm.

Artifact presence is much less than other trails but consists of non-diagnostic ceramics and lithic scatters. Where the trail originates, in proximity to the Gila River floodplain, a ground stone mano

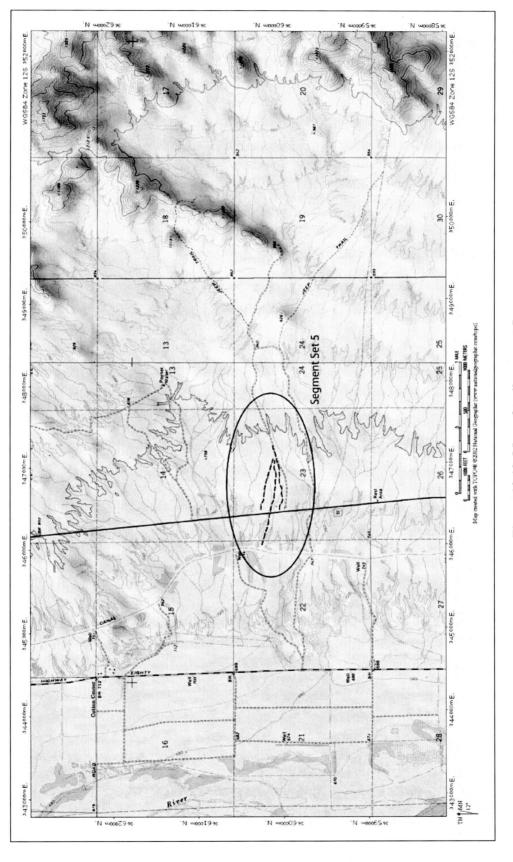

Figure 12.10. Map of trail segment 5.

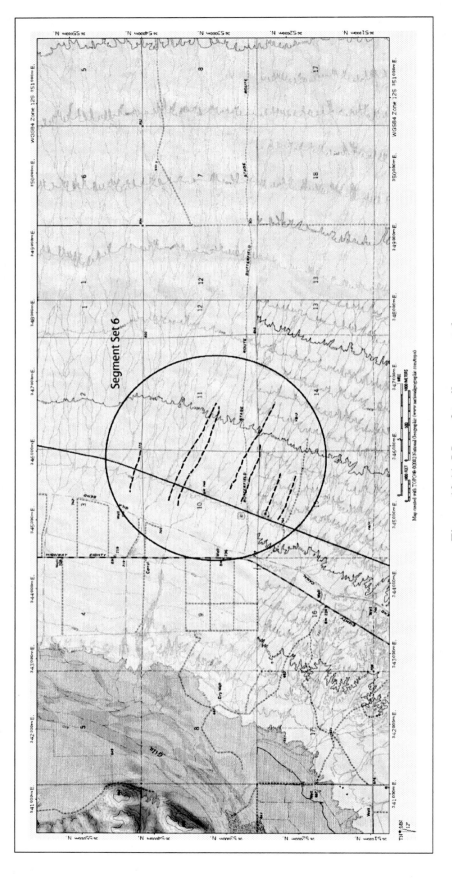

Figure 12.11. Map of trail segment 6.

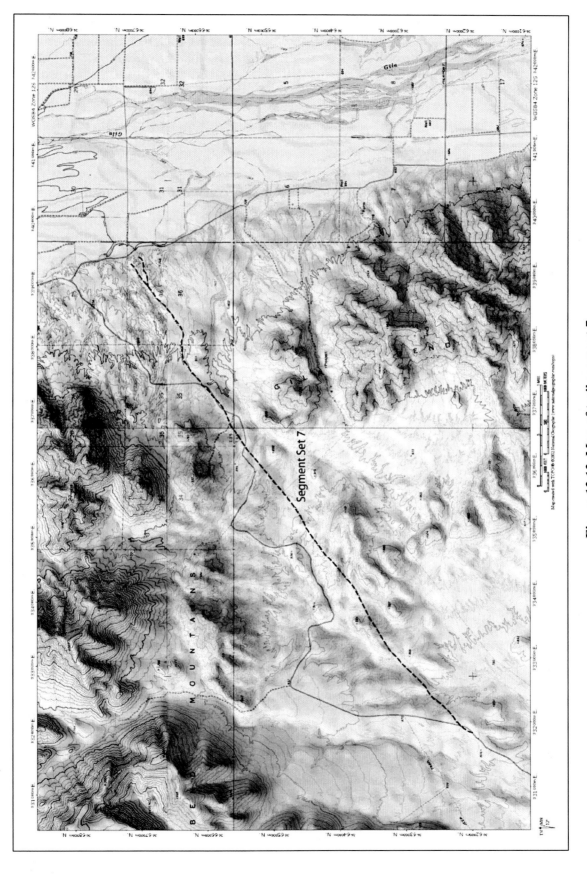

Figure 12.12. Map of trail segment 7.

fragment and red-on-buff ceramics were observed. Further along the trail, lithic artifacts tended to exhibit higher amounts of desert varnish, similar to artifacts found in Colorado or Mojave Desert environments. Formal features were also less common than on the Gila Bend Valley but were more discrete and included two quartz trail markers (Figure 12.13). The westernmost portion of the trail was reminiscent of Colorado Desert trails marked by a clear track with occasional ceramics.

Segment Set 8

Trail Segment Set 8 is 3.72 km. in length and is the easternmost documented section of the Oyadaibuic-Komatke Trail, which crosses the Estrella Mountains from the Rainbow Valley on the west to the Middle Gila Valley on the east (Figure 12.14). This trail is indicated primarily by a long linear artifact scatter dominated by Hohokam pottery jars of plain, buff, and red-on-buff wares and some lithics. Occasional trail segments were visible but have mainly washed out. When measurable, trail width ranged between 30 and 40 cm. Elevation change was dramatic from the trail's starting point on the west at 1350 ft asl to 2400 ft asl at the summit and a descent to 1835 ft asl at the limit the trail could be followed to the east.

In spite of the ephemeral nature of the trail segments, the artifact scatter clearly links a series of rock art panels or petroglyph sites, cairns (some of them modern), and shrines as well as passing by quartz outcrops which were evidently mined for material scatter along the trails. Probable shrines are large and formal with one shrine located below the trail summit represented by a large natural stone column with preclassic Hohokam cache vessels broken at its base (Figure 12.15). A split in the column also had a small stone shelf placed in it presumably to receive offerings. Rock rings and possible campsites were evident at the base of the Estrella Pass on the western side.

SUMMARY

Trail survey in connection with SR 85 data recovery in the Gila Bend Valley confirmed the existence and integrity of numerous unusually well preserved trails initially identified by surveys in the highway's right-of-way. The sheer quantity of trails seems attributable to the stability of Pleistocene terraces located on the bajada on the east side of the valley. As was shown through the current survey, it is likely that many more trail segments or individual tracks also may exist than was actually sampled by the earlier survey of SR 85.

The large number of trails on the bajada may also be attributed in part to the pattern by which trails enter from outside the valley into the Gila Bend. As trails emerge from mountain passes, they fan out or branch before descending off the bajada. These branches or secondary trails leave the passes and head toward village settlements scattered along the upper edge of the Gila River floodplain. The distance between trail segments is smallest on the bajada, nearest their branch points from the main trails, resulting in a high density of trail segments near gateways or passes into the next valley. In this way, mountain passes act as nodes or convergence points for numerous trails extending throughout the valley.

This pattern contrasts with Segment Set 6, which crosses the Butterfield Stage Line. In this area the trails exhibit a distinctly different orientation and direction. Trails on the bajada are parallel and show no tendency to converge on a main trail or pass. The pattern of these trails may be attributed to unobstructed travel. In contrast the Stage Line tends to crosscut existing ridges and may be characteristic of travel using domestic animals and wheeled conveyances.

Figure 12.13. Quartz trail marker.

Other trails are oriented less to inter-regional travel and seem to access particular bajada resource areas. This may be true of Segment Sets 3 and 5, where trails appear to approach usable lithic raw material sources. The occurrence of petroglyph boulders and fewer ceramics may be indicative of chronological differences or a different set of activities or behaviors associated with these trails. Further in-field analysis of these features is necessary to make these determinations. However, the lower density of artifacts, particularly ceramics, also suggests a lower level of traffic.

Level of traffic seems to be a good deal higher along Segment Sets 1 and 8, which are situated along the Oyadaibuic–Komatke Trail. Here, the regular occurrence of multiple parallel tracks, converging and branching trails, and numerous features suggest higher usage. Artifact abundance is higher and the consistent loss of jars, presumably used as transport vessels, and occasional special items, or raw material, such as shell indicate use over a long period. Furthermore, probable establishment of trail shrines and the use of quartz to mark the trail seem to prevail over evidence of resource extraction along the trail. This further supports the hypothesis that these trails were used for inter-regional travel. Uncertainty and the dangers associated with major thoroughfares most likely elicited different sorts of behaviors from travelers as opposed to individuals who used trails to gather resources.

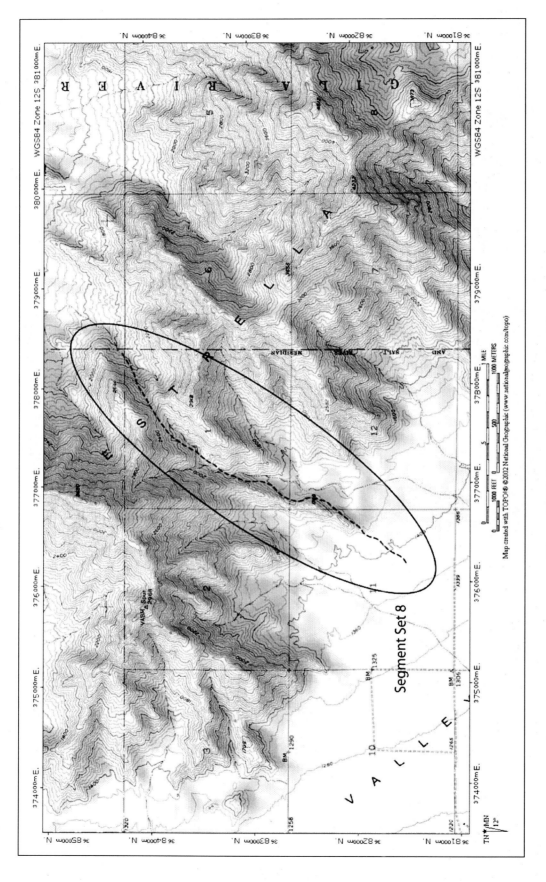

Figure 12.14. Map of trail segment set 8.

Figure 12.15. Shrine.

ANALYZING TRAIL NETWORKS

Analysis of trail systems is tied to studies of space and how sociocultural systems use it. Continuous space allows for straight-line connections between fixed locations or settlements. However, in the real world, space is discrete. Movement is constrained by physical features, social factors, or other elements in the landscape. As a result, networks of roads or trails determine or exhibit the ways in which energy and information flow between settlements (Gorenflo 1991). Travel or types of travel along these trails reflect the behavioral aspects of movement. As noted in the introduction to this chapter, trails may be used for many different kinds of travel. Thus, it is likely that the artifacts and features along trails are the combined residue of a variety of travelers who used them.

Contextual studies of trails, particularly their location and situation in a trail network may help to narrow down the range of travel types exhibited along them. Preliminary analysis of trails and a review of the Rogers record of trails in the Arid Southwest reveal that many inter-valley routes of travel cross-cut major drainage systems rather than paralleling river courses or streams (see Figure 12.1). As illustrated in this study all the trails examined were located on the bajada and therefore were trails to access bajada resources or to reach inter-regional routes of travel. The Oyadaibuic–Komatke Trail, for example, crosses three mountain passes and connects settlement areas in three river valleys along the Gila River.

This may be modeled in terms of modes of travel (Figure 12.16). Movement along Type I trails between zones of settlement (Zone A) through hinterlands (Zone B) characterizes intra-regional travel patterns. Type II trails provide access to resources and materials outside settlements. Movement along Type I trails consists of travel from zones of security (Zone A) to areas where loss of life and possessions increases (Zone B). Higher amounts of artifacts especially broken pottery jars as well as shrines, rock art, and other features in Zone B attest to the dangers of travel between settled areas particularly mountainous zones. Desert travel may be equally dangerous due to the lack of water. Along the Gila River drainage this may not be as much of an issue. However as shown by the trail record amassed by Malcolm Rogers, zones of security may consist of wells or water sources separated by large stretches of waterless desert (Zone B).

Type III trails are routes utilized for ritualized travel including salt journeys, warfare, pilgrimages, etc. Unlike Type I trails, Type III trails may bypass local settlements as travelers leave familiar landscapes or homelands for distant lands. Rituals of preparation as well as cleansing or purification upon their return are activities required of the traveler. Type III trails may be highly specialized and recapitulate itineraries stipulated in stories of historical events or songs.

HISTORICAL CONTEXT OF TRAILS AND THE TRAILS OF GILA BEND

As Ezell (1968) once noted, from the time of their first entry into the Desert Southwest to the end of the Mexican Period, it is likely that no European ever blazed a new trail across the desert and that all routes of travel were based on preexisting Indian trail networks. With increasing usage by Europeans, descriptions of these trails became available. In time, several major routes were recognized as significant ethnohistoric routes of travel including the Mohave Trail, the Coco-Maricopa Trail, the Yuma Trail, the Camino del Diablo, and the Gila Trail, among others. One such trail, the Oyadaibui-Komatke Trail, was described by Fr. Eusebio Francisco Kino and Captain Juan Mateo Manje in 1699. Its circuitous route across mountain passes proved less advantageous to explorers with horses and wagons and subsequently this route was forgotten, while other trails became enshrined in the annals of exploration. Nineteenth and twentieth century historians and archaeologists later confused this route with a route that followed the old Gila Trail or what became the Butterfield Stage Route. Data recovery along SR-85 has helped to clarify the historical record and relocate this important indigenous trail connecting the Gila Bend and Middle Gila River Valleys.

The Oyadaibuic – Komatke Trail

In the winter of 1699, while on an exploration trip to investigate the peninsularity of the once-believed island of Lower California, the Spanish explorers, Fr. Eusebio Francisco Kino and Captain Juan Mateo Manje, reluctantly turned their party back from the Colorado River, well short of their intended goal. They headed east, and several days later, they proceeded around the first curve of the

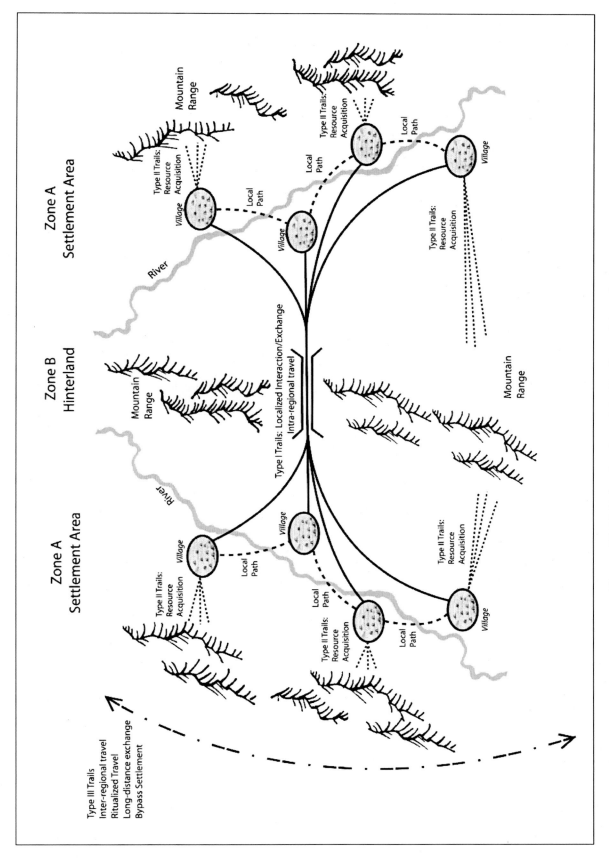

Figure 12.16. Behavioral model of trails and travel.

great bend of the Gila River. The explorers arrived at the O'odham (Pima) village of San Felipe y Santiago de Oyadoibuise (Oxibahibuiss) located approximately half way along the length of the large S-curve made by the river. Here they were greeted by as many as 132 Opa and Pima Indians (Manje reports a total of 150 adult males, having neglected to count the women and children).

Seeking a short-cut across the bend, the explorers and three Pima guides left the village after mass on Sunday, March 1, 1699. They headed east along a trail through the north Maricopa Mountains. After a ride of 11 leagues (36 kilometers) across the Rainbow Valley, the group stopped for the night at a small, unnamed ranchería, where pasturage and a small well were located. The following morning, the explorers continued their journey ascending 1000 feet along a narrow trail to the spine of the Estrella Mountains. Here a low pass offered an easy descent into the Middle Gila River Valley, the heartland of the Akimel O'odham (River People) and their ancestors the Huhugam (Hohokam).

From the summit of the Estrella Mountains, Kino and Manje observed the confluence of the Salt and Gila Rivers. Following the trail into the fertile valley, their guides led them to a Pima village, which they named San Barlolomé del Comac (Komatke or *Komatkĭ*). Having passed two days and approximately 48 kilometers along the Komatke Trail, they were greeted by 200 inhabitants, some of whom recognized them from previous exploratory trips to villages located further upstream.

Manje's account of this trip across the Maricopa and Estrella ranges is detailed and may be found in two sources—his journal of the fifth expedition undertaken with Kino from February 7 to March 14, 1699 (Burrus 1971:223–248) and Manje's memoir, *Luz de Tierra Incógnita*, which was written in 1716 (Karns 1954). Karns translation of the latter work, under the title *Unknown Arizona and Sonora, 1693–1721*, provides a nearly exact duplicate of Manje's original journal account. This description is provided below (the Spanish original of which is provided in a footnote).[4]

> On March 1, with guides furnished by the Indians, we left the river and turned left. We traveled east through rock-ribbed and arid hills, and after having gone 11 leagues, we camped for the night near a well of water, and a plain covered with pasture.
>
> On the 2nd, traveling east and climbing to the top of a small mountain, which the guides pointed out to us, we could see plainly the Verde River which takes its rise in the land of the Apaches, running northeast to southeast, with a grove of trees along its banks. It is joined by another salty river, running northeast to southeast, with a grove of trees along

---

[4] En primero de marzo, con guías que nos dieron, dejando el río a la izquierda, por una gran vuelta que da, caminamos, al oriente, por entre ceros pedregosos y estériles; y, a 11 leguas andadas, dormimos en un pozo y llano de buen pasto.

En 2, prosiguiendo al oriente y trasmontando el puerto de una sierrecilla, de la cumbre nos enseñaron los guías, que vimos patentemente, el río Verde que nace en la tierra de los apaches y corre de nordeste a sudueste, poblado de ancha y frondosa arboleda, ya florida, que lo guarnece; y, juntándosele otro río salobre de oriente a poniente, ya juntos, desaguan en este grande, cuya junta también vimos. Dijeron le llaman Verde, por pasar por una sierra de muchas vetas de piedras verdes, azules, y otros colores.

No sabemos si será ésta la Sierra Azul de que hay tradición de haber visto infinidad de minas de oro y plata, de que sacaron mucha ley repecto al poco metal que llevaron, y ensayaron en el Nuevo México, a los principios de su pacificación, y no pudieron vovler más, recelosos los pacificadores de que no se sublevasen los pueblos, como cristiandad nueva; y, habiendo pasado año, solo quedó la noticia de la Sierra Azul, rica de plata, sin haber hoy quien dé razón de ella.

Bajando de la cumbre al río, 3 leguas distante de la junta, y 13, de donde salimos, dormimos en una ranchería de pimas que intitulamos San Bartolomé del Comac, con 200 personas, dóciles y afables; y de fértiles tierras. Recibieron nos con júbilo y se les intimó el conocimiento de Dios; y bautizaron a 3 párvulos. [Manje (1699) in Burrus 1971: 400–401]

its banks. It is joined by another salty, river running from east to west, and the two merging together flow into this Río Grande River, the junction of which we were able to see. They told us its name was Verde and it flows by a mountain streaked with several veins of green, blue and variegated colored stones. We do not know if this could be the Blue Mountain range of which a tale is told to the effect that innumerable gold and silver mines, very rich and of high grade character of ore, have been discovered. The conquerors of New Mexico at the time, when they came to this place, took some ore to be refined; but they never returned. As the years passed only the tradition of the Blue Mountain, rich in silver, remained. However, no one could give its exact location.

Coming down from the hill to the river, three leagues distance from the junction, and 13 leagues from where we started on that day, we camped for the night in a Pima settlement, which we called San Bartolomé del Comac. It contained 200 peaceful and courteous Indians who welcomed us gladly. They were told about God, and three children were baptized. There are good fertile lands here. [Manje 1716 (Karns, trans. 1954:122–123)]

An Historical Controversy

Little did Kino or his companions realize that based on ceramic artifacts encountered 300 years later, they were traversing a trail used continuously by the Pima and the Hohokam and potentially earlier populations. Ironically, the actual location of the route followed by Kino and his companions on March 1st and 2nd, 1699, also appears to have been misidentified repeatedly by historians and archaeologists; first by Bolton (1919), and subsequently by Karns (1954), Schroeder (1961) and Burrus (1971).

Based on Kino and Manje's accounts, these scholars identified the village of San Felipe y Santiago de Oyadoibuise (Oxibahibuiss), at the southwest end of the Gila Bend in roughly the same location as the village of El Tutto or Aritutac, later identified by Ezell (1961, 1963:7). As Bolton and other scholars proposed, the explorers would have followed a route roughly approximating the later Butterfield Overland Trail, pioneered after 1850 (Figure 12.17). In 1699, this route would have brought the exploring party around the south end of the Estrella Mountain range, requiring that they pass several villages in the vicinity of Pima Butte (including Hueso Parado) without notice. From this location they would have had to travel north to Komatke, only to reverse their direction to continue on their journey. As Ezell proposes, the location of the village of Oxibahibuiss, midway along the north-south portion of the Gila Bend, concurs with Kino and Manje's description. This includes the presence of wells at the unidentified village still used into the twentieth century, as well as the panoramic view of the Salt-Gila River Valley, which would not have been visible on the misidentified route located too far to the south.

Period artifacts have not been found during archaeological survey of the Komatke Trail, which might verify the explorers' accounts. However, the Kino-Manje record serves to accomplish more by drawing attention to the centuries-old route of travel that communicated the Middle Gila River Valley with the Gila Bend and into the Painted Rocks Reservoir area to the west. Field identification of portions of the trail in passes in the Estrella Mountains, the Maricopa Mountains, and the Gila Bend Mountains provides sufficient evidence that this route extended from the central Hohokam region, dominated by such archaeological sites as Snaketown, to its western periphery. During the Historic Period, the trail communicated between Yuman (Patayan) areas along the river inhabited by the Cocamaricopa, the Opa (including Pima and Opa living in mixed villages in the Gila Bend), the Maricopa, and the Pima. Unusual preservation of the trails west of the Maricopa Mountains reveals extensive branching as the main Komatke Trail split into numerous smaller trails accessing villages along the length of the valley at Gila Bend.

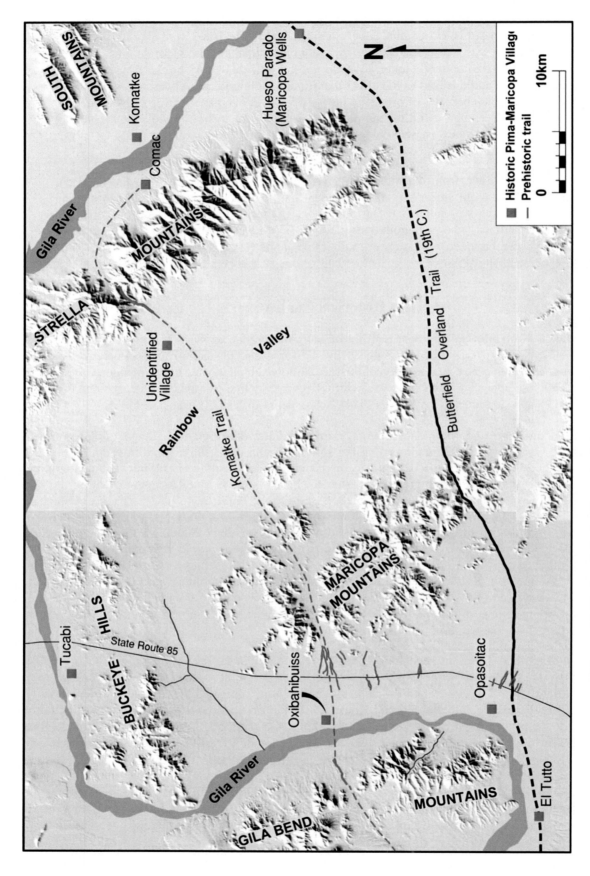

Figure 12.17. Oyodoibuic–Komatke Trail and the Butterfield Overland Trail.

CONCLUSION

The previous analysis reveals several useful observations about understanding trails:

1. Trails are regionally extensive archaeological features that cannot be fully understood without mapping and study well outside standard project areas (areas of potential effect) or road right-of-ways.

2. Recent advances in remote sensing and low elevation imaging (not available to this project) may be useful for identifying and mapping trails, and can be used in the design of research prior to entry into the field. These may provide data for hypothesis generation and network analysis testable through targeted data recovery efforts. We feel that emphasizing the behavioral aspects of different modes of travel in relation to decision-making processes will provide a productive avenue for research over previous typological studies.

3. The unusual preservation of trails in the Gila Bend provides a rare opportunity to understand travel as a cultural behavior and its relationship to indigenous infrastructures that existed long before Europeans entered on the scene. Clearly other areas up and down the Gila River maintained similarly complex, if not more complex trail networks, no longer visible today. Further work in the Gila Bend Valley is warranted to document this unusual and highly fragile cultural resource.

4. Much of the literature on indigenous trails and trail networks is dominated by European accounts reflecting the early explorers' reliance on Native Americans as guides and sources of information on local landscapes. The co-opting of Native American infrastructures and dramatic reshaping of them into stage lines and mail routes is a little understood process by which preexisting structures of information and communication were transformed. This has resulted in a not insignificant bias in the historical literature on trails in which only the preeminent trails used by Europeans continue to be recognized while the thousands of kilometers of Native American trails have been lost.

CHAPTER 13

TRAVEL AND FARMING IN THE GILA BEND AREA, A.D. 500 TO 1940

Glen E. Rice and John L. Czarzasty

INTRODUCTION

The Arizona Department of Transportation State Route 85 archaeological project investigated five prehistoric and one historic site along the highway between Gila Bend and Buckeye (more specifically, mileposts 121 through 147). The Arizona Department of Transportation plans to widen State Route 85 to a four-lane freeway, and the archaeological work was in response to that proposed undertaking. The study was conducted by a research team assembled by the Office of Cultural Resource Management at Arizona State University (ADOT-ECS Contract No 02-59).

The one historic site, AZ T:14:96 (ASM), was a Depression-era African-American homestead. Two of the prehistoric sites, AZ T:10:86 (ASM) and AZ Z:2:46 (ASM), were portions of Hohokam-era agricultural fields, and the remaining three sites, AZ T:14:92 (ASM), AZ T:14:94 (ASM) and AZ T:14:113 (ASM), were rock cairn features associated with prehistoric trails. There were an additional 44 trail sites (for a total of 47) at which no field work was conducted, but an overview study of trails (Chapter 12) and a compilation of settlement pattern data from archival sources (Chapter 4) were used to provide a regional context for understanding the trail systems in the Gila Bend region.

The findings of the study are summarized by addressing what has been learned concerning six research questions that structured the design of the project (Chapter 2). Five of the six sites are located on the west facing bajada of the Maricopa foothills and one site is located on the alluvial terrace of the Lower Gila River.

WHAT SUBSISTENCE ACTIVITIES WERE ASSOCIATED WITH THE SITES?

Two of the sites were associated with prehistoric agricultural fields and produced evidence for the planting and harvesting of maize. One was an example of an irrigated field on the floodplain of the Gila River (AZ T:10:86) and the other an *ak chin* field located on the bajada of the Maricopa Mountains AZ Z:2:46). A third example of agriculture was attempted in the historic period when an African-American family tried to drill a well so they could irrigate agricultural fields on the bajada (AZ T:14:96), but unfortunately they never reached the depth that produced water. They relied, instead on other economic activities such as harvesting and selling firewood and raising domestic animals.

Site AZ T:10:86 (ASM) consisted of a sparse surface distribution of artifacts and occasional occurrences of buried lenses of burned material. Wright (1995), working on an earlier ADOT archaeological project, found a very similar pattern at AZ T:10:85 (ASM) located about 1.3 miles directly to the west of site AZ T:10:86 (ASM). Both of the sites are locations of prehistoric agricultural fields on aggrading terraces of the Gila River. In addition to buried lenses of burned material, Wright (1995) also found evidence of ditches, a buried roasting pit, and a burned tree stump.

The lenses of burned materials at both of these sites included remains of maize, and it is likely that such materials accumulated on the surface of fields when the old stubble was burned to prepare the field for a new planting season. During heavy rains the burned material would float to low spots in the fields where they would accumulated, and then be buried by sediments during over-bank flooding of the river (Wright 1995:158–159). The fields at AZ T:10:85 and AZ T:10:86 were irrigated either by systems of ditches and canals or by overbank flooding of the river.

Feature 1 at AZ T:10:86 (ASM), a lense of burned material buried at a depth of 70 cm, was associated with a radiocarbon date of A.D. 650 to 870 (calibrated, one-sigma range). The burned material also yielded a burned fragment of corn. This indicates that the Gila has deposited about 70 cm of fill at this location in the past 1100 to 1300 years, and shows that the Hohokam were planting fields of maize in this area by the late Pioneer Period. The flotation studies (Chapter 9) also found that ironwood was being burned as firewood, and the pollen (Chapter 8) analysis indicates greens in the Cheno-am family of plants were being collected from, or possibly planted, in the fields.

Site AZ Z:2:46 (ASM) is a cluster of rock features and roasting pits in the Holocene sediments of a small wash on the bajada; the wash has cut into and is bordered on both sides by Pleistocene surfaces at a slightly higher elevation. The roasting pits were used and cleaned out on repeated occasions, and it is likely that some of the rock features around the roasting pits represent the contents of the pits that were removed and dumped nearby when the pits were cleaned. Pollen and flotation samples showed that maize was being cooked in the pit, and probably grown in nearby fields on the bajada. Wild grasses were also gathered and used in the roasting pit, probably as coverings over the food. Both mesquite and ironwood were used as fuel.

The maize probably came from agricultural fields planted on the narrow strip of Holocene deposits in the wash itself and watered using the *ak chin* technique. During and immediately following rainstorms on the bajada, water would flow into and down the wash; the Hohokam farmers would plant their crops in the wet soils of the wash, and hope for a few additional showers later in the summer to bring the crops to maturity. The wash was quite narrow, and a household would need to plant a number of small fields in neighboring washes to provide for all of its needs. The pollen evidence suggests that the farmers may also have been gathering wild seeds of a plant of the plantain family and the buds of the cholla cactus in the late spring and early summer during the months that preceded the ripening of the agricultural fields; the cholla buds could also have been baked in the roasting pits.

A suite of radiocarbon dates indicate the pits and associated fields were being used at a very early time. Three of the dates were obtained from materials in the roasting pit (Feature 3) and one was associated with a scatter of fire-cracked rock (Feature 2) that may have been the material cleaned out from the roasting pit. The pits were used during two intervals, first between A.D. 420 and 540, based on two dates from the roasting pit (calibrated, one-sigma range), and the second between A.D. 620 and 670, based on one date from the upper levels of the roasting pit and one date from a rock scatter (Feature 2). (As an alternative interpretation that gives a single date for the site, the two-sigma calibrated ranges of all four dates overlap between A.D. 550 and 610). The site was in use by the Vahki phase of the Hohokam Pioneer Period.

The Depression-era homestead established by the Goode family was also located on the bajada. However, their approach to farming on the bajada was to excavate a well, using heavy machinery, from which they hoped to obtain enough water to irrigate their agricultural fields. Unfortunately, despite nearly two years of effort, they were unable to strike water, and they were seldom successful in their attempts to raise crops using just rainfall. A picture (see Chapter 10) of one year's attempt at farming shows a field of short corn stalks and other vegetables. For household use the family hauled in water using 50-gallon drums.

A wash ran through their property, but it seldom flowed. Few non-Native Americans in the 20th century could have been expected to understand the techniques that were necessary for *ak chin* agriculture, but even had the Goode family attempted to use this long-lived southwestern agricultural technique, the homesteading laws would not have provided them with sufficient flexibility and range to be successful. *Ak chin* farming requires moving to the areas of the bajada where the rain is falling, which might vary considerably from year to year, and even seasonally, rather than waiting for the rainstorm to come to a particular 160 acre plot.

The Goode family used the bajada for another economic activity; cutting ironwood trees and selling the wood as fuel to people living in the Phoenix area. The Goode family would place their Model-T Ford on jacks, remove one of the rear tires and loop a belt from the car wheel to a pulley on a large table saw. In this way they used their car motor to drive the saw that cut the ironwood into the size that could fit into wood-burning stoves. Seventy years later, a large pile of ironwood chips continues to mark the location of the saw. The family also raised chickens, hogs and cows, and Mr. Goode also took on a number of other jobs in the nearby communities.

WHO USED THE LANDSCAPE AND DID THIS CHANGE OVER TIME?

At the start of the study we suspected that many of the trails were used only locally, by people living in communities along the Gila River, to collect resources such as wild grasses, cacti fruits, and lithic raw material from the neighboring bajada. We knew of one long-distance route at the south end of the study area (the Gila Trail, later used for the Butterfield Stage Coach Trail) that was used during ethnographic and early historic times (see Figure 12.17). So we expected to find evidence of local use of trails in the central part of the study area where most of our trail-associated sites were located (AZ T:14:92, AZ T:14:94 and AZ T:14:113), and for long-distance travel routes in the southern part of the study area where we had only one site (AZ Z:2:46).

This picture changed with the trail overview study and the detailed temper analysis of ceramics. The trail study conducted by Darling and Eiselt identified the ethnographically used Komatke trail that ran through the central part of the study area and linked the Gila Bend area with Pee Posh and Pima settlements on the Middle Gila (the area of the Gila River Indian Community) towards the east, and to Yuman settlements on the Lower Colorado river valley. Father Kino traveled this route in 1699, and Darling and Eiselt walked much of the trail to corroborate the written descriptions of Kino's trip (and resolved confusion in the literature on the route of Kino's 1699 journey).

Analysis of ceramics from AZ T:14:92 and AZ T:14:94, conducted by Kathleen Peterson and Arleyn Simon, demonstrates that the trail had been used during Hohokam times as well, and that had been used by populations living on the Lower Colorado River, the Gila Bend, the Lower Salt River and the Middle Gila (Chapter 6). In short, the prehistoric use of the trail was comparable in scale to the ethnographic use of the trail, with the addition that it also was used by Hohokam populations living in the Phoenix basin, an area that was unoccupied during the 1600s and 1700s when the early ethnographic records were compiled.

A number of the trails along State Route 85, it turns out, are segments of the prehistoric and historic Komatke trail that lead from the locations of ball court villages along the Gila River (see Doyel 2000) eastwards towards a pass in the Maricopa Mountains (see Figure 12.4). Or, viewed from the perspective of traveling to the west, as the Komatke trail exited from the pass in the Maricopa Mountains, it divided into a series of trails that fanned out across the bajada towards the main ball court centers and other villages on the west bank of the Gila River (Doyel 2000). One segment of the trail, however, continued directly westward and up the bajada of the Gila Bend Mountains through another pass and from there towards the Lower Colorado River (Figure 12.3).

The scattered rock features at AZ T:14:92 and AZ T:14:94 were very likely once rock cairns used perhaps as shrines, at which artifacts, especially sherds, were deposited. There are ethnographic accounts (see the quote from Ezell on page 15 of this volume) of Pima travelers who placed stone on piles by the side of the trail to ensure a speedy trip and avoid misfortune, and this practice may have applied to sherds in the past. The ceramic analysis determined that the ceramics associated with the rock features at these sites were not parts of pots that broke at those locations. Rather they were actually carried to the sites as sherds and left there for some currently unknown reason. (Darling and Eiselt, in walking other portions of the trails, did on occasion find true pot-busts consisting of plain ware sherds that all belonged to a single, entire vessel, as described in Chapter 12). Although we were unable to determine exactly why sherds were brought and left at the rock features, we were able to determine the original provenance, or production area, of the sherds, and from this it was possible to determine that the sherds had come from many different locations, at considerable distances.

The rock feature at AZ T:14:113 is too far north to be associated with the Komatke Trail, but it was possibly associated with a different trail and it contained exclusively sherds that had come from the lower Gila River and the Lower Colorado River. The absence of Hohokam Red-on-buff sherds suggests this trail may post-date the Hohokam period.

Some of the trails on the bajada of the Maricopa Mountains were apparently used locally for the procurement of resources, and these differed from the long distance trails in being associated with fewer ceramics, more lithics, including lithic reduction stations, and more petroglyph boulders. Darling and Eiselt found this to be the case for trails in Set 3 and Set 5 shown in Figure 12.3.

To summarize, it has been possible in this region to distinguish between local trails that led to resource areas on the bajada (Type II trails), and long distance trails that led to settlements in different regions (Type I trails). For this region, at least, these two types of trails seem to be associated with different categories of artifacts; non-local ceramic sherds on the long distance trails, and quarried lithics and petroglyph boulders on the local access trails.

Did the use of the trails on the landscape change over time? To some extent, the answer is a guarded yes. For instance, the lack of red-on-buff ceramics at AZ T:14:113 may indicate it was associated with a trail that post-dated the Hohokam (see Chapter 6). And the Komatke trail was used only once by Kino who found it too difficult to travel with horses and mules, which may explain why the trail ceased to be used in historic times (and its location became lost until re-established by Eiselt and Darling). But perhaps the more intriguing finding is that some trails were used for considerable lengths of time. The Komatke Trail itself was used from at least late Colonial times at about A.D. 900 to about A.D. 1700, a span of 800 years. The Gila Trail, that led from the Gila Bend area around the south end of the Maricopa Mountains towards the Middle Gila, became the Butterfield Stagecoach Trail, and subsequently a route for the Southern Pacific Railroad. Assuming a late Colonial date for the establishment of this route, it remains in use 1000 years later.

HOW WERE THE SITES USED FOR RESOURCE EXCHANGE?

Another surprise in studying the trails is that we did not learn very much about what kinds of items were being transported over the trails. In our sample of excavated features we determined that the associated sherds were NOT evidence of the vessels being carried along the trails, although clearly there was long distance exchange in ceramic vessels. The sherds associated with the rock clusters in our excavated sample had been brought to those sites as sherds, not as complete vessels, as determined by Peterson (see Chapter 6). Although we did not excavate or collect any "pot busts," Darling and Eiselt did find pot busts in other portions of the trails that lay beyond the right-of-way.

Nor did we find pieces of obsidian or large pieces of shell that would indicate trade in those items, although obsidian from the Sauceda source to the south of Gila Bend was traded widely in the Hohokam core area (Shackley 1988), and some of the important routes for the shell trade are thought to have gone through the Gila Bend area (McGuire and Howard 1987). However, Darling and Eiselt, by walking out longer stretches of the trails, did find one whole *Glycymeris* shell next to a trail.

This suggests that researchers need to walk very long stretches of trails in order to find enough artifacts to use as evidence of resource exchange. People did not often discard by the side of the trail the materials they were transporting from one location to another. Provenance or sourcing analyses seem to provide a more secure basis for studying the materials that were exchanged along trails. The artifact evidence from trails reveals the region from which travelers have come, but it is not very revealing about what they were carrying.

WHAT KINDS OF FEATURES AND ARTIFACTS OCCUR WITH TRAIL SITES?

Within the State Route 85 project area two kinds of rock features were found associated with trails, but in his more extensive survey of trail segments (not funded by the National Park Service and the Pima-Maricopa Irrigation Project), Darling and Eiselt found six additional categories of features. The combined list includes:

- trail markers
- trail shrines
- rock circles
- lithic working areas
- pot busts,
- pot or basket rests
- rock art, and
- intaglios.

Trail markers are large cobbles of white quartz or feldspar that help make the trail more visible under moon light. Trail shrines are usually piles of boulders to which pieces of material culture, such as sherds, were added as offerings; we have assumed that the scattered rock features (See Figure 5.23, this volume) found in the State Route 85 project area are eroded examples of trail shrines. Darling and Eiselt (Chapter 12) also describe a considerably more impressive trail shrine in a cleft boulder on the Komatke trail.

Distinctly circular arrangements of cobbles (see Figure 5.40) are sometimes called sleeping circles, but many are too small (ca. 1 meter in diameter) for such a purpose. The one rock circle excavated in this study was not associated with any artifacts. Lithic working areas, consisting of spent flakes and cores of locally available materials, are frequently found along trails used to access local resources. Pot busts are entire broken vessels that have been abandoned at the location where they broke. Pot or basket rests consist of three to six boulders arranged so as to hold upright vessels with conically shaped bottoms, such as baskets and ceramic jars. Rock art images pecked into the patina of a stone are sometimes found on large cobbles adjacent to trails. Intaglios are large images created by selectively removing the weathered desert pavement to reveal the lighter underlying dirt.

Trails can differ considerably with respect to the kinds of associated artifacts. In the Gila Bend area, trails used for long distance travel tend to be associated with ceramic artifacts, while local trails leading to resource areas on the bajada tend to be associated with lithic artifacts and rock art (see Chapter 12).

WHERE DO THE TRAILS GO?

The State Route 85 trails fell into two different categories depending on their destination. Two long distance trails led from the Gila Bend to settlements on the middle Gila (Darling and Eiselt's Type I trail). The Komatke trail went through passes in the Maricopa Mountains and the Sierra Estrella to reach the Middle Gila, while the Gila Trail passed around the southern end of both those mountain ranges and arrived at the Middle Gila further south. Sites AZ T:14:92 and AZ T:14:94 were associated with different segments of the Komatke trail route. In ethnographic times the Komatke trail also extended westward from the Middle Gila towards the Lower Gila and the Lower Colorado River areas; the ceramics recovered from these two sites indicate that the trail also extended that distance during the Hohokam period.

Site AZ T:14:113 was also associated with a trail, but it is too far north to be part of the general Komatke trail. It is situated on Holocene alluvium, and there are only a few faint impressions of trails on nearby patches of desert pavement. Nonetheless, the ceramics associated with AZ T:14:113 were manufactured at locations on the Lower Colorado River and Lower Gila. The rock feature at this site is the remains of a shrine associated with a Type I travel route between zones of settlements.

There were also Type II trails that led from settlements to parts of the landscape where resources were available. These tended to not be associated with trail shrines, and as a consequence none of the sites included in the archaeological project were trails of this kind. The survey work directed by Darling and Eiselt, however, found that such trails led to areas on the bajada with desirable lithic raw material; petroglyphs were also common along these trails.

Darling and Eiselt's Type III trail refers to those that were used for ritualized travel, including the salt journey, pilgrimages and perhaps warfare. Because of the need for ritual seclusion or military secrecy, these trails could often by-pass local settlements completely. Darling and Eiselt found one assent trail that went straight up the side of a small butte on the Maricopa bajada, and there was a rock enclosure at the top of the butte; they posited that this may have been a lookout post to warn against the approach of enemy forces

CONCLUDING THOUGHTS

The Arizona Department of Transportation's State Route 85 Archaeological Project and an overview of trails have documented significant events and processes in the human use of a bajada landscape in the Gila Bend area. Using settlement pattern data for the Gila Bend area, it was possible to compare how human populations living in settlements along the river used the bajada of the neighboring Maricopa Mountains where five of the six project sites were located.

The study found evidence for the remarkable antiquity and resilience of *ak chin* agriculture. *Ak chin* agricultural fields of maize were grown on the bajada as early as A.D. 500 and continued to be used into the following century; irrigated fields of maize were established on the Gila flood plain by the A.D. 600s as well. Why did people living on the flood plain also farm *ak chin* fields on the bajada? The agricultural productivity of the flood plains was considerably greater than that of the *ak chin* fields on the bajada, as demonstrated by the numbers of large villages that were subsequently established on the river during the Sedentary Period (ca. A.D. 900 to 1000). Despite the availability of ample land on the river terraces during the 6th and 7th centuries A.D., the early human populations were as willing to plant *ak chin* fields on the bajada as they were to plant irrigated fields on the flood plain. This study has found that both agricultural techniques were important early in the Hohokam period; the question of why the Hohokam, even in the absence of population pressure, employed the dual strategies is posed as a question for future research projects.

The history of the human use of the Maricopa Mountain bajada is unique, and differs from the history of other bajadas in the Hohokam region. The contrast is particular marked in comparison to the well documented case in Marana area of the Northern Tucson Basin (Fish et al. 1992). There residential settlements were located on the upper slope of the bajada as well as along the (Santa Cruz) flood plain, but in the Gila Bend area villages were located only along the edges of the (Gila River) flood plain. In the North Tucson Basin rock pile fields of agave were planted on the bajada, but no such evidence of rock-pile fields has been found on the Maricopa Mountain bajada. Here, the bajada was traversed by at least two major travel routes that extended for hundreds of miles, while the Tucson Basin bajada was used only by the local populations to collect resources. As a result, ceramic assemblages from the Maricopa Mountain bajada are far more cosmopolitan than those from the Tucson Basin bajada. This comparison illustrates the importance of fully understanding and documenting the different ways in which Hohokam populations used bajada landscapes.

Finally, the Maricopa Mountain bajada was also the setting for the unique history of an African American family, that of Warren and Clara Goode. Against great odds and the lack of a well for water, they managed to successfully establish and come to own a 160 acre homestead. Working against the harsher injustices of segregation, all eight children attended high school, five attended college, and all contributed to their communities. In one generation, the Goode family had gone from sharecroppers to professionals in education, health care, and public service (Stein, Chapter 11).

REFERENCES CITED

Abbott, D. R.
1994   *The Pueblo Grande Project, Volume 3: Ceramics and the Production and Exchange of Pottery in the Central Phoenix Basin.* Publications in Archaeology No. 20. Soil Systems, Inc., Phoenix.

2000   Hohokam Buff Ware Production and Distribution and the Provenance of Decorated Pottery from the BMGR. In *Procurement, Processing, and Passing Through, Volume II,* edited by J. D. Lyon, pp. 577–619. SWCA Cultural Resource Report No. 98-267. SWCA, Inc., Tucson.

2000   *Ceramics and Community Organization among the Hohokam.* University of Arizona Press, Tucson.

Adams, K. R.
1994   Macrobotanical Analyses. In *The Roosevelt Rural Studies, Changing Land use in the Tonto Basin, Volume,* edited by R. Ciolek-Torrello and J. R. Welch, pp. 167–187. Statistical Research Technical Series No. 28, Statistical Research, Inc., Tucson.

1997   Macrobotanical Analysis. In *Agriculture, Subsistence and Environmental Studies,* edited by J. A. Homburg and R. Ciolek-Torrell, pp. 149–178. SRI Press, Tucson.

2001   Looking Back Through Time: Southwestern U.S. Archaeobotany at the New Millennium. In *Ethnobiology at the Millennium: Past Promise and Future Prospects,* edited by R. I. Ford, pp. 49–99. Anthropological Papers No. 91, Museum of Anthropology, University of Michigan, Ann Arbor.

2003   Plant Remains. In *From the Desert to the Mountains. Archaeology of the Transition Zone. The State Route 87-Sycamore Creek Project,* edited by E. E. Klucas, R. Ciolek-Torrello, and R. Vanderpot. Statistical Research Technical Series No. 73, Statistical Research, Inc., Tucson.

Ahlstom, R. V. N., and D. B. Tucker
2000   Previous Research and Culture History. In *East TAC,* edited by Heidi Roberts, R. V. N. Ahlstrom, and D. B. Tucker, pp. 35–70. SWCA Cultural Resource Report No. 99-7, Tucson.

Ahnert, G. T.
1973   *Retracing the Butterfield Overland Trail Through Arizona. A Guide to the Route of 1857–1861.* Westernlore Press, Los Angeles, California.

Alschul, J. H., and Adrianne G. R, (editors)
2008   *Fragile Patterns. The Archaeology of the Western Papaguería.* SRI Press, Tucson.

Arizona Department of Transportation
2001   *Request for Proposal Package for Contract No. 02-30 SR 85, Gila Bend to Buckeye Interstate I-8 to Interstate10 Archaeological Investigations.* Engineering Consultants Section.

The Arizona Republic
1982   Obituary for Warner Goode. July 27, p. D2.

Ayres, J. E. and G. B. Seymour
  1993   *Life on a 1930s Homestead: Historical Archaeological Investigations of the Brown Homestead on the Middle Agua Fria River, Yavapai County, Arizona.* Anthropological Research Paper No. 2, SWCA Environmental Consultants, Phoenix.

Ayres, J. E., C. Griffith, and T. Majewski
  2001   *Historic Archaeology in Arizona: A Research Guide.* State Historic Preservation Office. Phoenix.

Bachman, L. N.
  1941   Roles Played by the Gila Bend Area in the Development of the Southwest. Master's Thesis, Arizona State Teachers' College. Copy on file, Northern Arizona University, Flagstaff.

Barrios, F. M.
  1989   Gillespie Dam. Paper presented at the 30th Annual Arizona Historical Convention, Yuma. Copy on file, Arizona Historical Society, Tucson.

Bates, P., K. Bates, and T. Bates
  n.d.   *Handbook of Embossed Soda Bottles.* Interactive Books, Goodlettsville, Tennessee.

Bayham, F. E., Morris, D. H. and Shackley, M. S.
  1986   *Prehistoric Hunter-Gatherers of South Central Arizona: The Picacho Reservoir Archaic Project.* Anthropological Field Studies, No. 13. Office of Cultural Resource Management, Department of Anthropology, Arizona State University, Tempe.

Bayman, J. M.
  2001   The Hohokam of Southwest North America. *Journal of World Prehistory*, Vol. 15. No. 3, pp. 257–311.

Bean, L. J.,
  1974   *Mukat's People: The Cahuilla Indians of Southern California.* University of California Press, Berkeley.

Becker, K. M. and J. H. Altschul
  2003   *Historic Context for Prehistoric and Protohistoric Trails and Related Features at Yuma Proving Ground, Arizona.* Technical Report 03-13. Statistical Research, Tucson.

Bohrer, V. L.
  1987   *The plant remains from La Ciudad, a Hohokam site in Phoenix. In Specialized studies in the economy, environment and culture of La Ciudad, Part III*, edited by J. Kisselburg, G. Rice, and B. Shears, pp. 67–202. Arizona State University Anthropological Field Studies 20, Tempe.

Bolton, H. E.
  1919   *Kino's Historical Memoir of Pimeria Alta.* 2 vols. Cleveland, 1919.

  1930   *Anza's California Expeditions.* 5 vols. University of California Press, Berkeley.

Bostwick, Todd W.
  1988   *An Investigation of Archaic Subsistence and Settlement in the Harquahala Valley, Maricopa County, Arizona.* Northland Research, Inc., Flagstaff.

Bostwick, T. W., and C. L. Stone
  1988   Hunters, Gatherers, and Farmers in the Harquahala Valley: Summary and Conclusions of the HVID Project. In *An Investigation of Archaic Subsistence and Settlement in the Harquahala Valley, Maricopa County, Arizona,* edited by T. W. Bostwick, pp. 320–355. Northland Research, Inc., Flagstaff.

Bowman, J. N., and R. F. Heizer
  1967   *Anza and the Northwest Frontier of New Spain.* Southwest Museum Papers No. 20. Southwest Museum, Los Angeles.

Breternitz, D. A.
  1957   A Brief Survey of the Lower Gila River. *The Kiva* 22 (2 & 3).

  1960   *Excavations at Three Sites in the Verde Valley, Arizona.* Museum of Northern Arizona, Bulletin 34. Flagstaff.

Brook, R. A., H. M. Davidson, A. H. Simmons, and P. H. Stein
  1977   *Archaeological studies of the Liberty to Gila Bend 230 kv transmission system.* Museum of Northern Arizona, Research Paper 5.

Brown, D. E.
  1994   *Biotic Communities: Southwestern United States and Northwestern Mexico.* University of Utah Press, Salt Lake City.

Brown, P. E., and C. L. Stone (editors)
  1982   *Granite Reef: A Study in Desert Archaeology.* Anthropological Research Papers No. 28. Arizona State University, Tempe.

Buckeye Review
  1935   Notice for Publication of the Warner Goode homestead. 15 February 1935.

Bureau of Land Management
  Nd   Phoenix Serial Record No. 065876. Copy on file, State Office, Bureau of Land Management, Phoenix.

  1936   Patent for the Warner Goode Homestead. Copy on file, State Office, Bureau of Land Management, Phoenix.

  1962   *Homesteads.* U.S. Government Printing Office, Washington, DC.

Burrus, Ernest J., S.J.
  1971   *Kino and Manje: Explorers of Sonora and Arizona.* Sources and Studies for the History of the Americas No. 10. Jesuit Historical Institute, Rome, Italy, and St. Louis.

Burton, J. H., and A. W. Simon
  1993   Acid Extraction as a Simple and Inexpensive Method for Compositional Characterization of Archaeological Ceramics. *American Antiquity* 58(1): 45–59.

  2002   *Geologic Reconnaissance of Potential Ceramic Temper Sources on Lands of the Gila River Indian Community.* Report on file with the Cultural Resource Program, GRIC, Sacaton, Arizona.

Cable, J. S., and D. E. Doyel
  1987   Pioneer Period Village Structure and Settlement Pattern in the Phoenix Basin. In *The Hohokam Village: Site Structure and Organization,* edited by David E. Doyel, pp. 21–70. Southwestern and Rocky Mountain Division of the American Association for the Advancement of Science, Glenwood Springs, Colorado.

Carlson, R. L.
  1982   The Polychrome Complexes. In *Southwestern Ceramics: A Comparative Review*, edited by A.H. Schroeder, pp. 201–234. School of American Research Advanced Seminar. The Arizona Archaeologist, No. 15. Arizona Archaeological Society, Inc.

Castetter, E. F.
  1936   Uncultivated native plants used as sources of food. *Ethnobiological Studies in the American Southwest.* The University of New Mexico Bulletin No. 266, Biological Series 4(1), Albuquerque.

Coe, C. A.
  1979   *Archaeological assessment of the Sells vicinity, Papago Indian Reservation, Arizona.* Arizona State Museum, Archaeological Series 131, Tucson.

Conkling, R. P., and M. B. Conkling
  1947   *Butterfield Overland Mail 1857–1869: Its Organization and Operation over the Southern Route to 1861; Subsequently over the CentralRoute to 1866; and under Wells, Fargo and Company in 1869.* Arthur H. Clark Co., Glendale, California.

Crownover, S.
  1994   *Archaeological Assessment of the North Landfill Project, Biscuit Flat, Arizona.* Ms. On file, Archaeological Consulting Services, Tempe, Arizona.

Darling, J. A., and B. V. Lewis
  2007   Songscapes and Calendar Sticks. In The Hohokam Millennium. Edited by S. K. Fish and P. R. Fish, pp. 131–139. School for Advanced Research Press, Santa Fe.

Davis, G. P. Jr.
  1982   *Man and Wildlife in Arizona: The Presettlement Era, 1823–1864.* Edited by N. B. Carmony and David E. Brown. The Arizona Game and Fish Department in Cooperation with the Arizona Cooperative Wildlife Research Unit, Phoenix.

Davis, J. T.
  1961   Trade Routes and Economic Exchange Among the Indian of California. *Reports of the University of California Archaeological Survey* 54: 1–73.

Dean, J. S.
  1991   Thoughts on Hohokam Chronology. In *Exploring the Hohokam: Prehistoric Desert Peoples of the American Southwest,* edited by G. J. Gummerman, pp. 61–150. University of New Mexico Press, Albuquerque.

Doebley, J. F.
  1984   "Seeds" of Wild Grasses: a Major Food of Southwestern Indians. *Economic Botany* 38(1):52–64.

Doelle, W. H.
  1976   *Desert Resources and Hohokam Subsistence: The Conoco Florence Project.* Archaeological Series No.103, Arizona State Museum, Tucson.

Douglas, D. L. and J. Crary
1993   *Archaeological Assessment of the Arizona Public Service Enterprise Ranch Powerline Replacement Right-of-Way, Maricopa County, Arizona.* Archaeological Consulting Services, Ltd., Tempe.

Downum, C. E.
1993   *Between Desert and River, Hohokam Settlement and land Use in the Los Robles Community.* Anthropological Papers of the University of Arizona Number 57, University of Arizona Press, Tucson.

Doyel, D. E.
1991   Hohokam Cultural Evolution in the Phoenix Basin. In *Exploring the Hohokam: Prehistoric Desert Peoples of the American Southwest,* edited by George J. Gummerman, pp. 61–150. University of New Mexico Press, Albuquerque.

2000   Settlement Organization at Gila Bend. In *The Hohokam Village Revisited,* edited by D. E. Doyel, S. K. Fish and P. R. Fish, pp. 101–138. Southwestern and Rocky Mountain Division of the American Association for the Advancement of Science, Fort Collins, Colorado.

Doyel, D. E., S. K. Fish and . R. Fish, (editors)
2000   *The Hohokam Village Revisited.* Southwestern and Rocky Mountain Division of the American Association for the Advancement of Science, Fort Collins, Colorado.

Effland, R. W., M. Green, and E. Robinson
1982   *Yuma 500KV Transmission Line: Technical Report on Findings.* Archaeological Consulting Services, Tempe.

Eiselt, B. S., and M. K. Woodson
2002   The Organization of Two Hohokam Platform Mound Communities Along the Casa Blanca Canal System: An Example from the middle Gila Valley. In *Visible Archaeology on the Gila River Indian Reservation.* Papers presented at the 67th Annual Meeting of the Society for American Archaeology, March 21–24, 2002, Denver, Colorado P-MIP Report No. 21, Gila River Indian Community, Sacaton, Arizona.

Euler, R. C.
1959   Comparative Comments on California Pottery. In *Archaeological resources of Borrego State Park,* edited by C. W. Meighan. Annual Report, University of California Archaeological Survey, Los Angeles.

1982   Ceramic Patterns of the Hakataya Tradition. In *Southwestern Ceramics: A Comparative Review,* edited by A. H. Schroeder, pp. 52–69. School of American Research Advanced Seminar. The Arizona Archaeologist, No. 15. Arizona Archaeological Society, Inc.

Ezell, P. H.
1954   An Archaeological Survey of the Northwest Papagueria. *The Kiva* 19:1–26.

1955   An archaeological delineation of a cultural boundary in Papagueria. *American Antiquity* 20:367–374.

1961   The Hispanic Acculturation of the Gila River Pimas. *Memoirs of the American Anthropological Association,* 90.

1963   *The Maricopas: an identification from documentary sources.* University of Arizona, Anthropological Papers 6.

1968   The Cocomaricopa Mail.   In *Brand Book Number One,* edited by R. Brandes, The San Diego Corral of the Westerners.

Ezzo, J. A., and J. H. Altschul (editors)
1993   *Glyphs and Quarries of the Lower Colorado River Valley.* Statistical Research Technical Series No. 44. Statistical Research, Inc., Tucson, Arizona.

Faegri, K. and J. Iverson
1989   *Textbook of Pollen Analysis,* Fourth Edition. John Wiley & Sons, Hoboken, New Jersey.

Faegri, K. and L. van der Pijl
1979   *The Principles of Pollination Ecology,* Third Edition. Pergamon Press, Oxford.

Farish, T. E.
1915   *History of Arizona, Volume II.* Filmer Brothers Electrotype Co., San Francisco.

Faulk, O. B.
1973   *Destiny Road: The Gila Trail and the Opening of the Southwest.* Oxford University Press, New York.

Felger, R. S.
1977   Mesquite in Indian cultures of Southwestern North America. In *Mesquite: Its biology in two desert ecosystems,* edited by B.B. Simpson. Dowden, Hutchinson and Ross, Inc. US/IBP Synthesis Series 4.

Felger, R. S., and M. B. Moser
1985   *People of the Desert and Sea: Ethnobotany of the Seri Indians.* The University of Arizona Press, Tucson.

Fish, S. K. and P. R. Fish (editors)
2007   *The Hohokam Millennium.* School for Advanced Research Press, Santa Fe.

Fish, S., P. Fish, and J. Madsen
1992   *The Marana Community in the Hohokam World.* University of Arizona Press, Tucson.

Fontana, B. L.
1994   Entrada: The Legacy of Spain and Mexico in the United States. Southwest Parks and Monuments Association, Tucson.

Funk, A.
1936   Letter dated 12 February 1936 to the Register (Registrar) of the Phoenix General Land Office. Copy on file, Warner Goode Homestead Case File, National Archives and Records Administration, Washington, DC.

Garate, D.
1994   Juan Bautista de Anza National Historic Trail. Southwest Parks and Monuments Association, Tucson.

Gasser, R. E., and S. M. Kwiatkowski
1991 Food for thought: Recognizing patterns in Hohokam subsistence. In *Exploring the Hohokam, Prehistoric desert peoples of the American Southwest,* edited by G. J. Gumerman, University of New Mexico Press, Albuquerque.

Gates, P. W.
1968 *History of Public Land Law Development (The Management of Public Lands in the United States).* Arno Press, New York.

General Land Office/GLO
1932 *Subdivision Plat for Township No. 3 South, Range No. 4 West, Gila and Salt River Meridian, Arizona.* Copy on file, State Office, Bureau of Land Management, Phoenix.

Gillio, D., F. Levine, and D. Scott
1980 *Some Common Artifacts Found at Historical Sites.* Cultural Resources Report No. 31. United States Department of Agriculture Forest Service, Albuquerque, New Mexico.

Gish, J. W.
1995 Pollen Analysis. In *Archaeological Investigations on the Gila River Floodplain: Test Excavations in the Robbins Butte Wildlife Area near Buckeye, Maricopa County, Arizona,* edited by T. W. Wright, pp. 145–152. Project Report No. 94-80, Archaeological Research Services, Inc., Tempe.

Gladwin, W., and H. S. Gladwin
1929a The Red-on-buff Culture of the Gila Basin. Medallion Papers, No. 3, Gila Pueblo, Globe, Arizona.

1929b The Red-on-buff Culture of the Papagueria. Medallion Papers, No. 4, Gila Pueblo, Globe, Arizona.

1930a The Western Range of Red-on-buff Culture. Medallion Papers, No. 5, Gila Pueblo, Globe, Arizona.

1930b An Archaeological Survey of the Verde Valley. Medallion Papers, No. 6, Gila Pueblo, Globe, Arizona.

1935 The Eastern Range of the Red-on-buff Culture. Medallion Papers, No. 16, Gila Pueblo, Globe, Arizona.

Gladwin, H. S., E. W. Haury, E. B. Sayles, and N. Gladwin
1938 *Excavations at Snaketown I: material culture.* Medallion Papers No. 25. Gila Pueblo, Globe, Arizona.

Goodyear, A. C., III
1975 *Hecla II and III: An Interpretive Study of Archaeological Remains from the Lakeshore Project, Papago Reservation, South Central Arizona.* Anthropological Research Paper No. 9, Arizona State University, Tempe.

Gorenflo, L. J. and T. L. Bell
1991 Network Analysis and the study of past regional organization. In *Ancient Road Networks and Settlement Hierarchies in the New World,* edited by C. D. Trombold, pp. 80–98. Cambridge University Press, Cambridge.

Government Land Office
  1936   Homestead Patent No. 1086176 dated October 12. On file, Bureau of Land Management State Office, Phoenix.

Granger, B. H.
  1983   *Arizona's Names (X Marks the Place).* Falconer Publishing Company, Tucson.

Greene, A. C.
  1994   *900 Miles on the Butterfield Trail.* University of North Texas Press, Denton, TX.

Greenleaf, J. C.
  1974   *Fortified Hill site.* Ms. on file, Archives A-1208, Arizona State Museum Library, Tucson.

  1975   The Fortified Hill Site Near Gila Bend, Arizona. *The Kiva* 40:213–218.

Gregonis, L. M.
  2000   Indigenous Ceramics, pp. 517-531. In Chapter 7: Artifact Analyses by L. M. Gregonis, J. D. Lyon, P. Montgomery, L. Myers, and A. W. Vokes, In *Procurement, Processing, and Passing Through, Volume II*, edited by J. D. Lyon, SWCA Cultural Resource Report No. 98-267. SWCA, Inc., Tucson.

Gregory, D. A. (editor)
  1999   *Excavations in the Santa Cruz River Floodplain: The Middle Archaic Component at Los Pozos.* Anthropological Papers, No. 20. Center for Desert Archaeology, Tucson.

Hackbarth, M.
  1995   *Survey of the Butterfield Stage Overland Route, Gila Bend to Mobile, Maricopa County, Arizona.* Northland Research, Flagstaff.

Harmon, E. H. and J. Beyer
  1995   *Cultural Resources Survey of Approximately 40 Miles of Proposed State Route 85 Right-of-Way (and Associated Alternative Routes) between Gila Bend and Buckeye, Southwestern Maricopa County, Arizona.* ADOT Project No. 085 MA 120 H 3225 01L. Archaeological Research Services Project No. 94-45. Archaeological Research Services Inc., Tempe.

Harris, R. E.
  1984   *The First Hundred Years: A History of Arizona Blacks.* Relmo Publishers, Apache Junction, Arizona.

Haury, E. W.
  1937   Pottery Types at Snaketown. In *Excavations at Snaketown: Material Culture*, edited by H. S. Gladwin, E. W. Haury, E. B. Sayles, and N. Gladwin, Medallion Papers No. XXV, Gila Pueblo, Globe, Arizona.

  1950   *The Stratigraphy and Arcahaeology of Ventana Cave.* University of Arizona Press, Tucson.

  1956   The Lehner Mammoth Site. *The Kiva* 21(3-4):23–24.

  1976   *The Hohokam, Desert Farmers and Craftsmen: Excavations at Snaketown, 1964–1965.* University of Arizona Press, Tucson.

Haury, E. W., E. B. Sayles, and W. W. Wasley
  1959   The Lehner Mammoth Site, Southeastern Arizona. *American Antiquity* 25:2–30.

Hayden, J. D.
1965 Fragile-Pattern Areas. *American Antiquity* 31:272–276.

1967 A Summary Prehistory and History of the Sierra Pinacate, Sonora. *American Antiquity* 32(3): 335–344.

1970 Of Hohokam Origins and Other Matters. *American Antiquity* 35:87–94.

1972 Hohokam Petroglyphs of the Sierra Pinacate, Sonora and Hohokam Shell Expeditions. *The Kiva* 37 (2): 74–83.

1976 Pre-Altithermal Archaeology in the Sierra Pinacate, Sonora, Mexico. *American Antiquity* 41:274–289.

Hemmings, E. T., and C. V. Haynes Jr.
1969 The Escapule Mammoth and Associated Projectile Points, San Pedro Valley, Arizona. In *Journal of the Arizona Academy of Science* 5(3):184–188.

Helbing, D., J. Keltsch, and P. Mohair
1997 Modeling the Evolution of Human Trail Systems. *Nature* 388:47–50.

Hill, W. D., and J. E. Clark
2001 Sports, Gambling, and Government: America's First Social Compact? *American Anthropologist* 103(2):331–345.

Hoffmeiser, D. F.
1986 *Mammals of Arizona*. The University of Arizona Press, Tucson.

Huckell, B. B.
1984 *The Archaic Occupation of the Rosemont Area, Northern Santa Rita Mountains, Southeastern Arizona.* Archaeological Series, No. 147, Vol. I. Cultural Resource Management Division, Arizona State Museum, University of Arizona, Tucson.

1990 *Late Preceramic Farmer-Foragers in Southeastern Arizona: A Cultural and Ecological Consideration of the Spread of Agriculture into the Arid Southwestern United States.* Unpublished Ph.D. dissertation, University of Arizona, Tucson.

1996a Middle to Late Holocene Stream Behavior and the Transition to Agriculture in Southeastern Arizona. In *Early Formative Adaptations in the Southern Southwest,* edited by B. J. Roth, pp. 27–36. Monographs in World Archaeology, No. 25. Prehistory Press, Madison.

1996b The Archaic Prehistory of the North American Southwest. *Journal of World Prehistory* 10(3):305–372.

Irwin-Williams, C.
1979 Post-Pleistocene Archaeology, 7000–2000 B.C. In *Southwest,* edited by A. Ortiz, pp. 31–42. Handbook of North American Indians, Vol. 9, Smithsonian Institution, Washington, DC.

Jett, S. C.
2001 *Navajo Placenames and Trails of the Canyon de Chelly System, Arizona.* Peter Lang Publishing, New York.

Johnson, A. E., and W. W. Wasley
    1961   *Pottery and artifact provenience data from sites in the Painted Rocks Reservoir, western Arizona.* Society for American Archaeology, Archives of Archaeology 18.

Johnson, W.
    1997   *Soil Survey of Gila Bend-Ajo Area, Arizona, Parts of Maricopa and Pima Counties.* Natural Resources Conservation Service, United States Department of Agriculture.

Johnston, F. J., and P. H. Johnston
    1957   An Indian Trail Complex of the Central Colorado Desert: A Preliminary Survey, pp. 22–39. Papers on California Archaeology 48. Reports from the University of California. Archaeological Survey 37.

Jones, L. T.
    1967   *Red Man's Trail.* The Naylor Company, San Antonio.

Jones, O., and C. Sullivan
    1985   *The Parks Canada Glass Glossary for the Description of Containers, Tableware, Closures, and Flat Glass.* National Historic Parks and Sites Branch, Parks Canada, Environment Canada, Ottawa.

Karns, H. J.
    1954   *Unknown Arizona and Sonora 1693–1721.* English Translation of Captain Juan Mateo Manje, Luz de Tierra Incógnita. Arizona Silhouettes, Tucson.

Kelly, R. L.
    1995   *The Foraging Spectrum. Diversity in Hunter-Gatherer Lifeways.* Smithsonian Institution Press, Washington, DC.

Keohane, P. J.
    1935   Memo dated 11 December 1935 to the Commissioner of the General Land Office. Copy on file, Warner Goode Homestead Case File, National Archives and Records Administration, Washington, DC.

Kino, E. F.
    1947   *Kino's Historical Memoir of Pimeria Alta*, edited by Herbert Eugene Bolton, University of California Press, Berkeley.

Kinsey, B. J.
    1931   Surveyor's notes for the subdivision survey of Township 3 South, Range 4 West. Copy on file, State Office, Bureau of Land Management, Phoenix.

Kroeber, C. B., and B. L. Fontana
    1986   *Massacre on the Gila, An Account of the Last Major Battle Between American Indians, with Reflections on the Origin of War.* The University of Arizona Press, Tucson.

Kwiatkowski, S.
    1995   Flotation and Wood Charcoal Results from the Robbins Butte Testing Project. In *Archaeological Investigations on the Gila River Floodplain: Test Excavations in the Robbins Butte Wildlife Area near Buckeye, Maricopa County, Arizona,* edited by Thomas W. Wright, pp.. 125–144. Project Report No. 94-80, Archaeological Research Services, Inc., Tempe, Arizona.

Laird, C.
    1976   *The Chemehuevis.* Malki Museum Press, Banning, California.

LeBlanc, S. A.
   1982   The Advent of Pottery in the Southwest. In *Southwestern Ceramics: A Comparative Review*, edited by A. H. Schroeder, pp. 27–51. School of American Research Advanced Seminar. The Arizona Archaeologist, No. 15. Arizona Archaeological Society, Inc.

Leckie, W. H.
   1967   *The Buffalo Soldiers: A Narrative of the Negro Cavalry in the West.* University of Oklahoma Press, Norman.

LeSeur, G.
   2000   *Not All Okies are White.* University of Missouri Press, Columbia.

Lief, A.
   1965   *A Close-Up of Closures.* Glass Container Manufacturers Institute, New York.

Lindauer, O.
   1988   *A Study of Vessel Forms and Painted Designs to Explore Regional Interaction of the Sedentary Period Hohokam.* Dissertation, Arizona State University, Tempe.

Loendorf, C. and G. E. Rice
   2004   Projectile Point Typology, Gila River Indian Community, Arizona. *Anthropological Research Papers* No. 2. Gila River Indian Community Cultural Resource Managmeent Program, Sacaton, Arizona.

Loomis, T. P.
   1980   Petrographic Analysis of Prehistoric Ceramics from Gu Achi. In *Excavations at Gu Achi: A Reappraisal of Hohokam Settlement and Subsistence in the Arizona Papagueria*, by W. Bruce Masse. Western Archaeological Center Publications in Anthropology, No. 12, National Park Service, Tucson.

MacPherson, E.
   1973   *Gillespie's Gold.* Southland press, Phoenix.

Manje, J. M.
   1954   *Unknown Arizona and Sonora 1693–1721.* English translation by Harry J. Karns, Arizona Silhouettes, Tucson.

   1971   *Kino and Manje, Explorers of Sonora and Arizona.* Jesuit Historical Institute, St. Louis University, St. Louis.

Maricopa County
   1940   Warranty Deed dated 5 August 1940 from Warner and Clara Goode to Mary A. Kinderman. Copy on file, Maricopa County Recorder's Office, Phoenix.

Masse, W. B.
   1980a Excavations at Gu Achi: A Reappraisal of Hohokam Settlement and Subsistence in the Arizona Papagueria. Western Archaeological Center Publications in Anthropology, No. 12, National Park Service, Tucson.

   1980b The Hohokam of the Lower San Pedro Valley and Northern Papagueria: Continuity and Variability in Two Regional Population. In *Current Issues in Hohokam Prehistory: Proceedings of a Symposium*, edited by D. Doyel and F. Plog. Arizona State University Anthropological Research Papers, No. 23, pp. 205–223, Tempe.

1982   Hohokam Ceramic Art: Regionalism and the Imprint of Societal Change. In *Southwestern Ceramics: A Comparative Review*, edited by A.H. Schroeder, pp. 70–105. School of American Research Advanced Seminar. The Arizona Archaeologist, No. 15. Arizona Archaeological Society, Inc.

Matson, R. G.
1991   *The Origins of Southwestern Agriculture.* University of Arizona Press, Tucson.

McGregor, J. C.
1965   *Southwestern Archaeology.* University of Illinois Press, Chicago.

McGuire, R. H.
1982   Problems in Culture History. In *Hohokam and Patayan: Prehistory of Southwestern Arizona,* edited by Randall McGuire and Michael B. Schiffer, pp. 153–222. Academic Press, New York.

1991   On the Outside Looking In: The Concept of Periphery in Hohokam Archaeology. In *Exploring the Hohokam*, edited by George J. Gumerman, pp.347–382. Amerind Foundation, Inc. Dragoon, Arizona.

McGuire, R. H., and A. V. Howard
1987   The Structure and Organization of Hohokam Shell Exchange. *The Kiva* 52 (2):113–146.

McGuire, R., and M. B. Schiffer (editors)
1982   *Hohokam and Patayan: Prehistory of Southwestern Arizona.* Academic Press, New York.

Meighan, C. W.
1959   *Archaeological resources of Borrego State Park*, edited by C. W. Meighan. Annual Report, University of California Archaeological Survey, Los Angeles.

Miksa, E. J.
2000a Temper Provenance Studies. In The Grewe Archaeological Research Project, Volume 2: Ceramic Studies, edited by D. R. Abbott. Anthropological Papers No. 99-1. Northland Research, Tempe.

2000b Appendix C: Petrofacies Summary Descriptions. In The Grewe Archaeological Research Project, Volume 2: Ceramic Studies, edited by D. R. Abbott. Anthropological Papers No. 99-1. Northland Research, Tempe.

Mitchell, D. R., and J. P. Solometo
2002   Introduction. In *Archaeology at Estrella Mountain Ranch: Prehistoric and Historic Settlement in the Foothills of the Sierra Estrella Mountains,* edited by Julie P. Solometo, pp. 1–14. Archaeological Report No. 01-349, SWCA Environmental Consultants, Phoenix, Arizona.

Moerman, D.
1998   *Native American Ethnobotany.* Timber Press, Portland, Oregon.

Morris, D. H.
1969   Red Mountain: An Early Pioneer Period Hohokam Site in the Salt River Valley of Central Arizona. *American Antiquity* 34(1): 40–53.

National Archives and Records Administration
1929a Homestead application dated 17 May 1929. On file, Warner Goode Homestead Case File, National Archives and Records Administration, Washington DC.

1929b Application for amendment dated 12 November 1929. On file, Warner Goode Homestead Case File, National Archives and Records Administration, Washington DC.

1935a Notice of intention to make proof dated 7 February 1935. On file, Warner Goode Homestead Case File, National Archives and Records Administration, Washington DC.

1935b Notice for publication dated 7 February 1935. On file, Warner Goode Homestead Case File, National Archives and Records Administration, Washington DC.

1935c Final proof: testimony of claimant dated 25 march 1935. On file, Warner Goode Homestead Case File, National Archives and Records Administration, Washington DC.

1935d Final proof: testimony of witness (Winfield F. Riley) dated 25 March 1935. On file, Warner Goode Homestead Case File, National Archives and Records Administration, Washington DC.

1935e Final proof: testimony of witness (Ruben Smith) dated 25 march 1935. On file, Warner Goode Homestead Case File, National Archives and Records Administration, Washington DC.

1936 Final certificate dated 18 February 1936. On file, Warner Goode Homestead Case File, National Archives and Records Administration, Washington DC.

National Park Service
1996 *Juan Bautista de Anza National Historic Trail: Comprehensive Management and Use Plan, Final Environmental Impact Statement.* U.S. Government Printing Office, Washington, DC.

Office of Cultural Resource Management
2002 *SR 85 Gila Bend to Buckeye, Interstate 8 to Interstate 10, Archaeological Investigations: A Treatment Plan.* Department of Anthropology, Arizona State University, Tempe.

Officer, J. E.
1987 *Hispanic Arizona, 1536–1856.* University of Arizona Press, Tucson.

Pendleton, L.
1986 *The Archaeology of Picacho Basin, Southeast California.* MS on file at the Cultural Resource Management San Diego State University.

Peterson, K., E. Vincent and G. E. Rice
2002 Who Used the Area Between the Rivers? Employing Ceramic Temper Analysis to study the Boundary Between the Gila and Salt River. In *Visible Archaeology on the Gila River Indian Reservation.* Papers presented at the 67th Annual Meeting of the Society for American Archaeology, March 21–24, 2002, Denver, CO. P-MIP Report No. 21, Gila River Indian Community, Sacaton, Arizona.

Phoenix City Directory
1931 *Phoenix City Directory 1931.* Arizona Directory Company, Phoenix.

Plog, F.
1980 Explaining Culture Change in the Hohokam Preclassic. In *Current Issues in Hohokam Prehistory: Proceedings of a Symposium,* edited by David Doyel and Fred Plog, pp. 4–22. Arizona State University Anthropological Research Papers 23.

Plog, S., F. Plog and W. Wait
  1978   Decision making in modern surveys. In *Advances in Archaeological Method and Theory* 1:383–421.

Putnam, H. E.
  n.d.   Bottle Identification (s.1.). Ms, Jamestown, California.

Rea, A. M.
  1997   *At the Desert's Green Edge*. The University of Arizona Press, Tucson.

Renfrew, C.
  1975   Trade as action at a distance: questions of integration and communication. In *Ancient Civilization and Trade*, edited by J. A. Sabloff and C. C. Lamberg-Karlovsky, pp.3–59. Albuquerque.

Rice, G. E.
  1985   A Strategy for the Excavation of Buried Sites. In A Research Design for the Investigation of the Marana Community Complex, edited by G. E. Rice, pp. 67–90. Arizona State University Anthropological Field Studies No. 10.

  2000   Hohokam and Salado Segmentary Organization: The Evidence from the Roosevelt Platform Mound Study. In *Salado,* edited by Jeffrey S. Dean, pp. 143–166. University of New Mexico Press, Albuquerque.

Rice, G. E., and A. J. Smith
  1999   *An Archaeological Survey of a Portion of the Robbins Butte Wildlife Area*. Office of Cultural Resource Management Report No. 97. Department of Anthropology, Arizona State University, Tempe.

Rice, G. E., C. Loendorf and J. C. Ravesloot
  2003   Archaic Research Design for Gila River Indian Community, Arizona. P-MIP Technical Report No. 2002-10, Cultural Resource Management Program, Gila River Indian Community, Sacaton, Arizona.

Rock, J.
  1981   *Glass Bottles: Basic Identification*. Klamath National Forest Region 5, United States Department of Aggriculture (s.1.).

Rockman, Marcy and James Steele (editors)
  2003   *Colonization of Unfamiliar Landscapes: The Archaeology of Adaptation*. Routledge, New York.

Rogers, J. B.
  1976   *An archaeological investigation of Buckeye Hills east, Maricopa County, Arizona*. Arizona State University, Anthropological Research Papers 10.

Rogers, M. J.
  1928   Remarks on the archaeology of the Gila River drainage. *The Arizona Museum Journal* 1(1):21–24.

  1939   *Early Lithic Industries of the Lower Basin of the Colorado River and Adjacent Desert Areas*. San Diego Museum Papers No. 3. San Diego.

  1945   An Outline of Yuman Prehistory. *Southwestern Journal of Anthropology* 1:167–198.

1958   San Dieguito Implements from the Terraces of the Rincon, Pantano, and Rillito Drainage System. *The Kiva* 24:1–23.

1966   *Ancient Hunters of the Far West.* The Union-Tribune Publishing Co., San Diego.

Rose, F. P.
   n.d.   Butterfield Overland Mail Co. In *.The Battle of Pea Ridge 1862.* edited by J. W. Bond. Pea Ridge National Park Series: 31–37. Pea Ridge National Park, Arkansas.

Ruble, E. C.
   1998   *Monitoring and Data Recovery along State Route 85 between Gila Bend and Buckeye, Maricopa County, Arizona.* Technical Report No. 98-12. Northland Research, Inc, Flagstaff.

Ryden, D. W.
   1999   *A Historic Resource Survey of Gila Bend, Arizona.* Copy on file, State Historic Preservation Office, Phoenix.

Sample, L.L.
   1950   *Trade and Trails in Aboriginal California.*   Berkeley, Reports of the University of California Survey 8, Department of Anthropology, University of California, Berkley.

Sayles, E. B., and E. Antevs
   1941   *The Cochise Culture.* Medallion Papers No. 29. Gila Pueblo, Globe, Arizona.

Schackley, S. M.
   1988   Sources of Archaeological Obsidian in the Southwest: An Archaeological, Petrological, and Geochemical Study. *American antiquity 53:752–772.*

   1995   Sources of Archaeological Obsidian in the American Southwest: An Update and Quantitative Analysis. *American Antiquity* 60 (3):531–551.

Schiffer, M. B., and R. McGuire
   1982a Introduction. In *Hohokam and Patayan: Prehistory of Southwestern Arizona,* edited by R. McGuire and M. B. Schiffer, pp. 1–12. Academic Press, New York.

   1982b The Study of Cultural Adaptaions. In *Hohokam and Patayan: Prehistory of Southwestern Arizona,* edited by R. McGuire and M.l B. Schiffer, pp. 223–274. Academic Press, New York.

Schiffer, M. B., and S. J. Wells
   1982   Archaeological Surveys: Past and Future. In *Hohokam and Patayan: Prehistory of Southwestern Arizona,* edited by R.l McGuire and M. B. Schiffer, pp. 345–384. Academic Press, New York.

Schroeder, A. H.
   1958   Lower Colorado Buff Ware: A Descriptive Revision. Museum of Northern Arizona Ceramic Series No. 3D, Flagstaff.

   1961   An archaeological survey of the Painted Rocks Reservoir, Western Arizona. *The Kiva* 27:1–28.

   1967   Comments on "Salvage Archaeology in the Painted Rock Reservoir, Western Arizona." *Arizona Archaeology* No. 1: 1–10.

1975   *The Hohokam, Sinagua, and the Hakataya.* Occasional Paper No. 3, Imperial Valley College Museum Society publication, El Centro. (originally Archives of Archaeology No. 5 (1960) on microcard).

1982   Historical Overview of Southwestern Ceramics. In *Southwestern Ceramics: A Comparative Review*, edited by A. H. Schroeder, pp. 1–26. School of American Research Advanced Seminar. The Arizona Archaeologist, No. 15. Arizona Archaeological Society, Inc.

Schroeder, A. H. (editor)
1982   *Southwestern Ceramics: A Comparative Review.* School of American Research Advanced Seminar. The Arizona Archaeologist, No. 15. Arizona Archaeological Society, Inc.

Schroeder, K. J.
1994   *Pioneer & Military Memorial Park Archaeological Project in Phoenix, Arizona 1990–1992, Volume 2: The Historic Component, Ethnographic Observations/Reconstructions, and The Future of Pioneer and Military Memorial Park.* Roadrunner Publications in Anthropology 3, Roadrunner Archaeology & Consulting, Tempe.

1996   *Archaeological Survey of Phoenix's Papago Park, Maricopa County, Arizona.* Pueblo Grande Museum Technical Report No. 96-2. City of Phoenix Parks, Recreation and Library Department, Phoenix.

2003   *Analysis of Selected Glass and Ceramic Artifacts from AZ T:14:96 (ASM).* Roadrunner Archaeology and Consulting, Tempe.

Sedelmayr, J.
1955   Jacobo Sedelmayr, Missionary Frontiersman, Explorer in Arizona and Sonora, edited by Peter Masten Dunne, Arizona Pioneer's Historical Society.

Shackley, M. S.
1996   Range and mobility in the Early Hunter-gatherer Southwest. In *Early Formative Adaptations in the Southern Southwest*, edited by B. J. Roth, pp. 5–16. Monographs in World Archaeology 25, Prehistory Press, Madison, Wisconsin.

Shepard, A. O.
1976   *Ceramics for the Archaeologist.* Carnegie Institution of Washington Publication 609, Washington, DC.

Shumaker, J. M.
2000   *A Class I Cultural Resource Overview of the Proposed Sonoran Desert National Monument, Maricopa and Pinal Counties, Arizona.* The Coalition for Sonoran Desert Monument.

Simon, A. (editor)
1998   *Salado Ceramics and Social Organization: Prehistoric Interactions in Tonto Basin, The Roosevelt Archaeology Studies, 1989 to 1998.* Roosevelt Monograph Series 11, Anthropological Field Studies, No. 40. Office of Cultural Resource Management, Department of Anthropology, Arizona State University, Tempe.

Simon, A. W., J. C. Komorowski, and J. H. Burton
1998   Ceramic Production and Exchange in the Tonto Basin: The Mineralogical Evidence. In *Salado Ceramics and Social Organization: Prehistoric Interactions in Tonto Basin: The*

Roosevelt Archaeology Studies 1989–1998, edited by A. W. Simon, pp. 93–128. Roosevelt Monograph Series 11, Anthropological Field Studies 40. Office of Cultural Resource Management, Department of Anthropology, Arizona State University, Tempe.

Sires, E. W.
1983   Excavations at El Polvorón. In *Hohokam Archaeology Along the Salt-Gila Aqueduct, Central Arizona Project,* edited by L.S. Teague and P.L. Crown. Arizona State Museum Archaeological Series 150(4), Tucson.

Sloane, E.
1958   *Butterfield Overland Mail across Arizona.* Arizona Pioneers' Historical Society, Tucson.

Smith, S.
2003   State Route 85, Pollen Results from Four Sites, AZ Z:2:46, AZ T:14;92, AZ T:14:94, and AZ T:10:86. Manuscript on file, Office of Cultural Resource Management, Gila River Indian Community, Arizona.

Social Security Death Index
n.d.   Social Security listing for Warner Goode. <www.ssdi@ancestry.com>.

Solometo, J. P. (editor)
2001   *Archaeology at Estrella Mountain Ranch: Prehistoric and Historic Settlement in the Foothills of the Sierra Estrella Mountains.* SWCA Cultural Resources Report No. 01-349. SWCA, Inc., Environmental Consultants, Phoenix.

Spier, L.
1933   *Yuman Tribes of the Gila River.* University of Chicago Press, Chicago. Reprinted 1970.

Spoerl, P.
1979   Prehistoric Cultural Development and Conflict in Central Arizona. Unpublished Ph.D. dissertation, Southern Illinois University, Carbondale.

Stein, P. H.
1981   Wintersburg: An Archaeological Archival and Folk Account of Homesteading in Arizona. In *The Palo Verde Archaeological Investigations,* Part 2. MNA Research Paper 21. Museum of Northern Arizona, Flagstaff.

1988   *Homesteading in the Depression: A Study of Two Short-Lived Homesteads in the Harquahala Valley, Arizona.* Northland Research, Flagstaff.

1990   *Homesteading in Arizona, 1862 to 1940: A Guide to Studying, Evaluating, and Preserving Historic Homesteads.* Copy on file, State Historic Preservation Office, Phoenix.

1994   Historic *Trails in Arizona from Coronado to 1940: Historic Context Study* (draft version). Report No, 94-72. SWCA Environmental Consultants, Inc., Flagstaff, Arizona.

Stone, B. W.
1997   *Supplemental Cultural Resources Survey along State Route 85 between Mileposts 137.14 and 138.19, Approximately 15 Miles South of Buckeye, Southwestern Maricopa County, Arizona.* Project Report No. 97:11. Archaeological Research Services, Inc. Tempe.

Stone, C. L.
   1986   *Deceptive Desolation: Prehistory of the Sonoran Desert in West Central Arizona.* Cultural Resource Series Monograph No. 1. Arizona State Office of the Bureau of Land Management, Phoenix.

   1991   *The Linear Oasis: Managing Cultural Resources Along the Lower Colorado River.* Cultural Resource Series Monograph No. 6. Arizona State Office of the Bureau of Land Management, Phoenix.

Sundell, E. G.
   1974   Vegetation and Flora of the Sierra Estrella Regional park, Maricopa County, Arizona. Master's Thesis, Arizona State University, Tempe.

Swanson, M. T.
   1992   *An Archaeological Investigation of the Historic Black Settlement of Mobile, Arizona.* Statistical Research Technical Series No. 34. Statistical Research, Inc. Tucson.

Teague, L. S.
   1981   *Test Excavations at Painted Rock Reservoir.* Archaeological Series No. 143, Arizona State Museum, Tucson.

   1988   The History of Occupation at Las Colinas. In *The 1982–1984 Excavations at Los Colinas: The Site and Its Features*, pp.121–152. Archaeological Series 162, Volume 2. Cultural Resource Management Division, Arizona State Museum, University of Arizona, Tucson.

Teague, L. S., and A. R. Baldwin
   1978   *Painted Rock Reservoir Project Phase 1: Preliminary Survey and Recommendations.* Arizona State Museum, Archaeological Series 126.

Toulouse, J. Harrison
   1971   *Bottle Makers and Their Marks.* Thomas Nelson, New York.

Thul, J. (editor and compiler)
   1990   *Blacks in Arizona from Early Settlement to 1990: A Historic Context Study.* Copy on file, State Historic Preservation Office, Phoenix.

Trafzer, C.
   1975   *Anza, Garces, and the Yuma Frontier during the Era of the American Revolution.* Monograph No. 2. Yuma County Historical Society, Yuma, Arizona.

Treutlein, T. E. (editor and translator)
   1949   *Sonora, a Description of the Province by Ignaz Pfefferkorn.* University of New Mexico, Albuquerque.

Trombold, C. D. (editor)
   1991   *Ancient Road Networks and Settlement Hierarchies in the New World.* Cambridge University Press, Cambridge.

Tucker, D. B., A. Lascaux, and R. V. N. Ahlstrom
   2000   Past Research and Culture History. In *Footsteps on the Bajada*, Volume 1, edited by David B. Tucker, pp.47–78. SWCA Cultural Resource Report No. 99-140.

Turner, R. M., and D. E. Brown
    1982   Sonoran Desert Scrub. In *Desert Plants Special Issue: Biotic Communities of the American Southwest-United States and Mexico 4*, edited by David E. Brown pp.181–222. The University of Arizona, Tucson.

University of Oregon
    Web de Anza. http://www.anza.uoregon.edu/.

Van Buren, M., J. M. Skibo, and A. P. Sullivan III
    1992   *The Archaeology of an Agave Roasting Location.* In The Marana Community in the Hohokam World, edited by S. K. Fish, P. R. Fish, and J. Madsen, pp. 88-96. Anthropological Papers of the University of Arizona, No. 56. University of Arizona Press, Tucson.

Vivian, R. G.
    1965   An Archaeological Survey of the Lower Gila River, Arizona. *The Kiva*, Vol. 30, No. 4: 95–146.

Vogler, L. E.
    1976   *Cultural Resources of Painted Rock Dam and Reservoir Preliminary Evaluation and Management Plan Recommendations.* Cultural Resources Management, Archaeological Series No. 99, Arizona State Museum, University of Arizona, Tucson.

von Werlhof, J.
    1988   Trails in Eastern San Diego County and Imperial County: An Interim Report. Pacific Coast *Archaeological Society Quarterly* 24 (1):51–75.

Wagoner, J. L.
    1975   *Early Arizona: Prehistory to the Civil War*. University of Arizona Press, Tucson.

Walker, H. P., and D. Bufkin
    1986   *Historical Atlas of Arizona* (second edition). University of Oklahoma Press, Norman.

Wallace, H. D.
    1989   *Archaeological Investigations at Petroglyph Sites in the Painted Rock Reservoir Area, Southwestern Arizona.* Institute for American Research Technical Report No. 89-5, Tucson, Arizona.

Wallace, H. D. and J. P. Holmlund
    1989   *Petroglyphs of the Picacho Mountains; South Central Arizona*, published by the Institute of American Research, Tucson.

Wasley, W. W.
    1960   A Hohokam Platform Mound at the Gatlin Site, Gila Bend, Arizona. *American Antiquity* 26:244–262.

    1965   *Report of surveys conducted by the Arizona State Museum for the National Park Service under Contract 14-10-0333-995.* Ms. on file, Arizona State Museum Library, Tucson.

Wasley, W. W., and A. E. Johnson
    1965   *Salvage Archaeology in Painted Rocks Reservoir Western Arizona.* The University of Arizona Press, Tucson.

Waters, M. R.

1982a The Lowland Patayan Ceramic Tradition. In *Hohokam and Patayan: Prehistory of Southwestern Arizona,* edited by Randall McGuire and Michael B. Schiffer, pp. 275–298. Academic Press, New York.

1982b The Lowland Patayan Ceramic Typology. In *Hohokam and Patayan: Prehistory of Southwestern Arizona*, edited by R. McGuire and M. B. Schiffer, pp. 537–590. Academic Press, New York.

1985   *The Geoarchaeology of Whitewater Draw, Arizona.*   Anthropological Papers of the University of Arizona, No. 45. University of Arizona Press, Tucson.

Waters, M. R., and J. R. Ravesloot

2000   Late Quaternary Geology of the Middle Gila River, Gila River Indian Reservation, Arizona. *Quaternary Research* 54:49–57.

Weisiger, M. L.

1995   *Land of Plenty: Oklahoans in the Cotton Fields of Arizona, 1933–1942.* University of Oklahoma Press, Norman.

Wheat, J. B.

1955   *Mogollon culture prior to A.D. 1000.* Society for American Archaeology, Memoirs 10.

Wilcox, D. R.

1979   The Hohokam Regional System. In *An Archaeological Test of Sites in the Gila Butte-Santan Region, South-central Arizona*, pp. 77–116. Anthropological Research Papers No. 18, Department of Anthropology, Arizona State University, Tempe.

Wilcox, D. R., and L. O. Shenk

1977   *The Architecture of the Casa Grande and its Interpretation.* Arizona State Museum Archaeological Series 115. Tucson.

Wilson, E. D., R. T. Moore, and P. Wesley

1957   *Geologic Map of Maricopa County, Arizona.* Arizona Bureau of Mines.

Woodall, G. R.

1995   *Reconnaissance Inventory and Preliminary Assessment of Forty-eight Trail Sites Crossed by the Proposed Right-of-Way for State Route 85 between Gila Bend and Buckeye, Southwestern Maricopa County, Arizona.* Project Report No. 95:86. Archaeological Research Services, Inc. Tempe.

1997   *Supplemental Data for Cultural Resources Report 94:45 (State Route 85 Right-of-Way between Gila Bend and Buckeye).* Project Report No. 94:45 (Supplement). Archaeological Research Services, Inc. Tempe.

Wright, T. E.

1995   *Archaeological Investigations on the Gila River Floodplain: Test Excavations in the Robbins Butte Wildlife Area near Buckeye, Maricopa County, Arizona.* Project Report No. 94-80. Archaeological Research Services, Inc., Tempe.

Table A.1. Site Inventory

Sites/ Names	Quad	Geomorph- ology	Evidence	Type	Size	Period/ Phase	Features	Condition	Context	Assem- blage	Diagnostics
T:10:38	Buckeye	Buckeye Hills	surface finds	camp site	not recorded	unknown	rock circle, ramada	not recorded	open air, surface	none	N/A
T:10:40	Buckeye	Buckeye Hills	trail, surface finds	trail w/activity area	not recorded	unknown	trail (1), artifact scatter (1)	good	open air, surface	C	not recorded
T:10:43	Buckeye	Gila River floodplain	surface finds	activity area	not recorded	unknown	artifact scatter (1)	not recorded	open air, surface	C, FS	not recorded
T:10:44	Buckeye	Buckeye Hills	masonry structure, rock ring	habitation	not recorded	unknown	rock ring (1), masonry (1)	not recorded	open air, surface	none	N/A
T:10:46	Buckeye	bajada	surface finds	activity area	not recorded	unknown	artifact scatter (1)	not recorded	open air, surface	C, FS	not recorded
T:10:48	Hassayampa	bajada	surface finds	activity area	not recorded	unknown	artifact scatter (1)	collected	open air, surface	C	not recorded
T:10:53	Hassayampa	bajada	trail, surface scatter	trail	not recorded	unknown	trail, artifact scatter (1)	disrupted	open air, surface	C	not recorded
T:10:54	Hassayampa	terrace	surface finds	activity area	not recorded	Gila Butte phase	artifact scatter (1)	not recorded	open air, surface	C, L	Hohokam buff, Gila Butte r/b
T:10:58	Hassayampa	terrace	surface finds	activity area	not recorded	Patayan I	artifact scatter (1)	eroded	open air, surface	C, L	L.C. buffware
T:10:60	Buckeye	bajada	rock rings, surface finds	camp site	not recorded	unknown	rock rings (3)	not recorded	open air, surface	C, L	not recorded
T:10:73	Buckeye	terrace	surface scatter	habitation	90x65m	Santa Cruz- Sacaton phases	artifact scatter (1), pithouse (1)	not recorded	buried	C, FS, FCR, GS	Santa Cruz r/b, Sacaton r/b, Gila plain
T:10:74	Hassayampa	bajada	trash mounds, surface finds	village	660x540m	Santa Cruz- Sacaton phases	trash mounds (14), artifact scatters	good	open air, surface	C, FS, GS, S	Hohokam r/b, plainware

Continued

Table A.1. Site Inventory (*Continued*)

Sites/Names	Quad	Geomorphology	Evidence	Type	Size	Period/Phase	Features	Condition	Context	Assemblage	Diagnostics
T:10:75	Hassayampa	bajada	rock piles, surface scatter	activity area	60x45m	Patayan II&III, Classic Period	rock piles (6), surface scatter (1)	not recorded	open air, surface	C	Palomas, Tumco, and Hohokam buff, Salt red, Gila plain
T:10:76	Hassayampa	bajada	rock piles, surface scatter	activity area	150x120m	Patayan I	rock features (2)	not recorded	open air, surface	C, FS, G, GS, FCR	Colorado beige
T:10:77	Hassayampa	bajada	rock feature	campsite	60x75m	unknown	rock feature (1)	not recorded	open air, surface	GS, FCR	N/A
T:10:79	Buckeye	bajada	trail, rock features	trail	60 x 180m	unknown	trails (2), rock features (2)	not recorded	open air, surface	C	Gila plain
T:10:85	Hassayampa	terrace	surface finds	activity area	not recorded	Santa Cruz through Polvoron phases	canals (2), artifact scatter (2), roasting pit (1)	disturbed	buried	C, FS, S, GS, FA, FCR, MB	Santa Cruz r/b, Sacaton r/b
T:10:86	Buckeye	terrace	surface finds	activity area	230x246m	Pioneer-Classic periods	ash stains (11), artifact scatters	disturbed	open air, surface	C, FS, GS	Salt red, Gila plain, Hohokam buff, Hohokam r/b
T:10:87 Cranky Site	Buckeye	bajada	rock rings, clearings	activity area	not recorded	unknown	artifact scatter (1), rock ring (5)	not recorded	open air, surface	FS, GS	N/A
T:10:88 Wards Site	Hassayampa	terrace	surface finds	activity area	not recorded	unknown	artifact scatter (1)	heavily disturbed	open air, surface	C, FS	Salt Gila plain
T:10:128	Hassayampa	bajada	surface finds	village	780x640m	Pioneer-Sedentary periods	artifact scatters	disturbed by modern berms	open air, surface	C, FS, GS, FCR	Gila Butte r/b, Sweetwater red-on-grey
T:10:129	Hassayampa	terrace	surface finds	activity area	30x70m	Pioneer-Sedentary periods	artifact scatters	excellent	open air, surface	C, FS, GS, S	Gila Butte r/b

Continued

Table A.1. Site Inventory *(Continued)*

Sites/Names	Quad	Geomorph-ology	Evidence	Type	Size	Period/Phase	Features	Condition	Context	Assem-blage	Diagnostics
T:10:130	Hassayampa	bajada	surface finds	village	80x60m	Pioneer-Sedentary periods	artifact scatters	excellent	open air, surface	C, FS, GS, FCR	Hohokam red-on-buff, plainware
T:10:131	Hassayampa	terrace	trash mound, surface finds	village	30x50m	Santa Cruz-Sacaton phases	trash mound, artifact scatters	good	open air, surface	C, FS, GS, S, FCR	Hohokam red-on-buff, plainware
T:10:184	Hassayampa	bajada	surface finds	activity area	30x30m	unknown	artifact scatter	good	open air, surface	C	Hohokam redware
T:10:186	Hassayampa	bajada	trail	trail	1x40m	unknown	trail	fair	open air, surface	none	N/A
T:10:187	Hassayampa	bajada	trails	trail	20x70m	unknown	trails (2)	fair	open air, surface	none	N/A
T:13:8 Fortified Hill Site	Citrus Valley East	bajada	structures, surface finds, petroglyphs	village	2 acres	Civano phase	artifact scatters, rooms (57), petroglyphs (200)	fair	open air, surface	C, FS, GS, S, FR	PW, redware, Tanque Verde red-on-brown, Gila Plain (Gila), L.C. Buff
T:13:9 Rock Ball Court Site	not within coverage area	terrace	pit houses, trash mounds, surface finds, ballcourt	village	200x300m	Colonial period	dwellings, trash mounds, ballcourt (1)	vandalized	open air, surface	C, FS, GS, S	Gila Butte r/b, Santa Cruz r/b, plainware, buffware
T:13:10	Cotton Center	bajada	surface finds	activity area	not recorded	unknown	artifact scatter (1)	not recorded	open air, surface	L	N/A
T:13:11	Cotton Center	bajada	surface finds	activity area	not recorded	Preclassic period	artifact scatter (1)	destroyed	open air, surface	C, L, FS, GS	not recorded
T:13:18	Spring Mountain	floodplain	surface finds, burials	village	600x800m	Classic period	burials (3), ramada (1), artifact scatters, canals	not recorded	open air, surface	C, FS, GS, S, FR, G	Hohokam red-on-buff

Continued

Table A.1. Site Inventory *(Continued)*

Sites/ Names	Quad	Geomorph- ology	Evidence	Type	Size	Period/ Phase	Features	Condition	Context	Assem- blage	Diagnostics
T:13:21	Spring Mountain	floodplain	surface finds	activity area	not recorded	unknown	artifact scatter (1)	not recorded	open air, surface	C	Pimeria brown, Gila plain
T:13:30	Citrus Valley East	floodplain	surface finds, petroglyphs	campsite	20x100m	unknown	rock rings (7), petroglyph panels (2), artifact scatters (2)	vandalized, eroded	open air, surface, and buried	C,FS	none
T:13:34	Cotton Center	Gila River floodplain	rock features, trails	trail with campsite	not recorded	unknown	rock features (3), trails	not recorded	open air, surface	FS	none
T:13:35	Cotton Center	Gila River floodplain	depression	habitation	6m diameter	"Archaic"	depression (1)	not recorded	open air, surface	FS	none
T:13:36	Cotton Center	bajada	rock features, surface finds	campsite	not recorded	unknown	rock feactures (5), artifact scatter (1)	not recorded	open air, surface	FS, GS	none
T:13:38	Cotton Center	terrace	rock ring	activity area	1m diameter	unknown	rock ring (1)	not recorded	open air, surface	none	N/A
T:13:42	Citrus Valley East	floodplain	surface finds	activity area	not recorded	unknown	lithic scatter (1)	not recorded	open air, surface	FS	none
T:13:43	Citrus Valley East	floodplain	surface finds	activity area	not recorded	unknown	artifact scatter (1)	not recorded	open air, surface	FS, GS, FCR	none
T:13:44	Citrus Valley East	floodplain	surface finds	activity area	not recorded	Patayan I	artifact scatter (1)	not recorded	open air, surface	C, FS	L. C. buff
T:13:45	Citrus Valley East	floodplain	surface finds	activity area	1x1m	unknown	rock feature (1)	not recorded	open air, surface	none	N/A
T:13:46	Cotton Center	terrace	rock feature	activity area	1m diameter	unknown	rock enclosure (1)	not recorded	open air, surface	none	N/A

Continued

Table A.1. Site Inventory *(Continued)*

Sites/ Names	Quad	Geomorph- ology	Evidence	Type	Size	Period/ Phase	Features	Condition	Context	Assem- blage	Diagnostics
T:13:47	Cotton Center	terrace	rock feature, surface finds	campsite	3x10m	unknown	rock features (2), artifact scatter (1)	not recorded	open air, surface	C, FS	not recorded
T:13:48	Cotton Center	terrace	surface finds	activity area	not recorded	unknown	artifact scatter (1)	eroded	buried	C, FS	not recorded
T:13:49 Figimag Site	Cotton Center	bajada	surface finds	activity area: knapping station	1 x 0.5m	unknown	lithic scatter (1)	not recorded	open air, surface	FS	none
T:13:53	Cotton Center	bajada	surface finds, pet- roglyphs, trail	trail w/activity area	not recorded	unknown	artifact scatter (2), trail (1), rock fea- tures (2), petroglyph (4)	not recorded	open air, surface	C, FS	not recorded
T:13:69	Citrus Valley East	rock outcrop	surface finds, petroglyph	activity area	1x1m	unknown	petroglyph (1), rock pile (1)	not recorded	open air, surface	FS	none
T:13:120	Spring Mountain	bajada	petroglyphs	activity area	not recorded	unknown	petroglyph panels (15-20)	not recorded	rock outcrop	none	N/A
T:13:121	Spring Mountain	bajada	petroglyphs	activity area	not recorded	unknown	petroglyph panels (<10)	not recorded	rock outcrop	none	N/A
T:14:11 Bartley Site	Cotton Center	terrace	surface finds, trash mound	village	not recorded	Classic period	artifact scatter, trash mound, burials, cremation	badly disturbed by agriculture and vandals	surface and buried	C, FS, GS, S, B	Casa Grande r/b, Tanque Verde red-on-brown, Gila Red, buffware, Gila Plain (Gila)

Continued

Table A.1. Site Inventory (*Continued*)

Sites/ Names	Quad	Geomorph- ology	Evidence	Type	Size	Period/ Phase	Features	Condition	Context	Assem- blage	Diagnostics
T:14:12	Cotton Center	terrace	surface finds, trash mound, structures	habitation	50x60m	Classic period	artifact scatters, perimeter wall, structure, trash mound, burial	good	surface and buried	C, FS, GS, S	Casa Grande r/b, Tanque Verde red-on-brown, Gila Red, buffware, Gila Plain (Gila)
T:14:14	Cotton Center	bajada	surface finds, ball court, trash mounds	village	not recorded	Sedentary period	artifact scatters, ball court, trash mounds	badly disturbed by agriculture and vandals	open air, surface	C	Sacaton r/b, L.C. buff, Mimbres black-on-white
T:14:15	Cotton Center	bajada	ball court	activity area	9.5x23.7m, 1.4m depth	Colonial-Sedentary periods	ball court	good	below surface	C, S	Sacaton r/b, Gila Butte r/b, Santa Cruz r/b
T:14:16 Hi-Vu Ranch	Cotton Center	terrace	plentiful surface finds	village	258x288m	Late Sedentary-Early Classic periods	ball courts (2), trash mounds (4), artifact scatters (5), rock feature (3)	disturbed	surface and buried	C, FS, S, G, GS, M	Gila plain
T:14:17 Enterprise South	Cotton Center	terrace	plentiful surface finds	village	273x369m	Colonial-Early Classic periods	trash mounds (10), depressions (5), rock features (2), artifact scatter (1)	heavily disturbed	surface and buried	C, FS, S, GS, FCR	Gila plain, Gila Butte r/b, Casa Grande r/b, Sacaton red, Tanque Verde red-on-brown
T:14:19 Enterprise Ranch	Cotton Center NW	bajada	surface finds and features	village	388x866m	Sedentary-Early Classic periods	ball courts (2), trash mounds (16), architecture	vandalized	surface and buried	C, FS, S, G, GS, FCR, M, W	Sacaton r/b, Gila plain, Sacaton red, Classic red
T:14:23	Cotton Center	bajada	petroglyph	petroglyph	one rock	unknown	petroglyph	not recorded	not recorded	none	N/A
T:14:24	Cotton Center	bajada	surface finds	activity area	5.5x6.5m	unknown	rock feature (1), artifact scatter (1)	good-moderate	open air, surface	C	not recorded

Continued

Table A.1. Site Inventory *(Continued)*

Sites/Names	Quad	Geomorphology	Evidence	Type	Size	Period/Phase	Features	Condition	Context	Assemblage	Diagnostics
T:14:26	Cotton Center	bajada	trails	trail	not recorded	unknown	trails (4)	good-moderate	open air, surface	none	N/A
T:14:28 Wide Trail Site	Cotton Center	bajada	surface finds, trail	trail w/campsite	60x1200m	Patayan I, Santa Cruz phase	trails (2), artifact scatter (1)	not recorded	open air, surface	C, FS	Hohokam buff, Santa Cruz r/b, L.C. buff, Gila plain
T:14:32 Gate Site	Cotton Center	bajada	surface finds, rock features	activity area	85x210m	Gila Butte-Sacaton phases	rock clusters (2), artifact scatter (1)	not recorded	open air, surface	C, FS, GS	Sacaton r/b, Gila Butte, PW, BW
T:14:39	Cotton Center	bajada	surface finds, petroglyphs	activity area	20x20m	unknown	petroglyph panels (3), artifact scatter (1)	not recorded	open air, surface	FS, GS	none
T:14:41	Cotton Center	Red Rock Canyon, Gila Bend Mountains	surface finds, petroglyphs, trail	trail w/activity area	52x90m	unknown	petroglyph panels (87), trail (1), lithic scatter (2)	unaltered	canyon and adjacent surfaces	FS	Patayan petroglyph elements
T:14:42	Cotton Center	Red Rock Canyon, Gila Bend Mountains	rock shelters, surface finds, petroglyphs	habitation	15x20m	Patayan I	petroglyph panels (3), pictogram panels (1), artifact scatter (1), rock alignment (1)	unaltered	rock shelters, surface	C, FS, GS	L.C. buff, stucco jar, Gila plain, redware, Patayan stuccoware
T:14:43	Cotton Center	Red Rock Canyon, Gila Bend Mountains	petroglyphs	activity area	not given	unknown	petroglyph panels (12)	vandalized	canyon	none	N/A
T:14:44 Wood Site	Cotton Center	Red Rock Canyon, Gila Bend Mountains	petroglyphs	activity area	3x50m	unknown	Patayan petroglyph panels (10)	severe erosion and vandalism	open air, canyon surfaces	none	N/A

Continued

Table A.1. Site Inventory *(Continued)*

Sites/ Names	Quad	Geomorph-ology	Evidence	Type	Size	Period/ Phase	Features	Condition	Context	Assem-blage	Diagnostics
T:14:52	Cotton Center	Gila Bend Mountains	interior finds	activity area	5x10m	unknown	rock shelter (1), artifact scatter (1)	graffiti present	rock shelter	FS	none
T:14:59	Cotton Center NW	Gila River floodplain	surface finds	activity area	not recorded	"late Archaic"	artifact scatter (1)	not recorded	open air, surface	FS, GS	none
T:14:61 Butterfield Stage Route	Cotton Center	bajada	trail	trail	2x435m within survey area	historic	trail	cut by SR 85	open air, surface	M	none
T:14:62	Cotton Center	bajada	surface finds, trails	trails w/ campsite	275x335m	Classic period	trails (7), artifact scatters	cut by SR 85	open air, surface	FCR, C	Hohokam buff and r/b, Salt red
T:14:63	Cotton Center	bajada	trails	trail	90m within SR85 row	unknown	trails (2)	cut by SR 85	open air, surface	none	N/A
T:14:64	Cotton Center	bajada	surface finds, trails	trails w/activity area	180x365m	unknown	trails (4), artifact scatter (1)	cut by SR 85	open air, surface	C, FS	Hohokam buff
T:14:66	Cotton Center	bajada	trails	trail	115m within SR85 row	unknown	trails (5)	cut by SR 85	open air, surface	none	N/A
T:14:67	Cotton Center	bajada	trails	trail	130m within SR85 row	unknown	trails (3)	cut by SR 85	open air, surface	none	N/A
T:14:68	Cotton Center	bajada	surface finds, trail, rock features	trails w/activity area	305x426m	unknown	trails (8), rock feature (1), lithic scatter (1)	vehicle tracks, cut by SR 85	open air, surface	FS	none
T:14:69	Cotton Center	bajada	surface finds, trail, rock features	trails w/ campsite	305x490m	Patayan I and Classic period	trails (13), rock features (3), roast pit (1), lithic scatter (2)	cut by SR 85	open air, surface	C, FS, FCR	Lower Colorado buff, Salt red, Hohokam buff

Continued

Table A.1. Site Inventory *(Continued)*

Sites/Names	Quad	Geomorphology	Evidence	Type	Size	Period/Phase	Features	Condition	Context	Assemblage	Diagnostics
T:14:70	Cotton Center	bajada	surface finds, rock features, trails	trails w/ campsite	275x400m	Patayan I	trails (6), rock features (6), clearings (5), ceramic scatter (1)	cut by SR 85	open air, surface	C, FS	Lower Colorado buff
T:14:71	Cotton Center	bajada	surface finds, rock features, trails	trails w/ campsite	180x460m	unknown	trails (4), rock features (6), petroglyph (1)	SR 85 and dozer disturbance	open air, surface	C, FS	Gila plain
T:14:72	Cotton Center	bajada	trails	trail	1x305m	unknown	trails (2)	SR 85 and dozer disturbance	open air, surface	none	N/A
T:14:73	Cotton Center	bajada	surface finds, rock features	trails w/activity area	180x365m	unknown	trails (5), lithic scatter (2), rock features (2)	cut by SR 85	open air, surface	FS	none
T:14:74	Cotton Center	bajada	surface finds, trails	trails w/activity area	180x365m	Patayan I	trails (6), artifact scatter (2)	SR 85 and vehicle disturbance	open air, surface	C, FS	L.C. buff, Gila plain
T:14:75	Cotton Center	bajada	trails	trail	1x275m	unknown	trails (2)	cut by SR 85	open air, surface	none	N/A
T:14:76	Cotton Center	bajada	surface finds, rock features, trails	trails w/activity area	105x230m	unknown	trails (3), rock fea-tures (3)	SR 85 and vehicle disturbance	open air, surface	FS	none
T:14:78	Cotton Center	bajada	surface finds, rock features, trails	trails w/activity area	120x470m	Patayan I	trails (2), rock features (2), artifact scatter (3)	SR 85 and dirt road	open air, surface	C, FS	Lower Colorado buff
T:14:79	Cotton Center	bajada	surface finds, trails	trails w/activity area	40x250m	unknown	trails (2), lithic scatter (1)	cut by SR 85	open air, surface	FS	none

Continued

Table A.1. Site Inventory *(Continued)*

Sites/Names	Quad	Geomorphology	Evidence	Type	Size	Period/Phase	Features	Condition	Context	Assemblage	Diagnostics
T:14:80	Cotton Center	bajada	surface finds, rock cluster, trails	trails w/activity area	240x305m	Patayan 1	trails (7), artifact scatters (6), rock features (1)	SR 85, vehicle, livestock impacts	open air, surface	C, FS	Lower Colorado beige & buff, Gila plain
T:14:81	Cotton Center	bajada	trails, scant artifacts	trail	150x275m	Patayan 1	trails (4)	SR 85 and vehicle disturbance	open air, surface	C, L	Colorado beige, Gila plain (Salt)
T:14:82	Cotton Center	bajada	surface finds, trails, ash stains	trails w/activity area	180x365m	unknown	ash stain (1), rock feature (1), trails (4)	SR 85 and machine disturbance	open air, surface	FS, FCR, W	none
T:14:83	Cotton Center	bajada	surface finds, trails, clearing	trails w/ campsite	245x600m	unknown	trails (4), rock ring (1), lithic scatter (1), petroglyph (1), rock features (2), clearing (1)	cut by SR 85	open air, surface	FS	none
T:14:84	Cotton Center	bajada	surface finds, trail	trail w/activity area	60x305m	unknown	trails (4), rock feature (1)	cut by SR 85 and dozer	open air, surface	L	none
T:14:85	Cotton Center	bajada	trails, surface finds	trails w/ campsite	90x365m	unknown	trails (3), rock ring (1), rock cluster	cut by SR 85	open air, surface	FS	none
T:14:86	Cotton Center	bajada	surface finds, trail, petroglyph	trail w/activity area	90x335m	unknown	petroglyphs (2), trail (1), rock features (2)	cut by SR 85 and dozer	open air, surface	FS	none
T:14:87	Cotton Center	bajada	trail, surface finds	trails w/ campsite	60x520m	unknown	trails (2), rock features (5)	cut by SR 85 and dozer	open air, surface	none	N/A
T:14:88	Cotton Center	bajada	trail, surface finds, petroglyphs	trail w/activity area	60m diameter	unknown	trail (1), petroglyph (1), rock features (5)	SR 85 cut area, but features good.	open air, surface	FS	none

Continued

Table A.1. Site Inventory *(Continued)*

Sites/ Names	Quad	Geomorph- ology	Evidence	Type	Size	Period/ Phase	Features	Condition	Context	Assem- blage	Diagnostics
T:14:89	Cotton Center	bajada	surface finds, trail	trail w/ campsite	60x365m	Patayan I	trail (1), rock features (1)	cut by SR 85 and secondary road	open air, surface	C, FCR	Gila plain (Salt), Colorado beige
T:14:90	Cotton Center	bajada	surface finds, trail	trails w/activity area	90x275m	unknown	trails (3), rock feature (1)	poor: dozer cuts	open air, surface	C, FS	Hohokam buff
T:14:91	Cotton Center NW	bajada	surface finds, trail	trails w/activity area	120x365m	unknown	trails (3), artifact scatter (1)	cut by SR 85	open air, surface	C	none
T:14:92	Cotton Center NW	bajada	surface finds, trail	trails w/activity area	170x425m	Patayan II-III and Colonial-Sedentary Periods	rock features (9), trails (3)	good	open air, surface	C, FS	Hohokam buff, PW, L.C. Buff
T:14:93	Cotton Center NW	bajada	surface finds, trail	trails w/ campsite	410x460m	Patayan II-III	trails (3), rock features (18)	disturbed	open air, surface	C, FS	Palomas buff
T:14:94	Cotton Center NW	bajada	surface finds, trail	trails w/activity area	60x365m	Patayan II-III and Sedentary-Classic period	trails (3), rock features (8)	good	open air, surface	C, FS	Colorado red, Colorado beige, Gila plain (Salt), Salt red
T:14:95	Cotton Center NW	bedrock	surface finds, petroglyph	activity area	not recorded	Patayan I	petroglyphs (6)	cut by road	open air, surface	C, FS	L.C. buff, Gila plain, Hohokam buff
T:14:97	Cotton Center NW	bedrock pediment	rock features	campsite	1x2m shelter interior	unknown	rock pile (1), rock alignment (1)	undisturbed	rock shelter	none	N/A
T:14:113	Cotton Center NW	bajada	surface finds	activity area	6x8m	Patayan II-III	rock feature (1), artifact scatter (1)	disturbed by sheet erosion	open air, surface	C	Lower Colorado buff

Continued

Table A.1. Site Inventory (Continued)

Sites/ Names	Quad	Geomorph- ology	Evidence	Type	Size	Period/ Phase	Features	Condition	Context	Assem- blage	Diagnostics
T:14:114	Cotton Center NW	bajada	trail	trail	0.4 m wide	unknown	trail (1)	good	open air, surface	C(1)	none
T:14:115	Cotton Center NW	bajada	petroglyphs	activity area	40x91m	Preclassic to Classic periods	petroglyphs (6)	not recirded	open air	none	N/A
T:14:116	Cotton Center SE	Maricopa Mountains	surface finds	campsite	103x125m	unknown	hearths (3), artifact scatter (1)	badly eroded	open air, surface	C, FS, GS, FR, FCR	thin brown-ware, r/b
T:14:117	Margies Peak	bajada	surface finds	activity area	80x240m	Patayan I	artifact scatter (1)	not recorded	open air, surface	C, FS	Gila plain, Hohokam buff, Hohokam r/b, L.C. red
T:14:118	Margies Peak	bajada	surface finds	activity area	60x82m	Patayan I and Classic period	artifact scatter (1)	not recorded	open air, surface	C, FS	Gila plain (Salt), Gila plain (Gila), Salt red, L.C. buff, L.C. red, Wingfield plain, Wingfield red
T:14:124 Hawk's Nest	Cotton Center	bajada	surface finds	activity area	34x112m	unknown	artifact scatter (1)	not recorded	open air, surface	C	Gila plain, Hohokam buff, Hohokam r/b, L.C. red
T:14:125	Cotton Center	bajada	surface finds	activity area	57x173m	Patayan I, Gila Butte-Santa Cruz phases	artifact scatter (1)	not recorded	open air, surface	C	Hohokam buff, Santa Cruz r/b, L.C. buff, Gila Butte r/b
T:14:130	Cotton Center NW	bajada	surface finds, architecture	village	164x333m	Colonial to Classic periods	ball courts (2), rooms (2), trash mound (1), artifact scatter (1)	vandalized, bulldozed	open air, eroding out	C, FS, S, GS, FCR	Gila plain (Gila & Salt), Sacaton r/b, Sacaton red, Gila Butte r/b

Continued

Table A.1. Site Inventory *(Continued)*

Sites/ Names	Quad	Geomorph- ology	Evidence	Type	Size	Period/ Phase	Features	Condition	Context	Assem- blage	Diagnostics
T:14:132	Cotton Center NW	bajada	surface finds, architecture	habitation	457x610m	Sacaton phase	trash mound (1), possible rooms (2), surface scatter (1)	vandalized, bulldozed	open air, surface	C, FS, G, GS, W, FCR	Gila plain (Salt & Gila), Sacaton red
T:15:6	Mobile NW	bajada	surface finds	habitation	90x160m	Colonial period	artifact scatter (1)	good	open air, surface	C, FS, S, GS	red-on-buff
T:15:7	Mobile NW	bajada	surface finds	activity area	70x160m	unknown	artifact scatter (1)	not recorded	open air, surface	C	none
Z:1:7	Not within coverage area.	terrace	surface finds	village	130x350m	Colonial and Sedentary periods	artifact scatter, structure, cremations, trash pits	poor, disturbed by agriculture & vandalism	sub- surface and open air, surface	C, FS, GS, S	Gila Butte r/b, Santa Cruz r/b, Sacaton r/b, Gila Plain, L.C. Buff
Z:1:8	Not within coverage area.	terrace	surface finds	village	300x400m	Sedentary period	artifact scatter, trash pit	poor, disturbed by agriculture	sub- surface and open air, surface	C, FS, GS, S, FCR	Sacaton r/b, Gila Plain, L.C. Buff
Z:1:11	Not within coverage area.	terrace	surface finds, trash mound	village	50x100m	Civano phase, Classic period	artifact scatter, trash mound, structure, cremations	disturbed by subsequent historic occupation	sub- surface and open air, surface	C, FS, GS, S	Gila Plain (Gila), Gila red, Gila smudged, L.C. Buff,
Z:1:20	Smurr	rock outcrop	surface finds, petroglyphs	activity area (quarry)	200x250m	Archaic through Hohokam	lithic quarry (1), petroglyph panels (7)	not recorded	open air, surface	FS, GS	Archaic and Gila style petroglyphs
Z:1:29 Mobak/ Aux 6 Site	Smurr	bajada	surface finds	agriculture activity area	1100 x 1300m	Sedentary-Classic periods	artifact scatters, rock piles, rock features	disturbed	open air, surface	C, FS, GS, S, FCR, G, W, M	red on buffs, Gila plain

Continued

Table A.1. Site Inventory *(Continued)*

Sites/ Names	Quad	Geomorph-ology	Evidence	Type	Size	Period/ Phase	Features	Condition	Context	Assem-blage	Diagnostics
Z:1:30 Rainy Day Site	Smurr	bajada	surface finds	activity area	115x150m	unknown	artifact scatter (1)	not recorded	open air, surface	C, GS, FCR	redware, Gila plain
Z:1:31 Wash Away Site	Smurr	bajada	surface finds	activity area	2x8m	Sedentary period	artifact scatter (1)	eroding out	buried in wash	C	red on buffs, brown plainware
Z:2:1 Gatlin Site	Gila Bend	bajada	platform & trash mounds, ball courts	village	385x410m	Colonial-to-Classic periods	platform mound (1), trash mounds (22), ball courts (2)	cut by road, vandalized	sub-surface and open air, surface	C, FS, GS, S, W, FR	Santa Cruz r/b, Sacaton r/b, Sacaton red, Gila plain, Sacaton buff
Z:2:2	Gila Bend	bajada	surface finds, trash mound	habitation	not recorded	Colonial-Sedentary periods	artifacts scatters, trash mound (1)	modern agriculture, fair-good	open air, surface	C, FS, GS, FCR, M	Gila plain (Gila)
Z:2:5	Gila Bend	bajada	surface finds	activity area	not recorded	historic	artifact scatter (1)	poor, eroded	open air, surface	C	Papago red, Papago r/b
Z:2:6 South Allentown Site	Gila Bend	bajada	houses, cremations	village	not recorded	recorded as Sacaton phase (by Wasley)	houses, cremations (2)	not recorded	sub-surface and open air, surface	C	not recorded
Z:2:7	Gila Bend	bajada	surface finds	habitation	30x30m	Patayan I	artifact scatter, midden (1)	plowed, graded, but good	open air, surface, and eroding out	C, FS, S	L. C. buff
Z:2:10	Gila Bend	bajada	surface finds	activity area	10m diameter	"Colonial period"	artifact scatter (1)	good	open air, surface	C	Hohokam sherds
Z:2:36	Bosque	bajada	surface finds	activity area	110x250m	Sedentary period	artifact scatter (1)	vehicle disturbance, but good	open air, surface	C, FS (1)	Gila plain (Gila), Gila r/b, PW

Continued

Table A.1. Site Inventory *(Continued)*

Sites/ Names	Quad	Geomorph- ology	Evidence	Type	Size	Period/ Phase	Features	Condition	Context	Assem- blage	Diagnostics
Z:2:38	Gila Bend	bajada	surface finds	activity area	150m diameter	unknown	artifact scatter (1)	cut by road and levee	open air, surface	C, S	none
Z:2:39	Gila Bend	bajada	trail	trail	15x215m	unknown	trail (1)	disturbed by vehicles	open air, surface	none	N/A
Z:2:41	Gila Bend	bajada	surface finds, trail	trail w/ campsite	60x245m	unknown	trails (2), rock feature (1)	disturbed by roads and dumping	open air, surface	L, FCR	none
Z:2:42	Gila Bend	bajada	surface finds, trail	trail w/activity area	215x305m	unknown	trails (3), rock feature (1)	disturbed by roads	open air, surface	FS, FCR, G	none
Z:2:44	Gila Bend	bajada	surface finds, trail	trails w/activity area	165x430m	Patayan I	trails (3), rock ring (1), artifact scatters (3)	cut by SR 85 and roads	open air, surface	C, FS, G	L.C. buff, Hohokam buff, Gila plain (Salt and Gila)
Z:2:45	Gila Bend	bajada	trails, pit features	trails w/ campsite	150x275m	Patayan I	trails (2), roasting pits (6)	disturbed by roads	open air, surface	C, FS, GS, W, FCR	L.C. buff, Hohokam r/b, Gila plain (Salt and Gila)
Z:2:46	Gila Bend	bajada	trail, rock features	trails w/ campsite	140x215m	Pioneer period	roasting pits (4), trails (2), rock features (5)	cut by SR 85 and roads	open air, surface	none	N/A
Z:2:47	Gila Bend	bajada	surface finds, trails, features	trails w/activity area	305x400m	Patayan I	artifact scatters (2), trails (2), rock features (5)	cut by SR 85, vehicle tracks	open air, surface	C, FS, G	Lower Colorado buff
Z:2:48	Gila Bend	bajada	surface finds, trails, features	trails w/ campsite	400x460m	Patayan I	artifact scatters (3), trails (15), rock features (5)	cut by SR85, vehicle tracks	open air, surface	C, FS, FCR	Lower Colorado buff, Gila plain (Salt)

Continued

Table A.1. Site Inventory *(Continued)*

Sites/ Names	Quad	Geomorph- ology	Evidence	Type	Size	Period/ Phase	Features	Condition	Context	Assem- blage	Diagnostics
Z:2:49	Gila Bend	bajada	surface finds, trail	trails w/activity area	100x240m	unknown	trails (2), clearings (2), artifact scatter (1)	slight vehicle disturbance	open air, surface	C, FS	Gila plain (Salt)
Z:2:50	Gila Bend	bajada	surface finds, trail, rock features	trails w/activity area	90x425m	unknown	trails (2), rock ring (1)	cut by SR 85, vehicle disturbance	open air, surface	FS	none
Z:2:51	Gila Bend	bajada	surface finds, trail, rock features	trails w/activity area	365m diameter	Classic period	trails (6), rock features (4)	cut by SR 85, vehicle disturbance	open air, surface	C, FS	Hohokam buff, Salt red
Z:2:52	Gila Bend	bajada	trails	trail	305x335m	unknown	trails (6)	cut by SR 85, vehicle disturbance	open air, surface	FS (1)	none
Z:2:53	Gila Bend	bajada	surface finds, trails	trail	215x275m	unknown	trails (4)	cut by SR 85, extensive vehicle disturbance	open air, surface	C, FS, W	Hohokam buff or Gila plain (Salt)
Z:2:54	Gila Bend	bajada	surface finds, trails	trails w/activity area	60x305m	unknown	trails (2), artifact scatter (1)	cut by SR 85	open air, surface	L	none
Z:2:55	Gila Bend	bajada	surface finds, trails	trails w/activity area	30x305m	unknown	trails (2), artifact scatter (1)	cut by SR 85 and dozer	open air, surface	C	Gila plain (Salt)
Z:2:57	Gila Bend	bajada	surface finds	activity area	40x128m	Patayan I	artifact scatter (1)	not given	open air, surface	C	Hohokam r/b, L.C. buff, Gila plain (Salt and Gila)
ASU											
T:9:3	Hassayampa	Gila River floodplain	surface finds	activity area	10x30m	unknown	artifact scatter (1)	eroded	eroding out of cut bank	FS, GS	none

Continued

Table A.1. Site Inventory *(Continued)*

Sites/Names	Quad	Geomorph-ology	Evidence	Type	Size	Period/Phase	Features	Condition	Context	Assem-blage	Diagnostics
T:10:6	Hassayampa	Robbins Butte	surface finds	activity area	10x10m	unknown	artifact scatter (1)	not recorded	open air, surface	C	not recorded
T:10:21	Buckeye	Buckeye Hills	surface finds	activity area	not recorded	unknown	artifact scatter (1)	not recorded	open air, surface	FS	none
T:10:22	Buckeye	Buckeye Hills	surface finds	activity area	3x5m	unknown	artifact scatter (1)	not recorded	open air, surface	FS	none
T:10:23	Buckeye	bajada	trail, rock feartures, surface finds	trail w/activity area	not recorded	unknown	trail (1), rock rings (2)	not recorded	open air, surface	none	N/A
T:10:24	Buckeye	terrace	rock features, surface finds	activity area	not recorded	recorded as Colonial to Sedentary	rock rings (3)	not recorded	open air, surface	C	not recorded
T:10:25	Buckeye	bajada	rock features, surface finds	campsite	1x6m	unknown	rock ring (1)	not recorded	open air, surface	FS	none
T:10:27	Buckeye	Buckeye Hills	rock feature	campsite	3x6m	unknown	rock ring (1)	not recorded	open air, surface	none	N/A
T:10:28	Buckeye	Buckeye Hills	rock features, surface finds	activity area	3x6m	Classic	rock platforms (2)	not recorded	open air, surface	FS	none
T:10:31	Buckeye	bajada	rock feature	activity area	1x1m	Classic	rock ring (1)	not recorded	open air, surface	none	N/A
T:10:34	Buckeye	Buckeye Hills	petroglyphs	activity area	not recorded	unknown	petroglyphs	some vandalism	open air, rock face	none	N/A
T:10:36	Buckeye	bajada	surface finds, petroglyphs	activity area	60x80m	unknown	petroglyphs	not recorded	open air, rock face	C, FS	not recorded
T:10:41	Buckeye	terrace	stone circle	campsite	not recorded	unknown	rock ring (1)	good	open air, surface	none	N/A

Continued

Table A.1. Site Inventory *(Continued)*

Sites/Names	Quad	Geomorphology	Evidence	Type	Size	Period/Phase	Features	Condition	Context	Assemblage	Diagnostics
T:10:42	Buckeye	Gila River floodplain	surface finds	activity area	40x150m	unknown	artifact scatter (1)	?	open air, surface	C,L,G,GS,M	not recorded
T:10:43	Buckeye	Gila River floodplain	surface finds	campsite	30x60m	unknown	artifact scatter (1)	not recorded	open air, surface	C, FS, GS, FR	not recorded
T:10:45	Buckeye	Gila River floodplain	surface finds	activity area	120x170m	Snaketown and Gila Butte phases	artifact scatter (1), hearth (1)	not recorded	open air, surface	C, FS	Gila plain, Gila Butte & Snaketown, r/b
Z:2:1 Gila Bend	Gila Bend	terrace	platform mound	activity area: ceremonial	40x80m	Classic	platform mound (1)	not recorded	open air, surface	none	N/A
BLM											
T:10:1	Hassayampa	Gila river floodplain	surface finds	activity area	15x70m	unknown	artifact scatter (1)	disturbed by erosion and building	buried, uncovered by canal	C, FS, GS	Hohokam r/b, PW
T:14:1	Cotton Center	bajada	surface finds, pithouse	habitation	200x300m	unknown	artifact scatter (1), pithouse (1)	not recorded	open air, surface	C, FS, GS	not recorded
T:14:3	Cotton Center	Gila Bend Mountains	surface finds, trail	trail w/activity area	14x25m	unknown	artifact scatter (1), trial (1)	eroded	open air, surface	C, FS	Gila plain, Gila r/b
T:14:4	Cotton Center SE	Maricopa Mountains	surface finds	activity area	160x220m	recorded as Santa Cruz phase	artifact scatters (21 knapping stations)	erosion and road cut	open air, surface	C,FS,GS	not recorded
T:14:5	Cotton Center	bajada	surface finds	activity area	4.5x5m	recorded as Santa Cruz phase	artifact scatter (1), rock feature (1)	disturbed	open air, surface	C, FS, GS	Hohokam r/b
T:14:6	Cotton Center	bajada	petroglyph	petroglyph	1x1m	unknown	petroglyph (1)	good	open air, surface	none	N/A

Continued

Table A.1. Site Inventory *(Continued)*

Sites/Names	Quad	Geomorphology	Evidence	Type	Size	Period/Phase	Features	Condition	Context	Assemblage	Diagnostics
T:14:7	Cotton Center	Red Rock Canyon	surface finds, trails	trails w/activity areas	1m x 15 km	unknown	trail system (1) artifact scatters	partially destroyed by erosion, roads, mining and vehicles	open air, surface	C, FS, GS	PW, redware, tanware
T:14:8	Cotton Center	terrace	surface finds	campsite	10x14m	unknown	rock features (3)	vehicle disturbance	open air, surface	C, FS	none
T:14:9	Cotton Center	bajada	trail, surface finds, rock features	trail w/activity area	9x21m	unknown	trail (1), rock features (4), artifact scatter (1)	vehicle disturbance	open air, surface	C, FS, GS	Gila plain, "Yuman PW"
T:14:10	Cotton Center	bajada	trail, surface finds, rock features	trail w/ activity area	1.5x24m	Patayan I	trail (1), rock feature (1), artifact scatter (1)	disturbed	open air, surface	C,FS	L.C. Buff
T:14:11	Cotton Center	bajada	trails, surface finds, rock features	trails w/ activity area	16x18m	unknown	trails (1), rock features (5)	disturbed	open air, surface	FS	none
T:14:12	Cotton Center	bajada	trail, surface finds	trail w/ activity area	8x8m	Patayan I	trail (1), rock feature (1)	good	open air, surface	C, FS, GS	L.C. Buff
T:14:15	Cotton Center SE	Maricopa Mountains	surface finds	campsite	103x125m	unknown	artifact scatter (1), hearths (2)	badly eroded	open air, surface	C, FS, GS, FR, FCR	Gila plain, brownware, r/b
Z:2:2	Bosque	bajada	surface finds	activity area	not recorded	unknown	intaglio (1)	road and erosion	open air, surfac	none	N/A
Z:2:3	Bosque	bajada	surface finds, roasing pit	campsite	10x10m	unknown	artifact scatter (1), roasting pit (1)	moderate disturbance	open air, surface	C, FCR	not recorded

Continued

Table A.1. Site Inventory *(Continued)*

Sites/ Names	Quad	Geomorph-ology	Evidence	Type	Size	Period/ Phase	Features	Condition	Context	Assem-blage	Diagnostics
Z:3:3	Estrella	Maricopa Mountains	surface finds	activity area	50x150m	recorded as Santa Cruz phase	artifact scatter (1)	good	open air, surface	C, FS, GS	not recorded
MNA											
T:14:5	Cotton Center	bajada	trails	trail	not recorded	unknown	trails (4)	good-moderate	open air, surface	none	N/A
NA											
12486/ T:10:53 (ASM)	Hassayampa	bajada	trail, petroglyph, surface finds	trail w/activity area	1m x 1.6km	unknown	trail (1), petroglyph (1)	good	open air, surface	C	Gila plain
13602/ T:10:57 (ASM)	Buckeye	bajada	petroglyphs	activity area	not recorded	unknown	petroglyphs	vandalized	open air, rock face	C	Pimeria brown, Gila plain
NMSU											
75-1	Margies Peak	bajada	surface finds, petroglyph	activity area	not recorded	Patayan I	artifact scatter (1), petroglyph panel (1)	good	open air, surface, and rock face	C	Lower Colorado buffware
Other											
Pierpont	Cotton Center	Gila Bend Mountains foothills									

Table B.1. List of Surveys

Survey	Quads	Survey Method	Survey Type	Acres Covered	Sites Found	Dominant Terrain
BLM-020-10-92-233	Hassayampa	pedestrian	block	6	0	terrace
BLM-020-10-92-239	Hassayampa	pedestrian	block	7.9	0	terrace
BLM-020-11-76-03	Cotton Center	pedestrian	block	40	0	Gila River floodplain & terrace
BLM-020-11-76-07	Buckeye	pedestrian	block	17	0	bajada
BLM-020-11-79-16	Hassayampa	pedestrian	linear	1.81	0	bajada
BLM-020-11-80-20	Buckeye	pedestrian	block	1	0	Buckeye Hills
BLM-020-11-82-26	Cotton Center	pedestrian	linear	2.28	0	terrace
BLM-020-11-82-27	Buckeye	pedestrian	linear	5	0	terrace & bajada
BLM-020-11-82-30	Hassayampa	pedestrian	block	25	1	Gila River floodplain
BLM-020-11-83-32	Gila Bend	pedestrian	linear	2	0	terrace
BLM-020-11-83-45	Buckeye	pedestrian	block	12,800	19	varied
BLM-020-11-84-47	Cotton Center	pedestrian	linear	0.5	0	bajada
BLM-020-11-84-50	Hassayampa	pedestrian	linear	16	4	terrace
BLM-020-11-86-55	Buckeye	pedestrian	linear	23	0	Buckeye Hills
BLM-020-11-86-61	Hassayampa	pedestrian	linear	26.7	0	all
BLM-020-11-86-67	Buckeye	pedestrian	block	54.6	0	bajada
BLM-020-11-89-72	Hassayampa	pedestrian	linear	5.9	0	terrace
BLM-020-11-90-79	Hassayampa	pedestrian	linear	0.7	0	Buckeye Hills
BLM-020-11-91-83	Buckeye	pedestrian & vehicular	linear & block	8.9	0	bajada & Buckeye Hills
BLM-020-11-91-85	Buckeye	pedestrian	block	16	0	bajada
BLM-020-11-92-88	Hassayampa	pedestrian	block	25	1	varied
BLM-020-11-92-89	Buckeye	pedestrian	block	7.28	0	Gila River floodplain
11-92	Cotton Center	pedestrian	linear & block	260	9	Red Rock Canyon
BLM-020-11-92-96	Cotton Center NW	pedestrian	linear	0.69	1	terrace
BLM-020-11-94-102	Hassayampa	pedestrian	block	150	0	terrace
BLM-020-11-96-110	Cotton Center NW	pedestrian	block	240	0	bajada & rock outcrops
BLM-020-11-96-111	Hassayampa	pedestrian	linear	2,643	66	bajada & terrace
BLM-020-11-98-126	Gila Bend	pedestrian	block	2.9	0	bajada
BLM-020-11-98-127	Cotton Center NW	pedestrian	linear	31	3	bajada
BLM-020-11-01-129	Cotton Center NW	pedestrian	linear	1,957	9	varied over 21.5 mile length
BLM-020-11-01-134	Cotton Center	pedestrian	linear	7.91	0	Gila Bend Mountains
BLM-020-12-77-06	Margies Peak	pedestrian	block	0.91	0	bajada
BLM-020-12-77-07	Margies Peak	pedestrian	block	0.51	0	bajada
BLM-020-12-78-11	Gila Bend	pedestrian	linear	0.29	1	terrace

Continued

Table B.1. List of Surveys *(Continued)*

Survey	Quads	Survey Method	Survey Type	Acres Covered	Sites Found	Dominant Terrain
BLM-020-12-79-13	Bosque	pedestrian	block	8	0	bajada
BLM-020-12-79-16	Buckeye	vehicular	linear	72.7	0	Buckeye Hills
BLM-020-12-79-17	Buckeye	pedestrian	linear	1.31	0	terrace
BLM-020-12-79-19	Margies Peak	pedestrian	block	4.8	0	bajada & mountains
BLM-020-12-80-20	Bosque	pedestrian	block	15.5	0	bajada
BLM-020-12-80-27	Margies Peak	pedestrian	block	0.73	0	Maricopa Mountains
BLM-020-12-81-30	Mobile NW	pedestrian	linear	0.62	0	bajada
BLM-020-12-81-31	Butterfield Pass	pedestrian	block	19.6	0	bajada
BLM-020-12-81-35	Mobile NW	pedestrian	linear	6	0	bajada
BLM-020-12-83-48	Bosque	pedestrian	block	260	0	bajada
BLM-020-12-83-55	Margies Peak	not recorded	linear	2,509	24	varied over 207 mi. length
BLM-020-12-83-57	Mobile NW	pedestrian	block	3.2	0	bajada
BLM-020-12-83-59	Bosque	pedestrian	linear	4,240	2	varied over 53 mi. length
BLM-020-12-80-60	Margies Peak	not recorded	block	80	1 (Yuman)	bajada
BLM-020-12-83-61	Buckeye	not recorded	?	?	4	terrace
BLM-020-12-84-63	Gila Bend	pedestrian	linear	1.7	0	terrace
BLM-020-12-84-70	Cotton Center	pedestrian & vehicular	linear & block	40	0	terrace
BLM-020-12-86-84	Margies Peak	pedestrian	linear	57.5	0	bajada
BLM-020-12-86-88	Butterfield Pass	pedestrian	block	1,162	3	bajada
12-89	Butterfield Pass	pedestrian	block	?	3	bajada
BLM-020-12-87-101	Mobile NW	pedestrian	linear	0.99	0	bajada
BLM-020-12-88-103	Bosque	pedestrian	linear	?	1	bajada & Maricopa Mountains
BLM-020-12-88-108	Bosque	pedestrian	linear	67.96	3 H-sites	varied over 18 mi., but crosses Maricopa Mountains
BLM-020-12-88-110	Mobile NW	pedestrian	block	10.9	0	bajada
BLM-020-12-90-124	Buckeye	pedestrian	linear & spot	5	0	bajada
BLM-020-12-90-126	Buckeye	pedestrian	linear	41.4	1	Gila River floodplain
BLM-020-12-90-127	Margies Peak	pedestrian	linear	7.7	0	bajada
BLM-020-12-90-130	Buckeye	pedestrian	block	996	0	bajada
BLM-020-12-91-133	Butterfield Pass	pedestrian	block	25.1	0	bajada
BLM-020-12-91-134	Gila Bend	vehicular	linear	330	0	bajada & mountains S. of I-8
BLM-020-12-91-135	Gila Bend	pedestrian	linear	32.4	0	bajada
BLM-020-12-91-143	Butterfield Pass	pedestrian	block	0.5	0	bajada

Continued

Table B.1. List of Surveys *(Continued)*

Survey	Quads	Survey Method	Survey Type	Acres Covered	Sites Found	Dominant Terrain
BLM-020-12-93-163	Estrella	pedestrian	block	2	0	Maricopa Mountains
BLM-020-12-93-164	Cotton Center SE	pedestrian	block	116	0	bajada
BLM-020-12-93-166	Butterfield Pass	pedestrian	block	1.1	0	bajada
BLM-020-12-93-167	Mobile NW	pedestrian	block	1.8	0	bajada
BLM-020-12-93-168	Cotton Center SE	pedestrian	block	1.3	0	Maricopa Mountains
BLM-020-12-93-169	Cotton Center SE	pedestrian	block	1.7	0	bajada
BLM-020-12-93-170	Margies Peak	not recorded	linear	0.01	0	bajada
BLM-020-12-94-173	Buckeye	pedestrian	linear	9.68	0	bajada
BLM-020-12-94-176	Estrella	pedestrian	linear	32.8	0	bajada
BLM-020-12-94-177	Estrella	pedestrian	block	1.6	0	bajada
BLM-020-12-94-179	Estrella	pedestrian	block	2	0	bajada
BLM-020-12-94-183	Butterfield Pass	pedestrian	linear	0.183	0	bajada
BLM-020-12-94-184	Cotton Center SE	pedestrian	linear	0.372	0	bajada
BLM-020-12-94-185	Mobile NW	pedestrian	linear	2.25	0	bajada
BLM-020-12-94-186	Margies Peak	pedestrian	linear	1.38	0	bajada
BLM-020-12-94-187	Cotton Center SE	pedestrian	block	6	0	bajada
BLM-020-12-94-188	Margies Peak	pedestrian	linear	0.115	0	bajada
BLM-020-12-94-191	Buckeye	pedestrian	block	160	2	bajada
12-196	Bosque	pedestrian	block	22.3	2	bajada
BLM-020-12-95-200	Butterfield Pass	pedestrian	linear & block	2.5	0	bajada
BLM-020-12-95-204	Margies Peak	pedestrian	block	11	0	Maricopa Mountains
BLM-020-12-95-205	Cotton Center SE	pedestrian	block	4	0	bajada
BLM-020-12-95-206	Cotton Center SE	pedestrian	block	2	1	bajada
BLM-020-12-95-207	Cotton Center SE	pedestrian	linear	21.8	1	Maricopa Mountains
BLM-020-12-95-209	Mobile NW	pedestrian	linear	72	0	bajada
BLM-020-12-96-216	Butterfield Pass	pedestrian	block	7.5	0	bajada
BLM-020-12-96-217	Mobile NW	pedestrian	block	7	0	bajada
BLM-020-12-96-218	Margies Peak	pedestrian	block	5.6	0	Maricopa Mountains
BLM-020-12-96-220	Cotton Center	not recorded	linear	247	6	varied, 37 km of Butterfield Trail
BLM-020-12-97-221	Cotton Center SE	pedestrian	linear	?	0	Maricopa Mountains
BLM-020-12-97-222	Bosque	not recorded	linear	<5	0	bajada
BLM-020-12-97-223	Buckeye	not recorded	?	1.31	0	bajada
BLM-020-12-97-228	Cotton Center SE	pedestrian	linear	?	0	bajada
BLM-020-12-97-229	Margies Peak	vehicular	linear	0.5	0	bajada
BLM-020-12-98-232	Buckeye	pedestrian	block	1.47	0	bajada
BLM-020-12-99-237	Buckeye	pedestrian	block	0.367	0	bajada

Continued

Table B.1. List of Surveys *(Continued)*

Survey	Quads	Survey Method	Survey Type	Acres Covered	Sites Found	Dominant Terrain
BLM-020-12-99-240	Cotton Center SE	pedestrian	block	2.6	0	bajada
BLM-020-12-99-241	Buckeye	pedestrian	block	71	0	terrace
BLM-020-12-00-242	Buckeye	pedestrian & vehicular	block	35	0	bajada
BLM-020-12-00-248	Butterfield Pass	pedestrian	block	0.23	0	Maricopa Mountains
BLM-020-14-78-24	Buckeye	pedestrian	block	?	0	Buckeye Hills & Maricopa Mountains
BLM-020-22-94-36	Gila Bend	pedestrian	block	26	1	mountains
BLM-020-22-96-47	Gila Bend	pedestrian	block	0.2	0	bajada
BLM-020-22-96-48	Gila Bend	pedestrian	linear	1,584	185	bajada
BLM-020-22-96-51	Gila Bend	pedestrian	block	2,076	0	bajada